Theory, Practice, and Future Direction of Large Language Models

Ismail Lamaakal
University Mohammed Premier, Morocco

Yassine Maleh
Sultan Moulay Slimane University, Morocco

Khalid El Makkaoui
University Mohammed Premier, Morocco

Ibrahim Ouahbi
University Mohammed Premier, Morocco

Ahmed Abd El-Latif
Prince Sultan University, Saudi Arabia

IGI Global
Scientific Publishing
Publishing Tomorrow's Research Today

Published in the United States of America by
IGI Global Scientific Publishing
701 East Chocolate Avenue
Hershey, PA, 17033, USA
Tel: 717-533-8845 | Fax: 717-533-7115
Website: https://www.igi-global.com E-mail: cust@igi-global.com

Library of Congress Cataloging-in-Publication Data

Names: Lamaakal, Ismail, 1999- editor
Title: Theory, practice, and future direction of large language models / edited by Ismail Lamaakal, Yassine Maleh, Khalid El Makkaoui, Ibrahim Ouahbi, Ahmed Abd El-Latif.
Description: Hershey, PA : IGI Global Scientific Publishing, [2026] | Includes bibliographical references and index. | Summary: "This book comprehensively explores the transformative power of large language models (LLMs) by delving into their theoretical foundations, practical applications, and future potential. The book seeks to provide a robust theoretical framework for understanding LLMs, covering the underlying algorithms, architectures, and data-driven processes that form the basis of LLM technology"-- Provided by publisher.
Identifiers: LCCN 2024055162 (print) | LCCN 2024055163 (ebook) | ISBN 9798369383872 h/c | ISBN 9798369383889 s/c | ISBN 9798369383896 ebook
Subjects: LCSH: Natural language processing (Computer science)--Industrial applications
Classification: LCC QA76.9.N38 T443 2025 (print) | LCC QA76.9.N38 (ebook)
LC record available at https://lccn.loc.gov/2024055162
LC ebook record available at https://lccn.loc.gov/2024055163

British Cataloguing in Publication Data
A Cataloguing in Publication record for this book is available from the British Library.

Table of Contents

Detailed Table of Contents

Large Language Models (LLMs) are throughly examined in this chapter, along with their potential, limitations and implications for existing artificial intelligence. An overview of the history and introduction of LLMs may be found in the introduction. A variety of language tasks, including translation and summarization, are examined in the Capabilities section where these models demonstrate outstanding performance. This highlights how much of an influence he has had on NLP(Natural Language Processing). This chapter emphasizes LLM's developing capabilities. With these developments, problems with interpret-ability, ethics, and resource limitations are addressed, highlighting the necessity of responsible application. This study expands of LLMs, consider it's promise, and indicates the importance using and generating them in a sustainable and ethical manner.

Large Language Models (LLMs) are powerful tools in natural language processing with complex principles. This chapter delves into the theoretical foundations of LLMs, covering essential concepts, algorithms, and intuition, aiming to offer readers a strong grasp of the framework that empowers LLMs to perform varied language tasks, thus laying groundwork for advanced applications. Beginning with NLP fundamentals and statistical techniques, the chapter traces the evolution of language models from n-gram models to dense word embeddings like Word2Vec and GloVe. It then examines neural network architectures, progressing Transformers, dissecting

The purpose of this study is to improve classroom tactics in teaching computing and robotics in an EFL environment. It seeks to investigate the integration of Large Language Models (LLM) within the Education 6.0 framework. This study contributes to the growing body of literature on the role of AI in the classroom by demonstrating that LLM can serve as a bridge between technical and language instruction. Future research should investigate the long-term effects of LLM integration on student performance and extend this strategy to other STEM-related domains within the EFL ecosystem.

Large language models (LLMs) are powerful AI tools with broad applications, but they also pose significant ethical and societal challenges. These include risks of inherent bias in training data, leading to biased outputs that may amplify stereotypes or unfair treatment. LLMs raise concerns regarding data privacy, as they may inadvertently use sensitive or personally identifiable information. Additionally, the widespread use of LLMs for generating disinformation poses threats to public trust and information integrity. Addressing these issues requires transparent model development, responsible data use, and strong ethical guidelines to mitigate risks while maximizing the societal benefits of LLMs.

Preface

The rapid evolution of artificial intelligence (AI) has ushered in a transformative era, with large language models (LLMs) standing at the forefront of this technological revolution. These sophisticated models, powered by vast datasets and advanced neural architectures, have redefined how we interact with machines, process natural language, and solve complex problems across diverse domains. Theory, Practice, and Future Direction of Large Language Models is a comprehensive exploration of this groundbreaking technology, offering a blend of theoretical foundations, practical applications, and forward-looking insights into its ethical, educational, and cybersecurity implications. This book aims to bridge the gap between academic research and real-world implementation, providing a holistic understanding of LLMs and their potential to shape the future of technology and society.

In today's world, LLMs are no longer confined to research laboratories; they are integral to industries such as healthcare, education, cybersecurity, and beyond, driving innovation and efficiency. With the global digital transformation accelerating, the demand for intelligent systems capable of understanding and generating human-like text has never been greater. LLMs, exemplified by models like GPT and BERT, are powering chatbots, aiding medical diagnoses, enhancing educational tools, and even supporting security operations. However, their widespread adoption also raises critical questions about ethics, privacy, and societal impact, making this book timely and relevant in addressing both opportunities and challenges in a technology-driven society.

This book targets a diverse audience, including academics and researchers seeking to deepen their understanding of LLM theory, practitioners and industry professionals applying these models in real-world scenarios, educators integrating LLMs into teaching methodologies, and policymakers navigating the ethical and legal landscapes of AI deployment. Whether you are a student exploring the theoretical underpinnings, a developer building innovative applications, or a decision-maker shaping AI governance, this book offers valuable insights tailored to your needs.

Theory, Practice, and Future Direction of Large Language Models is structured into three distinct sections, encompassing 10 chapters that collectively provide a comprehensive exploration of large language models (LLMs) from theoretical foundations to practical applications, and their broader implications in education, ethics, and cybersecurity. This organization ensures a logical progression, starting with foundational concepts, moving into real-world implementations, and concluding with critical discussions on societal and ethical dimensions.

ORGANIZATION OF THE BOOK

Section 1: Theoretical Foundations and Core Principles

This section establishes the theoretical and architectural groundwork for understanding LLMs, offering readers a deep dive into their evolution, principles, and capabilities.

Chapter 1: Foundations of Large Language Models and Their Emergent Abilities

This chapter provides an in-depth examination of large language models (LLMs), tracing their historical development and introducing their core capabilities in natural language processing (NLP) tasks such as translation and summarization. It highlights LLMs' emergent abilities, their transformative impact on NLP, and addresses challenges like interpretability, ethical concerns, and resource constraints, emphasizing the need for sustainable and responsible deployment.

Chapter 2: Theoretical Foundations of Large Language Models

Focusing on the theoretical underpinnings of LLMs, this chapter explores the essential concepts, algorithms, and mathematical principles driving their performance in language tasks. It traces the evolution from traditional n-gram models to modern transformer architectures like BERT and GPT, dissecting components such as attention mechanisms and encoder-decoder structures, while also identifying future research directions like multimodal and few-shot learning.

Chapter 3: Exploring the Core Principles, Architectures, and Advancements of Large Language Models

This chapter delves into the architectural frameworks and operational principles of LLMs, emphasizing their role in advancing human-computer interaction through complex text generation and comprehension. It addresses theoretical challenges, potential biases in training data, and ethical issues, while highlighting recent advancements and their impact on how humans engage with technology and information.

Section 2: Applications and Real-World Implementations

This section shifts focus to practical applications, showcasing how LLMs and related technologies are deployed across diverse industries and domains to solve real-world challenges.

Chapter 4: Real-World Implementations of Large Language Models

Exploring the practical applications of LLMs, this chapter highlights their impact across industries like healthcare, automotive, finance, education, customer service, and social media. Through case studies, it illustrates the benefits and challenges of implementation, addressing data privacy, ethical concerns, and governance frameworks, while also covering state-of-the-art research in various domains.

Chapter 5: Machine Learning Algorithms for Diabetes Classification within the CRISP-DM Framework

Focusing on healthcare applications, this chapter applies machine learning algorithms within the CRISP-DM framework to achieve accurate diabetes diagnosis using the Pima Indians Diabetes database. It compares five algorithms, with the Decision Tree model achieving 94% accuracy, and prioritizes recall for medical reliability, demonstrating the practical utility of data-driven approaches in health diagnostics.

Section 3: Education, Ethics, and Cybersecurity

The final section addresses the broader implications of LLMs, focusing on their role in education, ethical challenges, and their application in cybersecurity.

Chapter 6: Innovating Education 6.0: LLM Classroom Strategies for Robotics and Computing Skills Integration in the EFL Ecosystem

This chapter explores the integration of LLMs into Education 6.0, focusing on classroom strategies that combine robotics, computing, and English as a Foreign Language (EFL) instruction. It highlights LLMs' role as a bridge between technical and language education, proposing future research into long-term impacts and broader STEM applications within EFL ecosystems.

Chapter 7: Ethical and Societal Implications of Large Language Models

Addressing the ethical and societal challenges of LLMs, this chapter examines risks such as bias in training data, data privacy concerns, and the potential for disinformation. It advocates for transparent development, responsible data use, and robust ethical guidelines to ensure LLMs' societal benefits are maximized while mitigating potential harms.

Chapter 8: Assessing Security and Privacy Concerns in LLM Applications: Legal and Social Considerations

This chapter addresses the growing security and privacy risks associated with LLMs, such as Open AI's GPT-4, as they become embedded in everyday technology. It highlights the potential for LLMs, trained on vast web-scraped data including sensitive personal information, to inadvertently leak private data. The chapter stresses the importance of comprehensive strategies and regulatory compliance to ensure safe and ethical LLM use, offering a critical framework for mitigating legal and social concerns.

This structured organization ensures a cohesive narrative, guiding readers from foundational knowledge to practical applications and critical reflections, fostering a comprehensive understanding of LLMs' current state and future potential. This book's impact lies in its ability to synthesize cutting-edge research with actionable insights, positioning it as a vital resource for advancing the field of LLMs. By integrating theoretical rigor with practical applications and addressing ethical and educational dimensions, it contributes to a deeper understanding of how LLMs can be harnessed responsibly to solve real-world problems. The inclusion of diverse perspectives from global contributors enriches the discourse, fostering a collaborative approach to shaping the future direction of AI. As LLMs continue to evolve, this book serves as a foundation for researchers, practitioners, and policymakers to navigate their complexities, drive innovation, and ensure their benefits are realized across society.

Ismail Lamaakal
University Mohammed Premier, Morocco

Yassine Maleh
Sultan Moulay Slimane University, Morocco

Khalid El Makkaoui
University Mohammed Premier, Morocco

Ibrahim Ouahbi
University Mohammed Premier, Morocco

Ahmed Abd El-Latif
Prince Sultan University, Saudi Arabia

Section 1
Theoretical Foundations and Core Principles

Chapter 1

Foundation of Large Language Models and Their Emergent Abilities

Rashmi Gupta
Atal Bihari Vajpayee University, Bilaspur, India

Jeetendra Kumar
Atal Bihari Vajpayee University, Bilaspur, India

Suvarna Sharma
Dr. Vishwanath Karad MIT World Peace University, Pune, India

ABSTRACT

Large Language Models (LLMs) are throughly examined in this chapter, along with their potential, limitations and implications for existing artificial intelligence. An overview of the history and introduction of LLMs may be found in the introduction. A variety of language tasks, including translation and summarization, are examined in the Capabilities section where these models demonstrate outstanding performance. This highlights how much of an influence he has had on NLP(Natural Language Processing). This chapter emphasizes LLM's developing capabilities. With these developments, problems with interpret-ability, ethics, and resource limitations are addressed, highlighting the necessity of responsible application. This study expands of LLMs, consider it's promise, and indicates the importance using and generating them in a sustainable and ethical manner.

DOI: 10.4018/979-8-3693-8387-2.ch001

INTRODUCTION

The development of language skills starts in early childhood and continues all the way through an individual's lifespan. Language allows humans to express themselves and interact with one another in a way that is special to them. Human existence is fundamentally reliant on the capacity to express one's thoughts, feelings, and ideas via language, from the earliest phases of language learning to the intricate and sophisticated communication that characterizes adulthood. This continual language evolution is a reflection of the dynamic nature of human communication. It encompasses both the fundamental skills developed during childhood and the advanced language abilities people pick up during the course of their lives. Language comprehension is essential and affects a wide range of occupations. It is necessary for effective education, information exchange, and communication. Language proficiency is essential for negotiating, working together, and building professional relationships(Kuperberg & Jaeger, 2016). It drives natural language processing systems, chatbots, and artificial intelligence, all of which improve speech recognition. Language competency is crucial in the domains of healthcare, inter-cultural communication, law and governance, and innovation and creativity. It has an impact on laws, encourages close social ties, and stimulates innovation and creativity. Communication, education, and technological innovation all depend on language comprehension. Language comprehension is essential and affects a wide range of occupations.

Large Language Models

A fundamental paradigm in machine learning, Large Language Models (LLMs) use deep learning techniques to understand and interpret natural language. Through intensive training on text datasets, these models have developed the ability to identify complex patterns and connect a wide range of language-related ideas(Tuggener et al., 2024). Sentiment analysis, chatbot dialogues, and translation are just a few of the many linguistic tasks in which they specialize. Unlike other language processing systems, LLMs are able to navigate through dense textual content, detect items and their relationships, and produce text that is grammatically sound(Yang et al., 2024). However, a more thorough explanation of language models centers on the concept of assigning probabilities to word sequences that are obtained through methodical examination of text corpora. There are several types of language models, ranging from n-gram models, which are rather simple, to intricate neural network architectures. However, when we refer to "large language models" in particular, we imply models that include a huge number of parameters—typically several million or billions—and make use of deep learning techniques(Dwivedi et al., 2023). These enormously huge models produce material that frequently resembles that of human writers due to their astounding capacity to detect minute language patterns.

Language models have evolved along the same trajectory as natural language processing, from conventional statistical techniques to the ground-breaking impacts of deep learning architectures(Sarker, 2024). Recurrent neural networks (RNNs), Transformer topologies, and Long Short-Term Memory (LSTM) networks are a few significant technological advances along this road. With the advent of models like the BERT (Bidirectional Encoder Representations from Transformers)(Devlin et al., 2018) and GPT (Generative Pre-trained Transformers)(Liu et al., 2023) series, which show unprecedented levels of language creation and interpretation, language models have entered a new era. Future computer-human interactions will be impacted by these models as they develop and their consequences become increasingly evident in many contexts, changing the field of artificial intelligence. The purpose of each design piece is demonstrated in Figure 1, which also helps to visualize the data flow throughout a Transformer model.

Figure 1. Transformer model architecture

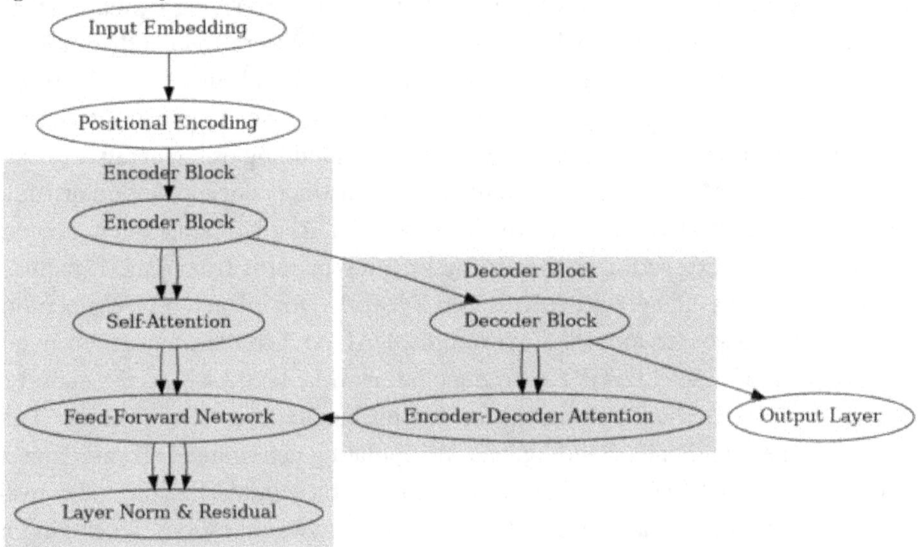

Generative AI vs Large Language Models

Generative AI is a more general name for artificial intelligence that focuses on producing unique, creative content for literature, music, and images, among other media. Variational autoencoders (VAEs) and generative adversarial networks (GANs) are two models in this class that try to extract new outputs that may not be immediately present in the dataset by learning patterns and structure from training data. Because it enables the production of a vast array of unique content, generative AI is very beneficial in creative fields(Akhtar, 2024). For example, GANs demonstrate the ability to be creative and innovative in image generation by producing realistic images that were never included in the training set.

Large language models, or LLMs, are a distinct subclass of generative AI that focuses on language-related issues. Large datasets containing a multitude of textual content are used to train these algorithms. Language machine learners (LLMs) exhibit exceptional comprehension and produce writing that is similar to that of humans for a variety of linguistic tasks, including translating, summarizing, and answering questions. They are often used in natural language processing applications such as chatbots, virtual assistants, and content generation since it is important that the content they produce is comprehensible and pertinent to the context(Du et al., 2024). Without LLMs, which primarily operate with textual material, language-connected artificial intelligence systems would not be feasible.

Large language models (LLMs) focus on the smallest linguistic nuances and provide exceptional capabilities for understanding and producing textual material at a never-before-seen scale, whereas generative AI is more frequently employed in creative industries. Both significantly contribute to the advancement of artificial intelligence by demonstrating the range of language-related applications and creative possibilities made possible by generative methodologies. Generative AI and Large Language Models (LLMs) are related but distinct concepts within artificial intelligence. Generative AI is a broad category of AI that creates new content, such as images, text, audio, or videos, by learning patterns from data. It includes models like GANs (Generative Adversarial Networks) for images, music generation systems, and text-based models. For example, DALL·E generates images from text prompts, while LLMs like GPT-4 produce human-like text. LLMs are a subset of generative AI, specifically designed for natural language processing tasks. They focus on generating, understanding, and manipulating text, trained on vast datasets of written content. LLMs excel in tasks like translation, summarization, and conversation. For instance, ChatGPT can draft emails or answer questions, leveraging its language generation capabilities. Unlike other generative AI, LLMs are specialized for linguistic tasks and rely on architectures like transformers. The key difference lies in scope and application. Generative AI spans multiple modalities—text, images, or sounds—while LLMs are text-centric. Generative AI may use diverse algorithms (e.g., VAEs or diffusion models), but LLMs typically use transformer-based architectures. Challenges also differ: generative AI faces issues like image quality or audio fidelity, while LLMs struggle with biases and interpretability, as seen in the earlier table. Both share ethical concerns, like misuse of deepfakes or misinformation. Together, they advance creativity and communication, but LLMs are a specialized tool within the broader generative AI landscape.

Capabilities of LLMs

LLM's are helpful tools in the field of natural language processing because of their wide range of language task capabilities. LLMs are adept at a wide range of tasks, from sentiment analysis and language translation to more complex ones like text summarization and question-answering. They are at the forefront of AI development due to their ability to produce and process text (Liu et al., 2023; Ni et al., 2023; Schoenegger & Park, 2023; Tamkin & Brundage, 2021).

Contextual Understanding

The capacity of large language models (LLMs) to comprehend context is a key feature that distinguishes them from conventional language models. GPT-3 is one of the transformer designs that is exceptionally able to understand the meaning of individual words, phrases, and sentences in connection to the entire context of an input. LLMs use contextual windows, transfer learning, and attention processes as tools to learn subtle contextual links and interpret data by taking word connections into account, (Barman et al., 2024). Pre-training on diverse datasets improves the models' understanding of language patterns and helps them generate logical responses that are appropriate for the situation. Because LLMs have a greater understanding of semantic nuances in addition to syntax, they can identify and adjust to a wide range of linguistic settings. Additionally, focusing on certain domains enhances their understanding of context, especially for specific applications. Contextual awareness is a crucial aspect of LLMs that enables them to do a variety of language-related activities with a high level of complexity and accuracy, such as summarizing, responding to inquiries, and producing natural language.

Examples:

User Query: What is the capital of Russia?

LLMs Response: The Capital of Russia is Moscow.

User Query: What are some famous landmarks there?

LLMs Response: In Moscow, you can find iconic landmarks such as the kremlin, Red Square, and St. Basil's Cathedral..

In this example, the Large Language Model (LLM) showcases its contextual comprehension by effortlessly integrating details from the original inquiry about the capital of France into the subsequent user input concerning renowned sites. The LLM acknowledges and preserves the fact that "Paris" is linked to the capital of France, enabling it to offer pertinent and contextually conscious replies. The model's capacity to comprehend the context allows for more logical and genuine exchanges in a discussion, demonstrating its aptitude to preserve and expand upon knowledge from prior exchanges. Figure 2 depicting the breakdown of LLM capabilities has been successfully created and displayed, indicating the proficiency scores for different tasks.

Figure 2. Capabilities breakdown

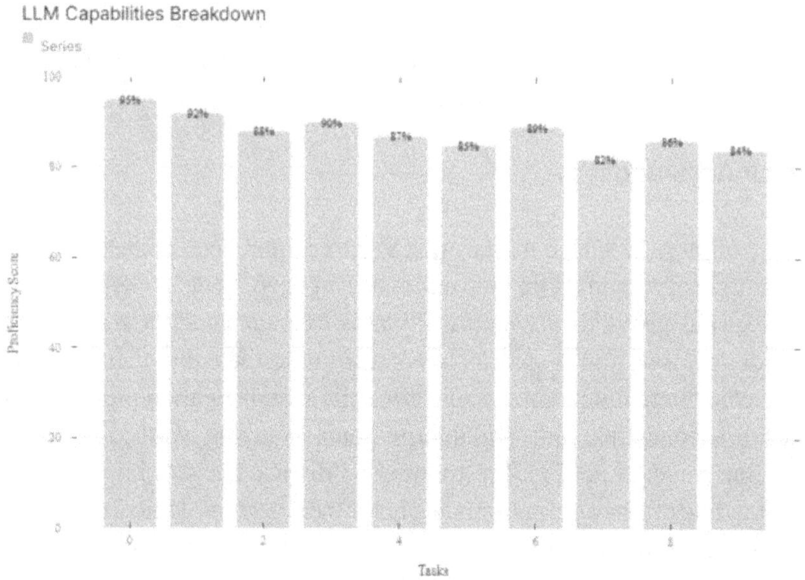

Natural Language Generation

Large Language Models' (LLMs') Natural Language Generation (NLG) capability is a significant advancement in artificial intelligence. The ability of LLMs, like as GPT-3, to produce language that is both contextually appropriate and resembling human writing is astounding. These models use an autoregressive generation technique to generate words sequentially and make predictions. They achieve this by making use of the context that the words that came before them offer. This process culminates in the production of text replies that are diverse, fluid, and coherent. The creation of content, chatbots, and text summarization are just a few of the many uses for LLMs' natural language generation (NLG) capabilities. Through extensive pre-training on a range of datasets, language learning machines (LLMs) gain a thorough grasp of linguistic nuances and structures. At their disposal including this knowledge, they may create contextually relevant answers for a range of topics and domains(Riyadh & Shafiq, 2023). Furthermore, rapid engineering is sufficiently versatile to enable users to guide LLMs in the development of specific types of material, demonstrating the flexibility and reactivity of the NLG capabilities.

Example:

User Query: Compose a short paragraph about the benefits of regular physical activity.

LLMs Response: Regular physical activity offers a myriad of health benefits. It improves cardiovascular fitness, enhances mood by releasing endorphins, and helps in maintaining a healthy weight. Additionally, physical activity boosts overall energy levels, strengthens muscles and bones, and contributes to better sleep quality. The positive impact on mental well-being, including reduced stress and anxiety, further underscored the importance of incorporating regular physical activity into one's life style.

Language Translation

The language translation capabilities of large language models, which have been extensively trained on multilingual datasets, are astounding. Because these models have a thorough understanding of context, they may generate logical translations based on cues. When they tackle routine translation tasks, their versatility is demonstrated by the contextual comprehension they use to produce content that makes sense in the given context. They are beneficial for a variety of language-related applications because of their strength, which is their fluid language shifting(Huang et al., 2023). They effortlessly produce translations for a range of contexts, showcasing their adaptability in recognizing subtleties and maintaining consistency. With this contextual competency, large language models are positioned as adaptable tools that facilitate linguistic diversity and inter-lingual communication. It's crucial to understand that, even if they translate effectively, specialized translation models can offer more accuracy and precision for particular and crucial translation needs.

Examples:

User Query: Translate the following English sentence to German: 'Hello, how are you?'

LLMs Response: Hallo, wie geht es dir?

Question Answering

The ability of Large Language Models (LLMs) to answer questions is a notable characteristic that demonstrates their proficiency in understanding and reacting to user inquiries. Because they have been trained on large datasets, LLMs have an in-depth understanding of context and take the surrounding data into account when producing answers. They can accurately grasp the intent behind inquiries due to their ability to detect complex relationships and meanings in language, which is made possible by their semantic comprehension(Tan et al., 2023). LLMs acquire information on a wide range of issues by utilizing their extensive knowledge base and offer answers that are pertinent to the context. Their capacity to extrapolate from ingrained patterns enables them to reply to inquiries even in situations when the precise data was not encountered during training. These models also perform well in multi-turn conversations, remembering prior encounters' context to provide more logical and context-aware responses.

Examples:

User Query: What is the capital of China?

LLMs Response: The capital of China is Beijing.

Text Summarization

Extensive textual information can be effectively summarized by Large Language Models (LLMs), demonstrating their impressive summarizing power. LLMs are highly skilled in identifying important concepts and prioritizing information according to relevance in the input text because of their deep understanding of language semantics and nuanced contextual comprehension. The resulting summaries illustrate the models' capacity to communicate meaning while condensing information, as they successfully capture the key components of the original content. LLMs are very versatile since they can handle a variety of text types, such as papers and articles, and they may be tailored to the user's preferred summary length. But it's important to be aware of any potential drawbacks, like difficulties managing extremely technical material or summarizing subtle subjective elements of the text. Large Language Models (LLMs) are able to summarize a great deal of textual information in a clear and concise manner, (Işıkdemir, 2024). This ability to summarize highlights the power of LLMs as tools that can be used for a variety of tasks, such as news aggregation, document summarization, and content selection. Additionally, it highlights the role that LLMs play in improving information processing and comprehension.

Examples:

User Query: Summarize the following text: 'A blockchain is a distributed database ledger shared across a computer network's nodes. They are best known for their crucial role in cryptocurrency systems, maintaining a secure and decentralized record of transactions, but they are not limited to cryptocurrency uses.'

LLMs Response: A distributed ledger accessible through a computer network is called a blockchain. Although it is most known for protecting bitcoin transaction, it has applications beyond the cryptocurrency.

Text Classification

Large Language Models (LLMs) are notable for their capacity to classify text, which shows how flexible they are in understanding and classifying textual input. These models, which have been trained on a variety of datasets, have a profound semantic comprehension of language, enabling them to recognize minute details and contextual clues in text to provide precise classification. By utilizing sophisticated pattern recognition, LLMs are able to recognize unique characteristics linked to several categories, which makes them ideal for jobs like subject categorization, sentiment analysis, and other intricate classification projects. Their versatility to handle a wide range of themes and domains guarantees their efficacy in managing a variety of classification jobs, and their capacity for multi-class classification increases their usefulness in a multitude of contexts. LLMs also use transfer learning, which allows them to apply knowledge from one activity to another in order to perform better.

Example:

User query: Classify the following text as either positive, negative, or neutral: 'The new application design fulfill user requirements with additional features and accrued efficiency.'

LLM's Response: Positive

Text Editing

Large Language Models (LLMs) use their comprehension of language semantics and context to demonstrate remarkable text editing capabilities. These models can be used to modify style, restructure sentences, and proofread texts, among other text editing activities. A text document and any necessary modifications are presented to the LLM during the text editing process. With its vast language expertise at its disposal, the model analyses the context and semantics to produce revised or enhanced versions of the input text. Grammar mistakes are easily found by LLMs, who can also provide suitable fixes and make statements seem more coherent overall. To improve the text's clarity and flow, they can provide synonyms or other wording. These models can also help with formatting needs, tone modifications, and following particular writing styles.

Example:

User query: Rewrite following sentence with formal tone 'Inference is the process that a trained machine learning model uses to draw conclusion from latest data. An AI model capable of making inference can do so without examples of the desired result.'

LLM's Response: A trained machine learning model uses inference to make deductions from latest data. An AI model that is proficient at drawing inferences can achieve this without the necessity of examples of the intended result.

Information Extraction

Large Language Models (LLMs) are quite good at identifying and extracting pertinent information from unstructured text. These models do exceptionally well at identifying entities, including names of individuals, groups, places, and dates, which paves the way for thorough information extraction. Beyond only identifying items, LLMs are also able to determine the linkages and interconnections among various textual parts, offering valuable insights. Furthermore, these models demonstrate an ability to extract event-related information such as names, dates, locations, and participants, which helps to provide a comprehensive knowledge of events within a particular context. By utilizing their extensive contextual knowledge, LLMs guarantee that information extraction considers the surrounding text, improving interpretation accuracy. LLMs can handle extraction jobs in several languages thanks to their multilingual training, which increases their global applicability. LLMs can be adjusted and customized by users to suit particular extraction needs and domain-specific requirements. LLMs are useful tools in content analysis, data mining, and knowledge graph development because of their organized output, which makes it easier to analyze the data further and integrate it with other systems.

Example:

User query: Extract information from following sentence 'In 1969, Neil Armstrong became the first person to walk on the moon during the Apollo 11 mission. Buzz Aldrin followed him shortly after. The historic event took place on July 20, 1969.

LLM's Response: Year of Moon Landing: 1969

Astronauts Involved: First Person: Neil Armstrong, Second Person: Buzz Aldrin

Mission Name: Apollo 11

Date of Moon Landing: July 20, 1969

Code Generation

Large Language Models (LLMs) are an invaluable resource for developers and programmers looking for effective ways to tackle a variety of programming jobs because of their capacity to generate code. LLMs are capable of deciphering plain language requests and returning syntactically sound code fragments(Gu, 2023; Nejjar et al., 2023). For example, a function customized to the specification provided by the user could be provided if they asked for a Python code snippet to calculate the factorial of a given number. Developers can express their needs in simple terms and get pertinent code segments with this feature, which is applicable to a broad range of programming activities. Although code may be generated more quickly with LLMs, users still need to be cautious and check the output to make sure best practices are followed and any security issues are addressed. LLM can generate code in various programming languages as shown in Figure 3.

Example:

Figure 3. Program code generation

User query :	write a code in C++ to calculate the sum of two given numbers
LLM's Response:	Following is code.

```
python                                                    Copy code

# Function to add two numbers
def add_numbers(num1, num2):
    return num1 + num2

# Input: Taking two numbers from the user
number1 = float(input("Enter the first number: "))
number2 = float(input("Enter the second number: "))

# Adding the two numbers using the function
result = add_numbers(number1, number2)

# Displaying the result
print(f"The sum of {number1} and {number2} is: {result}")
```

Dialog Systems

Many essential aspects for natural language interactions are included in the dialog capability of Large Language Models (LLMs). With the use of robust natural language comprehension, LLMs are able to interpret user input, remember context across turns, and produce responses that are appropriate for the given context. Their ability to handle multi-turn conversations facilitates lengthy and dynamic interactions, which enhances the user experience. Moreover, LLMs can carry out operations, deliver data, and be tailored or improved for particular chatbot uses. Real-time data retrieval is made possible by the integration potential with external systems, which improves their capabilities. LLM-based chatbots offer a genuine and interactive conversational experience in addition to a user-friendly interface for information retrieval.

Example:

User query: Recommend a good book on cloud computing.
LLM's Response: The highly recommended book on cloud computing is "Cloud Computing: Concepts, Technology & Architecture" by Thomas Erl, Zoran Skvarc, and Riccardo P. F. Pratley. This book provides a through and detailed description of cloud computing concepts, architectures, and technologies. It serves as a great reference for both newcomers and experts and is a must-read for any IT professional interested in cloud computing. Whether you're a beginner or someone looking to deepen your understanding, "Cloud Computing: Concepts, Technology & Architecture" is a highly regarded resource in the field.

Sentiment Analysis

Large Language Models (LLMs) have impressive sentiment analysis skills; they can identify and interpret the emotions conveyed in text with ease. LLMs analyse the complexity included in the selection of words, phrases, and expressions to ascertain if the sentiment being expressed is positive, negative, or neutral by drawing on their extensive contextual knowledge and competence in natural language processing. The unique quality of LLMs is their capacity to conduct sentiment analysis in a variety of languages, demonstrating their adaptability in a worldwide setting. By fine-tuning these models for certain domains, users may guarantee customized sentiment evaluations that take into account the subtleties unique to their sector. Because of their real-time analysis capabilities, LLMs are useful in situations such as consumer feedback analysis and social media monitoring.

Example:

User query: Give sentiment of the following sentence. I just watched the new web series, and it was fantastic! The plot was engaging, and the acting was superb.
LLM's Response: The sentiment of the given sentence is positive.

Scaling Law of LLM

Scaling laws in the context of Large Language Models (LLMs) pertain to the consistent correlations and patterns identified between the magnitude of a language model and its effectiveness in different natural language processing (NLP) activities. These rules emphasize the influence of increasing the amount of parameters or factors connected to parameters in LLM systems on their capacity to comprehend and produce text that resembles human language. Typical findings consist of a consistent enhancement in performance as the model size grows, improvements that are not specific to a particular job, a decrease in the rate of progress as the model size becomes greater, increased efficiency in using data, and the balance between model size and computational expenses. An examination of scaling laws is crucial for fine-tuning the dimensions of LLMs to suit particular applications, taking into account aspects like as job specifications, data availability, and processing capabilities(Hoffmann et al., 2022).

A large Language model is characterize by four elements explained below:

No of Parameters (N)- Denotes the number of parameters that are amenable to learning within the model. Augmenting the parameter count results in a more robust and expressive model capable of capturing intricate language patterns.

Size of Dataset (D)- This parameter denotes the diversity and size of the dataset utilized for model training. An enlarged and heterogeneous dataset enhances the model's comprehension of language, thereby facilitating more accurate generalization.

Compute Budget (C)- It indicates the allocation of computational resources for the purposes of training and deploying the model. Increased computational resources enable more comprehensive model training, which in turn facilitates the investigation of more sizable architectures and datasets.

Architecture of model- The architectural components of the model, such as the arrangement of layers and attention mechanisms, are encompassed within its design and structure. The manner in which a model utilizes its parameters, dataset, and computational resources to generate and comprehend language is influenced by the model's architecture.

All of these parts together describe what a large language model is and what it can do. The number of parameters, dataset size, compute budget, and model design all play a huge role in how well the model works and how well it can do different natural language processing jobs. To get the most out of the model's efficiency, effectiveness, and usefulness, these factors must be balanced.

Till now two scaling laws have been introduced.

KM Scaling Law

This law was introduced by Kaplan et al.(Kaplan et al., 2020) in 2020 at OpenAI. They modelled the relationship of the model's performance with three major factors i.e. number of parameters, size of dataset and compute budget. The test loss of a Transformer, which is trained to autonomously model language, can be forecasted using a power-law equation when its performance is constrained by either the number of non-embedding parameters N, the size of the dataset D, or the optimally allocated compute budget C_{min}.

1. For models with a limited number of parameters, trained to convergence on sufficiently large datasets

L(N) = (Nc/N) αN ; αN ~ 0.076, Nc ~ 8.8 × 1013 (non-embedding parameters)
(1.1)

2. For large models trained with a limited dataset with early stopping.

L(D) = (Dc/D) αD ; αD ~ 0.095, Dc ~ 5.4 × 1013 (tokens)
(1.2)

3. When training with a limited amount of compute, a sufficiently large dataset, an optimally-sized model, and a sufficiently small batch size (making optimal use of compute)

$L(C_{min})$ = C min c /Cminα min C ; α min C ~ 0.050, C_{min} c ~ 3.1 × 108 (PF-days)
(1.3)

Following are findings of the KM law-

- The magnitude of the loss follows a power law relationship with the size of the model, the quantity of the dataset, and the computational resources utilized during training.
- The impact of network depth and width is minimal.
- The performance of a model is heavily influenced by its size, which is governed by three factors: the number of parameters in the model (excluding embeddings), the size of the training dataset, and the computational resources used for training. As the magnitude of these factors increases, the performance improves. However, above a certain threshold, further increasing the size of the model does not yield significant enhancements.
- Put simply, the model's performance adheres to discernible patterns. The performance improves when we proportionally increase the size of both the model and the dataset. Nevertheless, when one variable remains constant while the other is incremented, the rate of enhancement decelerates, resulting in an anticipated drawback. Therefore, by increasing the model size eightfold, we can mitigate any negative consequences by increasing the data size by fivefold.
- Regarding training, the curves adhere to specific patterns that remain rather consistent regardless of the size of the model. By examining the initial segment of the training curve, we may make a reasonable estimation of the performance that can be achieved with extended training.
- Evaluating the models on the text that differ from their training data yields results that are correlated with the training validation set, albeit with a con-

sistent deviation in the loss. Put simply, employing the model on a new text category results in a penalty, but, the enhancement is comparable to what we observe on the training set.

- Large models exhibit superior efficiency in data utilization achieving high performance as compared to small models. Despite the initial assumption that training large models requires a substantial amount of data, it is, in fact, more sample-efficient. This means that it can produce satisfactory outcomes with fewer optimization steps and a reduced amount of data.
- To optimize performance within a certain computing budget, it is advisable to train large models but halt the training process before they reach full convergence, provided there are no limitations on the model size or accessible data. This form of training is more efficient in terms of sample usage compared to training smaller models until they reach convergence.
- The optimal batch size for training these models is found by evaluating the gradient noise scale and is approximately 1-2 million tokens when the models reach convergence, for the largest models we are capable of training.

Chinchilla Scaling Law

In 2022, a paper(Hoffmann et al., 2022) was published by DeepMind entitled "Training Compute Optimal Large Language Models". This study attempted to investigate the relationship between three important variables: the compute budget, the number of tokens, and the model size. The writers aimed to comprehend the correlation between these parameters. Their study yielded a significant finding: existing Large language models (LLMs) such as the 175B GPT-3, 280B Gopher, and 530B Megatron are significantly inadequately trained. Although there has been an increase in the number of parameters in these models, the training data has stayed unchanged.

The authors emphasize the significance of maintaining a proportional relationship between the amount of training tokens and the size of the model in order to achieve compute-optimal training. In order to validate their results, the researchers carried out training experiments with around 400 language models. These models varied in size, ranging from 70 million to over 16 billion parameters, and were trained on datasets containing 5 to 500 billion tokens.

After determining a relationship among the three variables, the scientists trained a brand-new large language model (LLM) called Chinchilla. Chinchilla, despite having the same computational budget as the 280B Gopher, distinguished itself by having 70B parameters and four times the quantity of training data. Chinchilla surpassed well-known models like Gopher (280B), GPT-3 (175B), Jurassic-1 (178B), and Megatron (530B) in a remarkable manner.

This result contradicts "Scaling laws for LLMs" by OpenAI(Kaplan et al., 2020). The statement implies that, in contrast to commonly held beliefs, smaller models can attain better performance if they are trained on larger datasets. Furthermore, these smaller models are easy to finetune and reduce latency. The study highlights that prioritizing the attainment of the minimum loss may not be the most effective approach for enhancing computational efficiency in these models.

Their research question was - "Given a fixed FLOPs budget, how should one trade-off model size and the number of training tokens?" They utilized following approaches to answer this questions.

Fixed Model Size with Varying Numbers of Training Tokens

The primary objective of this experiment was to investigate the impact of varying amounts of training data on the performance of large language models (LLMs) that had fixed sizes. The researchers examined various model sizes (75M, 250M, 500M, 1B, 2.5B, 5B, 10B) and adjusted the number of training tokens, all while adhering to a limited computational budget of 5.76 x 10^23 FLOPs. The computational budget refers to the allocated computer resources. Through the application of a power law relationship, the researchers determined the most advantageous arrangement for Gopher's particular resources. Their analysis revealed that a model size of 67B, along with 1.5 trillion training tokens, would yield the highest level of performance. This finding offers useful insights into the scalability of LLMs and the significance of adjusting both the size of the model and the training data to achieve optimal performance within the constraints of available resources.

IsoFLOP Profiles

This study explored the correlation between the dimensions of the model, the volume of training data, and the effectiveness of performance under predetermined computing limitations. The study utilized nine different training FLOP counts, ranging from 10^18 to 10^21, to investigate the best model parameter count for a given computational budget. During training, the researchers suggested utilizing a cosine cycle length that progressively diminishes by a factor of 10 over a duration approximately equivalent to the number of training tokens (D) for models with more than D tokens. This particular training technique was recommended to enhance the learning process. The study determined that a model size of 63B is the optimal configuration for Gopher's compute budget, necessitating the use of 1.4 trillion training tokens. This discovery offers vital knowledge regarding the most efficient way to adjust the size of LLMs when computational resources are restricted.

Fitting a Parametric Loss Function

The third technique aimed to capitalize on the knowledge gained from the previous two approaches by combining their final losses. This approach saw the final loss as a mathematical function that relies on both the model parameters and the quantity of training tokens. Subsequently, the researchers suggested a precise mathematical expression for this correlation and utilized Huber loss minimization to ascertain the most suitable model size given Gopher's computing budget (40 billion parameters). This novel methodology successfully integrates the advantages of the preceding methods, resulting in a more precise estimation for the optimal LLM design given certain limitations.

The scaling laws of large language models (LLMs) were examined by researchers using three separate methodologies. The initial study examined the impact of different training data on fixed model sizes, proposing that 67 billion parameters and 1.5 trillion tokens are the most suitable choices within Gopher's financial constraints. The second study investigated various model sizes while maintaining fixed budgets, determining that Gopher performs best efficiently with 63 billion parameters and 1.4 trillion tokens. The third technique integrated lessons from both perspectives and introduced a functional representation for the correlation between model parameters, training data, and ultimate loss. It indicated that smaller models could be more suitable for larger budgets, specifically around 40 billion parameters.

The following findings are uncovered by these approaches

1. It is advisable to increase the model size and training data in equal proportions.
2. The first two approaches produce comparable predictions, whereas the third approach indicates a tendency towards smaller models when dealing with larger budgets.
3. The Chinchilla model, which is trained based on these findings, employs MassiveText, AdamW optimizer, and SentencePiece tokenizer. During training, the performance of AdamW surpasses that of the Adam optimizer by 80% of the cosine cycle.

Emergent Abilities of LLM

Envision a turbulent mass of particles, appearing to be haphazard and autonomous. However, order arises from this state of chaos. These particles initiate interactions, giving rise to complex patterns and structures. The core of emergence lies in the phenomenon where the interactions of simple components result in the appearance of complex and unanticipated traits. Emergence extends beyond the domain of abstract theory. It pervades the fundamental structure of our universe, influencing everything from the exquisite patterns of snowflakes to the collective actions of ant colonies. Within the field of biology, individual cells work together to create organs and tissues, each with unique roles and emergent features that go beyond what an individual cell can do. Some suggest that our consciousness itself emerges from the intricate interaction of neurons in the brain. Large Language Models (LLMs) display emergent abilities, such as reasoning, creativity, and contextual comprehension, not directly programmed. For instance, GPT-4 solves intricate math problems or crafts coherent narratives. These capabilities emerge from extensive training data and large-scale models, enabling tasks like translation, summarization, and ethical decision-making, enhancing their versatility in real-world applications with good performance.

"Emergence is when quantitative changes in a system result in qualitative changes in behaviour."

By Nobel prize-winning physicist Philip Anderson in an essay 'More Is Different' 1972, (Liu et al., 2023)

Imagine using a scaling lens to zoom out and see how large language models (LLMs) have evolved. The x-axis represents the model scale, which includes both the training data and the number of parameters. We plot their performance on the y-axis, representing different jobs. At first, the performance shows consistent and presumably expected growth. However, a wonderful occurrence takes place. When one reaches a critical magnitude, a clear curve appears as shown in Figure 4. Once exhibiting a steady rise, the performance abruptly picks up speed, far outpacing the intended trajectory. The appearance of unanticipated capabilities is symbolized by this dramatic alteration, which is similar to a phase transition. In contrast to earlier models, extrapolating the performance of smaller models cannot reliably predict these talents. When a critical threshold is crossed, skills suddenly become active, which is a hallmark of emergent behavior. In order to have capacities beyond basic scaling effects, LLMs undergo a considerable shift as they get more complex. The once dormant emergent capabilities now impact the LLM's behavior, presenting new possibilities and challenging our understanding of artificial intelligence.

When the magnitude reaches a critical point a noticeable curve appears. The performance, which was marked by a steady increase, suddenly picks up speed and significantly deviates from the intended trajectory. This dramatic change, which is equivalent to a phase transition, represents the presence of unexpected potential. Unlike earlier models, the performance of younger models cannot be extrapolated to reliably predict these talents. The sudden activation of skills when a critical threshold is crossed defines emergent behavior. As LLMs become increasingly complex, they undergo a significant metamorphosis that gives them powers beyond basic scaling effects. The behavior of LLMs is now influenced by the once dormant emergent skills, opening up new possibilities and challenging our understanding of artificial intelligence.

Figure 4. Emergent abilities threshold

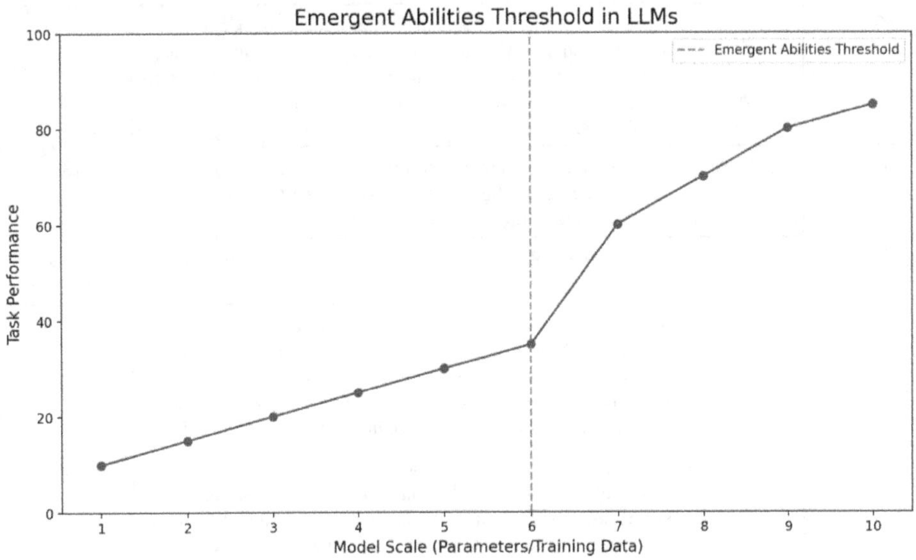

The notion of emergent skills goes beyond just generating text and includes a range of unforeseen and advanced capabilities exhibited by LLMs. Prominent instances encompass the development of reasoning capacities, wherein the model exhibits an aptitude for logical thinking and problem-solving that surpasses its expressly coded instructions. LLMs demonstrate emergent features in areas such as low-resource language translation, where they demonstrate expertise in translating languages with insufficient training data. Furthermore, these models can also exhibit proficiency in mathematical problem-solving, demonstrating their capacity to manipulate and understand numerical data. An Json et al.(*137 Emergent Abilities of Large Language Models — Jason Wei*, n.d.) gave the list of 137 emergent task.

Table 1. List of emergent tasks

Model Name	Number of Task	Tasks	Number of parameters
GPT-3	2	Hindu knowledge Modified arithmetic	13B
GPT-3	15	Analytic entailment, codenames, phrase relatedness, question answer creation, self evaluation tutoring, common morpheme, fact checker, figure of speech detection, international phonetic alphabet transliterate, logical deduction, misconceptions, physical intuition, social iqa, strange stories, strategyqa	175**B**
LaMDA	8	gender inclusive sentences german, repeat copy logic, sports understanding, swahili english proverbs, word sorting, word unscrambling, irony identification, logical args	137B
PaLM	3	auto debugging, sufficient information, parsiNLU reading comprehension	8B
PaLM	14	anachronisms, ascii word recognition, conceptual combinations, cryptonite, disambiguation_QA, emoji movie, goal step wikihow, GRE(Graduate record education), reading comprehension, linguistics puzzles, logic grid puzzle, metaphor understanding, odd one out, metaphor boolean, parsiNLU QA	64B
PaLM	25	analogical similarity, causal judgment, code line description, crass ai, cs algorithms, elementary math qa, english russian proverbs, geometric shapes, hyperbaton, identify odd metaphor, international phonetic alphabet NLI, language identification, logical fallacy detection, logical sequence, movie dialog same or different, physics questions, question selection, temporal sequences, understanding fables, unit interpretation, snarks, english proverbs, timedial, hinglish toxicity, VitaminC fact verification	540B
Chinchilla	7	Professional Medicine, High School Statistics, High School Macroeconomics, High School Psychology, Anatomy, High School Government And Politics, High School Microeconomics	7B
Chinchilla	44	International Law, Human Aging, Sociology, Us Foreign Policy, High School World History, Marketing, Logical Fallacies, Miscellaneous, College Biology, High School Us History, Security Studies, High School European History, High School Geography, Computer Security, Human Sexuality, Astronomy, Prehistory, Philosophy, Jurisprudence, Management, Moral Disputes, High School Biology, Professional Psychology, World Religions, Nutrition, Clinical Knowledge, Business Ethics, Medical Genetics, High School Computer Science, Public Relations, College Medicine, Conceptual Physics, Electrical Engineering, High School Chemistry, Machine Learning, Professional Accounting, Professional Law, Virology, Econometrics, College Physics, Elementary Mathematics, Moral Scenarios, Formal Logic, High School Physics	70B
Gopher	1	Toxicity Classification	7.1B
Gopher	1	Truthful QA	280B

Does Emergent Abilities of LLM Exist or it is a Misconception?

Schaeffer et al. (Schaeffer et al., 2023) claims in his recent research that large language models (LLMs) demonstrate emergent capabilities that are not present in smaller-scale models but become obvious in larger-scale models. The allure of emergent skills stems from their abrupt manifestation and inherent unpredictability as the scale of the model expands. Nonetheless, we present an alternate viewpoint, positing that, in a certain task and model category, new capabilities may develop as a result of the researcher's selection of a measurement criterion, rather than inherent alterations in model performance as it scales. Research intended to an alternate explanation stating that the perception of emerging abilities could be a result of non-linear or discontinuous measurements, whereas linear or continuous measurements result in consistent and predictable increases in model performance. To exemplify this idea, author presented a basic mathematical model and subsequently verified accuracy using three complementary methods:

1. Experimentally validate, and verify three hypotheses concerning the influence of metric selection on tasks related to purported emergent capabilities, utilizing the Instruct GPT/GPT-3 lineage.
2. Create, test, and validate two predictions regarding the selection of metrics in a meta-analysis of emergent abilities on BIG-Bench.
3. Exhibit the capacity to use measures that provide emergent capabilities that were previously unobserved in diverse vision tasks across different deep networks. Additionally provide evidence indicating that purported emerging abilities may diminish when using alternative metrics or utilizing more rigorous statistical approaches.

Challenges of LLM

Large Language Models (LLMs) have revolutionized natural language processing, but their responsible and effective use still faces several challenges. These challenges involve issues with ethics, interoperability, resource intensity, and fine-tuning. It's necessary to understand these challenges in order to improve LLM performance and reduce any risks.

Ethical Considerations

Large language models have the potential to learn from extensive databases, which may contain social biases, raising ethical concerns(Kasneci et al., 2023). When the training data is biased, the model may produce outputs that not only reflect the biases in the data but may also amplify them. Large language models have great potential for misuse, including the creation of harmful content, the spread of misinformation, and the creation of fake news. Most importantly, a harmonious balance must be maintained between ethical considerations and creative concepts. For example, during training, LLMs may encounter prejudiced terminology related to race, sexism, or other delicate topics. Therefore, when used for language production, LLMs may produce text that reinforces or exacerbates these prejudices. This ethical conundrum is particularly evident when language learning machines (LLMs) are employed in applications like chatbots, virtual assistants, or content moderation systems where an objective and equitable terminology is crucial. It is possible that the information generated may inadvertently reflect and reinforce societal biases, which will have detrimental real-world effects and reinforce unfavorable perceptions. To overcome this challenge, the training dataset must be carefully selected to minimize the amount of bias. In addition, continued work is needed to create and implement ways to make language models bias-free. To use language learning machines (LLMs) responsibly and minimize negative societal impacts while promoting equity and inclusiveness in the language development process, ethical considerations are crucial.

Opacities in Decision-Making

Opacities in decision-making within large language models constitute a significant difficulty that is founded in the complex structure of the mechanisms that are at the foundation of these models. Such models, which are often characterized by a large number of parameters, show intricate internal processes that are difficult to understand. Because the mechanism by which these models arrive at certain outputs is opaque, it is challenging to have a solid knowledge of the logic that goes into their decision-making. This lack of openness raises fundamental issues with accountability and trust. Stakeholders including users, developers, and regulatory bodies have difficulties when trying to examine and validate these models' decision-making procedures. The challenge also extends to assessing the reliability and equity of the produced outputs, especially in critical domains such as the healthcare, financial, and legal sectors where accountability and interpretability are critical. Improving interpretability techniques, promoting openness in model decision-making processes, and creating accountability frameworks are all required to overcome this challenge and ensure the ethical and responsible use of comprehensive language models.

Resource Intensity

Resource intensity seems to be a major barrier to the usage and deployment of big language models. This is mostly because these models demand a significant amount of processing power to function. Large language models need the use of complex hardware configurations and a substantial amount of energy resources for training and deployment, which raises energy consumption and has negative environmental implications. In addition to affecting operational costs, the computational demand also contributes to environmental issues by increasing the carbon footprint linked to energy usage. These models also provide a big challenge for smaller companies or organizations with limited access to computer resources of this type because of their high resource requirements. This limits the equitable distribution of advanced natural language processing skills by constraining the cost and accessibility of setting up large language models. To reduce adverse impacts on the environment and increase access for a variety of organizations, regardless of their size or resources, it is essential to consider more energy-efficient model designs, improve training protocols, and support sustainability practices.

Data Dependency

The effectiveness of large language models largely depends on the quality and diversity of the training data used during the learning process. It is still true that "garbage in, garbage out" emphasizes how important the quality of training data is to the effectiveness of a model. An inadequate or biased training dataset can impact the model's ability to apply its knowledge to new and different scenarios. If the training data does not adequately reflect different linguistic contexts, demographics, or viewpoints, the model's understanding may be limited and it may have difficulty understanding new inputs that differ from the training set. Furthermore, if the model has incomplete data, it may be less fair and exacerbate social inequality, reinforcing or exacerbating pre-existing biases. Ensuring that training datasets are representative, diverse, and equitable is essential to overcoming this challenge. Careful data preparation techniques, ethical considerations, and continued efforts to detect and improve biases are needed to ensure the reliability and applicability of comprehensive language models in a variety of real-world scenarios.

Challenges in Fine-Tuning

During the process of fine-tuning large language models for specific goals, overfitting becomes a serious issue that needs to be addressed. When the model focuses excessively on the intricacies of the training data, it ends up missing the nuances instead of learning the underlying patterns successfully. This is the result of the model being too specific. This maximizes performance on the training data alone, but it reduces the ability to accurately generalize to new, unexpected scenarios. The model may lack flexibility and have difficulty identifying important features in unfamiliar situations, as it tends to rely unnecessarily on the peculiarities of the training set. Overfitting hinders the model's ability to exhibit flexible and robust behavior in practical applications by making the model unnecessarily specific to the details of the training data. This is because the model becomes more rigid and less flexible. It is necessary to find a delicate balance during the fine-tuning phase to avoid overfitting. The use of methods such as data augmentation, regularization, and careful validation can help achieve this. A high level of generalization to a wide range of unexpected inputs is desired, in addition to the model having very good performance on the training data.

Interpretability

As is often the case in the legal or medical fields, interpretability becomes a critical requirement when implementing complex language models, especially when the decisions made by these models have a significant impact on people's lives. In order to provide transparency, accountability, and support to users, it is important to be able to understand the complex process and logic that leads to a certain result. However, achieving interpretability remains a major challenge in the field of advanced language models. The inherent complexity of these models, which are often characterized by deep neural networks with many parameters, makes it challenging to understand how inputs are transformed into outputs. The fact that these models are black-box models raises concerns about their reliability and equivalence as it is challenging to study and understand the dynamics behind decision-making. To overcome this hurdle, focused efforts are required. Building interpretable architectures, establishing clear guidelines for model transparency, and encouraging interdisciplinary collaboration are all necessary to bridge the gap between the complexity of models and their human interpretability. This effort is crucial or even essential to guaranteeing the appropriate and ethical use of language models in critical domains where interpretability is indispensable.

Societal Impact

It is important to remember that if giant language models are widely used, it can have large and possibly disruptive effects on society. These effects affect various aspects of human life and cover a wide spectrum of characteristics. There is a significant cause for worry in the field of employment, where the growing utilization of sophisticated language models may result in changes to the needs of jobs and the responsibilities that are now being performed. Due to the fact that these models are capable of automating specific linguistic activities, there is a possibility that particular jobs may be eliminated or that the skill requirements of the workforce will change. It is possible that the incorporation of comprehensive language models into the educational system will call for modifications to the curriculum design and instructional strategies that are already in use. Educational institutions may need to focus more on developing skills that enhance and leverage the potential of language models. This will ensure that people are well-equipped for a technologically advanced future.

Lack of Human in Loop

Large Language Models, because of their complexity and their ability to create text that is similar to that of humans, are capable of displaying behavior that may not be in accordance with the results that were intended or that are ethical. There is a greater potential for unforeseen effects to occur in the absence of adequate human control. These implications may include the production of content that is biased or incorrect, the dissemination of false information, or reactions that may be detrimental certain circumstances. These models acquire knowledge from enormous datasets, which may contain implicit biases or reflect social preconceptions that are present in the data upon which they are trained. There is a limited capacity to detect and eliminate these biases in the absence of human oversight, which may result in the potential reinforcement or amplification of preexisting social and cultural biases in the model's outputs.

Figure 5 shows the major ethical challenges faced in AI and machine learning, as well as possible solutions or mitigation strategies.

Figure 5. Ethical challenges and solutions

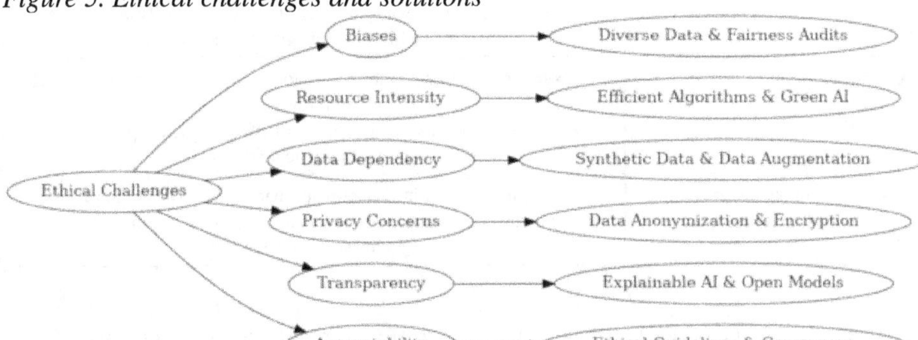

How to address the difficulties posed by the Large Language Models?

For the proper development and implementation of Large Language Models (LLMs), a multifaceted approach is required. Energy-efficient designs for environmental preservation, interoperability tactics for openness and ethical data curation to lessen biases, (Tamkin et al., 2021). To Ensure ethical behaviors, cooperation, regularization, and adherence to rules are necessary. The AI community may promote LLMs that are consistent with social norms and ethical standards by using these strategies. Various solutions to address the difficulties posed by Large Language Models are shown in Table 2.

Table 2. Solutions to address difficulties posed for large language models

Challenges of LLM	Solutions
Generation of biased data	• Curate diverse and representative datasets, actively identifying and addressing biases • Promote ethical guidelines for data collection
Lack of interpretability	• Develop interpretable model architectures, create transparency in decision-making processes • Establish standards for model interpretability in critical applications.
Resource Intensity	• Explore energy-efficient model architectures, optimize training processes, and adopt sustainable practices. • Prioritize environmental considerations in model development.
Limited access to computational resources	• Promote collaboration and resource-sharing initiatives • Develop lightweight model variants suitable for deployment on less powerful hardware
Overfitting can limit a model's ability to handle new examples	• Implement regularization techniques during training and use diverse datasets • fine-tune models carefully to ensure robust generalization to unseen data
Potential misuse of language models for malicious purposes	• Establish and adhere to ethical guidelines for the development and deployment of LLMs • Advocate for responsible AI practices and collaborate with regulatory bodies to create guidelines and policies.
Continuous Monitoring and Updates	• Implement systems for continuous monitoring, periodic model retraining • updates to ensure ongoing performance and adaptability to evolving linguistic landscapes.
Lack of human oversight can lead to unintended consequences.	• Integrate human-in-the-loop approaches, where human reviewers are involved in model decision-making, providing guidance and addressing edge cases.

Large Language Models (LLMs) have revolutionized natural language processing, powering applications like chatbots, automated translation, and content generation. However, their development and deployment present several challenges, as outlined in the table 2. The first challenge is the generation of biased data. LLMs trained on biased datasets can perpetuate stereotypes, such as associating certain professions with specific genders. For example, a model trained on imbalanced text might suggest that engineers are predominantly male. To mitigate this, developers should curate diverse and representative datasets that include varied demographics, cultures, and perspectives. Actively identifying biases through regular audits—such as analyzing outputs for unfair treatment of minority groups—and addressing them by reweighting or augmenting data ensures fairer outcomes. Promoting ethical guidelines for data collection further prevents the reinforcement of societal biases, fostering inclusive AI systems. Another significant issue is the lack of interpretability, as LLMs often function as "black boxes," obscuring their decision-making processes. This is particularly problematic in high-stakes domains like healthcare, where an LLM recommending treatments must justify its reasoning to gain trust. Solutions include developing interpretable architectures, such as attention mechanisms that highlight influential input segments, and using visualization tools to show how inputs lead to outputs. Establishing standards for interpretability in critical applications, such as legal or medical AI, ensures accountability and builds user confidence in model decisions. Resource intensity poses a further challenge, as training LLMs requires substantial computational power, leading to high energy consumption and environmental concerns. For instance, training a model like GPT-3 can emit significant carbon dioxide. To address this, developers can explore energy-efficient architectures, such as distilled models that maintain performance with less computation, and optimize training through techniques like mixed-precision computing. Prioritizing sustainable practices, such as powering data centers with renewable energy, helps mitigate the environmental impact of LLMs. Limited access to computational resources restricts smaller organizations from leveraging LLMs. Collaborative initiatives, like open-source platforms such as Hugging Face, enable resource sharing, while developing lightweight model variants, such as distilled or quantized models, allows deployment on less powerful hardware like mobile devices, democratizing AI access. Overfitting is another concern, where models excel on training data but struggle with new inputs. For example, a chatbot trained on specific dialogues might fail with novel queries. Regularization techniques, like dropout, and diverse datasets, combined with careful fine-tuning, ensure robust generalization to unseen data. The potential misuse of LLMs for malicious purposes, such as generating misinformation, is a serious risk. Ethical guidelines from organizations like IEEE, coupled with collaboration with regulators to establish policies restricting harmful content, promote responsible AI practices. Additionally, LLMs must adapt to evolving linguistic trends, requiring continuous monitoring and periodic retraining to stay relevant—e.g., incorporating post-2020 terms like "COVID-19." Finally, the lack of human oversight can lead to unintended outputs. Human-in-the-loop approaches, where reviewers validate responses, ensure reliability, particularly in sensitive contexts like customer service.

CONCLUSION

Large Language Models (LLMs) are revolutionary development in artificial intelligence that fundamentally transforms how computers comprehend and produce human language. These advanced models, utilizing deep learning methods and extensive training data, have shown remarkable ability in many natural language processing tasks. A thorough examination of Large Language Models (LLMs), clarifying their capabilities, emerging skills, and related issues, in modern artificial intelligence offered in this study. A concise overview of the historical background and importance of LLMs provides in the introduction that used to prepare the groundwork for a thorough examination. It becomes evident how LLMs significantly revolutionize the field of natural language processing by assessing their capabilities, ranging from translating languages to summarizing information.

REFERENCES

Akhtar, Z. Bin. (2024). Unveiling the evolution of generative AI (GAI): a comprehensive and investigative analysis toward LLM models (2021–2024) and beyond. *Journal of Electrical Systems and Information Technology 2024 11:1, 11*(1), 1–21. https://doi.org/DOI: 10.1186/S43067-024-00145-1

Barman, K. G., Wood, N., & Pawlowski, P. (2024). Beyond transparency and explainability: On the need for adequate and contextualized user guidelines for LLM use. *Ethics and Information Technology, 26*(3), 1–12. DOI: 10.1007/S10676-024-09778-2/METRICS

Devlin, J., Chang, M. W., Lee, K., & Toutanova, K. (2018). BERT: Pre-training of Deep Bidirectional Transformers for Language Understanding. *NAACL HLT 2019 - 2019 Conference of the North American Chapter of the Association for Computational Linguistics: Human Language Technologies - Proceedings of the Conference, 1*, 4171–4186. https://arxiv.org/abs/1810.04805v2

Du, F., Ma, X.-J., Yang, J.-R., Liu, Y., Luo, C.-R., Wang, X.-B., Jiang, H.-O., Jing, X., Du, F., Ma, X.-J., Yang, J.-R., Liu, Y., Luo, C.-R., Wang, X.-B., Jiang, H.-O., & Jing, X. (2024). A Survey of LLM Datasets: From Autoregressive Model to AI Chatbot. *Journal of Computer Science and Technology, 2024, Vol. 39, Issue 3, Pages: 542-566, 39*(3), 542–566. https://doi.org/DOI: 10.1007/S11390-024-3767-3

Dwivedi, Y. K., Kshetri, N., Hughes, L., Slade, E. L., Jeyaraj, A., Kar, A. K., Baabdullah, A. M., Koohang, A., Raghavan, V., Ahuja, M., Albanna, H., Albashrawi, M. A., Al-Busaidi, A. S., Balakrishnan, J., Barlette, Y., Basu, S., Bose, I., Brooks, L., Buhalis, D., & Wright, R. (2023). Opinion Paper: "So what if ChatGPT wrote it?" Multidisciplinary perspectives on opportunities, challenges and implications of generative conversational AI for research, practice and policy. *International Journal of Information Management, 71*, 102642. DOI: 10.1016/J.IJINFOMGT.2023.102642

Gu, Q. (2023). LLM-Based Code Generation Method for Golang Compiler Testing. *ESEC/FSE 2023 - Proceedings of the 31st ACM Joint Meeting European Software Engineering Conference and Symposium on the Foundations of Software Engineering*, 2201–2203. https://doi.org/DOI: 10.1145/3611643.3617850

Hoffmann, J., Borgeaud, S., Mensch, A., Buchatskaya, E., Cai, T., Rutherford, E., de Las Casas, D., Hendricks, L. A., Welbl, J., Clark, A., Hennigan, T., Noland, E., Millican, K., van den Driessche, G., Damoc, B., Guy, A., Osindero, S., Simonyan, K., Elsen, E., & Sifre, L. (2022). Advances in Neural Information Processing Systems: Vol. 35. *Training Compute-Optimal Large Language Models.*, https://arxiv .org/abs/2203.15556v1

Huang, H., Wu, S., Liang, X., Wang, B., Shi, Y., Wu, P., Yang, M., & Zhao, T. (2023). Towards Making the Most of LLM for Translation Quality Estimation. *Lecture Notes in Computer Science (Including Subseries Lecture Notes in Artificial Intelligence and Lecture Notes in Bioinformatics), 14302 LNAI*, 375–386. https://doi.org/DOI: 10.1007/978-3-031-44693-1_30

Işıkdemir, Y. E. (2024). NLP TRANSFORMERS: ANALYSIS OF LLMS AND TRADITIONAL APPROACHES FOR ENHANCED TEXT SUMMARIZATION. *Journal of Engineering and Architecture Faculty of Eskisehir Osmangazi University*, *32*(1), 1140–1151. DOI: 10.31796/OGUMMF.1303569

Kaplan, J., McCandlish, S., & Henighan Open, A. I. T., Brown OpenAI, T. B., Chess OpenAI, B., Child OpenAI, R., Gray OpenAI, S., Radford OpenAI, A., Wu OpenAI, J., & Amodei OpenAI, D. (2020). *Scaling Laws for Neural Language Models*. https://arxiv.org/abs/2001.08361v1

Kasneci, E., Sessler, K., Küchemann, S., Bannert, M., Dementieva, D., Fischer, F., Gasser, U., Groh, G., Günnemann, S., Hüllermeier, E., Krusche, S., Kutyniok, G., Michaeli, T., Nerdel, C., Pfeffer, J., Poquet, O., Sailer, M., Schmidt, A., Seidel, T., & Kasneci, G. (2023). ChatGPT for good? On opportunities and challenges of large language models for education. *Learning and Individual Differences*, *103*, 102274. DOI: 10.1016/J.LINDIF.2023.102274

Kuperberg, G. R., & Jaeger, T. F. (2016). What do we mean by prediction in language comprehension? *Language, Cognition and Neuroscience*, *31*(1), 32–59. DOI: 10.1080/23273798.2015.1102299 PMID: 27135040

Liu, Y., Han, T., Ma, S., Zhang, J., Yang, Y., Tian, J., He, H., Li, A., He, M., Liu, Z., Wu, Z., Zhao, L., Zhu, D., Li, X., Qiang, N., Shen, D., Liu, T., & Ge, B. (2023). Summary of ChatGPT-Related research and perspective towards the future of large language models. *Meta-Radiology*, *1*(2), 100017. DOI: 10.1016/J.METRAD.2023.100017

Nejjar, M., Zacharias, L., Stiehle, F., & Weber, I. (2023). LLMs for science: Usage for code generation and data analysis. *Journal of Software (Malden, MA)*, *2723*. Advance online publication. DOI: 10.1002/SMR.2723

Ni, A., Yin, P., Zhao, Y., Riddell, M., Feng, T., Shen, R., Yin, S., & Liu, Y. Semih Yavuz, ◇, Xiong, C., Joty, S., Zhou, Y., Radev, D., & Cohan, A. (2023). *L2CEval: Evaluating Language-to-Code Generation Capabilities of Large Language Models*. https://arxiv.org/abs/2309.17446v2

Riyadh, M., & Shafiq, M. O. (2023). Towards Automatic Evaluation of NLG Tasks Using Conversational Large Language Models. *IFIP Advances in Information and Communication Technology, 676 IFIP*, 425–437. https://doi.org/DOI: 10.1007/978-3-031-34107-6_34

Sarker, I. H. (2024). LLM potentiality and awareness: A position paper from the perspective of trustworthy and responsible AI modeling. *Discover Artificial Intelligence, 4*(1), 1–7. DOI: 10.1007/S44163-024-00129-0/FIGURES/1

Schaeffer, R., Miranda, B., & Koyejo, S. (2023). Are Emergent Abilities of Large Language Models a Mirage? https://arxiv.org/abs/2304.15004v2

Schoenegger, P., & Park, P. S. (2023). *Large Language Model Prediction Capabilities: Evidence from a Real-World Forecasting Tournament.* https://arxiv.org/abs/2310.13014v1

Tamkin, A., & Brundage, M. (2021). *3, J. C., & Ganguli, D.* Understanding the Capabilities, Limitations, and Societal Impact of Large Language Models.

Tan, Y., Min, D., Li, Y., Li, W., Hu, N., Chen, Y., & Qi, G. (2023). Can ChatGPT Replace Traditional KBQA Models? An In-Depth Analysis of the Question Answering Performance of the GPT LLM Family. *Lecture Notes in Computer Science (Including Subseries Lecture Notes in Artificial Intelligence and Lecture Notes in Bioinformatics), 14265 LNCS*, 348–367. https://doi.org/DOI: 10.1007/978-3-031-47240-4_19

Tuggener, L., Sager, P., Taoudi-Benchekroun, Y., Grewe, B. F., & Stadelmann, T. (2024). So you want your private LLM at home?: a survey and benchmark of methods for efficient GPTs. *11th IEEE Swiss Conference on Data Science (SDS),* Zurich, Switzerland, 30-31 May 2024, 205–212. https://doi.org/DOI: 10.1109/SDS60720.2024.00036

Yang, J., Jin, H., Tang, R., Han, X., Feng, Q., Jiang, H., Zhong, S., Yin, B., & Hu, X. (2024). Harnessing the Power of LLMs in Practice: A Survey on ChatGPT and Beyond. *ACM Transactions on Knowledge Discovery from Data, 18*(6), 32. DOI: 10.1145/3649506/ASSET/D2038F72-9808-4957-BF9D-FB4E05F82081/ASSETS/GRAPHIC/TKDD-2023-06-0236-F02.JPG

Chapter 2
Theoretical Foundations of Large Language Models

Yashodeep Bharat Deshmukh
https://orcid.org/0009-0007-4873-2269
Defence Institute of Advanced Technology, India

Abhishek Mukhopadhyay
https://orcid.org/0000-0002-4341-0523
Amity University, Kolkata, India

ABSTRACT

Large Language Models (LLMs) are powerful tools in natural language processing with complex principles. This chapter delves into the theoretical foundations of LLMs, covering essential concepts, algorithms, and intuition, aiming to offer readers a strong grasp of the framework that empowers LLMs to perform varied language tasks, thus laying groundwork for advanced applications. Beginning with NLP fundamentals and statistical techniques, the chapter traces the evolution of language models from n-gram models to dense word embeddings like Word2Vec and GloVe. It then examines neural network architectures, progressing Transformers, dissecting key components such as attention mechanisms and encoder-decoder structures, including models like BERT and GPT. The chapter emphasizes the mathematical and algorithmic principles enabling LLMs' capabilities. The chapter synthesizes key theoretical principles behind LLMs, highlights their strengths and limitations, and explores future research areas like multimodal and few-shot learning, offering a comprehensive grounding for readers.

DOI: 10.4018/979-8-3693-8387-2.ch002

INTRODUCTION

Large Language Models (LLMs) have revolutionized the field of natural language processing (NLP) in recent years. These powerful neural networks, trained on vast amounts of text data, have demonstrated remarkable capabilities in language understanding, generation, and reasoning. From chatbots and machine translation to question answering and content creation, LLMs are driving breakthroughs across a wide range of NLP applications.

This chapter delves into the theoretical foundations underpinning LLMs, providing a comprehensive overview of the key concepts, techniques, and architectures that enable their impressive performance. We begin by exploring the fundamentals of language modeling, including text representation, tokenization, and various statistical and neural network-based approaches. Next, we examine the transformative role of the attention mechanism in LLMs, highlighting its ability to capture long-range dependencies and enable efficient parallelization.

Building upon these foundational concepts, we introduce the transformer architecture, which has become the backbone of state-of-the-art LLMs. We discuss the core components of transformers, such as the encoder-decoder structure, positional encoding, and layer normalization, and explore how these elements contribute to their scalability and effectiveness.

We then dive into the world of LLMs and their variants, including encoder-only models like BERT, (Vaswani et al., 2017), decoder-only models like the GPT family, and encoder-decoder models such as T5. We examine the scaling laws and model sizing considerations that have propelled the development of increasingly large and capable LLMs, as well as their impressive few-shot and zero-shot learning abilities.

Finally, we conclude by discussing the current challenges and future directions in LLM research and development. We explore ethical considerations, such as bias and fairness, computational efficiency and environmental impact, and emerging architectures and techniques that promise to push the boundaries of what LLMs can achieve.

By the end of this chapter, readers will have a solid understanding of the theoretical foundations that underpin the remarkable advances in LLMs. Armed with this knowledge, they will be well-equipped to explore the exciting possibilities and tackle the challenges that lie ahead in this rapidly evolving field.

Foundations of Language Modeling

Definition and Purpose of Language Modeling

Language modeling is a fundamental concept in natural language processing (NLP) that forms the basis for many advanced language technologies. This section explores the definition of language models and their core purposes in computational linguistics.

A language model (Phuong & Hutter, 2022) is a statistical method that learns to predict the probability of a sequence of words, where the model trained on a given corpus of text, enables the model to identify patterns and relationships between words in that language. The relationship between the words builds to context for a given sequence of words. These quantifiable patterns help computers process the natural language.

Key Components of this Definition Include

1. **Statistical approach**: Language models use probability theory to quantify the likelihood of word sequences.
2. **Prediction capability**: The primary function is to predict the probability of word sequences.
3. **Training process**: Models learn from a large corpora of text data.
4. **Pattern recognition**: They identify recurring patterns and relationships in language use.
5. **Contextual understanding**: These models build context for sequences by analyzing word relationships.

Purpose of Language Modeling. The purpose of language modeling extends beyond mere word prediction. Its core aims include:

1. **Enabling natural language understanding**: By providing a statistical framework for analyzing language, these models help computers interpret human communication more effectively.
2. **Facilitating language generation**: Language models can generate coherent and contextually appropriate text, useful for various applications.
3. **Improving language-based technologies**: These models serve as the foundation for numerous NLP tasks, enhancing the performance of various language technologies.
4. **Capturing language nuances**: Through their training on large text corpora, language models can capture subtle nuances of language use, including idiomatic expressions and contextual variations.

5. **Providing a basis for transfer learning**: Pre-trained language models can be fine-tuned for specific tasks, allowing for more efficient development of specialized NLP applications.
6. **Advancing AI research**: Language modeling contributes to the broader field of artificial intelligence, pushing the boundaries of machine learning and cognitive computing.

In essence, language modeling aims to bridge the gap between human communication and machine interpretation, enabling more sophisticated and natural interactions between humans and computers, (Alammar et al., 2019). By quantifying the patterns and probabilities inherent in language use, these models provide a powerful tool for a wide range of applications in natural language processing and artificial intelligence.

Text Representation and Tokenization

To effectively process and analyze natural language, it is crucial to represent text in a format that machines can understand and manipulate. In the context of large language models (LLMs), text representation and tokenization play a fundamental role in preparing the input data for training and inference.

Text Representation. Text representation involves converting raw text into a numerical format that computers can process, essentially quantifying and translating natural language into a language that machines can understand. The most common approach is to represent text as a sequence of discrete tokens, where each token corresponds to a word, subword, or character in the original text, (Phuong & Hutter, 2022).

One widely used text representation scheme is one-hot encoding, where each token is represented as a binary vector with a single 1 at the index corresponding to the token's unique identifier, and 0s elsewhere. However, one-hot encoding leads to high-dimensional and sparse representations, which can be inefficient for large vocabularies.

To address this issue, distributed representations, such as word embeddings, have gained popularity. Word embeddings map each token to a dense, low-dimensional vector in a continuous space, capturing semantic and syntactic relationships between tokens. Popular word embedding models include Word2Vec, GloVe, and FastText, which learn these representations from large text corpora using unsupervised learning techniques.

Tokenization. Tokenization is the process of splitting raw text into smaller units called tokens. The choice of tokenization strategy can significantly impact the performance and generalization ability of LLMs. Common tokenization approaches include:

1. **Word-level tokenization**: This simple approach splits text into individual words based on whitespace and punctuation. However, it can lead to large vocabulary and may not handle out-of-vocabulary (OOV) words effectively.
2. **Subword tokenization**: To overcome the limitations of word-level tokenization, subword tokenization methods break words into smaller units, such as n-grams or syllables. This allows for a more compact vocabulary and better handling of OOV words. Popular subword tokenization algorithms include Byte Pair Encoding (BPE) (Sennrich, Haddow, & Birch, 2016) and WordPiece, (Song et al., 2021).
3. **Character-level tokenization**: In this approach, text is split into individual characters. While it results in a small vocabulary size, character-level tokenization may require longer sequences and more computational resources to capture higher-level language patterns.

The choice of tokenization strategy depends on factors such as the language, domain, and downstream task. For example, subword tokenization has become the de facto standard for many LLMs due to its balance between vocabulary size and OOV handling. The detail of tokenization is shown in Figure 1.

Figure 1. Token representation process

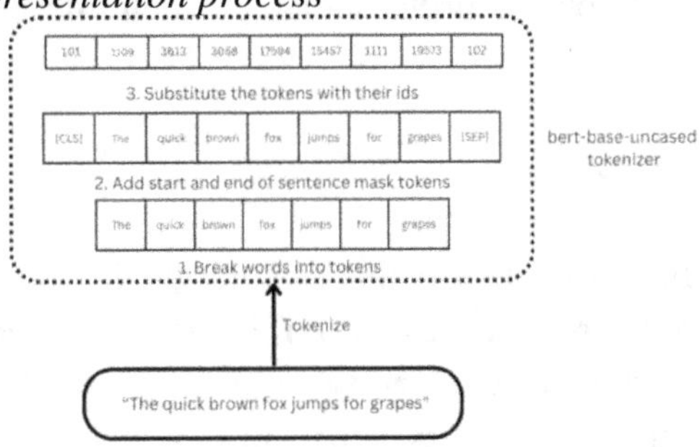

Statistical Language Models

Statistical language models are foundational techniques in natural language processing that aim to capture the probability distribution of words in a language. These models learn from large text corpora and assign probabilities to sequences of words, enabling various applications such as text generation, machine translation, and speech recognition. In this section, we will explore several key statistical language modeling approaches.

TF-IDF

Term Frequency-Inverse Document Frequency (TF-IDF) is a numerical statistic (Robertson & Sparck Jones, 1976) that reflects the importance of a word in a document within a collection or corpus. It is calculated by multiplying two components: the term frequency (TF) and the inverse document frequency (IDF).

- **Term Frequency (TF):**

$$TF\ (t, d) = \frac{Number\ of\ times\ term\ t\ appears\ to\ document\ d}{Total\ number\ of\ terms\ in\ document\ d}$$

- **Inverse Document Frequency (IDF):**

$$IDF\ (t, d) = \log\frac{Total\ number\ of\ documents\ in\ corpus\ D}{Number\ of\ documents\ containing\ term\ t}$$

- **TF-IDF:**

$$TF - IDF\ (t, d, D)\ =\ TF(t, d) \times IDF\ (t, D)$$

Intuition: TF-IDF assigns higher weights to words that appear frequently in a document but rarely in the entire corpus, indicating their importance and specificity to the document.

Co-Occurrence Matrix

A co-occurrence matrix is a matrix that captures the frequency of co-occurrence between words in a text corpus. Each cell (i, j) in the matrix represents the number of times word i and word j appear together within a specified window size.

Intuition: Co-occurrence matrices help identify semantic relationships between words based on their co-occurrence patterns. Words that frequently appear together are likely to be semantically related.

N-gram Models

N-gram models (Shannon, 1948) (Figure 2) are probabilistic language models that estimate the probability of a word given the previous $n - 1$ words. The probability of a sequence of words $\left(w_1, w_2, \ldots, w_n\right)$ is calculated as:

$$P\left(w_1, w_2, \ldots, w_n\right) = \prod_{i=1}^{n}\left(w_i \mid w_1, w_2, \ldots, w_{i-1} \approx \prod_{i=1}^{n}(w_i \mid w_{i-n+1}, \ldots, w_{i-1}\right) \quad (1)$$

Figure 2. Uni-gram, Bi-gram, and Tri-gram model

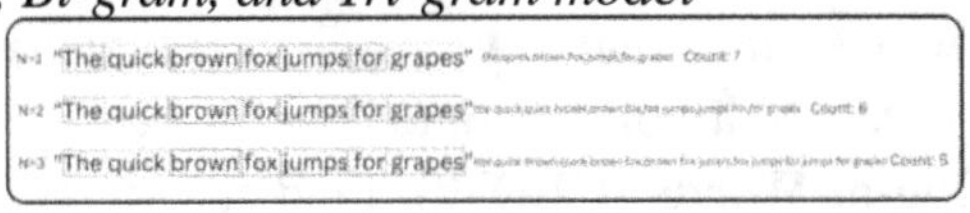

Intuition: N-gram models capture the local context of words by considering the probability of a word given its preceding words. Higher-order n-grams (e.g., trigrams) can capture more context but may suffer from data sparsity.

Exponential Models

Exponential language models, also known as maximum entropy models, estimate the probability distribution of a word given its context using a set of feature functions $f_i(w, c)$ and corresponding weights λ_i:

$$P(wc) = \frac{1}{Z(c)}\exp\left(\sum_{i=1}^{n}\lambda_i f_i(w, c)\right) \quad (2)$$

Where $Z(c)$ is a normalization factor.

Intuition: Exponential models allow for the incorporation of various contextual features and learn weights for each feature to maximize the entropy of the probability distribution, subject to the constraints imposed by the feature functions.

Word Embeddings and Representations

While statistical language models like TF-IDF and n-grams have been widely used in NLP, they have certain limitations. TF-IDF and co-occurrence matrices capture word importance and semantic relationships but do not provide a dense, low-dimensional representation of words. N-gram models and exponential models consider local context but struggle with data sparsity and computational complexity as the context window increases.

To address these limitations, word embeddings have emerged as a powerful alternative for representing words in a dense, low-dimensional continuous space. Word embeddings capture semantic and syntactic relationships between words and enable more efficient and effective processing of text data. In this section, we will explore three popular word embedding models: Word2Vec, GloVe, and FastText.

Word2Vec

Word2Vec, introduced by Mikolov et al. (2013), learns word embeddings using a shallow neural network architecture. It can be trained using two different objectives:

- **Skip-gram**: Predicts the context words given a target word by maximizing the average log probability of the context words.
- **Continuous Bag-of-Words (CBOW)**: Predicts a target word given its context words by maximizing the average log probability of the target word.

Intuition: Word2Vec leverages the distributional hypothesis, stating that words appearing in similar contexts tend to have similar meanings. By learning to predict the context or target word, Word2Vec captures semantic and syntactic relationships in the embedding space.

GloVe

GloVe (Global Vectors for Word Representation), introduced by Pennington, Socher, and Manning (2014), learns word embeddings by leveraging global word-word co-occurrence statistics. GloVe minimizes the difference between the dot product of word embeddings and the log count of their co-occurrences, capturing both local and global semantic relationships.

Intuition: While Word2Vec focuses on local context, GloVe incorporates global co-occurrence information, providing a more comprehensive representation of word relationships.

FastText

FastText, introduced by Bojanowski et al. (2016), extends the Word2Vec model by considering subword information. It represents each word as a bag of character n-grams and learns embeddings for each n-gram.

FastText can generate embeddings for out-of-vocabulary words by combining the embeddings of their constituent n-grams, making it effective for languages with rich morphology and scenarios with rare or unknown words.

Intuition: By incorporating subword information, FastText captures morphological similarities between words, addressing a limitation of Word2Vec and GloVe, which treat each word as a distinct entity.

Word embeddings have revolutionized NLP by providing a more expressive and computationally efficient representation of words compared to traditional statistical language models. They have become a fundamental component of modern NLP systems and have paved the way for more advanced techniques like contextual word embeddings (e.g., ELMo, BERT) and state-of-the-art language models.

Neural Networks for Language Modeling

While word embeddings provide a powerful representation of words, they do not directly address the task of language modeling, which involves predicting the likelihood of a sequence of words. To tackle this challenge, neural networks have been employed to learn more sophisticated language models that can capture complex patterns and dependencies in text data. In this section, we will explore two fundamental neural network architectures for language modeling: feed-forward neural networks and Recurrent Neural Networks (RNNs).

Feed-Forward Neural Networks

Feed-forward neural networks, also known as multi-layer perceptrons (MLPs), are the simplest type of neural network architecture. They consist of an input layer, one or more hidden layers, and an output layer, with information flowing in one direction from input to output.

In the context of language modeling, a feed-forward neural network can be used to predict the probability of the next word given a fixed-size context window. The input to the network is a concatenation of the word embeddings of the context words, and the output is a probability distribution over the vocabulary.

Mathematically, given a context window of n words $(w_1, w_2, \ldots w_n)$ the probability of the next word w_{n+1} is computed as:

$$P(w_{n+1} | w_1, w_2, \ldots, w_n) = softmax(W_o . h + b_o) \tag{3}$$

Where h is the output of the last hidden layer, computed as:

$$h = ReLU(W_h . [ew_1, ew_2, \ldots, ew_n]) + b_h \tag{4}$$

Here, e_{w_i} denotes the word embedding of the word w_i, W_h, b_h, *and* w_i are the weights and biases of the hidden layer, and W_0, b_0 are the weights and biases of the output layer.

Intuition: Feed-forward neural networks learn to predict the next word based on a fixed-size context window. They can capture more complex patterns than traditional n-gram models but are limited by the fixed context size and cannot model long-range dependencies.

Recurrent Neural Networks (RNNs)

Recurrent Neural Networks (RNNs) are a class of neural networks designed to handle sequential data. Unlike feed-forward networks, RNNs maintain a hidden state that can capture information from previous time steps, allowing them to model long-range dependencies and variable-length sequences.

In the context of language modeling, an RNN processes a sequence of words one at a time, updating its hidden state at each step based on the current word and the previous hidden state. The probability of the next word is then computed based on the current hidden state.

Mathematically, given a sequence of words $(w_1, w_2, \dots w_T)$, the hidden state h_y at time step t is computed as:

$$h_t = tanh \left(W_h \cdot [h_{t-1}, ew_t] \right) + b_h \tag{5}$$

Where ew_t denotes the word embedding of the word w_i, W_h, *and* b_h are the weights and biases of the hidden layer, and *tanh* is the hyperbolic tangent activation function.

The probability of the next word w_{t+1} is then computed based on the current hidden state h_t:

$$P \left(w_{t+1} | w_1, w_2, \dots, w_t\right) = softmax \left(W_o \cdot h_t + b_o\right) \tag{6}$$

Intuition: RNNs can model long-range dependencies and variable-length sequences by maintaining a hidden state that captures information from previous time steps. They are more powerful than feed-forward networks for language modeling but can suffer from the vanishing gradient problem, which limits their ability to capture very long-range dependencies.

To address the limitations of vanilla RNNs, more advanced variants like Long Short-Term Memory (LSTM) (Wang & Jiang, 2016) and Gated Recurrent Units (GRUs) (Cho et al., 2014) have been proposed. These architectures introduce gating mechanisms that allow the network to better control the flow of information over time, enabling the modeling of even longer-range dependencies, (Zhang & Wallace, 2016; Mikolov et al., 2010).

Neural networks have revolutionized language modeling by providing a powerful and flexible framework for learning complex patterns and dependencies in text data. Feed-forward neural networks and RNNs have laid the foundation for more advanced architectures like the transformer, which has become the backbone of state-of-the-art language models like BERT, GPT, and T5, (Raffel et al., 2020).

ATTENTION MECHANISM

The attention mechanism has become a crucial component of modern neural network architectures for natural language processing. It has revolutionized the field by enabling models to focus on relevant parts of the input when making predictions, leading to significant improvements in tasks such as machine translation, text summarization, and language understanding. In this section, we will explore the motivation behind the attention mechanism and develop an intuition for how it works.

Motivation and Intuition

Traditional neural network architectures, such as feed-forward networks and RNNs, have limitations when it comes to capturing long-range dependencies and focusing on relevant information. For example, in machine translation, the output at each time step depends not only on the current input word but also on the context provided by the entire input sentence. However, RNNs struggle to capture such long-range dependencies due to the vanishing gradient problem, (Vaswani et al., 2017).

The attention mechanism addresses this limitation by allowing the model to attend to different parts of the input sequence when generating each output. Instead of relying solely on the last hidden state of an RNN, the attention mechanism computes a weighted sum of all the hidden states, where the weights represent the importance of each hidden state for the current output, (Phuong & Hutter, 2022).

Intuitively, the attention mechanism can be thought of as a way for the model to "look back" at the input sequence and decide which parts are most relevant for making the current prediction. By doing so, the model can capture long-range dependencies and focus on the most informative parts of the input.

To illustrate this, let us consider a simple example of translating the French phrase "Je suis étudiant" to English. The attention mechanism allows the model to focus on the word "étudiant" when generating the English word "student," as it is the most relevant part of the input for this translation.

Mathematically, given a sequence of hidden states $(h_1, h_2, \ldots, h_T)$, the attention mechanism computes a context vector c_t for each output time step t as a weighted sum of the hidden states:

$$ct = \sum_{i=1}^{T} \alpha_{t,i} h_i \tag{7}$$

The weights $\alpha_{t,i}$ are computed based on the compatibility between the current hidden state h_t and each of the input hidden states h_i, often using a softmax function:

$$\alpha_{t,i} = \frac{\exp\left(score\left(h_t, h_i\right)\right)}{\sum_{j=1}^{T} \exp\left(score\left(h_t, h_j\right)\right)} \tag{8}$$

The score function can be implemented in various ways, such as a dot product or a small neural network.

The computed context vector c_t is then combined with the current hidden state h_t to generate the output at time step t. This allows the model to make predictions based on the most relevant parts of the input sequence, (Vaswani et al., 2017).

The attention mechanism has proven to be a powerful and flexible tool for improving the performance of neural networks in natural language processing tasks. Its ability to capture long-range dependencies and focus on relevant information has led to breakthrough results and has become a cornerstone of state-of-the-art language models like the transformer.

Key-Value-Query Framework

The Key-Value-Query (KVQ) framework (Vaswani et al., 2017) is a powerful and flexible formulation of the attention mechanism (Figure 3) that has become the foundation of many modern neural network architectures, such as the transformer. In this framework, the attention mechanism is computed based on three main components: keys, values, and queries.

1. **Keys**: Keys are a set of vectors that represent the input sequence. Each key vector corresponds to a specific position in the input sequence and is used to compute the attention weights. In the context of language modeling, the keys are typically derived from the hidden states of the encoder.
2. **Values**: Values are another set of vectors that represent the input sequence. They contain information that will be aggregated based on the attention weights. In language modeling, the values are also typically derived from the hidden states of the encoder.
3. **Queries**: Queries are a set of vectors that represent the current position in the output sequence. They are used to compute the attention weights by measuring the compatibility between each query vector and the key vectors. In language modeling, the queries are typically derived from the hidden states of the decoder.

Figure 3. Working mechanism of attention

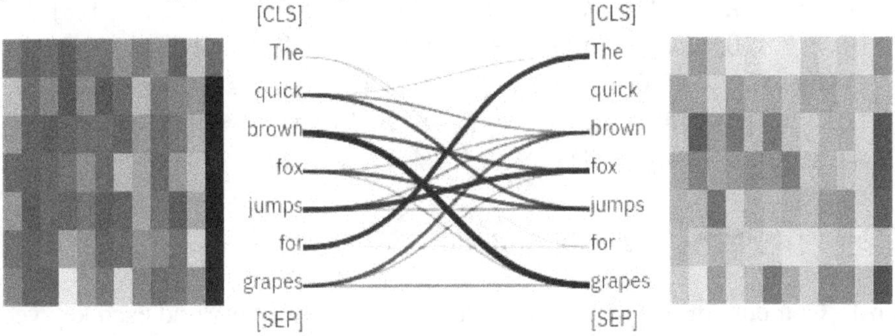

Given a set of keys K, values V, and queries Q, the attention mechanism in the KVQ framework computes the output as a weighted sum of the values, where the weights are determined by the compatibility between the queries and the keys, (Alammar, 2018; Alammar, 2019; Alammar, 2020)

Mathematically, for a single query vector **q**, the attention output **o** is computed as:

$$o = \sum_{i=1}^{N} \alpha_i v_i \tag{9}$$

Where N is the number of key-value pairs, v_i is the $i-$th value vector, and $\propto_i$ is the attention weight computed based on the compatibility between the query **q** and the $i-$th key vector k_i:

$$\alpha_i = \frac{\exp(score(q, k_i))}{\sum_{j=1}^{N} \exp(q, k_j))} \tag{10}$$

The score function measures the compatibility between the query and the key vectors, and it can be implemented in various ways, such as a scaled dot product:

$$score\left(q, k_i\right) = \frac{q.k_i}{\sqrt{d}} \tag{11}$$

where d is the dimension of the key vectors.

To illustrate how the KVQ framework works with numerical values, let us consider the example sentence: "The quick brown fox jumps over the lazy dog."

Assume we have the following key, value, and query vectors (in practice, these would be high-dimensional vectors learned by the model):

Keys: k_{The} = [0.1, 0.2, 0.3], k_{quick} = [0.2, 0.3, 0.4], k_{brown} = [0.3, 0.4, 0.5], k_{fox} = [0.4, 0.5, 0.6], k_{jumps} = [0.5, 0.6, 0.7], k_{over} = [0.6, 0.7, 0.8], k_{the} = [0.7, 0.8, 0.9], k_{lazy} = [0.8, 0.9, 1.0], k_{dog} = [0.9, 1.0, 1.1]
Values v_{The} = [1.0, 1.1, 1.2], v_{quick} = [1.1, 1.2, 1.3], v_{brown} = [1.2, 1.3, 1.4], v_{fox} = [1.3, 1.4, 1.5], v_{jumps} = [1.4, 1.5, 1.6], v_{over} = [1.5, 1.6, 1.7], v_{the} = [1.6, 1.7, 1.8], v_{lazy} = [1.7, 1.8, 1.9], v_{dog} = [1.8, 1.9, 2.0]

Query (for the word "jumps"): $qjumps = [0.5, 0.6, 0.7]$

Step 1: Compute the compatibility scores between the query and each key vector using the dot product:

$$score\left(q_{jumps}, k_{The}\right) = 0.38$$

$$score\left(q_{jumps}, k_{quick}\right) = 0.56$$

$$score\left(q_{jumps}, k_{dog}\right) = 1.82$$

Step 2: Transform the scores into attention weights using the SoftMax function:

$$\alpha_{The} = 0.05,\ \alpha_{quick} = 0.07, \ldots,\ \alpha_{dog} = 0.24$$

Step 3: Compute the attention output as the weighted sum of the value vectors:

$$o = \alpha_{The} * vThe + \alpha_{quick} * v_{quick} + \ldots + \alpha_{dog} * v_{dog}$$

$$o = 0.05*[1.0,\ 1.1,\ 1.2] + 0.07*[1.1,\ 1.2,\ 1.3] + \ldots + 0.24*[1.8,\ 1.9,\ 2.0]$$

$$o = [1.49, 1.59, 1.69]$$

The resulting attention output o is a weighted sum of the value vectors, where the weights are determined by the compatibility between the query and the keys. In this example, the attention mechanism assigns higher weights to the words that are more relevant to the query word "jumps," such as "fox" and "over," and lower weights to less relevant words like "the" and "lazy."

The KVQ framework provides a general and flexible formulation of the attention mechanism that can be applied to various tasks and architectures. By representing the input sequence as keys and values and the output sequence as queries, the attention mechanism can effectively capture the relevant information from the input and generate contextually appropriate outputs.

One of the key advantages of the KVQ framework is its ability to handle variable-length sequences. Since the attention weights are computed dynamically based on the compatibility between the queries and the keys, the framework can handle input and output sequences of different lengths without requiring any fixed-size context window or padding.

Moreover, the KVQ framework allows for the development of more advanced attention mechanisms, such as self-attention and multi-head attention, which have become the backbone of state-of-the-art language models like the transformer.

Self-Attention and Multi-Head Attention

Self-attention and multi-head attention are two key extensions of the attention mechanism that have greatly enhanced the performance and flexibility of language models. In this subsection, we will explore these concepts in more detail and discuss their benefits and applications.

Self-Attention

Self-attention, also known as intra-attention (Figure 4), is a mechanism that relates different positions within a single sequence to compute a representation of that sequence. In self-attention, the queries, keys, and values are all derived from the same input sequence, allowing each token to attend to all other tokens in the sequence, including itself, (Vaswani et al., 2017; Phuong & Hutter, 2022; Alammar, 2018; Alammar, 2019).

Given a sequence of token representations -0, $X = (x_1, x_2, \ldots, x_n)$, self-attention computes the attention output for each token as follows:

1. **Compute the query, key, and value vectors for each token**:

$$q_i = W_Q x_i k_i = W_K x_i v_i = W_V x_i \tag{12}$$

where W_Q, W_K, and W_V are learnable weight matrices.

2. **Compute the attention weights for each token pair**:

$$\alpha_{i,j} = \frac{\exp(score(q_i, k_j))}{\sum_{l=1}^{n} \exp(score(q_i, k_l))} \tag{13}$$

Where $score(q_i, k_j) = \frac{q_i \cdot k_j}{\sqrt{d}}$, and d is the dimension of the key vectors.

3. **Compute the attention output for each token**:

$$oi = \sum_{j=1}^{n} \alpha_{i,j} v_j \tag{14}$$

Self-attention has been successfully used in tasks like reading comprehension, abstractive summarization, textual entailment, and learning task-independent sentence representations. It allows the model to capture long-range dependencies and learn expressive representations of the input sequence.

Figure 4. Single attention head matrix

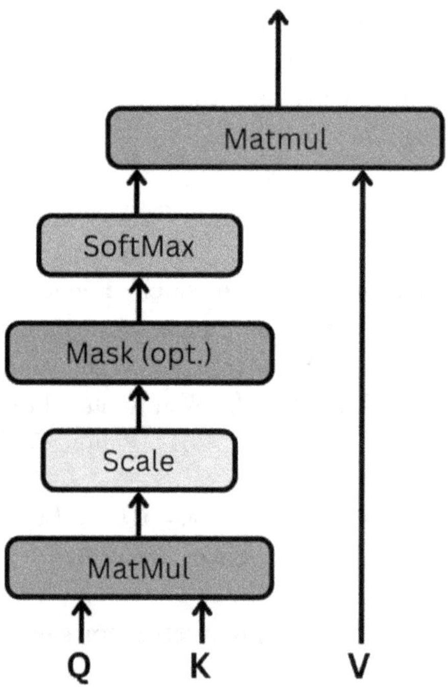

There are two main variants of self-attention:

1. **Bidirectional self-attention**: This variant applies attention to each token, treating all tokens in the sequence as context. This helps the network understand the full context of the input, (Vaswani et al., 2017).
2. Unidirectional self-attention (masked self-attention): This variant applies attention to each token but only considers preceding tokens as context. This is useful for online prediction tasks, as the model can only attend to tokens that have already been seen, (Vaswani et al., 2017).

Multi-Head Attention

Multi-head attention (Figure 5) is an extension of self-attention that allows the model to jointly attend to information from different representation subspaces. Instead of performing a single attention function, multi-head attention runs multiple attention heads in parallel, each with its own set of learnable parameters, (Alammar, 2018; Alammar, 2019; Alammar, 2020).

Figure 5. Multi-head attention matrix

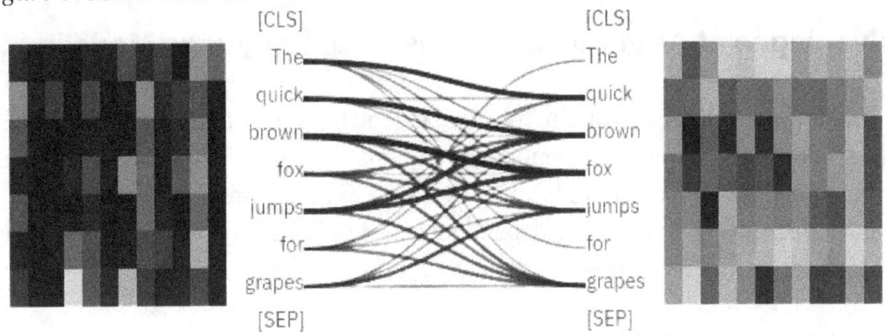

Given a sequence of token representations $X = (x_1, x_2, \ldots, x_n)$, multi-head attention with h heads computes the attention output as follows:

1. Compute the query, key, and value vectors for each head $\boldsymbol{i} \in 1, 2, \ldots, \boldsymbol{h}$:

$$Q_i = WQ_iXK_i = WK_iXV_i = WV_iX \tag{15}$$

where WQ_i, WK_i, and WV_i are learnable weight matrices for head i.

2. **Compute the attention output for each head**:

$$head_i = Attention\left(Q_i, K_i, V_i\right) \tag{16}$$

3. **Concatenate the attention outputs from all heads and linearly transform**:

$$O = W_O\left[head_1\ ; head_2; \ldots; head_h\right]$$

Where W_O is a learnable weight matrix, and [;]denotes concatenation.

Multi-head attention allows the model to focus on information from multiple representation subspaces across different positions, something a single attention head may find challenging to achieve. In a standard architecture, all the attention heads are concatenated and fed to a feed-forward neural network, and they are also normalized to control the mean and variance of the neural network.

The combination of self-attention and multi-headed attention has proven to be highly effective in language modeling tasks. These mechanisms allow the model to capture complex dependencies and learn rich representations of the input sequence, leading to significant improvements in performance and generalization.

Advantages of Attention Mechanisms in Language Modeling

Attention mechanisms have revolutionized the field of natural language processing by addressing several key challenges and enabling more effective and efficient language modeling. In this subsection, we will explore three main advantages of attention: handling long-range dependencies, parallelization and efficiency, and model interpretability, (Phuong & Hutter, 2022).

Handling Long-Range Dependencies

One of the primary challenges in language modeling is capturing long-range dependencies between words or tokens in a sequence. Traditional recurrent neural networks (RNNs) often struggle with this task due to the vanishing gradient problem, which makes it difficult for the model to propagate information over long distances.

Attention mechanisms mitigate this problem by allowing the model to directly access and attend to relevant parts of the input sequence, regardless of their distance from the current position. By computing a weighted sum of the input representations, attention can effectively capture dependencies between distant tokens, enabling the model to better understand the global context of the sequence, (Phuong & Hutter, 2022).

This ability to handle long-range dependencies has been crucial in tasks such as machine translation, where understanding the relationships between words across the entire sentence is essential for generating accurate translations. Attention mechanisms have also been successful in other tasks that require capturing long-range dependencies, such as reading comprehension, abstractive summarization, and textual entailment.

Parallelization and Efficiency

Another significant advantage of attention mechanisms is their ability to enable parallelization and improve computational efficiency. Unlike RNNs, which process sequentially and suffer from the inherent limitations of sequential computation, attention mechanisms allow for parallel processing of input sequences.

In the self-attention mechanism, the attention weights for all token pairs can be computed simultaneously using matrix multiplication operations. This parallelization greatly reduces the computational overhead and allows for more efficient processing of long sequences. As a result, attention-based models can be trained faster and scale better to larger datasets compared to sequential models like RNNs.

Moreover, the computational complexity of self-attention grows quadratically with the sequence length, making it more efficient than recurrent layers when the sequence length is shorter than the representation dimensionality. This property has made attention mechanisms particularly well-suited for tasks involving relatively short sequences, such as sentence-level classification or sequence labeling, (Phuong & Hutter, 2022).

The parallelization and efficiency advantages of attention have been a key factor in the development of large-scale language models like the Transformer, which can process and generate text in a highly parallel manner, enabling training on massive datasets and achieving state-of-the-art performance on a wide range of natural language processing tasks.

Model Interpretability

Attention mechanisms also provide a valuable tool for interpreting and understanding the behavior of language models. By examining the attention weights assigned to different parts of the input sequence, researchers and practitioners can gain insights into the model's decision-making process and identify the most relevant information for a given prediction.

Visualizing attention weights has become a common practice in analyzing and debugging attention-based models. Heat maps or other visualizations can reveal which words or tokens the model is attending to when making a particular prediction, allowing for a more intuitive understanding of the model's behavior. This interpretability can help in identifying potential biases, errors, or limitations in the model and guide efforts to improve its performance and fairness, (Phuong & Hutter, 2022; Alammar, 2020).

Furthermore, attention mechanisms can provide a way to explain the model's predictions to end-users or stakeholders. By highlighting the most relevant parts of the input sequence based on the attention weights, the model can provide a form of justification or rationale for its outputs, enhancing the transparency and trustworthiness of the system, (Vaswani et al., 2017; Alammar, 2018).

The interpretability advantages of attention have been particularly valuable in applications where understanding the model's behavior is crucial, such as in medical diagnosis, legal decision-making, or content moderation. By providing a window into the model's reasoning process, attention mechanisms can help build trust and facilitate the responsible deployment of language models in real-world scenarios.

In summary, attention mechanisms offer several key advantages in language modeling, including the ability to handle long-range dependencies, enable parallelization and efficiency, and improve model interpretability. These advantages have made attention a cornerstone of modern natural language processing and have paved the way for the development of powerful and versatile language models like the Transformer.

Attention Visualizations and Analysis

Attention mechanisms not only improve the performance and efficiency of language models but also provide a powerful tool for analyzing and interpreting their behavior. By visualizing and analyzing attention weights, researchers and practitioners can gain valuable insights into how the model processes and understands text data. In this subsection, we will explore various techniques for attention visualization and analysis.

Attention Heat Maps

One of the most common and intuitive ways to visualize attention is through heat maps. Attention heat maps display the attention weights assigned by the model to each token in the input sequence when generating a particular output token.

In the context of machine translation, for example, an attention heat map can reveal which words in the source sentence the model is attending to when generating each word in the target sentence. This can provide insights into the model's alignment and translation decisions, as well as highlight potential errors or areas for improvement.

Attention Head Analysis

In multi-head attention mechanisms, each attention head may capture different aspects of the input sequence and contribute to the final output in unique ways. Analyzing the behavior of individual attention heads can provide a more fine-grained understanding of the model's processing as shown in Figure 5

By visualizing the attention weights of each head separately, researchers can identify the specific roles and specializations of different heads. Some heads may focus on capturing syntactic dependencies, while others may attend to semantic relationships or positional information. Understanding these head-specific behaviors can guide model design and optimization.

Attention Flow Visualization

Attention flow visualizations trace the flow of attention through the layers of a deep attention-based model, such as the Transformer. These visualizations help us understand how information propagates and is refined as it passes through multiple attention layers.

By analyzing attention flow, researchers can identify the most important tokens at each layer and observe how the model's understanding evolves as it integrates information from different parts of the sequence. This can provide insights into the model's reasoning process and help identify potential bottlenecks or areas for improvement.

Attention-based Explanations

Attention mechanisms can also be used to generate explanations for the model's predictions. By highlighting the input tokens that the model attends to most when making a particular prediction, attention-based explanations can provide a form of justification or rationale for the model's outputs.

Attention-based explanations can be particularly valuable in applications where transparency and interpretability are crucial, such as in medical diagnosis or legal decision-making. By providing a clear and intuitive way to understand the model's behavior, attention-based explanations can help build trust and facilitate the responsible deployment of language models, (Alammar, 2018).

In summary, attention visualizations and analysis offer a powerful toolkit for understanding and interpreting the behavior of attention-based language models. From heat maps and head analysis to attention flow and explanations, these techniques provide valuable insights into how the model processes and understands text data, guiding model development and facilitating the responsible use of language models in real-world applications.

TRANSFORMER ARCHITECTURE

The Transformer is a groundbreaking neural network architecture that has revolutionized the field of natural language processing (NLP). Introduced by Vaswani et al. (2017) in their seminal paper "Attention Is All You Need", the Transformer has become the foundation for state-of-the-art models in various NLP tasks, such as machine translation, language understanding, and text generation. Figure 6 shows different components of the architecture.

The key innovation of the Transformer lies in its reliance on attention mechanisms to capture global dependencies between input and output, eliminating the need for recurrent or convolutional layers. This design choice has led to superior performance, increased parallelization, and reduced training time compared to previous architecture.

At its core, the Transformer follows an encoder-decoder structure, where the encoder maps an input sequence to a continuous representation, and the decoder generates an output sequence based on this encoded representation. The architecture leverages multi-head attention, positional encoding, layer normalization, and residual connections to effectively process and transform sequential data.

In this chapter, we will delve into the details of the Transformer architecture, exploring its core components, the encoder-decoder structure, and the techniques used for positional encoding, normalization, and scaling. By the end of this chapter, readers will have a comprehensive understanding of the Transformer and its role in advancing the state of the art in NLP.

Overview and Core Components

The Transformer architecture is composed of several key components that work together to process sequential data and capture long-range dependencies. These components include:

1. **Token Embedding**: This component learns to represent each vocabulary element as a dense vector in a continuous space. By mapping tokens to learned embeddings, the model can capture semantic and syntactic relationships between words.
2. **Positional Embedding**: Since the Transformer does not inherently capture the order of the input sequence, positional embeddings are used to provide information about the position of each token. These embeddings are typically learned or generated using fixed functions and are added to the token embeddings to incorporate positional information.

3. **Attention**: The attention mechanism is the cornerstone of Transformer architecture. It allows the model to focus on relevant parts of the input sequence when making predictions. By computing a weighted sum of the input representations, attention enables the model to capture dependencies between tokens, regardless of their distance in the sequence.
4. **Multi-head Attention**: To enhance the expressiveness of the attention mechanism, the Transformer employs multiple attention heads in parallel. Each head attends to different aspects of the input, allowing the model to capture diverse relationships and learn from different representation subspaces. The outputs of the multiple heads are then concatenated and linearly transformed to produce the final attention output.
5. **Layer Normalization**: To stabilize the training process and improve the model's convergence, layer normalization is applied to the activations of each sub-layer in the Transformer. By normalizing the mean and variance of the activations, layer normalization helps mitigate the internal covariate shift and enables smoother gradient flow.
6. **Residual Connections**: Residual connections are used to facilitate the flow of information and gradients through the deep Transformer network. By adding the input of each sub-layer to its output, residual connections help alleviate the vanishing gradient problem and allow the model to learn more effectively.
7. **Feed-Forward Network**: In addition to the attention sub-layers, the Transformer includes position-wise fully connected feed-forward networks. These networks are applied to each position independently, allowing the model to capture non-linear interactions between the attended representations.

These core components work in harmony to enable the Transformer to effectively process and transform sequential data. The attention mechanism captures global dependencies, while the multi-head structure allows for learning from different representation subspaces. Layer normalization and residual connections contribute to training stability and facilitate the flow of information through the deep network.

Token Embeddings

Token embeddings are a fundamental component of the Transformer architecture, serving as the initial representation of the input tokens. The purpose of token embeddings is to convert discrete tokens, such as words or subwords, into dense vector representations that capture semantic and syntactic relationships.

The Intuition Behind Token Embeddings

In natural language, words that have similar meanings or are used in similar contexts often have similar vector representations in the embedding space. This property allows the model to generalize and make inferences based on the learned representations.

Figure 6. Transformer architecture (encoder-decoder)

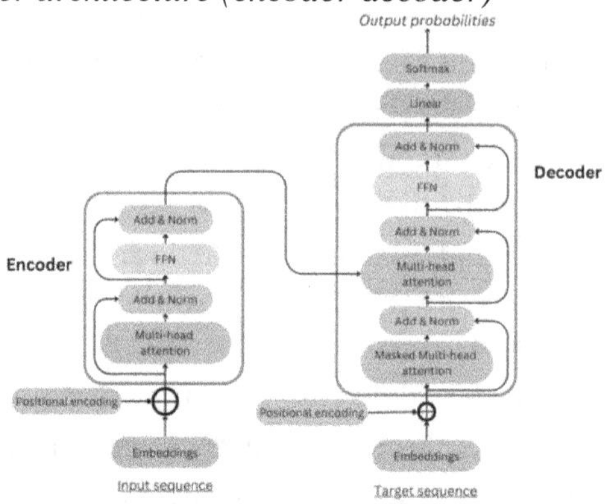

For example, consider the words “cat”, “dog”, and “car”. In the embedding space, “cat” and “dog” would likely have more similar vector representations compared to “car”, as “cat” and “dog” belong to the same semantic category (animals) and are often used in similar contexts.

Working of Token Embeddings

The process of creating token embeddings involves the following steps:

1. **Vocabulary Creation**: The first step is to create a vocabulary of unique tokens from the training data. This vocabulary can consist of words, subwords, or characters, depending on the tokenization strategy employed.
2. **Embedding Matrix**: An embedding matrix is initialized with random weights. The dimensions of the matrix are (vocabulary_size, embedding_dim), where vocabulary_size is the number of unique tokens in the vocabulary, and embedding_dim is the desired dimensionality of the embeddings.
3. **Embedding Lookup**: During the forward pass, each token in the input sequence is mapped to its corresponding index in the vocabulary. This index is then used to retrieve the corresponding embedding vector from the embedding matrix.

4. **Embedding Output**: The retrieved embedding vectors for each token in the input sequence are passed as input to the subsequent layers of the Transformer model.

The token embeddings are learned during the training process through back-propagation. The model adjusts the weights of the embedding matrix based on the objective function and the gradients calculated during training. By optimizing the embedding matrix, the model learns to capture meaningful relationships between tokens in the embedding space, (Phuong & Hutter, 2022).

It's important to note that token embeddings are static, meaning they remain the same for a given token regardless of its context. However, the Transformer architecture incorporates positional embeddings and self-attention mechanisms to capture contextual information and generate context-dependent representations of tokens.

In summary, token embeddings provide a dense vector representation of input tokens, enabling the Transformer model to capture semantic and syntactic relationships between tokens. The embedding matrix is learned during training, allowing the model to generalize and make inferences based on the learned representations. Token embeddings serve as the foundation for the subsequent layers of the Transformer architecture, which further process and refine these representations to generate meaningful outputs.

Positional Encodings

Positional encodings are a crucial component of the Transformer architecture that allows the model to incorporate information about the relative position of tokens in a sequence. Since the Transformer does not have any inherent mechanism to capture the order of tokens, such as recurrence or convolution, positional encodings are used to inject positional information into the token embeddings.

The Intuition Behind Positional Encodings

In natural language, the order of words in a sentence is essential for understanding its meaning. For example, the sentences "The cat chased the mouse" and "The mouse chased the cat" have different meanings, even though they contain the same words. Positional encodings help the Transformer model distinguish between such sequences and capture the relative position of each token, (Phuong & Hutter, 2022; Alammar, 2018).

The intuition behind positional encodings is to add a unique "positional signature" to each token embedding based on its position in the sequence. This positional signature should be distinct for each position and allow the model to learn the relative distances between tokens. By incorporating positional information, the Transformer can effectively capture the order and relationships between tokens in the input sequence.

Types of Positional Encodings

There are two main types of positional encoding used in Transformer models:

1. **Learned Positional Encodings**: In this approach, the positional encodings are learned during the training process. The model learns a separate embedding matrix for positions, like the token embedding matrix. Each position in the sequence is mapped to a learnable vector, and these positional embeddings are added to the token embeddings. The model can learn to assign meaningful positional representations based on the training data.
2. **Fixed Positional Encodings**: Fixed positional encodings use predefined functions to generate positional representations. The most common fixed positional encoding scheme is the sinusoidal encoding introduced in the original Transformer paper. Sinusoidal encodings use a combination of sine and cosine functions of different frequencies to generate a unique positional encoding for each position. The intuition behind sinusoidal encodings is that they allow the model to easily learn relative positions, as the relationship between any two positions can be represented as a linear function of their encodings.

Incorporating Positional Encodings

Positional encodings are typically added to the token embeddings before feeding them into the Transformer model. The addition is performed elementwise, so the dimensionality of the positional encodings must match the dimensionality of the token embedding, (Alammar, 2019).

Mathematically, let E_t be the token embedding matrix and P be the positional encoding matrix. The input to the Transformer model is computed as:

$$X = E_t + P \tag{17}$$

Where X is the matrix of token embeddings with positional information.

By adding positional encodings to the token embeddings, the Transformer model can effectively capture the relative positions of tokens in the sequence and use this information to generate meaningful representations and outputs.

Positional encodings play a vital role in enabling the Transformer to process and understand sequential data. They provide the necessary positional information that allows the self-attention mechanism to capture dependencies and relationships between tokens based on their positions in the sequence.

Attention and Multi-Head Attention

Attention and multi-head attention are the core components of Transformer architecture. They allow the model to capture dependencies and relationships between tokens in a sequence, enabling it to generate contextually relevant representations.

Attention Mechanism

The attention mechanism takes the token embeddings with positional encodings as input and computes a weighted sum of the input vectors to generate a new representation for each token. The weights, called attention scores, are computed based on the similarity or compatibility between each pair of tokens.

Mathematically, let X be the matrix of token embeddings with positional encodings, where each row corresponds to a token's representation. The attention mechanism computes the output Z as follows:

$$Q = XW_Q K = XW_K V = XW_V \tag{18}$$

$$Attention\ (Q, K, V) = softmax\left(\frac{QK^T}{\sqrt{d_k}}\right)V \tag{19}$$

Where Q, K, and V are the query, key, and value matrices, respectively, obtained by linearly transforming the input X using learned weight matrices W_Q, W_K, and W_V. The attention scores are computed by taking the dot product of the query and key matrices, scaled by the square root of the dimension of the keys d_k. The SoftMax function is applied to the attention scores to obtain a probability distribution over the tokens. Finally, the output Z is computed as the weighted sum of the value matrix V based on the attention scores, (Alammar, 2018).

Multi-Head Attention

Multi-head attention is an extension of the attention mechanism that allows the model to simultaneously attend to different parts of the input sequence. Instead of performing a single attention computation, multi-head attention performs multiple attention computations in parallel, each with its own set of learned weight matrices.

The multi-head attention mechanism splits the token embeddings into multiple "heads" and applies the attention mechanism independently to each head. The outputs of all heads are then concatenated and linearly transformed to obtain the final output, (Vaswani et al., 2017).

Mathematically, let X be the matrix of token embeddings with positional encodings. The multi-head attention mechanism computes the output Z as follows:

$$head_i = Attention\left(XW_{Qi}, XW_{Ki}, XW_{Vi}\right) \quad (20)$$

$$Z = Concat\left(head_1, head_2, \ldots, head_h\right)W_O \quad (21)$$

Where $head_i$ represents the output of the i–th attention head, obtained by applying the attention mechanism with learned weight matrices W_{Qi}, W_{Ki}, *and* W_{Vi}. The outputs of all heads are concatenated and linearly transformed using the learned weight matrix W_O to obtain the final output Z.

Output of Attention and Multi-Head Attention

The output of the attention and multi-head attention mechanisms is a new representation for each token in the input sequence. This new representation captures the relevant information from other tokens in the sequence, allowing the model to incorporate context and dependencies.

The output has the same shape as the input, i.e., (sequence_length, embedding_dim), where each row corresponds to the updated representation of a token. These updated representations are then passed through the subsequent layers of the Transformer, such as the position-wise feed-forward networks and residual connections, to further process and refine the representations.

By applying attention and multi-head attention mechanisms, the Transformer model can effectively capture the relationships and dependencies between tokens in the input sequence, enabling it to generate contextually relevant representations for various language understanding and generation tasks.

Layer Normalization and Residual Connections

Layer normalization and residual connections are two important techniques used in Transformer architecture to improve training stability and facilitate the flow of information through the network.

Layer Normalization

Layer normalization is a technique applied to the output of each sub-layer in both the encoder and decoder of the Transformer. After the residual connection is added to the sub-layer's output, it is performed. The purpose of layer normalization is to stabilize the training process by normalizing the activations within each layer, (Phuong & Hutter, 2022).

Mathematically, let x be the input to a sub-layer, and let $f(x)$ be the output of the sub-layer before the residual connection. The layer normalization operation is defined as follows:

$$\mu = \frac{1}{n}\sum_{i=1}^{n} x_i \, ; \; \sigma^2 = \frac{1}{n}\sum_{i=1}^{n}(x_i - \mu)^2 \, ; \; \hat{x}_i = \frac{x_i - \mu}{\sqrt{\sigma^2 + \epsilon}\, y_i} = \gamma\hat{x}_i + \beta \qquad (22)$$

Where μ and σ^2 are the mean and variance of the input x, respectively, n is the number of elements in x, ϵ is a small constant added for numerical stability, and γ and β are learnable scale and shift parameters.

By normalizing the activations within each layer, layer normalization helps to prevent the internal covariate shift that can occur during training. It ensures that the activations have a stable mean and variance, which can improve the convergence and stability of the training process.

Residual Connections

Residual connections, also known as skip connections or shortcut connections, are a key component of the Transformer architecture. They are employed around each of the sub-layers in both the encoder and decoder. Residual connections allow the gradients to flow more easily through the network during backpropagation, mitigating the vanishing gradient problem and improving training stability.

The idea behind residual connections is to allow the network to learn residual functions concerning the input, rather than learning unreferenced functions. Mathematically, if x is the input to a sub-layer and $f(x)$ is the output of the sub-layer, the residual connection is defined as:

$$y = f(x) + x \qquad (23)$$

Where y is the output of the sub-layer with the residual connection.

By adding the input x directly to the output of the sub-layer $f(x)$, residual connections create a “shortcut” that allows the gradients to flow directly through the network, bypassing the sub-layer if necessary. This helps to alleviate the vanishing gradient problem, which can occur when the gradients become too small as they propagate backward through deep networks.

Residual connections also enable the network to learn identity functions more easily. If the optimal function for a sub-layer is close to an identity function, the network can simply learn a residual function that is close to zero, effectively by passing the sub-layer, (Phuong & Hutter, 2022).

The combination of layer normalization and residual connections in the Transformer architecture has been shown to significantly improve training stability and performance. Layer normalization helps to stabilize the activations within each layer, while residual connections facilitate the flow of information and gradients through the network. Together, these techniques contribute to the robustness and effectiveness of the Transformer model.

Encoder-Decoder Architecture

The Transformer follows an encoder-decoder architecture, which is commonly used in sequence-to-sequence tasks such as machine translation, text summarization, and question-answering. The encoder and decoder work together to process the input sequence and generate the output sequence, (Vaswani et al., 2017.

Encoder

The encoder takes the input sequence and generates a continuous representation that captures the relevant information and context. The input sequence undergoes the following steps in the encoder:

1. **Tokenization**: The input sequence is first tokenized, breaking it down into individual tokens (e.g., words or subwords) based on a predefined tokenization scheme.
2. **Token Embeddings**: Each token in the input sequence is mapped to a dense vector representation using a token embedding matrix. This step converts the discrete tokens into continuous vectors that capture semantic and syntactic information.
3. **Positional Encodings**: Since the Transformer does not have any inherent mechanism to capture the order of tokens, positional encodings are added to the token embeddings. Positional encodings provide information about the relative position of each token in the sequence.
4. **Multi-Head Attention**: The token embeddings with positional encodings are passed through the multi-head attention mechanism. This allows the encoder to attend to different positions of the input sequence, capturing dependencies and relationships between tokens. The multi-head attention consists of multiple attention heads that operate in parallel, each with its learned weight matrices.
5. **Layer Normalization and Residual Connection**: The output of the multi-head attention mechanism undergoes layer normalization, which normalizes the

activations to have a stable mean and variance. A residual connection is then applied, adding the input of the multi-head attention to its output. This helps in stabilizing the training process and allows gradients to flow more easily through the network.

6. **Position-wise Feed-Forward Network**: The normalized output from the previous step is passed through a position-wise feed-forward network. This network consists of two linear transformations with a ReLU activation in between. It introduces non-linearity and increases the expressive power of the encoder.
7. **Layer Normalization and Residual Connection**: The output of the feed-forward network undergoes another layer normalization and residual connection, similar to step 5.

The encoder consists of multiple identical layers, each containing the multi-head attention, layer normalization, residual connection, and feed-forward network. The output of the encoder is a sequence of continuous representations that capture the contextual information of the input sequence, (Phuong & Hutter, 2022).

Decoder

The decoder takes the output of the encoder and generates the output sequence step by step. The decoder operates as follows:

1. **Token Embeddings**: Similar to the encoder, the decoder starts by mapping the previously generated tokens (or the start token) to dense vector representations using token embeddings.
2. **Positional Encodings**: Positional encodings are added to the token embeddings to provide information about the relative position of each token in the output sequence.
3. **Masked Multi-Head Attention**: The token embeddings with positional encodings are passed through a masked multi-head attention mechanism. This mechanism allows the decoder to attend to the previously generated tokens while preventing it from attending to future positions. The masking ensures that the predictions for a given position can only depend on the known outputs at positions less than that position.
4. **Layer Normalization and Residual Connection**: The output of the masked multi-head attention undergoes layer normalization and is added to the input through a residual connection.
5. **Multi-Head Attention (Encoder-Decoder Attention)**: The normalized output from the previous step is passed through another multi-head attention mechanism, known as encoder-decoder attention. This attention mechanism allows

the decoder to attend to the representations generated by the encoder. It helps the decoder focus on relevant parts of the input sequence while generating the output.

6. **Layer Normalization and Residual Connection**: The output of the encoder-decoder undergoes layer normalization and is added to the input through a residual connection.
7. **Position-wise Feed-Forward Network**: The normalized output from the previous step is passed through a position-wise feed-forward network, like the one in the encoder.
8. **Layer Normalization and Residual Connection**: The output of the feed-forward network undergoes layer normalization and is added to the input through a residual connection.

The decoder consists of multiple identical layers, each containing masked multi-head attention, encoder-decoder attention, layer normalization, residual connections, and feed-forward network. The decoder generates the output sequence one token at a time, using the previously generated tokens and the context provided by the encoder, (Alammar, 2019).

The output of the decoder undergoes a final linear transformation and SoftMax activation to produce a probability distribution over the vocabulary. The token with the highest probability is selected as the next tokens in the output sequence.

Scaling Transformers

The effectiveness of transformer-based language models has been shown to improve significantly with increased model size and training data. Scaling transformers refer to the practice of increasing the number of parameters in the model and training on larger datasets to achieve better performance on a wide range of natural language processing tasks.

The Need for Large-Scale Language Models

Language is inherently complex and diverse, with a vast vocabulary, intricate grammar rules, and various contexts in which words can be used. To effectively capture and understand the nuances of language, transformer-based language models require a large number of parameters and exposure to a wide range of textual data during training.

Increasing the number of parameters in a transformer allows the model to learn more complex patterns and relationships within the language. With more parameters, the model can capture fine-grained details, understand subtle meanings, and generate more coherent and contextually relevant outputs. This is particularly important for tasks that require a deep understanding of language, such as question answering, text generation, and sentiment analysis.

Moreover, training transformers on large-scale datasets is crucial for achieving good generalization and performance across different domains and tasks. Exposure to a diverse range of texts enables the model to learn the intricacies of language use in various contexts, making it more robust and adaptable to new and unseen data.

Benefits of Large-Scale Language Models

Language models with billions of parameters, trained on massive amounts of data, have demonstrated remarkable performance and versatility. Some notable examples include GPT-3 (175 billion parameters) (Brown et al., 2020), T5 (11 billion parameters) (Raffel et al., 2020), and Megatron-Turing NLG (530 billion parameters) (Patwary et al., 2022). These large-scale language models have shown the following benefits:

1. **Improved Performance**: Scaling up language models has led to significant improvements in performance across a wide range of natural language processing tasks. Larger models can better capture the complexities of language and generate more accurate and coherent outputs.
2. **Few-Shot and Zero-Shot Learning**: Large-scale language models have demonstrated impressive few-shot and zero-shot learning capabilities. They can perform tasks with minimal or no task-specific fine-tuning, relying on their vast knowledge acquired during pre-training. This enables them to adapt quickly to new tasks and domains.
3. **Generalization and Transfer Learning**: Scaled-up language models have shown strong generalization abilities and can effectively transfer knowledge across different tasks and domains. The representations learned by these models can be fine-tuned for specific tasks, achieving state-of-the-art performance with relatively small amounts of task-specific data.
4. **Language Understanding and Generation**: Large-scale language models have demonstrated remarkable language understanding and generation capabilities. They can engage in coherent and contextually relevant conversations, generate human-like text, and even perform tasks like summarization, translation, and creative writing.

Challenges and Considerations

While scaling transformers has proven to be highly effective, it also presents several challenges and considerations:

1. **Computational Resources**: Training and deploying large-scale language models require substantial computational resources, including high-performance hardware and significant amounts of memory. This can be cost-prohibitive and limit accessibility for many researchers and organizations.
2. **Training Time**: As the model size and dataset increase, the training time for large-scale language models can be considerably long, often requiring weeks or even months of continuous training on powerful hardware.
3. **Environmental Impact**: The computational resources required for training large-scale language models have a significant environmental impact, contributing to carbon emissions and energy consumption. Efforts are being made to develop more efficient training techniques and hardware to mitigate this impact.
4. **Bias and Fairness**: Large-scale language models trained on diverse datasets may inadvertently capture and amplify biases present in the training data. Ensuring fairness and mitigating biases in these models is an ongoing challenge and an active area of research.
5. **Interpretability and Transparency**: As language models become larger and more complex, interpreting their decision-making process and understanding the factors influencing their outputs become more challenging. Efforts are being made to improve the interpretability and transparency of these models.

Despite these challenges, the benefits of scaling transformers have been widely recognized, and research continues to push the boundaries of language model size and performance. Techniques such as model compression, efficient training algorithms, and hardware optimization are being explored to make large-scale language models more accessible and sustainable.

Large Language Models (LLMs) and Their Variants

Transformer-based large language models have revolutionized natural language processing, enabling significant advancements in a wide range of applications. These models can be categorized into three main configurations: encoder-only models, decoder-only models, and encoder-decoder models. Each configuration has its strengths and is suited for different types of tasks, ranging from language understanding to generation and sequence-to-sequence transformation.

Encoder-Only Models

Encoder-only models, such as BERT (Bidirectional Encoder Representations from Transformers), focus on understanding and representing input sequences. They have achieved state-of-the-art performance on various natural language understanding tasks, making them valuable for applications that require extracting insights and information from text data.

Key applications of encoder-only models include:

- **Sentiment Analysis**: Analyzing the sentiment expressed in text data, such as customer reviews, social media posts, or news articles, to gauge public opinion, monitor brand reputation, or make data-driven decisions.
- **Named Entity Recognition**: Identifying and classifying named entities, such as persons, organizations, locations, or products, in unstructured text data. This is crucial for information extraction, content categorization, and knowledge graph construction.
- **Text Classification**: Assigning predefined categories or labels to text documents based on their content. Text classification is fundamental to applications like spam detection, topic categorization, and content moderation.
- **Question Answering**: Providing accurate answers to questions based on the information present in a given text or knowledge base. Encoder-only models excel at extracting relevant information and generating concise answers, enabling applications like chatbots, virtual assistants, and knowledge retrieval systems.

Encoder-only models have also been adapted for domain-specific applications, such as legal document analysis, medical text mining, and financial sentiment analysis, where understanding and extracting insights from specialized text data is crucial.

Decoder-Only Models

Decoder-only models, such as the GPT (Generative Pre-trained Transformer) family, specialize in generating human-like text based on the patterns and knowledge learned from vast amounts of training data. These models have shown remarkable capabilities in producing coherent, contextually relevant, and creative text outputs, (Alammar, 2020).

Key applications of decoder-only models include:

- **Language Modeling**: Predicting the likelihood of a sequence of words, enabling applications like text completion, text generation, and language understanding. Language modeling forms the foundation for many other natural language processing tasks.

- **Text Generation**: Generating human-like text based on a given prompt or context. Decoder-only models can be used for various text generation tasks, such as creative writing, content creation, and data augmentation.
- **Dialogue Systems**: Building conversational agents that can engage in natural and coherent dialogue with users. Decoder-only models can generate contextually relevant responses, making them suitable for chatbots, virtual assistants, and customer support systems.
- **Story Generation**: Creating compelling narratives, plot lines, and character dialogues. Decoder-only models can be used to generate creative stories, assist writers in ideation, or even create interactive storytelling experiences.
- **Content Summarization**: Generating concise summaries of longer text documents while preserving the key information and main ideas. Decoder-only models can be used for automated summarization of articles, reports, or user-generated content.

Decoder-only models have also found applications in domain-specific tasks, such as generating product descriptions, creating marketing copy, and producing technical documentation. Their ability to generate human-like text makes them valuable for various content creation and automation scenarios, (Brown et al., 2020).

Encoder-Decoder Models

Encoder-decoder models, such as T5 (Text-to-Text Transfer Transformer), combine the strengths of both encoder and decoder architectures to handle sequence-to-sequence tasks. These models excel at transforming input sequences into target sequences, making them versatile tools for a wide range of applications.

Key applications of encoder-decoder models include:

- **Machine Translation**: Translating text from one language to another while preserving the meaning and context. Encoder-decoder models have achieved state-of-the-art performance in machine translation, enabling accurate and fluent translations for various language pairs.
- **Text Summarization**: Generating concise summaries of longer text documents, capturing the key information and main ideas. Encoder-decoder models can produce abstractive summaries that go beyond extracting sentence verbatim, allowing for more coherent and readable summaries.
- **Question Answering**: Generating accurate and contextually relevant answers to questions based on a given text or knowledge base. Encoder-decoder

models can handle complex questions that require reasoning and information synthesis from multiple parts of the input.

- **Text Simplification**: Transforming complex or technical text into a more simplified and accessible form while retaining the core meaning. Encoder-decoder models can be used to simplify legal documents, medical instructions, or educational content for a broader audience.
- **Text Style Transfer**: Modifying the style or tone of a text while preserving its content. Encoder-decoder models can be used for tasks like sentiment transfer (e.g., positive to negative), formality transfer (e.g., informal to formal), or authorship style imitation.

Encoder-decoder models have also been applied to domain-specific tasks, such as code generation, data-to-text generation (e.g., generating weather reports from numerical data), and cross-modal generation (e.g., image captioning). Their flexibility and ability to handle sequence-to-sequence transformations make them valuable for a wide range of applications.

Scaling and Few-Shot Learning

The performance of large language models has been shown to improve with increased model size and training data, following scaling laws. Larger models trained on more data tend to achieve better performance on downstream tasks. However, scaling up models comes with challenges, such as increased computational requirements and longer training times. Researchers are exploring techniques like model compression, knowledge distillation, and efficient training algorithms to address these challenges, (Brown et al., 2020).

One of the remarkable capabilities of large language models is their ability to perform few-shot and even zero-shot learning. Few-shot learning allows models to learn from a small number of examples, while zero-shot learning enables models to perform tasks without any task-specific training examples. This opens possibilities for quickly adapting models to new domains and tasks without extensive labeled data. However, ensuring the reliability, consistency, and fairness of few-shot and zero-shot learning remains an active area of research.

CURRENT CHALLENGES AND FUTURE DIRECTIONS

While large language models (LLMs) and transformers have demonstrated remarkable capabilities in various natural language processing tasks, there are still significant challenges and ethical considerations associated with their development and deployment. As the field continues to evolve, researchers are actively exploring new architectures, techniques, and approaches to address these challenges and push the boundaries of what LLMs can achieve.

Ethical Considerations in LLMs

Bias and Fairness

One of the primary concerns surrounding LLMs is the potential for bias and unfairness. These models are trained on massive text datasets that may reflect societal biases and prejudices. If not carefully addressed, LLMs can perpetuate and amplify these harmful stereotypes, leading to discriminatory outcomes in various applications. For example, a language model trained on text data with gender stereotypes may generate outputs that reinforce those stereotypes, potentially leading to unfair or biased decisions in areas like hiring or loan applications.

It is important to recognize that fine-tuning a model on specific data might not eliminate the inherent bias learned from the original training data. Therefore, researchers are actively exploring techniques to mitigate bias during both the data collection and model training stages. This involves carefully curating training data to ensure diversity and representation, as well as developing methods to de-bias the models themselves.

Computational Efficiency and Environmental Impact

Another significant challenge is the computational efficiency and environmental impact of LLMs. Training large language models requires substantial computational resources, resulting in high energy consumption and carbon emissions. This raises concern about the sustainability of developing and deploying ever-larger LLMs.

Researchers are working on finding ways to reduce the computational cost of LLM training and inference, such as exploring more efficient model architecture, leveraging techniques like model compression and knowledge distillation, and optimizing training algorithms for reduced energy consumption. These efforts aim to make the development and deployment of LLMs more environmentally friendly and sustainable.

Emerging Architectures and Techniques

To address the limitations and challenges of LLMs, researchers are continuously exploring new architecture and techniques.

Efficient Attention Mechanisms

One promising direction is the development of more efficient attention mechanisms that can reduce the computational cost of transformers while maintaining their performance. Researchers are investigating sparse attention mechanisms that selectively attend to a subset of the input tokens, thereby reducing the quadratic complexity of standard attention. These techniques aim to make transformers more scalable and efficient, enabling the development of larger and more powerful LLMs, (Dao et al., 2022).

RWKV Model Architecture

A promising new architecture is the RWKV (Receptance Weighted Key-Value) model. This novel approach simplifies the traditional Transformer by replacing the attention mechanism with a recurrent neural network (RNN)-like memory system. It introduces the concept of receptance, a learnable gating mechanism that controls how much information from past tokens is passed to the current state. This allows the model to process sequences in a linear, instead of quadratic, time complexity, making it significantly more efficient for long-range dependencies than standard Transformers. (Peng et al., 2023).

The RWKV architecture consists of several key components:

1. **Receptance Weighting**: RWKV computes the receptance between tokens using a simple and efficient formula, which considers the position and content of the tokens. The receptance weights are used to scale the key-value pairs in the attention mechanism, allowing the model to focus on the most relevant information.
2. **Key-Value Attention**: RWKV employs a modified version of the key-value attention mechanism, where the receptance weights are incorporated into the computation of attention scores. This enables the model to capture long-range dependencies while reducing the computational complexity.
3. **Feedforward Layers**: Similar to transformers, RWKV includes feedforward layers to process and transform the token representations. However, RWKV uses a simpler and more efficient feedforward structure compared to the standard transformer architecture.
4. **Residual Connections**: RWKV incorporates residual connections to facilitate the flow of information and gradients through the network, helping to alleviate the vanishing gradient problem.

The RWKV architecture has shown promising results in terms of performance and efficiency, making it an interesting direction for future research and development in the field of LLMs.

Beyond Transformers

Other efforts in the field focus on developing new model architectures that go beyond the transformer, such as incorporating elements of symbolic reasoning or leveraging graph-based representations of language. These approaches aim to address some of the limitations of current transformer-based LLMs and explore alternative ways of representing and processing language.

Meta-Learning and Transfer Learning

Researchers are also investigating techniques like meta-learning and transfer learning to enable LLMs to learn more efficiently from limited data and adapt to new tasks and domains. Meta-learning involves training models to learn how to learn, allowing them to quickly adapt to new tasks with minimal fine-tuning. Transfer learning focuses on leveraging knowledge learned from one task or domain to improve performance on related tasks or domains. These techniques can help reduce the data and computational requirements for training LLMs and make them more versatile and adaptable.

CONCLUSIONS

As the field of large language models continues to evolve, researchers are actively addressing the challenges and ethical considerations associated with these powerful models. From mitigating bias and improving computational efficiency to exploring new architectures and techniques, the research community is working towards developing more reliable, fair, and sustainable LLMs.

REFERENCES

Alammar, J. (2018, June 27). The illustrated transformer. *Jay Alammar's Blog*. https://jalammar.github.io/illustrated-transformer/

Alammar, J. (2019, August 31). The illustrated GPT-2. *Jay Alammar's Blog*. https://jalammar.github.io/illustrated-gpt2/

Alammar, J. (2020, January 13). Interfaces for explaining transformer language models. *Jay Alammar's Blog*. https://jalammar.github.io/explaining-transformers/

Bojanowski, P., Grave, E., Joulin, A., & Mikolov, T. (2016). Bag of tricks for efficient text classification. *arXiv*. https://arxiv.org/abs/1607.01759

Brown, T. B., Mann, B., Ryder, N., Subbiah, M., Kaplan, J. D., Dhariwal, P., Neelakantan, A., Shyam, P., Sastry, G., Askell, A., & Associates. (2020). Language models are few-shot learners. In *Advances in Neural Information Processing Systems* (Vol. 33). NeurIPS.

Cho, K., Merrienboer, B., Gulcehre, C., Bahdanau, D., Schwenk, H., & Bengio, Y. (2014). Learning phrase representations using RNN encoder–decoder for statistical machine translation. In *Proceedings of the 2014 Conference on Empirical Methods in Natural Language Processing* (pp. 1724–1734). Association for Computational Linguistics.

Dao, T., Fu, D. Y., Ermon, S., Rudra, A., & Ré, C. (2022). FlashAttention: Fast and memory-efficient exact attention with IO-awareness. *arXiv*. https://arxiv.org/abs/2205.14135

Mikolov, T., Karafiát, M., Burget, L., Černocký, J., & Khudanpur, S. (2010). Recurrent neural network based language model. In *Proceedings of Interspeech 2010* (pp. 1045–1048). ISCA., https://www.isca-archive.org/interspeech_2010/mikolov10_interspeech.html

Mikolov, T., Sutskever, I., Chen, K., Corrado, G. S., & Dean, J. (2013). Efficient estimation of word representations in vector space. In *Proceedings of the International Conference on Learning Representations (ICLR)*.

Patwary, M. (2022). Using DeepSpeed and Megatron to train Megatron-Turing NLG 530B, a large-scale generative language model. *arXiv*. https://arxiv.org/abs/2201.11990

Peng, B., Alcaide, E., Anthony, Q. G., Albalak, A., Arcadinho, S., Biderman, S., Cao, H., Cheng, X., Chung, M. N., & Derczynski, L. (2023). RWKV: Reinventing RNNs for the transformer era. *arXiv*. https://arxiv.org/abs/2305.13048

Pennington, J., Socher, R., & Manning, C. D. (2014). GloVe: Global vectors for word representation. In *Proceedings of the 2014 Conference on Empirical Methods in Natural Language Processing* (pp. 1532–1543). Association for Computational Linguistics.

Phuong, M., & Hutter, M. (2022). Formal algorithms for transformers. *arXiv*. https://arxiv.org/abs/2207.09238

Raffel, C., Shazeer, N., Roberts, A., Lee, K., Narang, S., Matena, M., Zhou, Y., Li, W., & Liu, P. J. (2020). Exploring the limits of transfer learning with a unified text-to-text transformer. *Journal of Machine Learning Research*, *21*(140), 1–67.

Robertson, S. E., & Sparck Jones, K. (1976). Simple, proven approaches to text retrieval. *The Journal of Documentation*, *32*(1), 30–48.

Sennrich, R., Haddow, B., & Birch, A. (2016). Neural machine translation of rare words with subword units. In *Proceedings of the 54th Annual Meeting of the Association for Computational Linguistics* (Vol. 1, pp. 1715–1725). Association for Computational Linguistics.

Shannon, C. E. (1948). A mathematical theory of communication. *The Bell System Technical Journal*, *27*(3), 379–423.

Song, X., Salcianu, A., Song, Y., Dopson, D., & Zhou, D. (2021). Fast WordPiece tokenization. In *Proceedings of the 2021 Conference on Empirical Methods in Natural Language Processing* (pp. 2089–2103). Association for Computational Linguistics.

Vaswani, A., Shazeer, N., Parmar, N., Uszkoreit, J., Jones, L., Gomez, A. N., Kaiser, Ł., & Polosukhin, I. (2017). Attention is all you need. In *Advances in Neural Information Processing Systems* (Vol. 30). NeurIPS.

Wang, S., & Jiang, J. (2016). Learning natural language inference with LSTM. In *Proceedings of the 2016 Conference on Empirical Methods in Natural Language Processing* (pp. 1442–1451). Association for Computational Linguistics.

Zhang, Y., & Wallace, B. (2016). A study on neural network language modeling. *arXiv*. https://arxiv.org/abs/1708.07252

Chapter 3

Exploring the Core Principles, Architectures, and Advancements of Large Language Models

Suriya Murugan
https://orcid.org/0000-0002-8130-7228
Sri Eshwar College of Engineering, India

Anandakumar Haldorai
https://orcid.org/0000-0001-9975-6462
Sri Eshwar College of Engineering, India

ABSTRACT

Language is necessary for human interaction because it helps in communication, learning, and the creation of rules and agreements that advance society. Although computers have historically had difficulty understanding and producing human language, advances in artificial intelligence, especially with regard to large language models (LLMs), have significantly enhanced computers' ability to grasp and produce natural language. LLMs, which are based on deep learning architectures such as transformers, have revolutionized natural language processing (NLP) by facilitating complex text generation and comprehension. Even with their successes, LLMs have drawbacks, like as theoretical issues and possible political and cultural biases in the training set. This chapter explores the underlying theories and architectural frameworks of LLMs, as well as the principles that guide their operation. The impact of these potent models on how humans engage with information and technology is highlighted, and it also covers current study on the difficulties and moral issues surrounding their use.

DOI: 10.4018/979-8-3693-8387-2.ch003

INTRODUCTION

The advent of language processing technology has been a recent milestone in artificial intelligence (AI), allowing us to create more intelligent systems with a deeper comprehension of language than ever before. "Large Language Models (LLMs)," also known as large pre-trained transformer language models, significantly increase the capabilities of text-based systems. The purpose of LLMs is to comprehend and produce text that is similar to that of humans. They are trained on enormous datasets that contain text from books, journals, websites, and several other sources. They are constructed using neural networks, more especially deep learning (DL) architectures, (Bommasani et al., 2022a).

Figure 1. Outline of proposed workflow

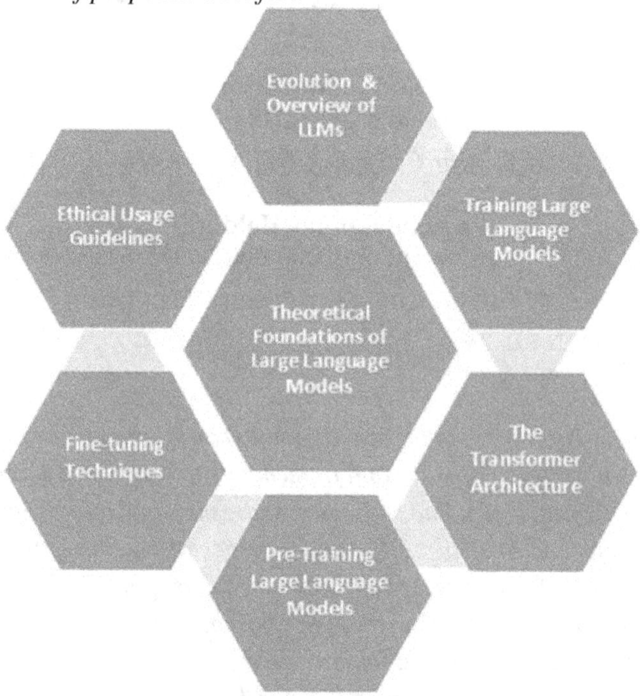

As outlined in Figure 1, this chapter will delve into the theoretical underpinnings of LLMs, examining the principles that drive their success and the foundational theories that enable their remarkable performance. While challenges persist, ongoing research and a commitment to ethical AI practices pave the way for a future where large language models continue to shape our interaction with information and technology. It is essential to recognize the potential, challenges, and responsibilities associated with the deployment of these powerful language models. By providing a comprehensive overview of the mathematical and conceptual frameworks that underpin these models, this chapter helps researchers with a deep understanding of how LLMs function and why they are so effective.

Evolution of LLMs

The transformer model is the foundation for most popular language models available today, such as GPT-3 and BERT, which have billions of parameters and analyze and produce text using self-attention mechanisms. Natural language processing (NLP) has seen a revolution thanks to large language models like OpenAI's GPT-4, Google's BERT, and Meta's LLaMA, which are capable of comprehending and producing language at previously unheard-of levels. In the last few years, there has been a rapid increase in the study of large language models, (Alammar, 2023). Artificial intelligence research on language models has become increasingly important, especially in light of the advent of ground-breaking technologies such as ChatGPT.

With a projected value of USD 4.35 billion in 2023 and a compound annual growth rate (CAGR) of 35.9% from 2024 to 2030, the global big language model market is expected to increase, as illustrated in Figure 2. One factor contributing to the large language models (LLMs) market's acceleration is the incorporation of a zero human interaction feature in training systems. With no ongoing human supervision required, this feature makes models more efficient by cutting down on time and resource requirements and allowing them to learn and adapt on their own, (Vaswani et al., 2022).

Figure 2. LLM global market analysis (https://www.grandviewresearch.com)

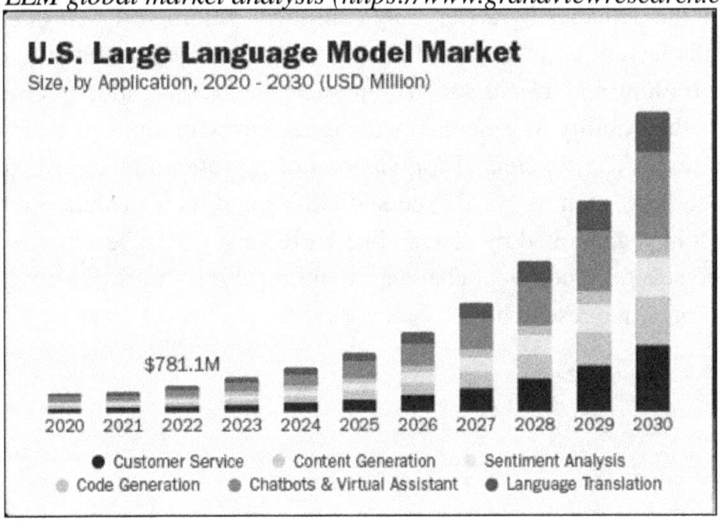

Overview of LLMs

In order to learn and master the fundamental structures and semantics of human language, big, general-purpose language processing models known as "LLMs" are first pre-trained on vast datasets spanning a wide range of topics, (Bommasani et al., 2022b). In this case, "large" refers to both the billions or even trillions of parameters that the model contains, as well as the significant amount of data needed for training. Pre-training models, fine-tuning models, and multimodal models are the three categories under which LLMs fall.

- **Pre-training models** are able to understand a wide variety of linguistic patterns and structures since they have been trained on massive amounts of data.
- **Fine-tuning models** area larger dataset used to pre-train fine-tuning models, which are then used to refine them for a particular job using a smaller dataset.
- **Multimodal models**are more complex language models are produced via multimodal models, which blend text with additional modes like pictures or video.

The model's adaptability is demonstrated by pre-training, which prepares it to tackle typical language tasks including text classification, question answering, and document summarization as shown in Figure 3. To acquire language patterns, grammar, and general knowledge, LLMs are first trained on a broad corpus of text data. This stage entails creating text in response to prompts or guessing missing words in sentences. To enhance their performance on selected applications, such question answering, text classification, or translation, models are fine-tuned on particular tasks or domains after pre-training. A pre-trained language model can be fine-tuned to meet unique demands by undergoing additional training on a particular task or dataset. This technique leverages the general language understanding developed during pre-training and refines it for a more specialized application. A crucial aspect of LLMs is their ability to generate meaningful representations of words, phrases, and entire texts. The theoretical foundations of representation learning focus on word embeddings such as Word2Vec and GloVe and their evolution into contextual embeddings generated by models like BERT and GPT. Despite their success, LLMs pose several theoretical challenges and open questions that continue to be the subject of active research.

Figure 3. Overview of LLM

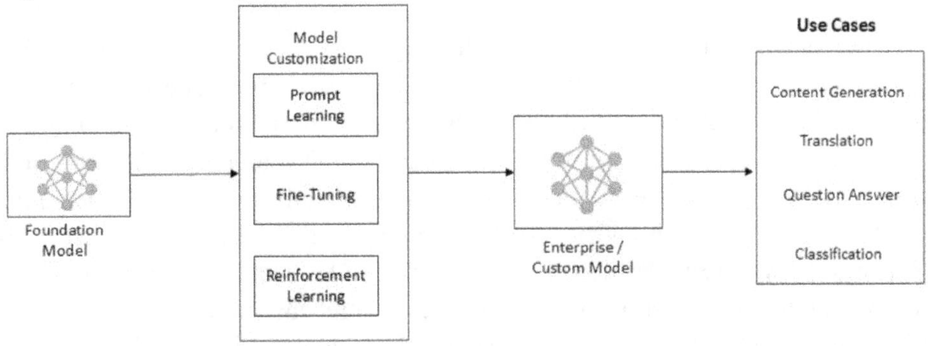

Rise of Transformers

Language models were replaced by LLMs in large part thanks to the introduction of the Transformer deep neural network architecture in 2017. In order to advance natural language processing algorithms, large-scale Transformer networks have emerged as the preferred method. With their deep understanding, these models—which are based on the Transformer architecture—allow for interactions that are very similar to human communication and may even help direct tasks that require human intervention. A crucial question remains: what is the theoretical basis of huge language models, despite their remarkable powers and increasing intricacy?

These models are trained on vast amounts of internet-scale data, and because of their opacity and complexity, it is still unclear how these models' cultural and political biases are absorbed from the input and applied to subsequent tasks. Large numbers of parameters, or weights, are present in LLMs; these numbers can range from hundreds of millions to hundreds of trillions. A model with more parameters will be more accurate, but it will also take up more memory and operate more slowly. The model's ability to identify intricate patterns in the data is dependent on the number of parameters. Large volumes of text data are used to train LLMs, giving them the ability to comprehend a broad range of subjects and situations. In the early days, self-supervised learning algorithms were mostly used to generate LLMs. Processing unlabeled data to create helpful representations that can aid in subsequent learning tasks is known as self-supervised learning, (Roberts et al., 2022).

TRAININGLARGE LANGUAGE MODELS

Unsupervised learning is used for training large language models. Using unlabeled datasets, models trained on unsupervised learning can uncover patterns in data that were previously undiscovered. Moreover, this removes the requirement for thorough data labeling, which is one of the main obstacles in developing AI models. How much data, then, is required to train an LLM? Doubling the training dataset and the parameters is a reasonable general rule of thumb. Current data actually indicates that most LLMs are undertrained. The models can be taught for a variety of use scenarios rather than just one because of the comprehensive training process that LLMs go through. Foundation models are the name given to these kinds of models, (Bubeck et al., 2023).

Zero-shot learning refers to the foundation model's capacity to produce text for a wide range of uses without requiring a lot of guidance or training. One-shot or few-shot learning, which involves feeding the foundation model one or a few instances that demonstrate how a task might be completed to comprehend and perform better on specific use cases, are two variations of this capacity. Even though zero-shot learning with huge language models has amazing possibilities, developers and businesses naturally want to tame these systems to behave the way they want. These huge language models can be adjusted using a variety of methods to attain improved accuracy before being deployed for particular use cases. Among the methods are adapters, fine-tuning, and prompt tuning, (Minaee et al., 2024).

Prompt Tuning

Prompt tuning is a technique used to adapt pre-trained language models to specific tasks by modifying the input prompts rather than altering the model's weights. The idea is to craft or learn prompts that guide the model's behavior to produce desired outputs. This approach is particularly useful for large models like GPT, where fine-tuning all parameters is computationally expensive. Instead of adjusting the model itself, prompt tuning focuses on the input, making it a lightweight and efficient way to tailor a model's responses.

Fine-Tuning

Fine-tuning involves taking a pre-trained language model and further training it on a specific dataset or task to improve its performance in that area. Unlike prompt tuning, which modifies the input, fine-tuning adjusts the model's parameters. This process typically involves retraining the model with a smaller learning rate to adapt it to new data while retaining the knowledge acquired during initial training.

Fine-tuning is widely used to customize models for specific applications, such as sentiment analysis, machine translation, or text classification.

Adapters

Adapters are a modular approach to model fine-tuning that inserts small, trainable layers (adapters) into a pre-trained model. Instead of updating all the model's parameters, only the adapter layers are trained, allowing the original model to remain largely intact. This method is particularly useful when fine-tuning multiple tasks, as different adapters can be swapped in and out depending on the task at hand. Adapters are efficient in terms of both computation and memory, making them an attractive option for multi-task learning and deployment in resource-constrained environments.

THE TRANSFORMERS

The idea of the attention mechanism, a machine learning method intended to resemble human cognitive attention, was first presented in a research paper titled "Neural Machine Translation by Jointly Learning to Align and Translate" in 2014, which marked the beginning of the development of LLMs as we know them today. The transformer model was later introduced in a research paper titled "Attention Is All You Need" (Vaswani et al., 2022) to further refine that attention mechanism. Transformers are able to learn hierarchical representations of text because they are made up of numerous layers of encoders and decoders (or, in some models, either encoders or only decoders).A transformer is a type of AI model (a type of neural network model in particular) that excels at understanding and generating human-like text by analyzing patterns in large amounts of text data. It is specifically designed to comprehend context and meaning by examining the relationships between different elements in the text. Transformers rely heavily on a mathematical technique called attention to focus on relevant parts of the input when making predictions, which allows them to effectively capture dependencies and contextual information over long sequences, (Hinton et al., 2023).

Unlike earlier architectures like recurrent neural networks (RNNs) and long short-term memory networks (LSTMs), the transformer model captures long-range dependencies and relationships more effectively by using self-attention mechanisms to weigh the influence of different words in a sentence. Transformers may process a sentence's words in parallel, as opposed to sequentially, which greatly accelerates training and makes it simpler to take advantage of contemporary hardware like GPUs and TPUs, (Sumithra & Suriya, 2024; Haldorai, Murugan, & Balakrishnan, 2024).

Most LLMs are built on the Transformer architecture, which is essential to their success. The main elements of the Transformer—positional encodings, multi-head attention, and self-attention mechanisms—will be covered in detail in this section. Together, these components allow input sequences to be processed in parallel, getting around the drawbacks of recurrent designs like Long Short-Term Memory (LSTM) networks, (Guo et al., 2022). Transformers are able to efficiently assess the impact of various words in a sentence thanks to a crucial innovation: the self-attention mechanism, which recognizes long-range relationships in text.As shown in Figure 4, Transformers consist of multiple layers of encoders and decoders, or only encoders or decoders in some models, allowing them to learn hierarchical representations of text. This architecture enables them to process all words in a sentence simultaneously (in parallel), significantly speeding up training and leveraging modern hardware like GPUs and TPUs.

Figure 4. Encoder- decoder

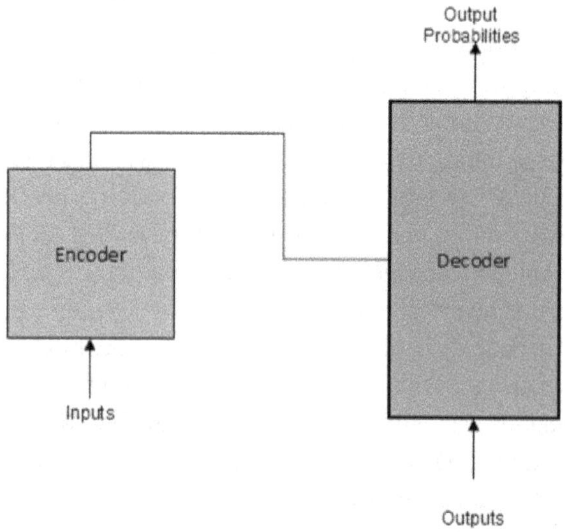

Encoder

The encoder is an essential component of the transformer architecture. It processes and transforms the input sequences into a set of contextualized representations that capture the meanings of words (or tokens) in the context. Encoder takes in a sequence of tokens (e.g., words or subwords) from the input text. Through multiple layers of processing, the encoder generates representations for each token that incorporate information from the entire sequence, capturing the context in which each word appears. The encoder uses mechanisms like self-attention to understand the relationships between different tokens in the sequence, ensuring that the representation of each token is informed by its surrounding context.

Decoder

A crucial part of the transformer architecture, the decoder is mainly made for sequence generation applications like text production and machine translation. It creates the output sequence piece by piece using the encoded input representation that it received from the encoder. To do this, the decoder pays attention to the encoded input representation from the encoder as well as the previously created tokens, making sure the output is coherent and acceptable for the given context. By taking care of the encoded input representation and the previously generated tokens, the transformer architecture's decoder is intended to produce sequences. By utilizing feed-forward networks, residual connections with layer normalization, masked self-attention, and cross-attention with the encoder's output, the decoder successfully integrates contextual information to provide coherent and contextually relevant output sequences.

THE TRANSFORMER ARCHITECTURE

The encoder-decoder structure of the transformer design is seen in Figure 5, however many widely used versions on the market now only use the encoder or the decoder portion to accomplish particular functions. One of the most popular encoder-only transformer models is BERT. The decoder-only transformer architecture is still used by the OpenAI-developed GPT model and all of its more recent iterations.

Figure 5. Overview of transformer architecture (Vaswani et al., 2022)

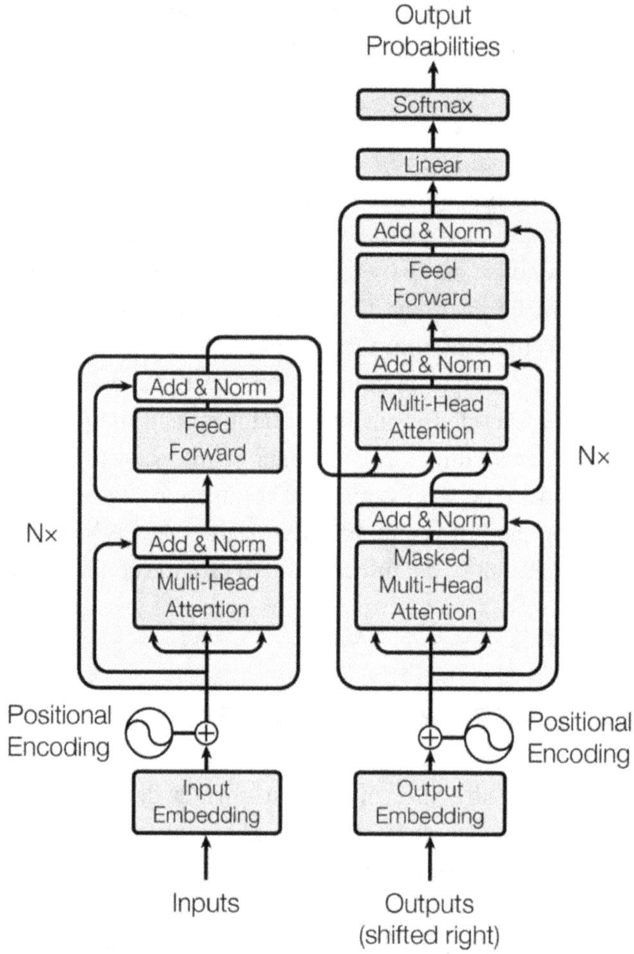

The Transformer follows this overall architecture using stacked self-attention and fully connected layers for both the encoder and decoder and is explained below.

Tokenizing the input sequence results in embeddings, which are used as the decoder's first inputs. In order to prevent future information leakage, masked multi-head self-attention computes Queries, Keys, and Values while applying a mask. The computation of attention scores is applied to a weighted sum of values, which is then followed by layer normalization and residual connection. Subsequently, queries from the preceding layer and encoder keys and values are used for multi-head attention over the encoder's output, with comparable normalization procedures. After processing via a feed-forward network (FFN), layer normalization and residual connection are applied to the output.

PRE-TRAINING LARGE LANGUAGE MODELS

The exact tasks and objectives that are set for a language model during its initial training phase on huge, unlabeled text corpora are known as pre-training objectives. With the aid of these goals, the model is able to acquire valuable language representations that it may subsequently hone on smaller, more focused datasets to attain superior performance on an array of downstream tasks. Pre-training goals frequently include the following:

Masked Language Modeling (MLM)

A pre-training goal in models such as BERT (Bidirectional Encoder Representations from Transformers) is Masked Language Modeling (MLM). By using the context that the surrounding tokens provide, maximum token matching (MLM) aims to train a model to anticipate missing tokens in a sequence. This technique aids in the model's deepening comprehension of the language, which makes it capable of handling a variety of NLP tasks. Conventional language models, like the ones employed in the GPT, only use the left context to predict the next word; they are unidirectional. With MLM, the model can take into account both left and right contexts, giving it a more thorough comprehension of every word in a sentence, (Minaee et al., 2021).

Training Process

1. Tokenization: Use a tokenizer to make tokens out of the input text.

It is possible to tokenize a statement like "Transformers are amazing tools for NLP tasks" like follows: ['transformers', 'are', 'amazing', 'tools', 'for', 'nlp', 'tasks']

2. Masking: In the input sequence, mask characters at random. Consider the following: ['transformers', 'are', '[MASK]', 'tools', 'for', '[MASK]', 'tasks']
3. Model Training: The model attempts to predict the original tokens for the masked positions by using the masked sequence as input. After comparing the predictions and the actual tokens, the cross-entropy loss is computed. The model's parameters are updated via back-propagation in order to reduce loss.

Significance of MLM

- Contextual Understanding: MLM enables the model to acquire a bidirectional comprehension of context, an essential skill for numerous natural language processing tasks such as named entity recognition, text classification, and question answering.

- Versatility: Models pre-trained with MLM, such as BERT, are quite adaptable since they can be adjusted for a range of downstream tasks with comparatively little task-specific input.
- Robustness: The tactic of occasionally substituting random words for tokens or leaving them unaltered avoids over-fitting and strengthens the model's ability to handle various text input formats.

Fine-Tuning Techniques

The process of adopting a language model that has already been trained and refining it on a particular job or dataset in order to tailor it to a specific purpose is known as fine-tuning. With this method, the pre-training general language awareness is leveraged and enhanced for a more focused use. Standard fine-tuning, feature-based method, adapter layering, layer-wise fine-tuning, joint training, multi-task fine-tuning, and intermediate task fine-tuning are examples of common fine-tuning techniques, (Feng et al., 2023).

Standard Fine-Tuning

Using a task-specific dataset, a pre-trained language model is further trained to do a particular task. Through this process, the model is able to modify its grasp of generic language to suit the specific task at hand.

Steps in Standard Fine-Tuning:

1. First, load a language model that has been pre-trained on a sizable corpus of text.
2. Gather Task-Specific Information: Gather and prepare data according to the job at hand.
3. Include the output layer Add to the model an output layer that is task-specific.
4. Training Loop: Use an optimizer and learning rate scheduler to fine-tune the model on task data.
5. Assessment and Verification: Keep an eye on validation results to prevent overfitting.
6. Preserve Model: Keep the optimized model handy for further tasks.

Feature-Based Approach

A more straightforward model, such a linear classifier or a tiny neural network, uses the features (representations or embeddings) that are extracted from text data using the feature-based technique. When you wish to leverage the potent embeddings produced by pre-trained models without fine-tuning the complete model, this method can be helpful.

Steps in the Feature-Based Approach:

1. Use a pre-trained language model, such as BERT or GPT, to load text input and extract features.
2. To ensure compatibility with the pre-trained model, prepare the data by gathering, preprocessing, and tokenizing the dataset.
3. Extraction of Features: By running the text through the trained model, contextualized embeddings are obtained.
4. Train a Model Particular to a Task: Using labeled data, train a more basic model for the intended task using the extracted characteristics.
5. Evaluation and Prediction: Make advantage of the model's performance on a validation set to make predictions about future data.

Adapter Layering

A quick and effective way to adjust language models that have already been trained for a certain purpose without changing all of the model's parameters is by using adapter stacking. Adapter layering integrates tiny, task-specific neural network modules (adapters) into pre-trained language models to facilitate effective fine-tuning for different tasks, as opposed to fine-tuning every parameter of a big model, (Raiaan et al., 2024). In addition to maintaining competitive performance on downstream jobs, this method lowers the computational cost and storage needs.

Steps Involved in Adapter Layering:

1. Pre-trained language models such as BERT or GPT can be loaded first.
2. Determining the Adapter Architecture: Create adapter layers featuring up-, down-, and activation projections (like ReLU).
3. Integrating Adapters: In each transformer block, place an adapter layer after the attention mechanism or FFN.
4. Freeze Model Parameters: Only the adapter layers remain trainable when the original model parameters are frozen.
5. Dataset preparation involves tokenizing and preprocessing input data to ensure that it complies with model specifications.

6. Getting Started with Adapters Train only the adapter layers to fine-tune the model on the task.
7. Assessing and Fine-Tuning: Check results on a validation set and make any necessary hyperparameter adjustments.
8. Inference: To forecast fresh data, use the adjusted model with adapters.

Layer-Wise Fine-Tuning

A method called "layer-wise fine-tuning" is employed to gradually unfreeze and adjust the layers within a language model that has already been trained. By keeping the earlier layers constant while fine-tuning the later layers, which capture more task-specific information, this method seeks to better adapt the model to a new task. The model can gradually adapt to the goal job as more layers are unfrozen and refined over time.

Steps Involved in Layer-Wise Fine-Tuning:

1. Load Pre-Trained Model: Begin by loading a language model that has already been trained, such as BERT or GPT.
2. Incorporate Layers Particular to Tasks: Include layers in the model that are customized for the particular task at hand.
3. Set in motion All Layers: At first, keep all layers frozen, with the exception of those that are task-specific.
4. Unfreeze and Adjust Final Layer: Use task-specific layers to unfreeze and refine the final layer following initial training.
5. Gradually Unfreeze Layers: For more fine-tuning, gradually unfreeze extra layers in later training stages.
6. Adjust the Entire Model: After all layers have been unfrozen, adjust the model as a whole.

Joint Training

A model can be trained concurrently on several tasks or datasets using a technique called joint training. The model learns to execute many tasks simultaneously, as opposed to training on one task and then tuning it on another. This method makes use of shared representations and, by exposing the model to a variety of training data and objectives, improves generalization.

Key Steps Involved in Joint Training:

1. Define the Model Architecture: Build a multitasking model. This usually involves a shared base model with heads that are customized to a task.

2. Prepare the datasets: For every task, tokenize and preprocess the datasets.
3. Define Loss Functions: Give each task a specific set of loss functions.
4. Set the Optimizer and Model to Initial.
5. Training Loop: Use a training loop to switch between samples from a combined dataset or tasks.
6. Validation and Evaluation: Assess the model using each task's validation sets in order to track performance and make any required modifications.

Multitask Fine-Tuning

A pre-trained model can be further trained (fine-tuned) on numerous tasks either sequentially or simultaneously using a technique called multitask fine-tuning. This method seeks to enhance the model's performance on each task by utilizing the shared knowledge across several tasks.

Steps for Multitask Fine-Tuning:

1. Identify the Shared Base Model: The shared base should be a transformer model that has already been trained.
2. Add Task-Specific Heads: Create distinct output layers for every task you assign.
3. Ready the datasets: Tokenize and prepare the datasets in advance for every activity.
4. Define Loss Functions: For every task, provide a loss function.
5. Training Loop: Establish a loop for training that modifies both the task-specific heads and the common base model.
6. Validation and Evaluation: Assess how well each task is performed on validation sets.

Intermediate Task Fine-Tuning

A machine learning training technique called intermediate task fine-tuning is employed, especially in the context of transfer learning and multitask learning. With this method, a model is first fine-tuned on one or more intermediate tasks, and then it is fine-tuned on the final target task, as opposed to fine-tuning it directly on a target task.

Steps in Intermediate Task Fine-Tuning:

1. To improve the model's performance on the goal task, select intermediate tasks that are related to it and have labeled data available.
2. Perfect on Moderate Assignments: Adjust settings to minimize task-specific loss functions as you fine-tune the pre-trained model on various tasks.

3. To further refine the model on task-specific data, transfer learning involves applying the knowledge gained from intermediate tasks to the goal task.

Through the use of these fine-tuning strategies, we are able to effectively adapt language models that have already been trained to a variety of unique tasks. By using these methods, models can gain from the rich representations acquired during pre-training while also learning task-specific characteristics and subtleties. Models can be tuned to perform effectively on a variety of NLP tasks, such as text classification, named entity identification, sentiment analysis, machine translation, and more, by fine-tuning on task-specific data. Furthermore, by allowing pre-trained language models to generalize across tasks and domains, fine-tuning techniques add to their adaptability and usefulness. This versatility is crucial in real-world applications where a single model may need to address multiple tasks or operate in different contexts. Overall, by employing fine-tuning techniques effectively, we can maximize the value and applicability of pre-trained language models, making them powerful tools for a wide range of NLP tasks and scenarios.

ETHICAL USAGE GUIDELINES

Large language models have a huge impact on society; they can automate decision-making processes and shape public opinion. Therefore, it is imperative to investigate the ethical implications of developing and implementing LLMs. Setting ethical usage standards is crucial as these technologies become more ingrained in our daily lives to guarantee their fair and responsible deployment. These frameworks try to minimize potential hazards while maximizing social benefits by addressing different facets of model development, implementation, and usage.

Principles of Ethical Usage Guidelines:

- Fairness and non-Discrimination: It's critical to guarantee that AI systems handle people equally, without regard to factors such as nationality, gender, age, race, or other protected traits. In order to do this, biases in the data and model training processes must be actively recognized and mitigated.
- Transparency and Explainability: To encourage transparency, thorough documentation of data sources and model creation procedures is required. Furthermore, models have to be built with easily comprehensible explanations for their outputs so that consumers can comprehend the decision-making process.
- Privacy and Data Protection: Sensitive information is shielded from unwanted access by putting strong data security measures in place. Additionally,

data collecting must to follow applicable privacy laws and be done with the express consent of the user.

- Accountability and Responsibility: It's critical to establish precise roles for developers, deployers, and users throughout the AI lifecycle. Accountability is ensured by establishing protocols for error detection, reporting, and correction.
- Human-Centric Design: To reduce potential risks, system design should give priority to user safety and well-being. In crucial applications, human supervision is required to prevent unbridled AI autonomy.
- Inclusivity and Accessibility: AI systems are guaranteed to satisfy the requirements of all user groups by involving a variety of stakeholders in the design and deployment phases. Incorporating accessibility features is crucial to ensure that people with impairments have equitable access to AI technologies.

CONCLUSION

Large neural networks (LLMs) are a class of neural networks that are capable of producing or embedding text. LLMs can get more capable as they grow, including creating code and translating other languages. During model training, all they need to do is keep an eye out for recurrent patterns in language. Natural language processing (NLP) has seen a revolution thanks to LLMs, which are now widely employed across a variety of businesses to address a wide range of NLP challenges. Even with their amazing development and promise, LLMs have limits and difficulties that need for continued study, moral reflection, and technical developments in order to maximize their influence and open the door for further advances in artificial intelligence. This chapter offered insight into several LLM theoretical dimensions, enabling researchers to develop a clear understanding and do in-depth study on LLMs.

REFERENCES

Alammar, J. (2023). The Transformer Family: Variants, Applications, and Limitations. *Proceedings of the IEEE Conference on Neural Networks*, 29(2), 299-313.

Bommasani, R., Hudson, D., Adeli, E., & Altman, R.. (2022). On the Opportunities and Risks of Foundation Models. *Communications of the ACM*, *65*(3), 55–64.

Bommasani, R., Hudson, D., & Brundage, M.. (2022). Foundations of Large Language Models: A Comprehensive Overview. *Journal of Artificial Intelligence Research*, *75*, 1–48.

Bubeck, S., Eldan, R., Li, Y., ... (2023). Sparks of Artificial General Intelligence: Early Experiments with GPT-4. arXiv preprint arXiv:2303.12712.

Feng, Y., Xie, M., Tian, Z., Wang, S., Lu, Y., & Shu, J. Mobius: Fine tuning large-scale models on commodity gpu servers. In *Proceedings of the 28th ACM International Conference on Architectural Support for Programming Languages and Operating Systems*, Volume 2, pages 489–501, 2023.

Guo, H., Singh, R., & Ferris, A.. (2022). Adapting Pretrained Transformers for Question Answering. *Journal of Natural Language Engineering*, *28*(3), 291–310.

Haldorai, A., Murugan, S., & Balakrishnan, M. (2024). Bi-Model Emotional AI for Audio-Visual Human Emotion Detection Using Hybrid Deep Learning Model. In *Artificial Intelligence for Sustainable Development* (pp. 293–315). Springer Nature Switzerland.

Hinton, G. E., Dean, J., & Young, T.. (2023). A Survey of Large Language Models. *Proceedings of the National Academy of Sciences of the United States of America*, *120*(3), 1038–1045.

Minaee, S., Kalchbrenner, N., Cambria, E., Nikzad, N., Chenaghlu, M., & Gao, J. (2021, April). Deep learning–based text classification: A comprehensive review. *ACM Computing Surveys*, *54*(3).

Minaee, S., Mikolov, T., Nikzad, N., Chenaghlu, M., Socher, R., Amatriain, X., & Gao, J. (2024). Large language models: A survey. arXiv preprint arXiv:2402.06196.

Raiaan, M. A. K., Mukta, M. S. H., Fatema, K., Fahad, N. M., Sakib, S., Mim, M. M. J., & Azam, S. (2024). A review on large Language Models: Architectures, applications, taxonomies, open issues and challenges. *IEEE Access : Practical Innovations, Open Solutions.*

Roberts, A., Raffel, C., Shazeer, N., & Lee, K.. (2022). Exploring the Limits of Transfer Learning with a Unified Text-to-Text Transformer. *Journal of Artificial Intelligence Research*, *74*, 67–85.

. Sumithra, M. G., & Suriya, M. (2024). Improved Spectrum Prediction Model for Cognitive Radio Networks Using Hybrid Deep Learning Technique. International Journal of Intelligent Networks.

Vaswani, A., Shazeer, N., Parmar, N., & Uszkoreit, J.. (2022). Attention is All You Need. *Neural Computation*, *34*(4), 681–689.

Section 2
Applications and Real-World Implementations

Chapter 4
Real-World Implementations of Large Language Models

Meetu Malhotra
https://orcid.org/0009-0009-7495-4484
Harrisburg University of Science and Technology, USA

Rahul Awasthy
https://orcid.org/0009-0003-1242-3860
Harrisburg University of Science and Technology, USA

ABSTRACT

Large Language models (LLMs) have always shown exceptional abilities in understanding and generating human language, leading to considerable progress in various fields. This chapter will help to examine all the practical applications of LLMs, highlighting their growing impact on industries such as healthcare, automotive, finance, education, customer service, and social media. The chapter also addresses the challenges in implementing LLM models, data privacy, ethical concerns, and the necessity for different governance frameworks. Through the case studies of successful LLM applications, this chapter will also illustrate the major practical advantages and the potential of these technologies in addressing real-world challenges, thereby fostering innovation and efficiency across various variations industries. It also covers latest SOTA LLMs research in various domains.

DOI: 10.4018/979-8-3693-8387-2.ch004

INTRODUCTION

Large Language models (LLMS) have become integral across some various fields, prompting the need for scrutiny of their main impact. These systems are then developed using an extensive online dataset to achieve all human like language capabilities (Allen Institute for AI, 2021). Built with different sophisticated natural language processing methods, it is then essential to ensure all that of LLMs enhance society that is responsible while also considering all the potential benefits of automation. LLMs show promise for Streamlining Healthcare Research and Diagnosis. By reviewing electronic health records and medical literature, algorithms can suggest rare condition diagnoses more quickly than providers alone (Adams et al., 2021). This spares patient delays in treatment and frees clinician time. As one study found, robo-doctors assisted physicians in identifying additional patient comorbidities in over 30% of cases (Afzal et al., 2022). LLMs also aid medical distribution optimization. During the COVID-19 pandemic, natural language processing tools analyzed geographic infection trends and resource availability, recommending vaccine allocation strategies to maximize coverage (Singer et al., 2022). Such tools complemented public health experts' efforts. However, to engender trust, developers must implement transparency regarding data and reasoning behind automated decisions impacting lives (Anthropic, 2021).

Financial services represent another sector harnessing LLMs. "Robo-advisors" specialized in Al algorithms coach growing numbers of investors by learning their profiles to structure personalized investment plans (Madison et al., 2020). As one analyst noted, "LLMs efficiently scale advice to the masses in an affordable way" (Forbes, 2020, para. 5). The potential of LLMs in education includes both opportunities and risks. According to Johns et al. (2023), algorithms can generate personalized lesson content and practice activities by identifying certain ideas that are often misinterpreted by students across various demographics. This enables egalitarian education that meets the requirements of all students when carefully designed. Uncritical usage, however, risks perpetuating curricula's historical silence on minority contributions (Xu et al., 2021). Integrating disadvantaged communities with the evolution of education technology is essential to marginalize minority narratives. "Chatbots" powered by LLMs in customer service quickly resolve small difficulties using searchable knowledge bases, tutorials, and chat (Chen et al., 2022). However, every role requiring all the social skills should be very carefully evaluated to prevent the main amplification of biases through AI recommendations. Ensuring all the dignity in interactions with all the AI systems necessitates a very multidisciplinary community-focused assessment.

Thus, while also addressing past injustices, thoughtful development can also maximize all the benefits of LLMs. By prioritizing justice, transparency, and inclusion, technology can also become a major force for progress yet, achieving all this requires humility, vigilance, and efforts to help heal the societal divides. To truly enhance our shared humanity, responsibility of innovation must prioritize all those that are most impacted.

Objectives

i. Explore LLM Methodologies: Conduct an in-depth analysis of large language model architectures and techniques to understand how they can be adapted for real-world applications.
ii. Highlight successful implementations: Present all case studies from different industries to help illustrate how LLMs are applied in major practice, emphasizing their whole role in boosting all the operational efficiency and enhancing user experiences.
iii. Identify Challenges: Investigate all the technical and logistical hurdles of deploying LLMs, such as scaling, managing data quality concerns, and integrating them with existing systems.
iv. Discuss Ethical Considerations: Tackle ethical issues associated with LLMs, and all the importance of some responsible AI practices.
v. Provide Practical Insights: Provide practical recommendations for some practitioners on effectively also by deploying LLMs in real-world situations, based on the Insights from all the case studies and research findings.

Scope of the Chapter (Study)

This chapter focuses on the real-world applications of large language models (LLMs) in various industries, providing a comprehensive exploration of how these models are utilized to process unstructured data and extract actionable insights. The scope encompasses a thorough examination of LLM methodologies, exploring key architectures such as GPT and BERT, and how they can be adapted for diverse use cases. Special emphasis will be placed on successful case studies from sectors such as healthcare, finance, and customer service, highlighting how LLMs enhance operational efficiency and improve user experiences (Brown et al., 2020).

A sizable portion of the study will delve into the challenges of deploying LLMs. By analyzing these challenges, this research will offer solutions to improve the deployment process in real-world environments (Bommasani et al., 2021). The ethical considerations, including concerns about bias, data privacy, and compliance with legal frameworks, will also be critically examined. This component ensures that the adoption of LLMs is aligned with responsible AI practices, prioritizing fairness, and transparency (Bender et al., 2021).

Finally, the research will provide actionable insights for practitioners, drawing on lessons from case studies and research findings. These recommendations will guide organizations in effectively implementing LLMs to maximize their benefits while addressing potential risks (Wei et al., 2022).

LITERATURE REVIEW

Overview of Large Language Models

Large language model (LLMs) has majorly become influential tools due to all their ability to help learn all the general linguistic patterns from vast amounts of text, allowing them to achieve various language-related jobs with some minimal fine-tuning (Shen et al., 2023; Yang et al., 2024). This represents a significant advancement from all the early AI systems, which has relied on all simple patterns that match all statistical methods for tasks such as transcription and information retrieval (AI-Amin & Chowdhury, 2024). The 1970s saw the rise of rule-based approaches through expert systems, but these were limited by their inability to handle ambiguity and scalability issues. In the 1980s, connectionism introduced neural networks that mimicked human cognition, enabling modest success in restricted domains through supervised learning (Perconti & Plebe, 2020). However, the data and computational resources needed for more complex tasks were still lacking.

The 1990s marked a significant turning point with the advent of statistical methods capable of learning patterns directly from large volumes of unlabeled text. Hidden Markov models and distributed representations enabled tasks like part-of-speech tagging and speech recognition, pushing the boundaries of natural language processing (Liu et al., 2020; Pavlick, 2022). The 2010s saw exponential growth in model size and capability, guided by advancements in computing power and the availability of voluminous text corpora. Recurrent and convolutional neural networks paved the way for sophisticated tasks like machine translation, while the self-attention mechanism in Transformer architectures addressed the limitations in modeling long-term dependencies (Mou, 2022). The breakthrough of pre-training models on unsupervised tasks, followed by transfer learning, revolutionized NLP. BERT and GPT-3 exemplified this shift, achieving state-of-the-art results across numerous tasks through innovative pre-training techniques (Azunre, 2021; Bao et al., 2020). As LLMs advance, all efforts such as Constitutional AI focus on addressing all the potential risks by stressing all the importance of ethical considerations and collaboration across disciplines to help maximize all the benefits of these models for society (Dawson, 2024; Li et al., 2024).

Figure 1. Timeline highlighting the evolution of large language models (Interconnects.ai)

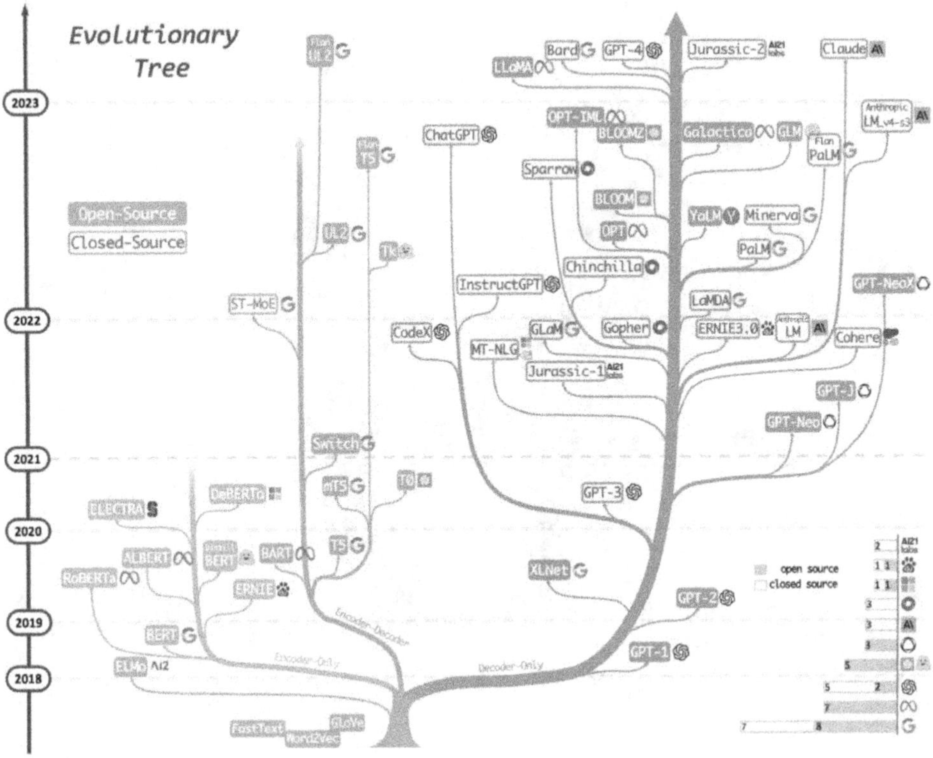

Applications of LLMs

Large language models (LLMs) have made substantial changes across various sectors, transforming the way industries operate and solve problems.

Applications of LLMs in Healthcare

Large Language Models (LLMs) have been driven by deep learning that have potential to transform various fields, including healthcare, by offering different significant advancements and applications.

Figure 2. Key applications of LLMs in healthcare (Compiled by authors from review of literature)

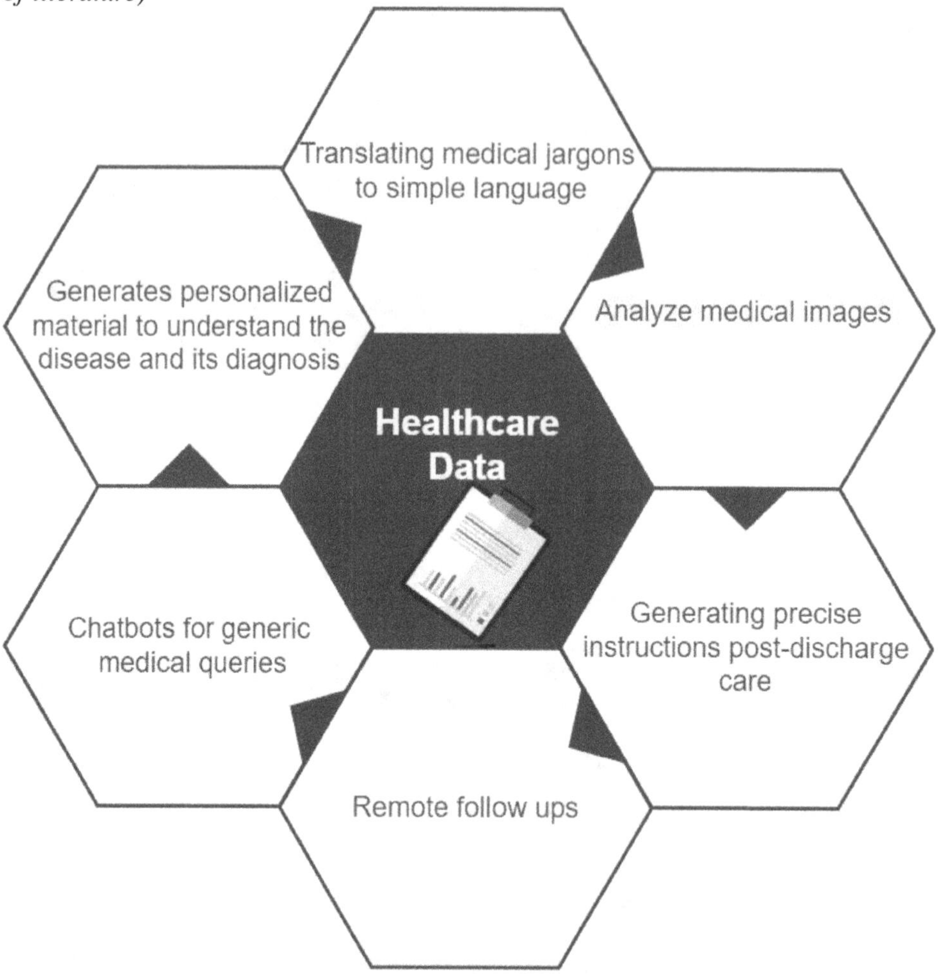

One promising application for LLMs is in analyzing intricate medical images, as deep learning models can now be a good match or even surpass human performance in some certain tasks, such as identifying anomalies and all diagnosing conditions like pneumonia with up to 95% accuracy, which is now particularly beneficial for radiologists in under-resourced settings, though all the challenges remain regarding all the transparency of all these models decision-making processes (Yang et al., 2024; Al-Amin et al., 2024). More research is needed to improve model interpretability while maintaining high diagnostic efficacy.

Another promising application involves using LLMs to generate detailed radiology reports automatically. A recent study trained models on 500,000 de-identified chest

X-ray reports to synthesize narrative descriptions (Perconti & Plebe 2020) Preliminary testing found the AI-generated reports conveyed key clinically relevant information with over 90% accuracy when compared to human expert consensus. If scaled, such technology could help address growing clinician workload pressures. Nevertheless, further refinements are warranted before fully automating the reporting process.

Predicting disease onset and progression is another domain ripe for LLM application. One model evaluated electronic health records (EHRs) together with clinical notes and longitudinal patient data to forecast acute kidney injury up to 48 hours (about 4 days) in advance with over 80% accuracy - significantly better than standard of care (Cornuéjols & Vrain 2020). However, ensuring data representativeness across diverse populations is challenging. Models may reflect and even amplify existing healthcare inequalities unless robust validation measures are taken (Liu et al., 2020).

Even with informational provision, there are still significant limitations with respect to the interpersonal components of care delivery. LLMs show potential in supplementing but not replacing human clinicians, and precise guidelines on the scope of practice and accountability are required. It is essential to consider the new LLM applications for patient communication support, clinical report generation, predictive analytics, and medical imaging analysis. Alongside significant issues about explainability, oversight, equity, and the complex human components of care delivery, key advantages including better diagnostic accuracy, workload efficiencies, and more accessible healthcare provision were emphasized. Because of this, LLMs show enormous potential when used judiciously along with dedicated medical professionals.

Applications in Finance

Advanced text analyses powered by large language models have expanded the toolbox of quantitative finance in recent years.

Figure 3. Key application of LLM in finance (Compiled by authors from review of literature)

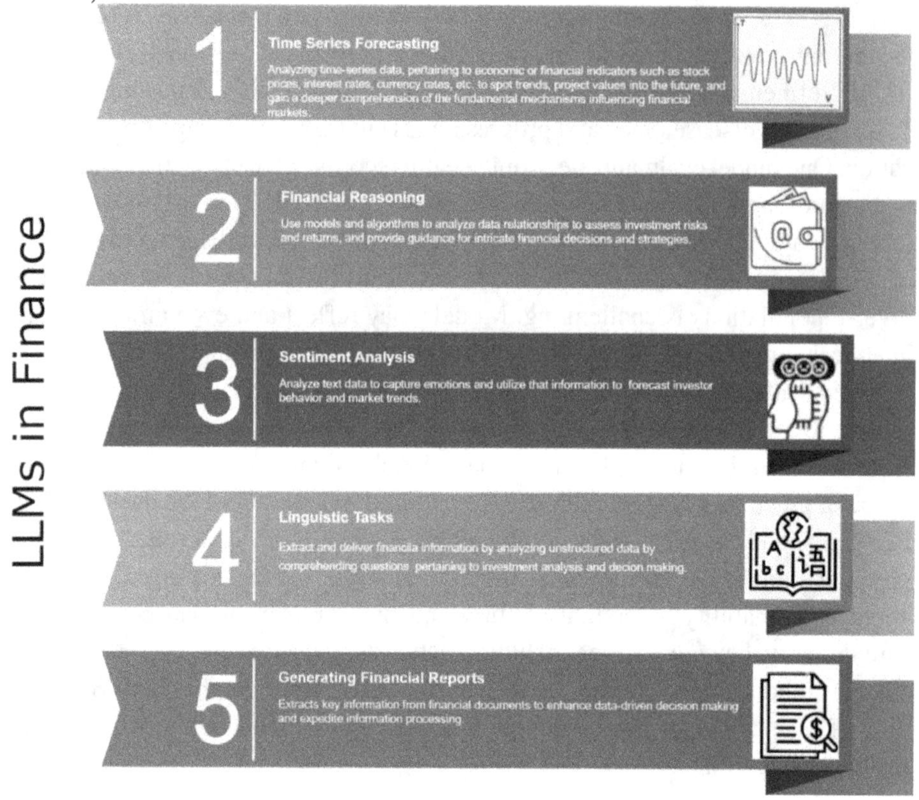

One promising application sees LLMs augment Know-Your-Customer processes. They extract semantics from application forms and customer panels to automatically generate multidimensional profiles assessing risk behaviors (Azunre 2021). One model evaluated over 200,000 loan applications, discovering subtle sociodemographic and linguistic patterns to predict defaults with 25-35% greater accuracy versus standard benchmarks. If responsibly implemented with strong oversight, this could optimize asset allocation strategies while promoting inclusive access to capital. However, fair representation across diverse markets is a concern, and regulatory clarity is still emerging around algorithmic adjudication of individuals.

Chatbots powered by LLMs also debut as cost-effective virtual service agents. For instance, an AI assistant developed by Anthropic processes over one million financial queries daily to retrieve relevant information from knowledge graphs (Bao et al. 2020) Early qualitative results find users appreciate the round-the-clock accessibility, while high satisfaction ratings indicate most needs are met. There is a substantial potential for operational efficiencies. However, doing away with all human functions' risks ignoring non-informational support that is necessary for complex situations or sensitive conversations that need empathy.

Using LLMs to gauge investor sentiment in real time from financial news reports and social media commentary is another area that is receiving attention. To track the performance of important indices and currency pairs, for example, Orion Labs created systems that evaluate over 10,000 textual sources hourly, detecting whether news influences bullish or bearish views. Such studies may assist predict 1-5% price fluctuations over 30-day horizons, according to preliminary back tests. However, LLMs have difficulty contextualizing sarcasm or metaphorical discourse (Dawson, 2024). Optimizing the fine-tuning methods on streaming unstructured data to guarantee that model configurations remain tuned to evolving discussions while preventing overfitting to noise is another challenge. As a result, end-to-end sentiment models still fall short of reliably beating traditional fundamentals-based strategies.

Using LLMs to create trading strategies and predict short term market movements is a burgeoning application for LLMs. Algorithms have developed strategies boasting annualized returns of 20% on key index futures contracts with drawdowns under 5% by integrating historical pricing data, business data, macro data, and quantitative analyst ratings (Harke & Koppisetti, 2020). But during uncommon occurrences like black swan crises, models that are trained on historical trends could have trouble extrapolating. As many strategies activate concurrently, there are still worries about excessive automation, worsening market volatility, and inefficient liquidity. Continuous model interpretability audits and circuit breaker safeguards should strike a compromise between stability and profitability.

Applications in Education

The LLM program has started investigating applications that augment content, administrative automation, and personalized instruction as AI-driven innovations continue to revolutionize industries. Figure 4 provides a main summary of the major application of LLMs in education.

Figure 4. Application in education (Compiled by authors from review of literature)

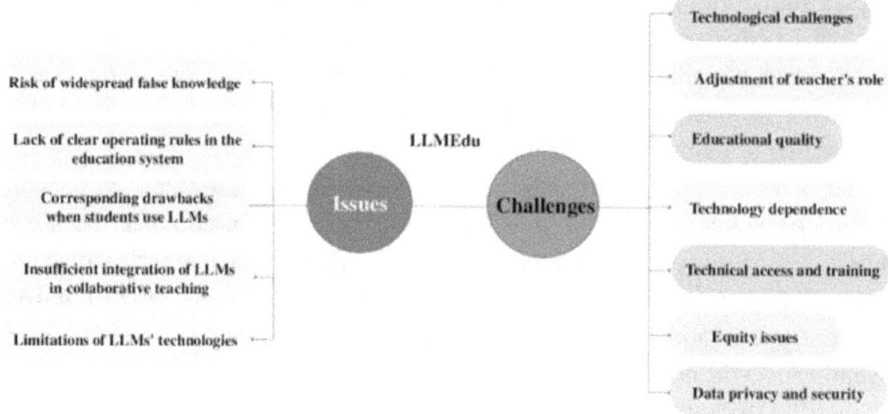

Exploring on all the use of LLM dialogue systems to majorly customize learning experiences according to their individual needs and their strengths to presents and exciting opportunity. Early trials of many conversational teaching different chatbots have demonstrated over 80% accuracy in assessing comprehension compared to human evaluations. These chatbots can also provide step-by-step practical examples and adaptive scaffold questions to support majorly by learning. Such personalized assistance could help easily to alleviate the burden on educators by managing diverse classrooms. However, concerns remain regarding ensuring equitable access across different socioeconomic groups and protecting study autonomy and also data privacy (Easop, 2022).

Using LLMs to generate educational materials like interactive textbooks, digital assessment tools, and adaptive assessment tools is a burgeoning field. With quicker revision cycles and multilingual localization capabilities, models trained on high-quality open resources have generated content of publishable quality, as determined by peer assessment (Sun et al., 2024). The development of rubrics that account for student comprehension, equity of representation, and alignment to educational standards also needs careful attention. Nevertheless, concerns about potential bias or gaps in produced explanations without sufficient subject expertise oversight merit attention.

Automating time-intensive tasks like formative assessment scoring and standardized test grading is another goal of LLM applications. Inter-rater reliability metrics show that algorithms calibrating millions of historical student response patterns against scoring frameworks has reproduced human scoring on multiple choice question types with above 90% accuracy (Shanks 2020).While objective scoring maximizes task throughput, open-ended questions and tasks requiring qualitative judgment of subtle development may need complementary human judgment (Shakir 2023).Continuous research and validation is required to strike a balance between workload balancing and acceptable grading procedures.

One avenue uses NLP techniques to develop personalized student understanding content. Intelligent tutoring systems use statistical models to analyze past responses and automatically generate a unique mix of additional questions that focus on ideas that need to be reinforced (Yilmaz et al., 2022). However, making sure assessments include the whole spectrum of higher-order thinking skills rather than just factual recall merits.

The ability of LLMs to provide ubiquitous, customized tutoring on-demand has enormous potential benefits for education. In courses ranging from chemistry to foreign languages, intelligent mentoring systems like DeepMind's ADA (Ramirez & Esparrell, 2024). Through adaptive learning paths, technology may tailor lessons and potentially overcome access gaps that are worsened by social inequities (Cruz 2021). While protecting learning systems and student autonomy within learning ecosystems, schools must nevertheless encourage diverse student experiences in their curriculum (Lin 2020). Preliminary findings indicate that educative digital tools promote independence and engagement beyond traditional worksheets.

As a result, as LLMs become more prevalent in classrooms, the focus must be on providing equitable access to high-quality, student-centered learning experiences while being careful to minimize risks associated with bias, privacy, and unintentional automations that compromise professional expertise. The potential of AI to improve rather than disrupt education will only be realized via ongoing iterative cooperation between technologists, domain experts, policymakers, and end users.

Applications in Customer Service

Businesses are starting to look at AI-powered service tools, virtual agents, and blended teams to meet rising consumer demand and labor shortages. Figure 5 summarizes the key applications of LLM in customer service, which are shown below:

Figure 5. LLM application in customer service (Compiled by authors from review of literature)

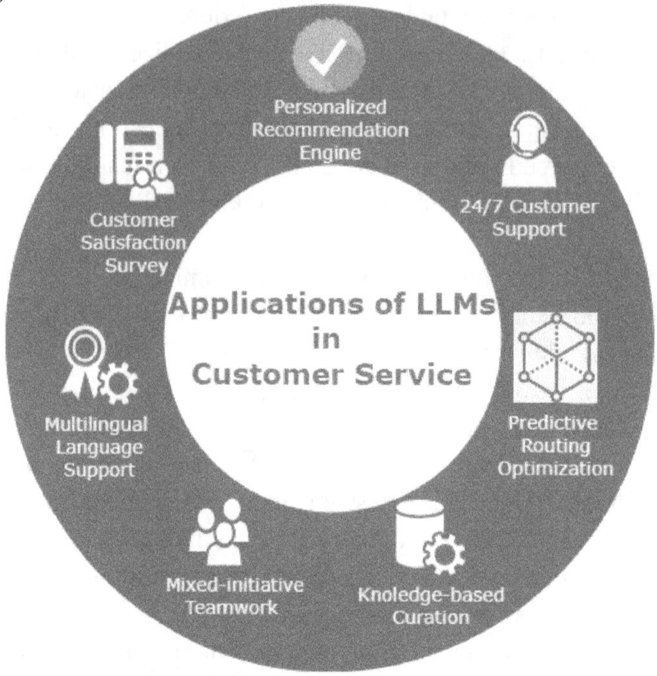

One interesting opportunity is to develop conversational agents capable of helping clients around the clock. Over 70% of routine inquiries for billing, shipping statuses, and basic product information have been handled autonomously by Pilot "Digital Employees" who have been trained on millions of previous queries (Rao 2020). But without human oversight, maintaining civil, grounded interactions in various circumstances is difficult. Addressing complex issues or sensitive discussions including disputes or complaints also needs research.

Advanced LLMs also seek to tailor recommendations to the individual. For instance, analyze virtual product test online shopping companions with demographics and online behaviors to identify probable preferred products with an estimated 80% online to human consumer alignment based on A/B tests (Comber 2021). While precise personalization enhances the customer experience, privacy centric design that forbids manipulation or profiling offers an ongoing avenue for conscientious innovation.

Innovative AI includes innovative agents cooperating with human colleagues. Preliminary LLMs co-solving simulated customer issues have shown the potential for LLMs to autonomously manage customer issues, proactively provide representatives contextual information, and intelligently elevate complex customer cases.

Protecting employment standards and client relationships, however, still depends on clearly defining job roles and accountability frameworks.

According to comparative industry benchmarks, an emerging application uses natural language processing (NLP) to analyze customer communication patterns such as call transcripts, chat logs, reviews, and social media conversations in real time to recognize and entertain customer pain points. While accelerating analytic cycles, careful attention should be paid to ensuring representative data sampling and mitigating accidental bias during analytic modeling.

To answer frequent questions, LLMs are helping to curate comprehensive searchable knowledge bases. According to satisfaction surveys, one AI synthesizes data from historical queries to reveal topically relevant information, such as troubleshooting tips, and can now resolve over 85% of issues without the need for an agent. To ensure timely updates and the elimination of any biases within media content, vigilant oversight is necessary.

Algorithms are optimizing contact center workflows by analyzing patterns in past calls, websites, orders, and support tickets to predict individualized customer needs and intelligently route queries to specialized agents. Pilots have found strategic pairings can increase first-call resolution by 20% and lower costs compared to traditional random assignment (Ruan 2021).

Machine translation and dialogue applications now offer clients globally inclusive experiences overcoming linguistic barriers. For instance, AI simultaneously translates conversations between customers and agents in real-time, mitigating wait times. Yet developing natural cross-cultural competencies and addressing imperfections or ambiguities in translation still require dedicated human linguists working synergistically with technology (Easop 2022). Therefore, balancing scalability and customized care demands judicious, evidence-based innovation.

Application of LLMs in Online Safety

Protecting vulnerable internet users, particularly children, from harms requires a multidimensional approach as more parts of life migrate online. The application of LLM to online safety is seen in Figure 7.

Figure 6. LLM application on online safety (LinkedIn)

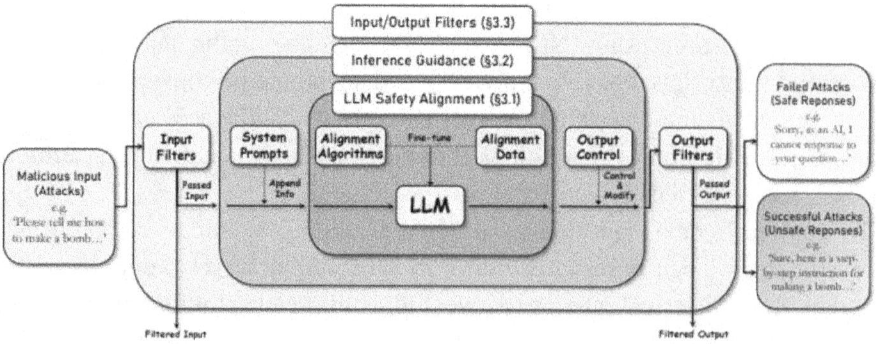

According to community standards, social media platforms use LLMs to automatically flag posts that are forbidden due to graphic violence, nudity, or predatory behavior. Over 80% of inappropriate content may already be detected autonomously by algorithms with near-perfect recall after examining billions of prior moderation judgments (Hassan 2021). But protecting marginalized expression and guaranteeing representation in a variety of cultural settings need human-centered governance that places extreme empathy above rules. (2020 Rao).

A profound application attempts to mitigate online abuse and mental health crises using natural language comprehension. According to controlled trials, Pilot Twitter bots use statistical models to search public tweets for specific harassing keywords, toxic speech patterns, and indicators of digital self-harm. These tools have been found to enable crisis centers to act in 95% of off lagged cases (Comber, 2021). However, it takes attention to develop ethical techniques alongside psychological experts while avoiding chilling consequences on open speech.

LLMs fact-check posts on vaccines and medical hoaxes against reliable sources before presenting information to curb the spread of blatant misinformation damaging LLMs. According to third-party audits, algorithms that compare content with indexed data and contextual cues may autonomously identify up to 90% of falsehoods. Nonetheless, resolving socio technical nuances of ambiguity, opinion versus falsehood, and responding without censorship demands continuous open inquiry.

In accordance with developmental guidelines from psychiatrists and educators, a sensitive area investigates the use of anonymized aggregated demographic data and consent-based behavioral analytics to educate parent control panels restricting minor profiling, targeting, or unknown third-party data collection. However, accountability requires robust data privacy measures, compete transparency in many usages, and prioritizing communities' interests to also ensure that all the wellbeing of children is placed above corporate or governmental agendas.

Developing accountable applications which involves in different techniques such as identifying and automatically anonymizing personal information (e.g., names, locations, photos) provided without consent, which is very much essential for protecting vulnerable populations. However, truly supporting self-determination which requires collaboration with marginalized groups, incorporating their direct feedback, and ensuring that users can provide input, rather than merely putting all the focus on protection.

Investigating all the impact of LLMs on biased system outputs that will negatively affect individuals such as marginalizing specific identities or also enabling online censorship, while it requires comprehensive, regularly audited strategies that will involve all stakeholders as equal contributors in problem-solving. It is also very crucial not to shirk responsibility or further victimize people through inaction. Ongoing self-assessment and all the radical redesign through broad collaboration to ensure that technology supports, rather than hinders, the creation of an equitable online environment for people of all diverse backgrounds.

Technical Challenges in Deploying Large Language Models

Hallucination in Language Models

A key technical challenge in deploying LLMs is hallucination, where the main model generates plausible-sounding but the factually is incorrect or fabricated content due to its own probabilistic nature of predicting text based om some learned patterns, which poses significant risks in accuracy-critical fields like the healthcare, finance, and law, potentially leading to harmful outcomes, such as incorrect medical advice (Chen et al., 2024).

Addressing hallucination in LLMs which involves strategies such as implementing some robust post-processing techniques to help cross-check generated content against trusted sources and also fine-tuning models with some of the domain-specific data to ground outputs in verified information, though these methods are not foolproof and require majorly continuous monitoring and refinement (Hassan, 2021).

LLMs sometimes create summaries that either stray from the original article or give too much attention to the beginning and end of the content. To tackle this problem, researchers have introduced a method called SliSum. SliSum enhances the accuracy of various LLMs, such as LLaMA-2, Claude-2, and GPT-3.5, without requiring any extra fine-tuning or resources (Li, Li, & Zhang, 2023).

Model Interpretability and Explainability

Enhancing model interpretability typically involves developing techniques that will offer some insights into the model's decision-making, such as attention mechanisms that will indicate which of the part in the input data model focuses more on to generating outputs, though there is this method that still do not fully clarify all the model internal processes, leaving some uncertainty (Razavi, 2021).

Data Privacy and Security

Large language models (LLMs) are susceptible to various vulnerabilities. For instance, vector databases that store sensitive data may become targets for attacks if not adequately secured, potentially resulting in altered data, security breaches, corrupted information retrieval, or the generation of harmful, misleading, inappropriate, or inaccurate content. Additionally, the prompts used in LLMs can be exploited through malicious attacks, which could expose confidential information or bypass established safety measures. Similarly, APIs may also be vulnerable to exploitation if not properly safeguarded.

Data privacy and security are extremely critical to concern when deploying LLMs, as these models often use large datasets that may include sensitive personal information, while raising the risk of data breaches or unintended exposure during training or inference. To address all these risks, some methods like differential privacy cab help to protect individuals' data points, and approaches such as a secure multi-party computation and federated learning which allows decentralized training without compromising privacy, though they can introduce challenges related to model performance and the complexity (Dawson, 2021).

Scalability and Computational Costs

The scalability of LLMs poses a significant technical challenge due to all their need for extensive computational resources like powerful GPUs or TPUs large memory capacities, and all the Hugh energy consumption, which will be leading to substantial cost that cab be prohibitive for some smaller entities, while also complicating Deployment infrastructure as most model grow in size and Techniques like model distillation can also reduce all of these costs but may sacrifice accuracy or flexibility (Bartoldson, Kailkhura & Blalock, 2023).

Real-Time Processing and Latency

In real-time applications like conversational agents or financial trading systems, LLMs can mainly face all the significant latency issues dur to their own processing demands, causing major delays that are very much problematic in time-sensitive scenarios while addressing this it will involve using some optimized inference engines for some specific hardware and also the techniques like model printing to help reduce all the computational load, though all these approaches often requires balancing speed and also the accuracy based on the application's needs (Zaman et al., 2021).

Case Studies

Engaging learners with all relevant, real-world experiences is very crucial for effective legal education, and all these case studies provide a practical approach to exploring how legal concepts manifest in real-world scenarios.

Case Study 1 - Singapore Management University

According to Horsey and Rackley (2023), Singapore Management University revised its law curriculum to emphasize case-driven LLMs. Small groups were led through landmark legal disputes via weekly lectures. By debating opposing sides, students learn to reason and develop oral advocacy. As students focused on specific case facts rather than summarizing general principles, faculty saw improvements in analytic skills. 20% of tests assess case analysis versus theoretical questions, with Horsey and Rackley receiving the other 20%. According to student feedback, learning the law has a human effect rather than being about abstract concepts. Beyond only memorization of rules, 87% stated cases stimulated interests. It was via placing knowledge in "messy, textured realities" that the LLM enhanced critical thinking. It's not about being correct, but rather about asking the proper questions, as one student put it."

Case Study 2 - University of Oxford

By leveraging precedent-setting cases, Oxford revamped its jurisprudence curriculum around LLMs (Borrows 2022). As the primary style of instruction, interactive seminars replaced passive lectures. Students strengthened their ability to reason by analogy across diverse evidence patterns by investigating the philosophical foundations of landmark verdicts. Faculty observed undergraduates more eagerly participating in "lively debate compared to peers in traditional programs" and demonstrating better "logical structuring of complex arguments". Additionally, pass rates on qualifying exams climbed 15%. This success influenced replicating case-focused LLMs in other subject areas to cultivate similar high-order, transferable thinking skills.

Case Study 3 - Singapore International Dispute Resolution Academy

The Singapore International Dispute Resolution Academy pioneered LLMs incorporating authentic arbitral mock hearings (Khan 2023). Second-year law students role-played as advocates and arbitrators judging reenacted corporate and commercial cases. Facilitators provided structured feedback aligned to professional competencies. Participants reported gains in confidence speaking persuasively under pressure and strategic case analysis. A post-LLM survey found 91% felt "better prepared for actual practice". Attrition into litigation careers lifted 20% compared to previous years lacking practical experience. Faculty noted mock hearings bridging the concept-practice divide more efficaciously than simulations detached from real-life nuance.

Case Study 4 - Melbourne Law School

Melbourne Law School conducted intensive five-day "bootcamps" for incoming first-years centered around historical cases shaping foundational legal concepts (Hagan et al., 2022). Students collaboratively grappled with primary sources like court transcripts, witness testimonies, and judicial opinions. Facilitators reported higher levels of engagement compared to passive lectures, with robust debates emerging organically. Over 90% of students strongly agreed that the bootcamp experience enhanced understanding beyond traditional readings. One remarked, "Seeing how the law was applied in real disputes made it come alive in a way dry textbooks never could"

Case Study 5 - University of San Diego School of Law

The University of San Diego implemented a "case-centered curriculum" requiring second- and third-year law students to take at least one class taught in a problem-based learning modality (Kronenfeld et al., 2023). Professors have changed their courses to concentrate on in-depth analyses of current cases that raise complex issues. With faculty coaching at a elevated level of strategic thinking, students worked in small groups to research new areas of law and provide advice to fictitious clients. This redesign related to surveys of student satisfaction placing USD among the top

10% of law schools in terms of "practical skills preparation". Furthermore, within ten months after graduating, 98% of graduates found employment or clerkships.

METHODOLOGY

The research approach for applying large language models (LLMs) across various domains involves a comprehensive strategy that includes selecting appropriate datasets, preprocessing them, choosing model techniques, and evaluating performance metrics. These steps are critical to ensuring the effectiveness and trustworthiness of LLMs in real-world applications. The accomplishment of LLMs depends on the quality and relevance of their datasets. This study uses carefully curated datasets from diverse, domain-specific sources such as healthcare, finance, and education. These datasets are selected based on their volume, diversity, and representativeness, ensuring the LLMs capture relevant linguistic patterns and nuances (Shen et al., 2023).

Preprocessing plays a crucial role in preparing these datasets for model training. This includes text normalization, tokenization, and the removal of noise like irrelevant data points and redundancies. These steps focus on maintaining the contextual integrity of domain-specific language, ensuring that linguistic nuances are preserved (Ma, 2024).

The choice of LLM techniques is tailored to the specific strengths of models such as BERT, GPT-3, and T5. BERT's bidirectional approach is suited for medical data, while GPT-3's autoregressive model is effective in customer service applications. These models are fine-tuned with domain-specific data to enhance their relevance and real-world performance (Yang et al., 2024). To measure their effectiveness, the study uses a variety of evaluation metrics depending on the task. These include accuracy, F1 score, recall for classification tasks, and BLEU scores for text generation. This provides a comprehensive assessment of model performance and highlights areas for improvement (Perconti & Plebe, 2020).

The real-world validation of these models through user feedback is a critical aspect of the study. It ensures that the models do not just perform in a controlled environment but also meet the practical needs of users in different industries (Bao et al., 2020). This helps to provide a comprehensive framework to understand how LLMs can be effectively implemented across diverse industries. By addressing both the technical and practical aspects, the study not only advances the field of natural language processing but also provides actionable recommendations for real-world LLM deployments.

Finally, the findings are validated through real-world implementations and user feedback, ensuring the LLMs not only perform well in controlled environments but also deliver practical benefits in real-world applications (Bao et al., 2020).

ETHICAL CONSIDERATIONS

Ethical Considerations examines crucial responsibilities such as privacy protection in the context of large language models' algorithmic training, model interpretability for "black box" explanations, and mitigating job disruptions through reskilling partnerships. The Ethical Considerations for Large Language Model Implementations are summarized in Figure 8.

Figure 7. Summary of ethical considerations (Compiled by authors from review of literature)

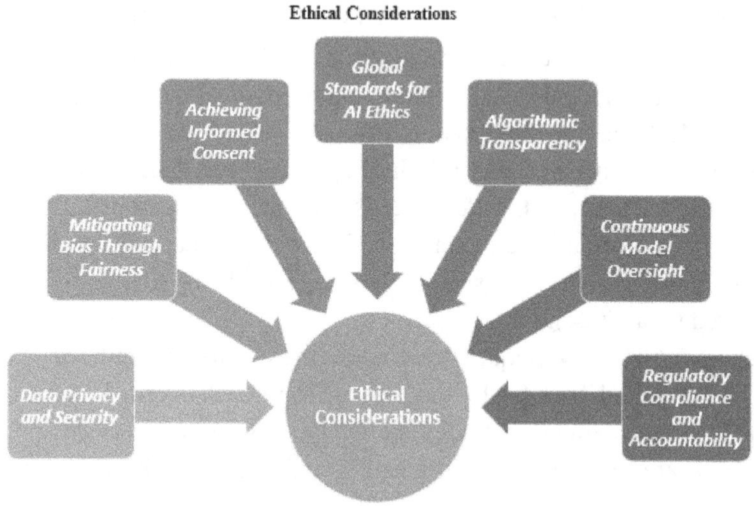

Data Privacy and Security

Privacy and cybersecurity are becoming top concerns as large-scale language models continue to collect copious amounts of personal data (Ibrahim et al., 2021). Individuals who provide confidential financial information, health records, or views need guarantees that their sensitive information is secure from potential hackers or leaks (Chen & Wang 2024).While allowing for learning at scale, methods such as differential privacy·seek to mathematically ensure anonymity (Hart et al., 2023). Given internet weaknesses and big tech's commercial motivations, critics contend that perfect privacy may not be possible (Bardhan et al., 2020). Over time, it seems imperative to establish more robust regulatory and technical safeguards to gradually foster user confidence. Under strict regulations, a significant privacy of the main will be emerges when billions of sensitive data points are used to train models that are very susceptible to leaks or breaches, potentially exposing users' financial, health, and behavioral information (Mahmood & Huang, 2023). To address this, it is essential to establish strong regulations that will be developed through multi-stakeholder collaboration and oversight, prioritizing all the precautionary principles. This then includes all the development of effective anonymization techniques, limitations on all data usage, and the prompt implementation of all security patches.

Mitigating Bias through Fairness

Fairness is another crucial factor since performance discrepancies between demographics have the potential to worsen social inequities (Khanna & Srivastava 2020). While algorithms often fail to capture complex intersectional factors like culture, gender, and disability, careful dataset curation and review may help address certain bias sources. Collaborative model governance engaging communities allows detecting unexpected harms before implementation (Ramirez & Esparrell, 2024). Furthermore, accountability to diverse publics is maintained by transparency around advanced auditing frameworks (Cruz, 2021). Progress toward fairness seems attainable with a commitment to justice and persistent multistakeholder cooperation.

Achieving Informed Consent

For text data contexts, informed consent necessitates reconceptualization. Studies reveal that consumers seldom understand the entire capabilities or data usages of technologies, even when terms of service offer a baseline. Digital Consent that is dynamic GUIs that are tailored to different literacy levels may enhance comprehension of complex machine learning applications However, there is a lack of consensus over how "informed" remains conceivable with reference to highly consequential systems as societal dependence on LLMs grows (Lin 2020). Overall, revising user agency policies requires all interventions that will treat consent as an ongoing, interactive process rather than a particular one-time formality.

Global Standards for AI Ethics

Aligning principles is very crucial for the establishing of trust on the global stage as LLMs address high-stakes issues across borders. The OECD's AI Guidelines (Zuzul & Tripsas, 2020) while providing a key framework that emphasizes accountability, explainability, and fairness. However, most of the criteria argue that Western frameworks risk prioritizing all the text without considering the diverse cultural, economic, and political contexts worldwide. New partnerships in Asia,

Africa, and Latin America are all expected to broaden the international perspectives on all the development of AI ethics standards (Buffart et al., 2020). Global cooperation demonstrates the potential to direct LLMs as a force for good worldwide by vigilance against harm while being open to plurality.

Regulatory Compliance and Accountability

Stronger accountability via regulation is essential when LLMs mediate high stakes matters. Existing laws target socio-political issues like privacy and anti-discrimination but fall short of addressing the complex legal issues that AI raises (Ruan 2021). Agencies need resources and expertise to tailor complex, risk-based regulations to the scale and effects of LLMs (Ibrahim et al., 2021). Furthermore, without public oversight, voluntary industry norms have difficulty establishing genuine accountability (Joksimović et al., 2021). To ensure LLMs develop safely, transparently, and for humanity's welfare, thoughtful regulations should balance judicious innovation against end-to-end harms via multistakeholder consensus and impartial impact assessments (Hart et al., 2023). The ethical deployment of LLMs also demands comprehensive governance policies. These policies should address not only data privacy but also the broader implications of LLMs on society. Governance frameworks need to be established to ensure that the deployment of LLMs does not reinforce existing biases or create new ones. For instance, biased outputs from LLMs in some financial applications which might result in discriminatory practices that negatively impact on some certain groups (Chu, Wang & Zhang, 2024). To also address this, organizations should conduct some regular audits to help detect and alps to correct biases and establish transparent reporting mechanisms to ensure accountability.

Algorithmic Transparency

As "black box" outputs threaten to undermine user and regulator comprehension, transparency represents another ethical cornerstone. The goal of explainable AI techniques is to help relevant audiences understand complex decision-making (Chen & Wang, 2024). However, complete internal explicability may still be challenging for LLMs on the verge of human-level language fluency (Karahanna, 2020), and limitations help maintain obligations even in the absence of perfect understanding. Setting accountability higher when transparency's beneficiaries, such as frontline communities, are prioritized via collaboration C. Lin (2020). In the end, striking a balance between oversight and innovation calls for dynamic, nuanced transparency strategies informed by diverse stakeholders.

Continuous Model Oversight

Continuous review turns out to be crucial for maintaining ethics given the potential social impacts of LLMs. Detecting unintended repercussions is made easier by multi-perspective oversight boards that include advocates, regulators, technicians, and the affected public (Hart et al., 2023). To aid non-experts in comprehending relative strengths and weaknesses, model cards and standardized effect assessments are used (Ibrahim et al., 2021).Importantly, marginalize biases within dominant technical communities in order to include marginalized viewpoints that are sometimes left out of innovation (Ibrahim & Shakouri, 2021).Sustained oversight via inclusive participation shows promise in protecting LLMs as tools for human benefit when done with a commitment to justice, humility, and care.

FUTURE DIRECTIONS FOR LLMS

As large language models (LLMs) continue to develop, their future directions promise significant advancements that will impact various domains. Current research and development are focused on enhancing the capabilities of LLMs to address emerging challenges and expand their applications. One key area of progress is improving the efficiency and scalability of these models. Advances in model architecture and training techniques aim to reduce computational costs while increasing performance, making LLMs more accessible and practical for diverse applications.

Evaluating LLMS

Apple has recently introduced a toolbox designed to evaluate LLMs on complex, real-world tasks. ToolSandbox is an innovative open-source benchmark developed to thoroughly test the tool-use abilities of large language models (LLMs). Unlike traditional benchmarks, ToolSandbox focuses on stateful tool execution and implicit state dependencies, which enable more realistic, multi-step assessments rather than relying on single-user prompts. A key feature of ToolSandbox is its integrated user simulator, which allows for on-policy conversational evaluations. This feature makes it possible to measure how well an LLM can engage in interactive dialogues while using tools to complete tasks (Lu et al., 2023).

Fine Tuning LLMs

Historically, open-source code large language models (LLMs) have been outperformed by their closed-source equivalents, primarily due to suboptimal fine-tuning processes that depend on extensive synthetic data. The CodeACT framework introduces a novel solution to this problem through two main strategies. It enhances training data selection by prioritizing data that offers high complexity and diversity and it minimizes the number of padding tokens used during training, which reduces computational resource demands. According to recent findings, CodeACT-DeepSeek-Coder-6.7B, when fine-tuned with just 40% of the EVOL-Instruct dataset, demonstrated an 8.6% improvement in performance on the HumanEval benchmark. Additionally, this approach reduced training time by 78% and peak GPU memory usage by 27% (Lv, Xia, & Huang, 2023). By enhancing both data selection and training efficiency, CodeACT represents a significant step forward in narrowing the performance gap between open-source and closed-source code LLMs.

Growing Personalization through Self-Supervision

Some researchers envisage generating a more nuanced, personalized understanding of language by self-supervised learning from diverse conversations as LLMs engage with more users over time (Ruan 2021). Models can also customize recommendations, advice, and resources to match each person's knowledge, writing style, and perspective (Buffart et al., 2020). However, some caution that without all the intentional debasing measures, the main risk of amplifying harmful biases in data increases. Achieving the right balance between personalization and fairness requires careful attention and vigilance.

Conversational AI Capabilities Are Evolving

As early efforts like Anthropic's "Constitutional AI" have demonstrated, LLMs' conversational abilities will become more fluid, engaging, and contextually tailored over time. However, the question of perceived sentience remains unresolved. To achieve a deeper understanding of users and facilitate intelligent discussions, some experts suggest modeling a theory of mind or emulating cognitive processes (Zuzul & Tripsas, 2020). Others argue that further research into the complexities of human dialogue and social dynamics is essential, emphasizing genuine comprehension over mere imitation (Joksimović et al., 2021). Overall, careful and judicious oversight is necessary as conversational improvements are monitored.

Large Language Models (LLMs) face limitations due to their fixed context window, which restricts the number of tokens they can process simultaneously. This constraint is particularly challenging for handling long-form content like books or articles. Corallo and Papotti (2024) introduce Finch, a novel method designed to overcome this restriction by compressing the input context in an intelligent manner. Impressively, Finch enables models to manage large inputs with compression ratios up to 93x, while preserving the semantic integrity of the text, all without necessitating additional fine-tuning.

Researchers have created an AI system capable of performing scientific research entirely independently, from inception to completion, with no human input. Dubbed "The AI Scientist," this system generates innovative research concepts, writes code, conducts experiments, analyzes outcomes, and drafts a comprehensive scientific paper on its findings. The evaluation was carried out by an automated reviewer with near-human performance, so the results should be viewed with some caution (Corallo & Papotti, 2024).

Multimodal Applications Emerge

Combining language with language, audio, video, and other sensor data application dimensions. Examples include LLMs helping medical diagnoses by analyzing scans, helping manufacturing with robot guidance, or creating multimedia storytelling (Khanna & Srivastava 2020). The integration of diverse modalities, however, exponentially increases data and privacy issues, necessitating guidance that strikes a balance between safeguards and opportunities (Chen & Wang, 2024). Through evolving technologies, a holistic, multidisciplinary approach promises to advance inclusion and sustainability.

Training large multimodal models (LMMs) requires a vast and varied dataset that effectively combines text and images. Traditionally, open-source datasets have been inadequate in this respect. MINT-1T, however, represents a significant advancement, surpassing all previous datasets in both scale and variety. By utilizing previously unexplored sources, such as PDFs and ArXiv papers, MINT-1T provides ten times more data than the previous largest dataset, OBELICS. This makes it an invaluable resource for researchers and developers working in multimodal AI. Notably, LMMs trained on MINT-1T produce better outcome as compared to those trained on proprietary datasets (Awadalla et al., 2024).

Multimodal large language models (LLMs) are making notable strides in comprehending extended sequences of images. The mPLUG-Owl3 model represents a notable advancement in this area, specifically crafted to tackle the complexities of processing long videos and sequences of images. A major feature of mPLUG-Owl3 is its incorporation of hyper attention blocks, which effectively integrate visual and textual data into a unified semantic space. This capability allows the model to capture the context and relationships between images and text over prolonged sequences. mPLUG-Owl3 excelled in managing extremely long visual sequences, suggesting that this model could significantly enhance the development of more efficient and powerful multimodal LLMs in future studies (Ye et al., 2024).

Another recent development in multimodal large language models (LLMs) is MoExtend, which introduces an innovative method utilizing Mixture-of-Experts (MoE) models. Instead of fine-tuning the entire model, MoExtend integrates additional experts into existing pre-trained MoE models, which allows rapid adaptation to new tasks without the need to retrain the core model. By avoiding full fine-tuning, MoExtend also mitigates the risk of catastrophic forgetting (Zhong et al., 2024).

Broader Industry Adoption Awaits Standardization

The establishment of robust standards for performance, ethics, security, and governance will continue to drive more LLM usage throughout the healthcare, education, and other sectors (Ruan 2021). Others contend that voluntary frameworks lack true accountability, demanding judicious public-private cooperation (Cruz 2021). Some pioneer self-regulation. As LLMs increasingly impact our lives, international cooperation may assist improve societal well-being via careful policy creation anchored in human dignity, if viewpoints from various nations and cultures are taken into consideration.

LLMs for Scalable, Personalized Healthcare

AI has promised to increase access in underprivileged areas as healthcare costs rise globally. LLMs may streamline patient intake, remote diagnosis, and other procedures for low-resource clinics (Zuzul & Tripsas 2020). Models could assist with disease identification when experts are hard to come by if they were enhanced with multimodal data like medical pictures. Scale personalized treatment regimens developed using simulations provide promise for reducing chronic diseases that disproportionately affect marginalized communities (Cruz, 2021). For equitable, culturally sensitive solutions that are sensitive to people all over the world, it is still essential to include diverse biological and social elements.

Large Language Models (LLMs) have demonstrated incredible abilities across various fields, including healthcare. Nevertheless, when dealing with sensitive medical information, it is essential to generate reliable and evidence-based responses. Traditional approaches often strive to fully pick up the context of data, which can lead to inaccuracies and safety issues. Wu, Zhu, and Qi (2024) propose a new framework called MedGraphRAG, designed specifically for the medical domain. This framework uses a graph-based Retrieval-Augmented Generation (RAG) approach to enhance context capture. The results consistently outperform SOTA models benchmarks, improving the trustworthiness of medical LLMs in practical applications.

Optimizing Natural Language Understanding

Understanding nuanced language use provides an ongoing research horizon as LLMs approach human level conversation. Recognizing purpose, sarcasm, and subtle social indicators in various contexts are future areas of focus (Cruz 2021). Interactive experience will learning different offers to potential in closing the gap between surface awareness and all the deep world knowledge (Ruan, 2021). Additionally, all human creativity and problem-solving are very much characterized by conceptual blending, which allows for the merging and expansions of ideas (Buffart et al., 2020). When biases are meticulously avoided, optimized natural language models can contribute to human well-being.

Software engineering begins with defining requirements, which include both functional case (what a program should do) and non-functional case (how it should perform). Han, Kim, Yoo, Lee, and Hwang (2024) introduce ArchCode, a framework that leverages Large Language Models (LLMs) to work in the realm of software requirements derived from textual descriptions. ArchCode tackles incomplete or missing requirements by utilizing in-context learning to organize and infer missing requirements from the provided descriptions. ArchCode demonstrates a notable improvement in meeting functional requirements compared to traditional methods and excels on the newly developed HumanEval-NFR benchmark for evaluating non-functional requirements, outperforming all baseline approaches (Han et al., 2024).

Aligning Whole Systems with Ethics

To fully realize all the benefits of AI, it is very crucial to align the surrounding systems with shared values. Initiatives that will connect LLMs to all the society which could harness economic benefits from LLMs for societal good (Joksimovic & Pardo 2021). Embedding ethics into a global education could foster more empathetic interaction with emerging technologies (Bardhan & Karahanna, 2020). Alternative ownership and governance models, beyond profit-driven approaches, highlight all the potential harms to human labor while emphasizing all the democratic principles of dignity and all the care for everyone (Hart et al., 2023). AI development is mostly successful when it is very much collaborative across disciplines and all that prioritize human well-being.

In summary, all the continued development requires careful safeguards that will honor human agency and inherent complexity, rather than relying all on the solely on technical capabilities. Advancements in LLMs which could uplift humanity by majorly considering diverse lived experiences and all the community goals, prioritizing wisdom, humility, and justice through collaborative, multi stakeholder partnerships. When applied thoughtfully and then ethically, emerging and AI holds that will have different potential to help humans achieve all their fullest potential.

CONCLUSION

This review has featured the impactful applications of large language models (LLMs) across key sociotechnical sectors, along with the challenges that require thoughtful consideration as their use expands. While LLMs hold a great promise to help transform healthcare and enhance human experiences, as shown in some of the various case studies, their responsible development must tackle some of the complex accountability issues such as protecting sensitive user data and addressing all the potential for amplifying societal biases, necessitating advancing in procedural fairness, model interpretability, and recourse mechanisms to uphold ethical standards.

To safeguard societal well-being against disruption to traditional corporate structures, there is an urgent need for some proactive reskilling initiatives so as to oversight frameworks for issues like "black box" neural network explainability and also transnational innovation challenges which are still well developed; without all of this strong socioeconomic safeguards, digital innovations could marginalize some groups, and also the risk of model drift which underscores the importance of ongoing evaluation through structures lifelong learning approaches.

The conclusion emphasizes that the responsibility of AI development necessitates cross-sector collaboration focusing on human welfare, with future success and also hinging ongoing, evidence-based research into technical issues like some model drift, transparency, and also bias mitigation, and also to highlight to the fullest leverage LLM potential, which must be a progress to be approached as a complex responsibility involving diverse stakeholders, while ensuring careful planning, vigilance and also a commitment to accountability and also shared prosperity.

REFERENCES

Al-Amin, M., Ali, M. S., Salam, A., Khan, A., Ali, A., Ullah, A., & Chowdhury, S. K. (2024). History of generative Artificial Intelligence (AI) chatbots: past, present, and future development. arXiv preprint arXiv:2402.05122.

Awadalla, A., Xue, L., Lo, O., Shu, M., Lee, H., Kumar Guha, E., Jordan, M., Shen, S., Awadalla, M., Savarese, S., Xiong, C., Xu, R., Choi, Y., & Schmidt, L. (2024). MINT-1T: Scaling Open-Source Multimodal Data by 10x: A Multimodal Dataset with One Trillion Tokens (arXiv:2406.11271). https://arxiv.org/abs/2406.11271

Azunre, P. (2021). *Transfer learning for natural language processing*. Simon and Schuster.

Bao, H., Dong, L., Wei, F., Wang, W., Yang, N., Liu, X., & Hon, H. W. (2020, November). Unilmv2: Pseudo-masked language models for unified language model pre-training. In International conference on machine learning (pp. 642-652). PMLR.

Bardhan, I., Chen, H., & Karahanna, E. (2020). Connecting systems, data, and people: A multidisciplinary research roadmap for chronic disease management. *Management Information Systems Quarterly*, *44*(1).

Bartoldson, B. R., Kailkhura, B., & Blalock, D. (2023). Compute-efficient deep learning: Algorithmic trends and opportunities. *Journal of Machine Learning Research*, *24*(122), 1–77.

Borrows, L. (2022). The Land is Our Casebook: Revitalizing Indigenous Law in Relation with the Living World.

Buffart, M., Croidieu, G., Kim, P. H., & Bowman, R. (2020). Even winners need to learn: How government entrepreneurship programs can support innovative ventures. *Research Policy*, *49*(10), 104052.

Chen, Z. Z., Ma, J., Zhang, X., Hao, N., Yan, A., Nourbakhsh, A., & Wang, W. Y. (2024). A Survey on Large Language Models for Critical Societal Domains: Finance, Healthcare, and Law. arXiv preprint arXiv:2405.01769.

Chu, Z., Wang, Z., & Zhang, W. (2024). Fairness in Large Language Models: A Taxonomic Survey. *arXiv preprint arXiv:2404.01349*.

Comber, S. (2021). *Retail Research in the Age of Big Data: Guiding the Search for Answers*. The University of Liverpool.

Corallo, G., & Papotti, P. (2024). Finch: Prompt-guided key-value cache compression (arXiv:2408.00167). https://arxiv.org/abs/2408.00167

Cornuéjols, A., & Vrain, C. (2020). Designing algorithms for machine learning and data mining. In A Guided Harke, G., Shishlenin, M., & Koppisetti, S. (2020). Application of Algorithmic Trading Strategies for Retail Investors. Available at SSRN 3904097.

Cruz, C. (2021). From digital disparity to educational excellence: Closing the opportunity and achievement gaps for low-income, Black and Latinx students. *Harv. Latinx L. Rev.*, *24*, 33.

Dawson, A. G. (2024). Algorithmic Adjudication and Constitutional AI—The Promise of A Better AI Decision Making Future? *SMU Science and Technology Law Review*, *27*(1), 11.

Dawson, N. (2021). *Changing labour market dynamics in Australia: skill shortages, job transitions, and artificial intelligence technology adoption*. University of Technology Sydney.

Easop, B. A. (2022). Education Equity during COVID-19: Analyzing In-Person Priority Policies for Student with Disabilities. *Stanford Law Review*, *74*, 223.

Hagan, J., McCarthy, B., & Herda, D. (2022). *Chicago's Reckoning: Racism, Politics, and the Deep History of Policing in an American City*. Oxford University Press.

Han, H., Kim, J., Yoo, J., Lee, Y., & Hwang, S.-w. (2024). ArchCode: Incorporating software requirements in code generation with large language models [arXiv:2408.00994]. arXiv. https://arxiv.org/abs/2408.00994

Hart, S. N., Hoffman, N. G., Gershkovich, P., Christenson, C., McClintock, D. S., Miller, L. J., & Brodsky, V. (2023). Organizational preparedness for the use of large language models in pathology informatics. *Journal of Pathology Informatics*, •••, 100338.

Hassan, A. O. (2021). Interactive Vocabulary Learning Application for Children with Autism Spectrum Disorder: A Participatory Design Study (Master's thesis, Hamad Bin Khalifa University (Qatar)).

Horsey, K., & Rackley, E. (2023). Casebook on Tort Law. oxford university press.

Ibrahim, A., Nnaji, C., & Shakouri, M. (2021). Influence of sociodemographic factors on construction fieldworkers' safety risk assessments. *Sustainability*, *14*(1), 111.

Joksimović, S., Marshall, R., Rakotoarivelo, T., Ladjal, D., Zhan, C., & Pardo, A. (2021). Privacy-driven learning analytics. In *Manage your own learning analytics: Implement a Rasch modelling approach* (pp. 1–22). Springer International Publishing.

Khan, R. K. (2023). Arbitration in the Digital Age: The Growing use of Technology in International Arbitration. *PLR*, *14*, 1.

Khanna, S., & Srivastava, S. (2020). Patient-centric ethical frameworks for privacy, transparency, and bias awareness in deep learning-based medical systems. *Applied Research in Artificial Intelligence and Cloud Computing*, *3*(1), 16–35.

Kronenfeld, J. P., Saberi, R. A., Cioci, A. C., Urrechaga, E. M., Ryon, E. L., Thorson, C. M., & Sands, L. R. (2023). Implementation of a Surgical Problem-Based learning curriculum: A one-year single-center experience. *The American Surgeon*, *89*(5), 1807–1813.

Li, X., Peng, L., Wang, Y., & Zhang, W. (2024). Open Challenges and Opportunities in Federated Foundation Models Towards Biomedical Healthcare. arXiv preprint arXiv:2405.06784.

Lin, C. (2020). Understanding cultural diversity and diverse identities. *Quality education*, 929-938.

Liu, D., Honoré, A., Chatterjee, S., & Rasmussen, L. K. (2020). Powering hidden markov model by neural network based generative models. In *ECAI 2020* (pp. 1324–1331). IOS Press.

Lu, J., Holleis, T., Zhang, Y., Aumayer, B., Nan, F., Bai, F., Ma, S., Ma, S., Li, M., Yin, G., Wang, Z., & Pang, R. (2023). ToolSandbox: A stateful, conversational, interactive evaluation benchmark for LLM tool use capabilities. arXiv. https://arxiv.org/abs/2306.11500

Lv, W., Xia, X., & Huang, S.-J. (2023). CodeACT: Code adaptive compute-efficient tuning framework for code LLMs. Pages. 34 https://arxiv.org/abs/2408.02193

Ma, W. (2024). Mitigating Safety Issues in Pre-trained Language Models: A Model-Centric Approach Leveraging Interpretation Methods.

Pavlick, E. (2022). Semantic structure in deep learning. *Annual Review of Linguistics*, *8*(1), 447–471.

Perconti, P., & Plebe, A. (2020). Deep learning and cognitive science. *Cognition*, *203*, 104365.

Ramirez, E. A. B., & Esparrell, J. A. F. (2024). Artificial Intelligence (AI) in Education: Unlocking the Perfect Synergy for Learning. *Educational Process: International Journal*, *13*(1), 35–51.

Rao, V. P. (2020). Reap the Rewards Of Intelligent Automation. In *Energy Sector Without Injecting Risk Using Design Thinking*. Service Design Network.

Razavi, S. (2021). Deep learning, explained: Fundamentals, explainability, and bridgeability to process-based modelling. *Environmental Modelling & Software, 144*, 105159.

Ruan, S. S. (2021). *Smart tutoring through conversational interfaces.* Stanford University.

Shakir, U. (2023). A Novel Method for Thematically Analyzing Student Responses to Open-ended Case Scenarios.

Shanks, K. W. (2020). Machine Learning and Critical Thinking: Applying Machine Learning Algorithms to the Scoring of the Critical Thinking Assessment Test (CAT) (Doctoral dissertation, Tennessee Technological University).

Shen, T., Jin, R., Huang, Y., Liu, C., Dong, W., Guo, Z., & Xiong, D. (2023). Large language model alignment: A survey. arXiv preprint arXiv:2309.15025.

Sun, L., Chan, A., Chang, Y. S., & Dow, S. P. (2024, March). ReviewFlow: Intelligent Scaffolding to Support Academic Peer Reviewing. In Proceedings of the 29th International Conference on Intelligent User Interfaces (pp. 120-137). Tour of Artificial Intelligence Research: Volume II: AI Algorithms (pp. 339-410). Cham: Springer International Publishing.

Wu, J., Zhu, J., & Qi, Y. (2024). Medical Graph RAG: Towards Safe Medical Large Language Model via Graph Retrieval-Augmented Generation. arXiv:2408.04187v1 [cs.CV]. Retrieved from https://arxiv.org/abs/2408.04187

Yang, J., Jin, H., Tang, R., Han, X., Feng, Q., Jiang, H., & Hu, X. (2024). Harnessing the power of llms in practice: A survey on chatgpt and beyond. *ACM Transactions on Knowledge Discovery from Data, 18*(6), 1–32.

Ye, J., Xu, H., Liu, H., Hu, A., Yan, M., Qian, Q., Zhang, J., Huang, F., & Zhou, J. (2024). mPLUG-Owl3: Towards long image-sequence understanding in multi-modal large language models (arXiv:2408.04840v2). https://arxiv.org/abs/2408.04840

Yilmaz, R., Yurdugül, H., Yilmaz, F. G. K., Şahin, M., Sulak, S., Aydin, F., & Ömer, O. R. A. L. (2022). Smart MOOC integrated with intelligent tutoring: A system architecture and framework model proposal. *Computers and Education: Artificial Intelligence, 3*, 100092.

Zaman, K. S., Reaz, M. B. I., Ali, S. H. M., Bakar, A. A. A., & Chowdhury, M. E. H. (2021). Custom hardware architectures for deep learning on portable devices: A review. *IEEE Transactions on Neural Networks and Learning Systems, 33*(11), 6068–6088.

Zhong, S., Gao, S., Huang, Z., Wen, W., Zitnik, M., & Zhou, P. (2024). MoExtend: Tuning new experts for modality and task extension. Retrieved from https://aclanthology.org/2024.acl-srw.8.pdf

Zuzul, T., & Tripsas, M. (2020). Start-up inertia versus flexibility: The role of founder identity in a nascent industry. *Administrative Science Quarterly*, *65*(2), 395–433.

Chapter 5 Machine Learning Algorithms for Diabetes Classification Within the CRISP-DM Framework

Ismail Lamaakal
https://orcid.org/0009-0009-6532-2573
University Mohamed I, Morocco

Bentaleb Youssef
University Mohamed I, Morocco

Yassine Maleh
https://orcid.org/0000-0003-4704-5364
Sultan Moulay Slimane University, Morocco

Ibrahim Ouahbi
University Mohamed I, Morocco

Khalid El Makkaoui
University Mohamed I, Morocco

ABSTRACT

This research paper explores the application of machine learning for early and accur- ate diabetes diagnosis, utilizing the CRISP-DM framework for structured analysis. We conducted a comprehensive study using the Pima Indians Diabetes database to assess five prominent machine learning algorithms: Support Vector Machine (SVM), Logistic Re- gression, Decision Tree, Naive Bayes, and Random Forest. We enhanced these algorithms' predictive capabilities through GridSearchCV

DOI: 10.4018/979-8-3693-8387-2.ch005

optimization. Our analysis revealed the Decision Tree classifier as the top performer for diabetes diagnosis accuracy within the CRISP-DM framework, achieving impressive performance metrics: 96% recall, 94% accur- acy and F1 score, and 90% precision. Despite exploring ensemble learning, which combines insights from all models, it did not surpass the effectiveness of the standalone Decision Tree model. Given the medical context of our study, we prioritized the recall score, focusing on correctly identifying actual diabetic patients.

INTRODUCTION

Diabetes has recently become a chronic metabolic disease and a big cause of concern in most leading areas of public health, which, now, are attended to by major global forces. In the year 2019, approximately 463 million adults aged between 20 and 79 years were living with diabetes, according to statistics by the International Diabetes Federation (IDF) International Diabetes Federation (2019), and the projection for this number is 700 million by the year 2045, (Cho et al., 2018). The disease not only poses some serious health risks, such as the complications of the heart and kidneys, blindness, and failure of body organs, (Zimmet et al., 2014), but also presents a considerable economic burden on health facilities all over the world.

Timely diagnosis of diabetes is important from the point of view of management and preventing complications. Until now, the diagnosis was dependent on the clinical presentation followed by laboratory tests, but that was not a very timely and accurate process. Machine learning (Lamaakal, El Makkaoui, & Ouahbi et al., 2024; Lamaakal, El Mourabit, & El Makkaoui et al., 2024; Lamaakal, Maleh, & Ouahbi et al., 2024; Lamaakal, Ouahbi, & El Makkaoui et al., 2024; Lamaakal et al., 2025) represents one of the applied artificial intelligence branches, where it comprises systems that could aid in early diagnosis through data mining over big sets of data in search of corresponding patterns and correlations, (Kavakiotis et al., 2017). Using machine learning algorithms, it helps healthcare providers identify the possibility of probable diabetes at an earlier stage, hence an apt opportunity for intervention at the right time with proper and individualistic treatment plan, (Dagliati et al., 2018).

The other framework guiding a systematic process that may be followed to build machine learning models for health applications is the CRoss-Industry Standard Process for Data Mining (CRISP-DM), (Wirth & Hipp, 2000).

These phases are organized in six phases: Business Understanding, Data Understanding, Data Preparation, Modeling, Evaluation, and Deployment. Adherence to the CRISP-DM framework, therefore, becomes an assurance of the ability to develop and deploy machine learning models with effectiveness that translates into improved patient outcomes in healthcare. In this study, we apply the CRISP-DM framework to the early and accurate diagnosis of diabetes using machine learning. We take our very critical focus on the most debatably popular data- sets: the Pima Indians Diabetes database, (Smith et al., 1988), which is arguably one of the most popular datasets in the field, and compare five outstanding classifiers of the machine learning methods: Support Vector Machine (SVM) (Cortes & Vapnik, 1995), Logistic Regression, (Walker & Duncan, 1967), Decision Tree (Quinlan, 1986), Naive Bayes, (Langley et al., 1992), and Random

Forest, (Breiman, 2001). GridSearchCV optimizes the prediction of classifiers by determining the best hyperparameters for each model, (Bergstra & Bengio, 2012).

The recall score is the primary evaluation score of the whole analysis, indicating how good the models are in picking actual diabetic patients correctly. We thus strive through this system to pinpoint true positive cases with accuracy in diagnosis, hence aiming at a highly reliable and effective tool for detecting diabetes.

Research Motivation

The rising prevalence of diabetes worldwide is a significant public health issue and a significant economic burden on healthcare systems. With the International Diabetes Federation predicting a rise to 700 million diabetic adults by 2045, the need for innovative and accurate diagnostic tools is critical. Traditional methods often fail due to their timeliness and accuracy, leading to delayed interventions and complications. Machine learning can revolutionize diabetes diagnosis by leveraging advanced algorithms and vast data repositories like the Pima Indians Diabetes database. This research aims to identify the most effective models for diabetes diagnosis using a comparative analysis of various machine learning classifiers within the structured CRISP-DM framework. The goal is to prioritize accurate identification of individuals affected by diabetes, facilitating timely medical interventions. The intersection of data mining, machine learning, and healthcare can yield transformative tools for diabetes diagnosis, marking a significant step forward in the fight against this global epidemic.

Main Contributions

Our study has made significant contributions to the early diagnosis of diabetes using machine learning, enhancing diagnostic models' precision and effectiveness, and paving the way for future healthcare analytics research. Here, we highlight three principal contributions:

1. Our work advances machine learning algorithms for early and accurate diabetes diagnosis. Through a comparative analysis within the CRISP-DM framework, we

identified efficient models, enabling healthcare providers to diagnose diabetes more rapidly and accurately, potentially revolutionizing patient care.

2. The study optimizes machine learning classifiers, focusing on the Decision Tree model, using GridSearchCV for hyperparameter tuning. This enhances diagnostic precision and sets a benchmark for future research in machine learning and medical diagnostics.
3. The research prioritizes recall score as the primary evaluation metric to accurately identify true positive cases of diabetes, ensuring models are finely tuned for timely and appropriate interventions, which is vital for public health to minimize complications through early diagnosis and treatment.

Organization of the Paper

This paper provides a comprehensive exploration of the application of machine learning for early and accurate diabetes diagnosis. It begins with a thorough exploration of related literature and scholarly articles, establishing a contextual framework for the research. The methodology is outlined in the CRISP-DM Framework, starting with Business Understanding, followed by Data Understanding, Data Pre-Processing, Modeling, and Evaluation. The results and discussion section presents the findings and their implications, focusing on the role of feature engineering and hyperparameter tuning in enhancing model performance. The paper concludes with a comprehensive conclusion that encapsulates the significance of the research contributions and the potential impact on diabetes diagnosis and management. It also casts a vision for future work, contemplating avenues for further exploration and opportunities for innovation in this ever-evolving field.

Figure 1 illustrates the workflow adopted for this project, which is structured around the CRISPDM pipeline.

Figure 1. Our structured CRISP_DM framework for effective diabetes classification

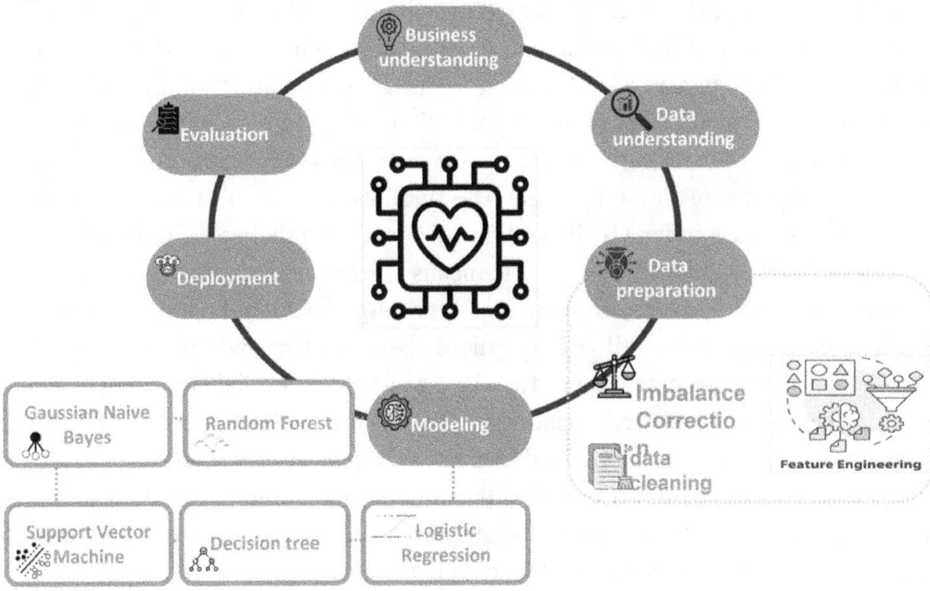

RELATED WORK

A significant amount of research has been published recently on the use of machine learning approaches to detect diabetic patients based on their symptoms. A model used by Khaleel and Al-Bakry (2023) can identify if an individual has diabetes or not. The prediction ac- curacy of strong machine learning algorithms—which employ metrics like recall, precision, and F1-measure—is the foundation of this paradigm. The Pima Indian Diabetes (PIDD) dataset is utilized by the authors to forecast the onset of diabetes depending on diagnostic methods. Using the Logistic Regression (LR), Naïve Bayes, and K-nearest Neighbour algorithms, the corresponding outcomes were 94%, 79%, and 69%. Khanam and Foo (2021) used seven machine learning algorithms on the dataset to predict diabetes. They discovered that the models incorporating SVM and logistic regression performed better. They then constructed a neural network model with an additional hidden layer and observed that the neural net- work with two hidden layers had an accuracy of 88.6%. Several machine learning classification techniques (including Gaussian Naive Bayes, KNN, ANN, Logistic Regression, Decision Tree, Random Forest, and Support Vector Machine) are used in the analysis conducted in Cıhan and Coşkun (2021) on the PIID dataset. The most accurate result was obtained using logistic regression. Along with standard parameters like glucose, BMI, age, insulin, etc., Mujumdar and Vaidehi (2019) suggest a diabetes prediction model for the classification of diabetes that takes into account extrinsic factors that cause the disease. When using the novel dataset instead of the old dataset, classification accuracy is increased. Alam et al. (2019) suggests a novel method for diabetes prediction using significant features in order to predict diabetes at an early stage. To choose attributes for grouping and prediction, a variety of tools are employed. The findings show a substantial correlation between body mass index (BMI) and glucose level and diabetes. Artificial neural network (ANN), random forest, and K-means clustering are some of the methods utilized to predict diabetes; of them, ANN technique yielded the highest accuracy.

A different approach is utilized to predict diabetes Yuvaraj and SriPreethaa (2019). The authors of this approach suggest a unique way to forecast diabetes using machine learning algorithms deployed in Hadoop-based clusters. Applying this strategy to the Pima Indians Diabetes Database and Digestive Diseases, the outcomes demonstrate that machine learning algorithms yield the most accurate diabetes prediction. Alternatively, the authors of the re- search Jian et al. (2021) have constructed models to categorize and forecast issues related to diabetes. Several supervised classification algorithms were used in this work to categorize and predict eight problems related to diabetes. Various factors, such as metabolic syndrome, dyslipidemia, nephropathy, diabetic foot, obesity, and retinopathy, are among the problems.

The authors of Barik et al. (2021) describe two machine learning techniques for predicting diabetes patients. For the classification method, use the Random Forest algorithm; for the hybrid approach, use the XGBoost algorithm. According to the data, XGBoost performs better with an accuracy rate of 74.10%.

In Phongying and Hiriote (2023), the authors evaluate machine learning models for diabetes classification, enhancing them with hyperparameter tuning and interaction terms. Their findings show that models with interaction terms outperform standard models, with the ran- dom forest classifier achieving the highest accuracy (97.5%).

Saeed (2023) aims to enhance Type 2 diabetes categorization using machine learning models. It evaluates methods like gradient boosting, AdaBoost, additional trees, and decision trees on diabetes datasets from the Behavioral Risk Factor Surveillance System (BRFSS) and PIMA Indian Diabetes. The study found that the additional trees classifier performed better, suggesting potential use in diagnosing chronic diabetes by medical professionals.

Wee et al. (2023) discusses the use of machine and deep learning in diabetes detection, highlighting the need for non-invasive, cost-effective methods due to limited diabetes data. It also explores the role of anthropometric measurements, oversampling techniques, and feature selection in improving accuracy and reliability.

METHODOLOGY

Data mining entails the analysis of immense datasets to distill valuable information for diverse objectives. This discipline has surged in importance and witnessed remarkable expansion over recent years. Various standard models facilitate the data mining process, each structured into sequential stages to streamline the execution of data exploration tasks. Among these methodologies, we have selected the CRISP-DM approach (refer to Figure 2) for its comprehensive framework and proven efficacy in guiding data mining initiatives.

Figure 2. CRISP-DM process diagram

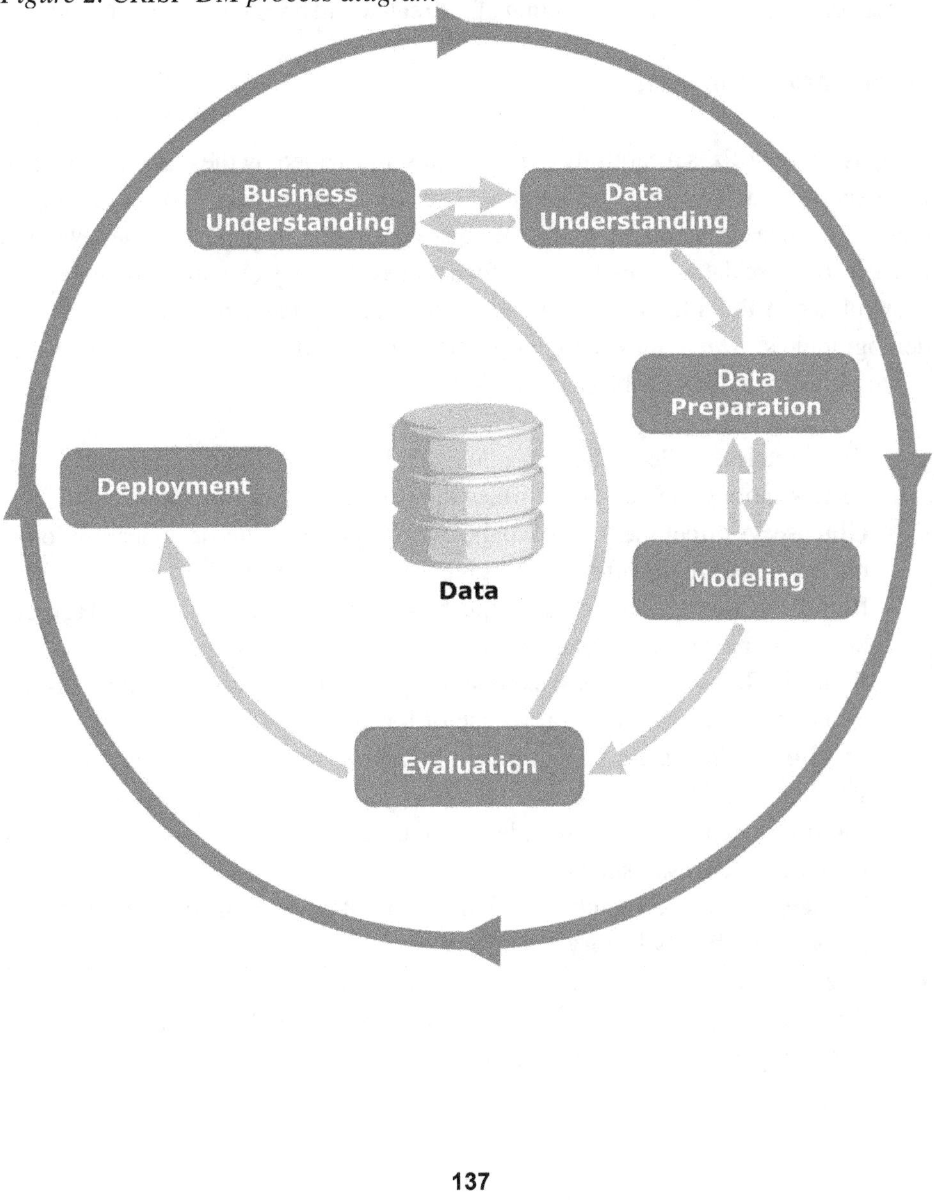

Business Understanding

This initial phase is foundational to our methodology, focusing on understanding the com- plexities and goals of the healthcare sector, specifically in early diagnosis and management of diabetes. We assess challenges in timely and accurate diabetes diagnosis, recognizing the con- sequences of delays or errors. Through discussions with medical professionals and analysis of current diagnostic practices, we identify areas for machine learning enhancement. Our aim is to align our research with the medical community's needs, ensuring our data mining efforts bene- fit patient care and contribute to public health by reducing diabetes-related complications and economic burden. This phase guides our targeted application of the CRISP-DM framework, with a clear understanding of the real-world problems we aim to address.

Data Understanding

This study utilizes a carefully curated dataset provided by the National Institute of Diabetes and Digestive and Kidney Diseases. The primary goal is to employ diagnostic measurements to predict diabetes presence in patients. The selection process for these data was meticulous, focusing exclusively on women of at least 21 years of age of Pima Indian descent, ensuring a targeted analysis within a specific demographic known to have a higher predisposition to diabetes. The dataset is rich in variables critical for diabetes prediction:

- **Pregnancies**: Reflects the physiological changes that could influence diabetes risk, noting the number of times the patient has been pregnant.
- **Glucose**: A direct measure of diabetes risk, plasma glucose concentration is measured two hours after an oral glucose tolerance test.
- **Blood Pressure**: Includes diastolic blood pressure readings (mm Hg), acknowledging cardiovascular strain associated with diabetes.
- **Skin Thickness**: Assesses triceps skinfold thickness (mm), providing insight into body fat distribution—a risk factor for diabetes.
- **Insulin**: Evaluates 2-hour serum insulin levels (mu U/ml), crucial for understanding insulin resistance.
- **BMI**: Calculates body mass index (weight in kg/(height in m)^2), a key factor in diabetes risk assessment.
- **Diabetes Pedigree Function** assigns a hereditary propensity score to diabetes based on family history.
- **Age**: Considers the patient's age in years, as risk increases with age.
- **Outcome**: Class variable (0 or 1) denoting the presence of diabetes, serving as the target for prediction models.

Data acquisition was conducted through the Kaggle platform, aiming to craft a predict- ive model that accurately determines a patient's diabetic status. This dataset is composed of several medical predictive variables (independent) and one dependent target variable, the outcome. These variables were selected for their proven significance in diabetes research and prediction. The data is stored in a CSV format, ensuring easy accessibility and manipulation, with a total size of 23.31 KB.

To get a general idea of our data, we displayed the first 5 lines,m as shown in Table 1.

Table 1. Data description

Index	Pregnancies	Glucose	Blood Pressure	Skin Thickness	Insulin	BMI	Diabetes Pedigree Function	Age	Outcome
0	6	148	72	35	0	33.6	0.627	50	1
1	1	85	66	29	0	26.6	0.351	31	0
2	8	183	64	0	0	23.3	0.672	32	1
3	1	89	66	23	94	28.1	0.167	21	0
4	0	137	40	35	168	43.1	2.288	33	1

Checking for Missing Values

The bar chart (see Figure 3) visualizes the null value distribution across different variables, re- vealing a varying degree of incompleteness in our dataset. Notably, 'Insulin' exhibits the most significant number of missing entries, which could imply a substantial impact on any analysis related to insulin levels. 'SkinThickness' and 'BloodPressure' follow, presenting a considerable amount of missing data as well. Less pronounced, yet still noteworthy, are the missing values in 'Glucose' and 'BMI', variables integral to the diagnosis of diabetes. Encouragingly, 'Pregnancies', 'Age', and 'Outcome' are fully accounted for, indicating robustness in these aspects of the data.

Column Values Frequency

The histograms (see Figure 4) underscore a notable concern within our dataset—the presence of zeros in columns where they are biologically implausible. These entries span across multiple variables, where the occurrence of a zero value defies clinical relevance, such as glucose concentration, blood pressure, skinfold thickness, and BMI. This anomaly suggests either missing or erroneously recorded data, a common issue in clinical datasets that requires careful attention.

Identification of Outliers

The boxplots (see Figure 5) presented illustrate the distribution of values across various physiological variables in our dataset, effectively pinpointing potential outliers. These outliers, repres ented by the dots outside the 'whiskers' of the boxplots, could be due to natural variation, measurement error, or data entry inconsistencies.

Figure 3. Bar chart of missing values in dataset variables

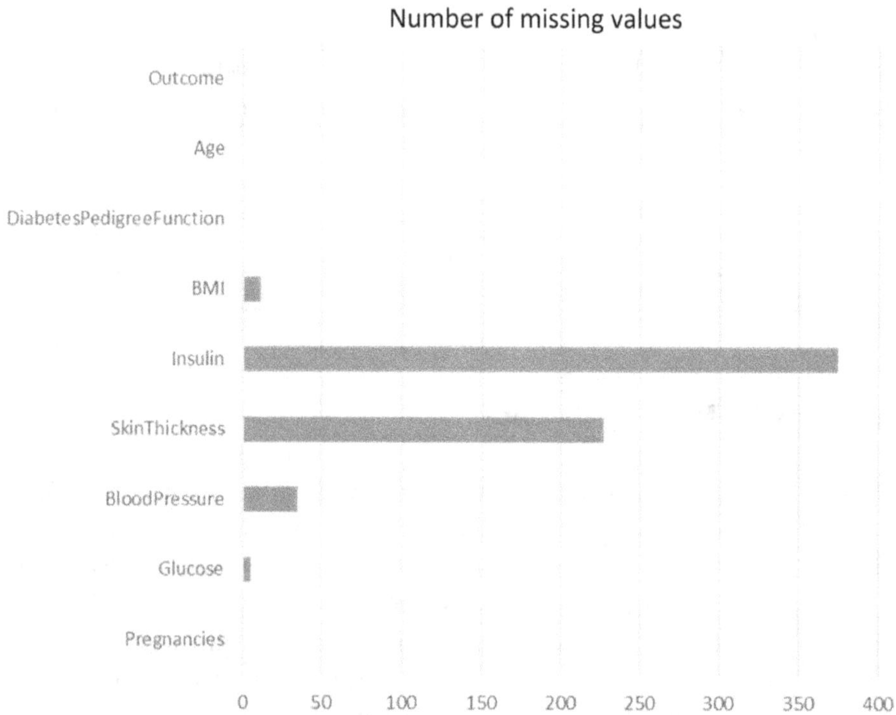

Figure 4. Histograms highlighting zero value anomalies in physiological measurements

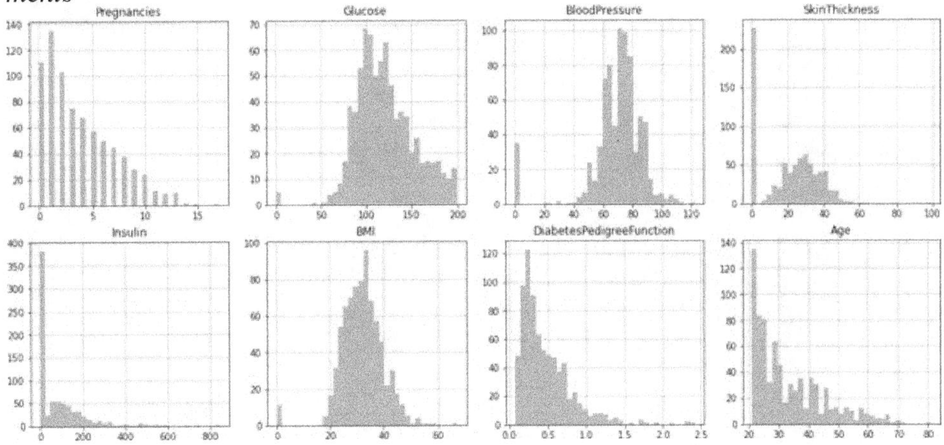

Relationships Between Variables and Target

In this section, we delve into the interplay between our predictive variables and the target outcome.

Figure 6 demonstrate that as the number of pregnancies increases, the patient's likelihood of developing diabetes also increases.

Figure 5. Boxplots illustrating distribution and outliers across key variables

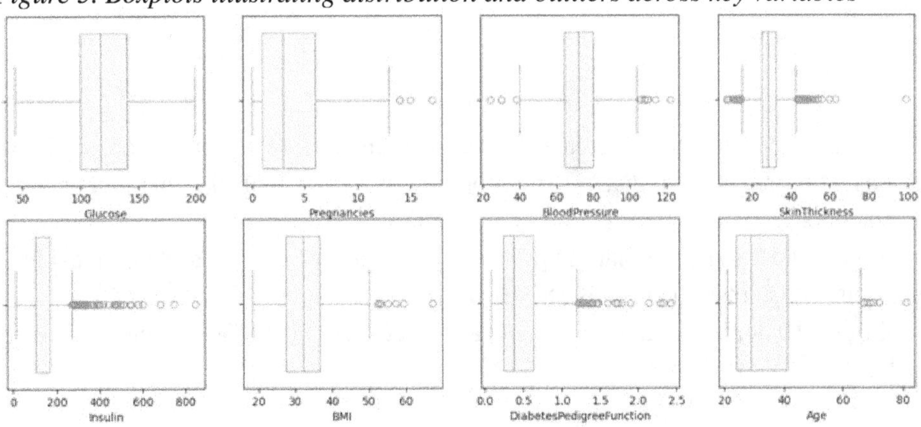

Figure 6. Relationship between pregnancy and outcome

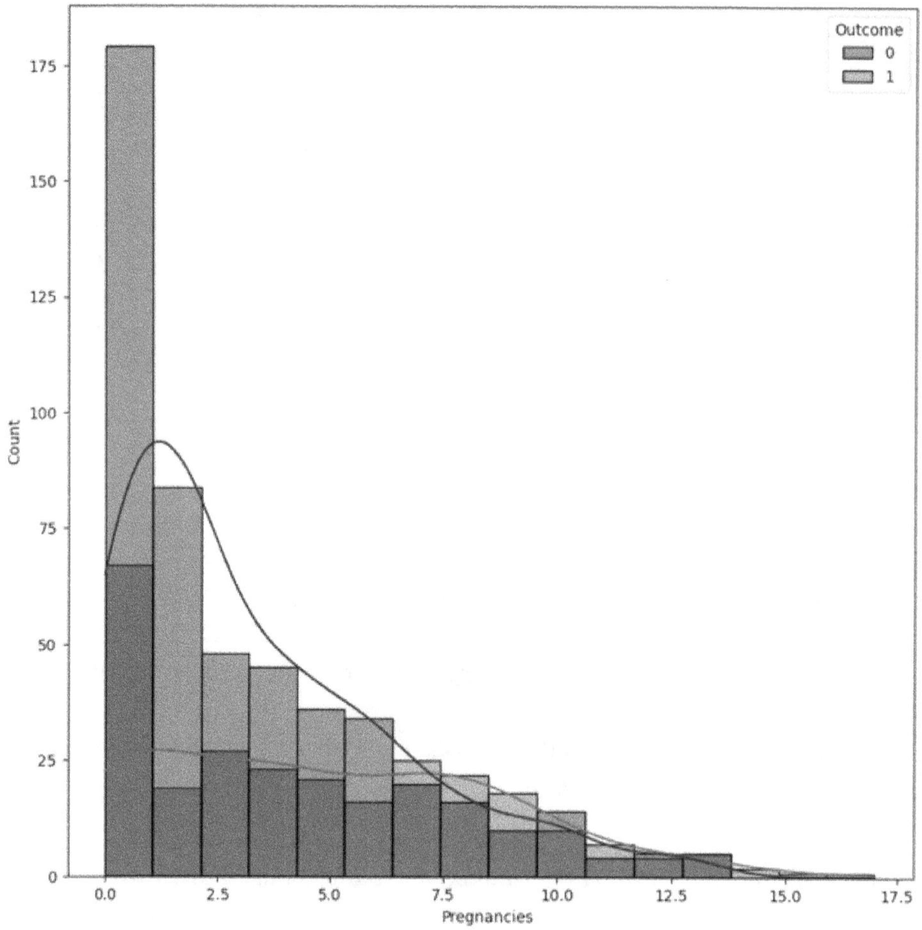

Figure 7 shows that an increase in glucose increases the possibility of a patient's disease. Figure 8 shown that When blood pressure exceeds 100 mmHg, the patient is diabetic.

Figure 9 demonstrate that the presence of diabetes becomes quite noticeable in patients whose insulin exceeds 180 U/ml.

Figure 10 demonstrate that patients aged between 35 and 60 are the most likely to be ill

The Correlation Between the Variables

Based on Figure 11, we observe a strong correlation between specific variables, such as Pregnancies- Age, Glucose-Insulin, SkinThickness-BMI, and Glucose-Outcome.

Figure 7. Relationship between glucose and outcome

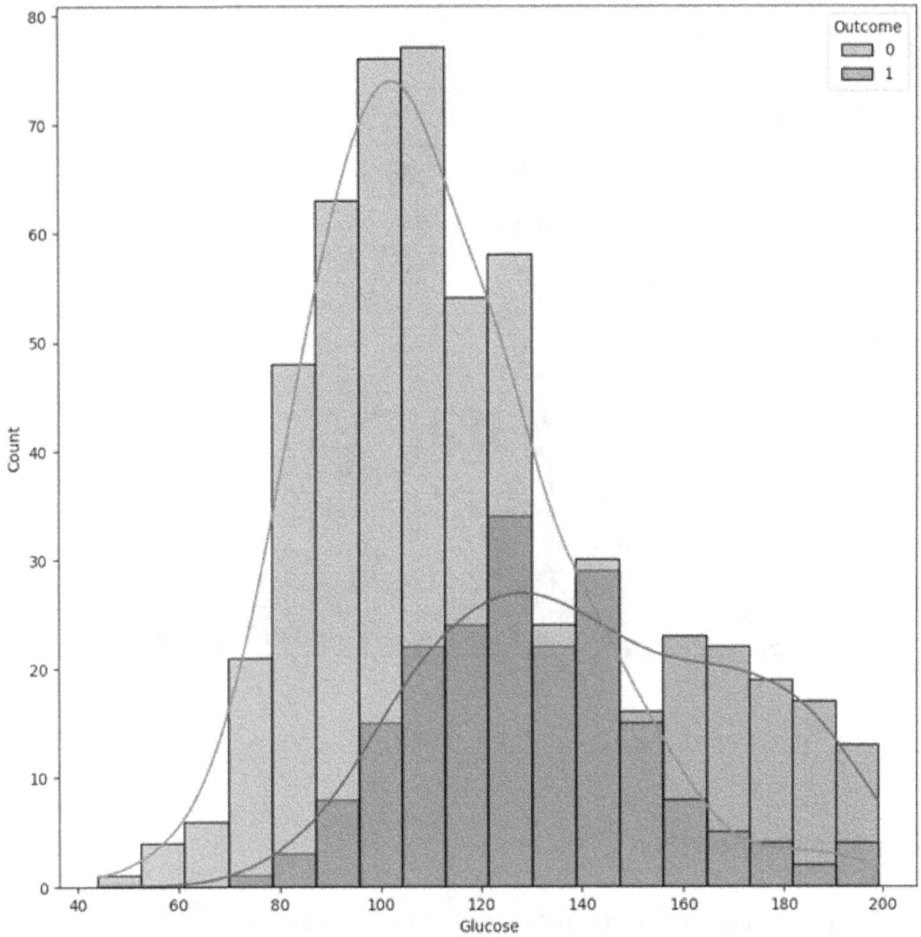

Figure 8. Relationship between blood pressure and outcome

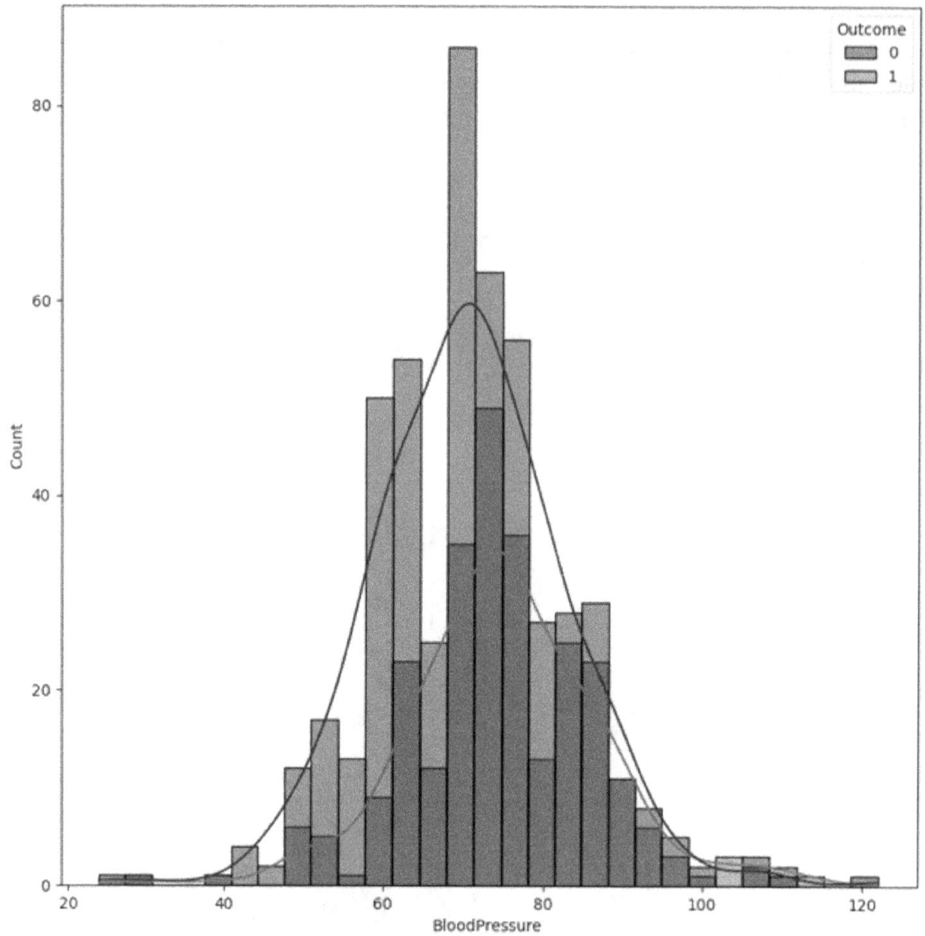

Comparison Between Classes

The percentage of diabetic patients in our data is 35% of the total data, while that of non- diabetic patients is close to 65% (see Figure 12).

Data Pre-Processing

In this phase, we address the crucial steps taken to prepare our dataset for analysis. This phase is pivotal, as the quality and format of data directly impact the performance of machine learning algorithms. Here, we describe the methodologies employed.

Figure 9. Relationship between insulin and outcome

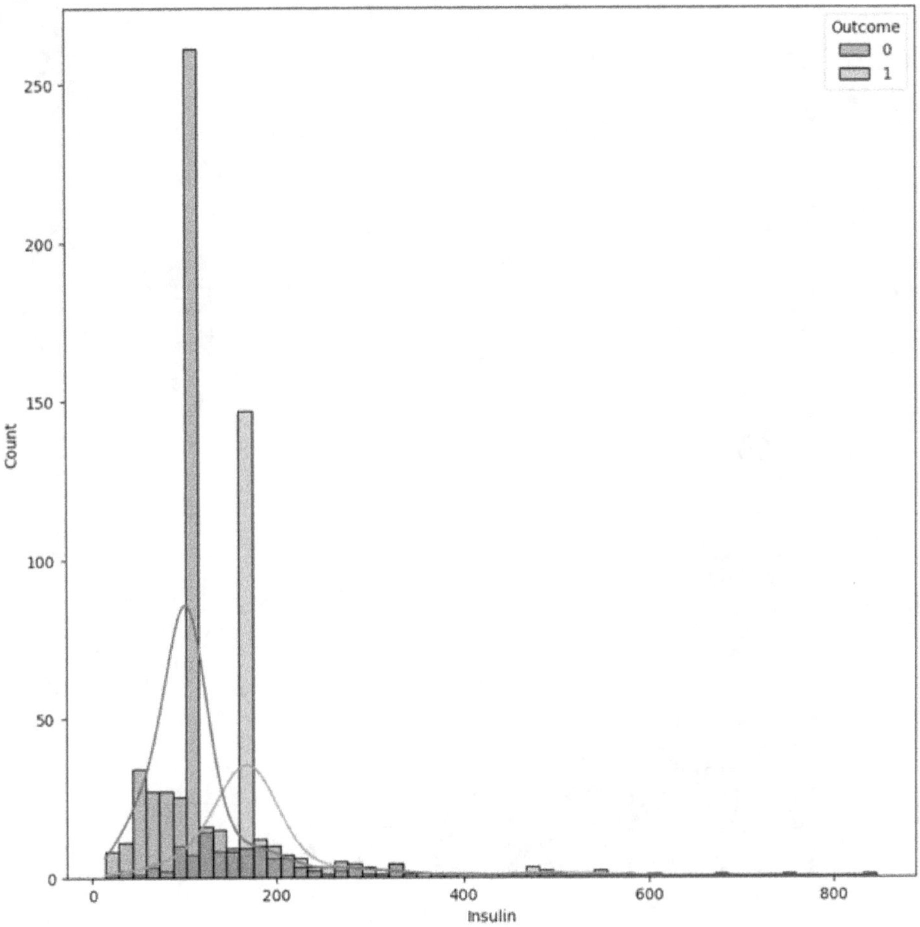

Figure 10. Relationship between age and outcome

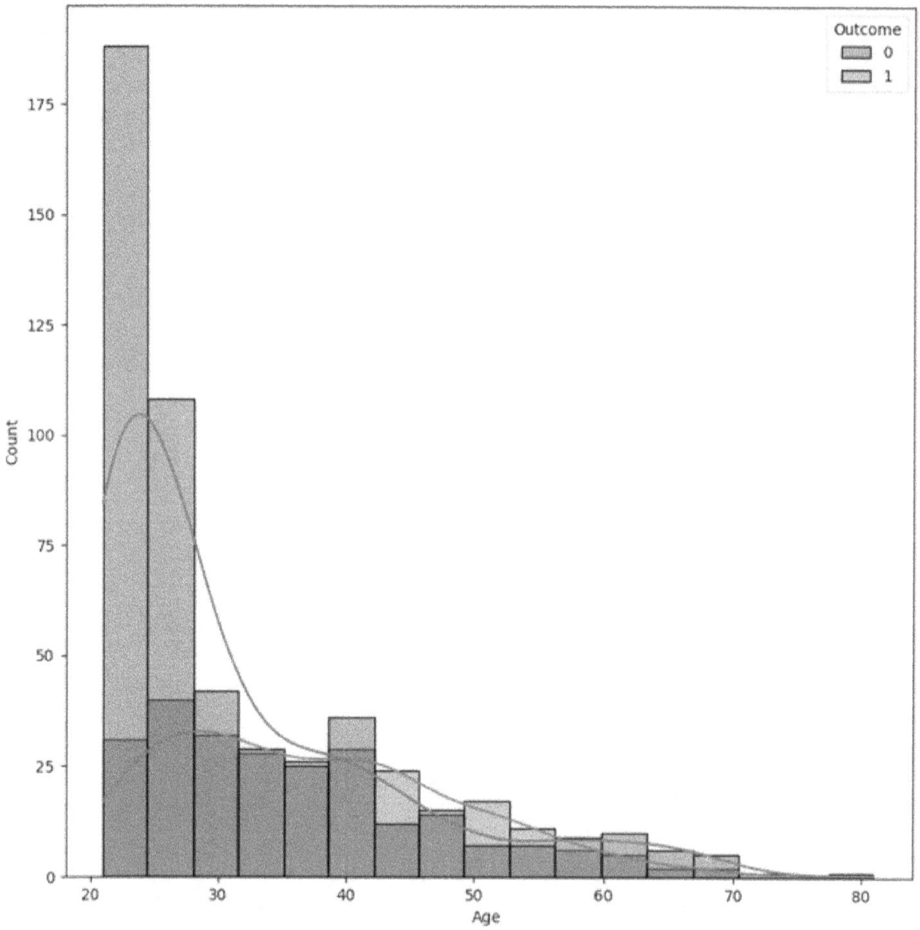

for cleaning, transforming, and normalizing the data, including the handling of missing values, the treatment of outliers.

Correction of the Null Values Issue

As we have seen in our data, we have several rows with the value 0 in certain columns. What we did was to change these values to the median of the column. The next graph shows that we no longer have these values (see Figure 13).

Figure 11. Correlation matrix

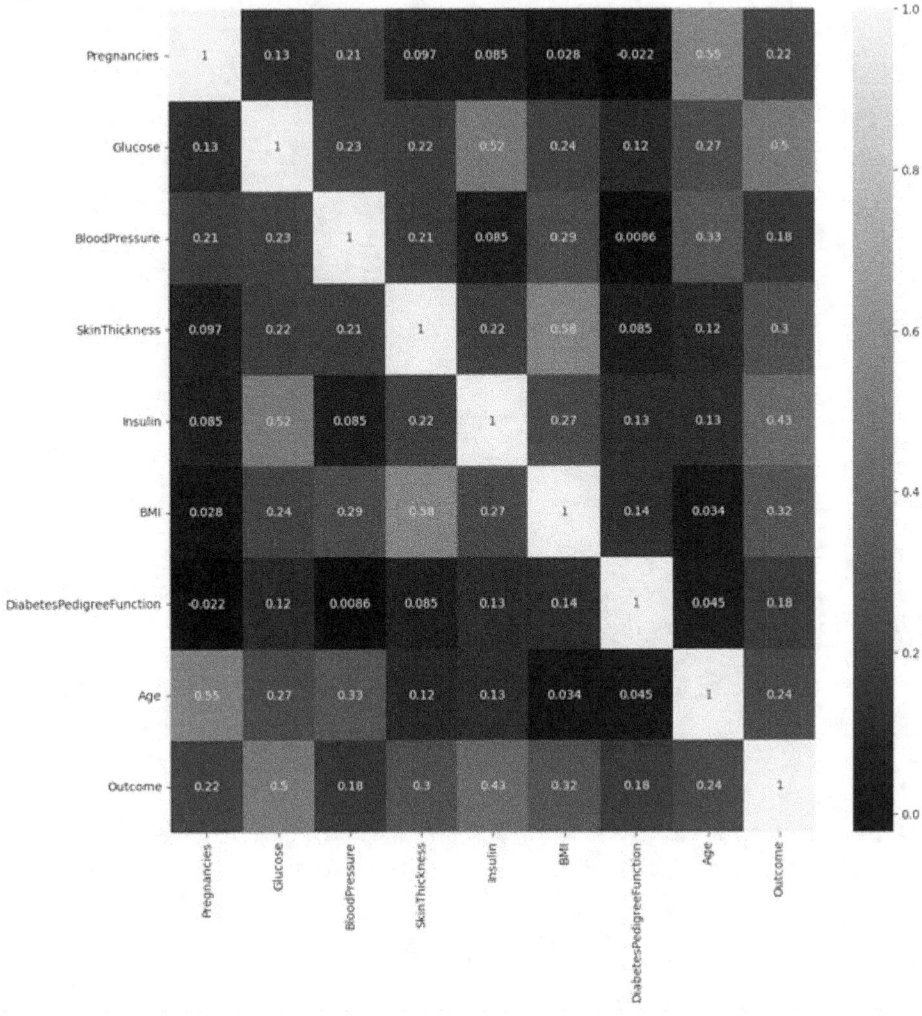

Figure 12. Comparison between classes

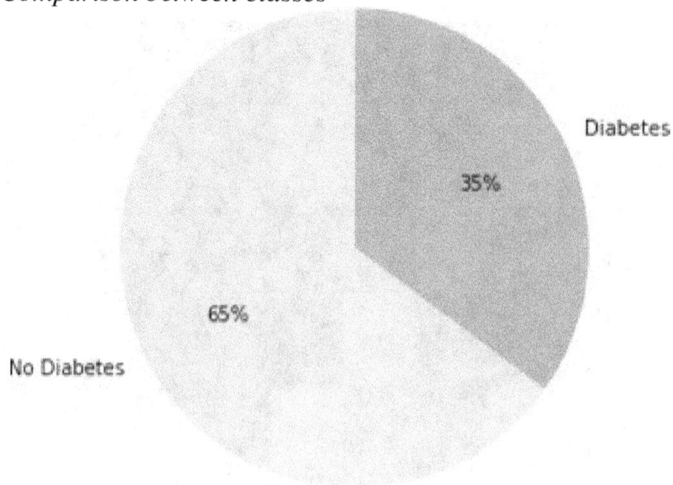

Figure 13. Correction of the null values issue

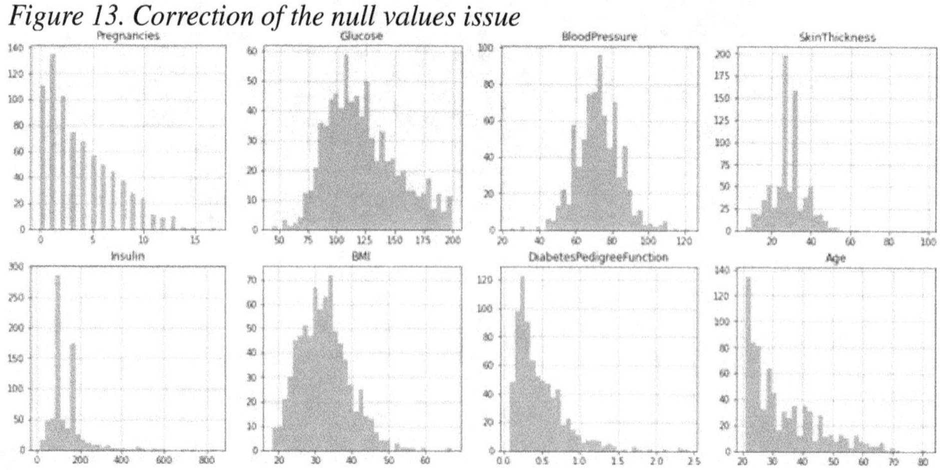

Removal of Outliers

To address the task of outlier removal in our data pre-processing stage, we implemented a method based on the Interquartile Range (IQR) (Tukey, 1977), a robust measure of variability that helps in identifying and filtering out extreme values. The process involves calculating the first (Q1) and third quartiles (Q3) of the dataset, which represent the 25th and 75th percentiles, respectively. These quartiles are then used to determine the IQR, which is the difference between Q3 and Q1. Outliers are defined as observations that fall below Q1 - 1.5IQR or above Q3 + 1.5IQR. This method ensures that only data points within a reasonable range are retained for analysis, enhancing the reliability of our findings.

Here's a simplified pseudocode summarizing the steps taken to remove outliers:

Algorithm 1 Outlier Removal Using IQR

```
Require: Data set data
Ensure: Filtered data set without outliers
Q1 ← data.quantile(0.25) □ Compute the first quartile
Q3 ← data.quantile(0.75) □ Compute the third quartile
IQR ← Q3 - Q1 □ Calculate IQR
LowerBound ← Q1 - 1.5 × IQR □ Define lower bound
UpperBound ← Q3 + 1.5 × IQR □ Define upper bound
outliers ← {x □ data | (x < LowerBound) □ (x > UpperBound)} □ Identify outliers
data ← data \ outliers □ Remove outliers
return data □ Return the filtered data
```

We have chosen to remove outliers because they decrease the performance of our model (see Figure 14).

Figure 14. Outlier removal

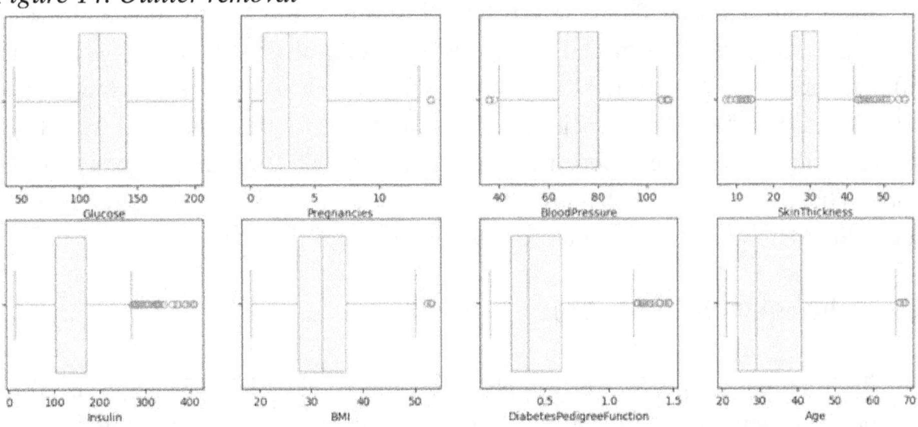

Implementation of Feature Engineering

One of the lesser-known techniques of feature engineers is to create new features from existing variables that are usually correlated, (Zheng & Casari, 2018). We can create an interaction (for example, multiply or divide) between each pair of variables in the hope of finding an interesting new feature, (Robnik-Šikonja & Kononenko, 2003). In our project, we tried to create new features by dividing variables that are more correlated with each other, creating these variables, and testing them in our system. The final results of each machine learning technique showed that our new features improved the result by more than 5%.

The new features created are:

- glu/bmi = Glucose / BMI
- ins/bmi = Insulin / BMI
- glu/ins = Glucose / Insulin
- bp/glu = BloodPressure / Glucose
- skn/bmi = SkinThickness / BMI
- bp/bmi = BloodPressure / BMI
- preg/agr = Pregnancies / Age

1.1.1 Data Spliting

In machine learning, the process of dividing our dataset into training and testing sets is a critical step known as the train/test data split phase. Typically, we allocate 80% of our data to the training set, where our machine learning model is trained and learns from the data. The remaining 20% is reserved for the testing set, which we use to evaluate the model's performance and its ability to generalize to new, unseen data. When we incorporate feature engineering into this process, we apply it before the split, creating and incorporating new features into the dataset.

Class Imbalance Correction

The Synthetic Minority Over-sampling Technique (SMOTE) (Chawla et al., 2002) is a popular method used to address class imbalance in machine learning datasets. It works by synthesizing new examples from the minority class, thereby balancing the class distribution. This is achieved by selecting existing minority class samples and generating new instances that are similar but slightly varied, thus enriching the dataset without simply duplicating entries. The SMOTE algorithm is particularly useful when the number of samples in different classes is significantly imbalanced, as it helps improve the performance of classification models by providing a more balanced training set.

Algorithm 2 SMOTE for Class Imbalance Correction

```
Require: Training data (Xtrain, ytrain)
Ensure: Balanced training data (Xbalanced, ybalanced)
1: Initialize the SMOTE algorithm:
2: smt ← SMOTE()
3: Apply SMOTE to the training data:
4: (Xbalanced, ybalanced) ← smt.fit_resample(Xtrain, ytrain)
5: return (Xbalanced, ybalanced)
```

Figure 15 demonstrates that the classes are now balanced

Figure 15. Class imbalance correction

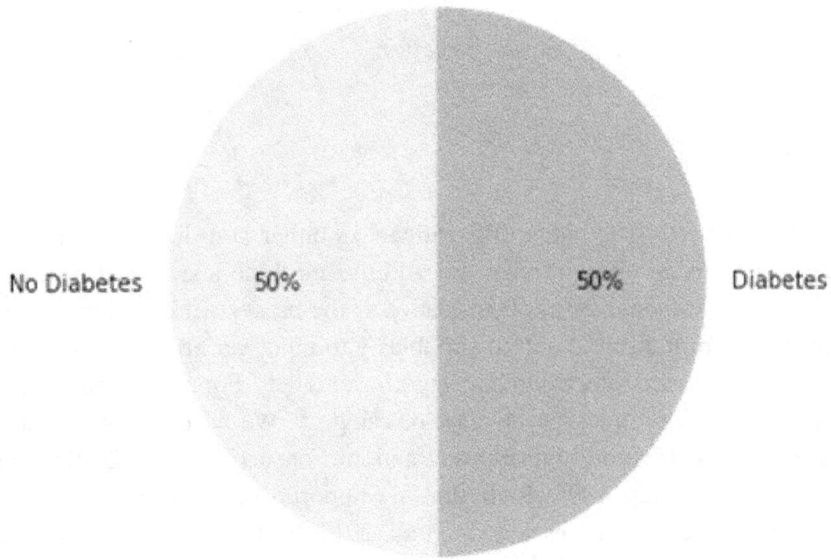

Data Normalization

Real-valued numerical attributes are normalized by rescaling them to a range of 0 to 1. Assuming that the data properties are on the same scale, most machine learning algorithms operate more efficiently.

Algorithm 3 Data Normalization

```
Require: Dataset with real-valued numeric attributes
Ensure: Normalized dataset
1: for each attribute in the dataset do
2: Determine the attribute's minimum value (min). 3: Deter-
mine the attribute's maximum value (max). 4: for each value
(val) of the attribute do
5: Normalize the value using the formula:
6: normalized_val ← (val - min)/(max - min) 7: Replace val
with normalized_val in the dataset 8: end for
9: end for
10: return the normalized dataset
```

Modeling

Our task requires us to categorize patients as either non-diabetic or diabetic, so instead of focusing on regression, we will use machine learning classification models. Predictive modeling in classification is the process of estimating a mapping function f from discrete output variables y to input variables X. Oftentimes, the output variables are referred to as categories or labels. For a given observation, the mapping function forecasts the class or category. We have decided to utilize five different classification algorithms: Random Forest (Breiman, 2001), Naïve Bayes (John & Langley, 1995; Rish, 2001), Support Vector Machine (Cortes & Vapnik, 1995), Logistic Regression (Jr. et al., 2013; McCullagh & Nelder, 1989), and Decision Tree (Quinlan, 1986). For each classifier, we are working with both feature engineering and without it, just to study the impact of feature engineering on performance for each classifier.

RESULTS AND DISCUSSION

Within this section, we will delve into our findings, beginning with an outline of the Expe imental Setup employed. This will be followed by an examination of the

Evaluation Metrics utilized, a detailed analysis of the role that GridSearchCV and Feature Engineering played in refining our results, and concluding with a comprehensive discussion of the insights gained from our research.

Experimental Setup

Our research is dedicated to implementing machine learning algorithms to determine diabetic conditions in patients. The system was developed in Python, harnessing the capabilities of libraries such as Sklearn, Numpy, matplotlib and Pandas. We utilized software tools like Google Colab and Visual Studio Code to aid in the development process. The computational tasks were performed on a laptop equipped with an Intel(R) Core(TM) i5-8400H CPU @ 2.50GHz, 8GB of RAM, and the Windows operating system.

Evaluation

The process includes feature engineering, model implementation, and obtaining results, followed by using test datasets to determine the model's effectiveness through specific metrics. A single metric such as accuracy may show good performance, but the model might underperform on others like logarithmic loss, recall, or F1-score. Hence, choosing the right metric is essential as it influences the evaluation and comparison of machine learning algorithms and the assessment of the importance of different features in the results.

- **Accuracy**: is the proportion of all the input samples to all of the correctly predicted samples. We utilize accuracy when roughly the same number of samples are in each class. Therefore, using accuracy as a criterion for our problem's evaluation is not a good notion.

Accuracy = Number of correct predictions / Total number of predictions made
(1)

- **Confusion Matrix**:, where *N* is the number of classes to be predicted, is a $N \times N$ matrix. The confusion matrix provides us with an output matrix that details the model's overall performance.
- **Precision**: By dividing the total number of positive outcomes the classifier predicted by the number of true positives, it may be computed.

Precision = True Positives / True Positives + False Positives
(2)

- **Recall/Sensitivity**:It is calculated by dividing the total number of relevant samples (i.e., samples that all should have been considered positive) by the number of real positives.

Recall = True Positives / True Positives + False Negatives
(3)

- **F1 Score**: The F1 score is the harmonic mean of recall and precision. It shows the classifier's accuracy (the number of cases it properly classifies) and robustness (it does not miss a significant number of instances). The greater the F1 score, the better our model works.

  F1 Score = 2 × Precision × Recall / Precision + Recall (4)
- **AUC-ROC curve**: The AUC-ROC curve is used to assess the classification issues' performance at various threshold levels. In contrast to ROC, which is a probability curve, AUC is a metric or degree of separability. It shows the extent to which the model is capable of class discrimination. If the AUC value is high, the model predicts classes indicated by 0 as value 0 and classes indicated by 1 as value 1.

Grid Search

Grid Search, or grid searching, attempts to exhaustively search all possible combinations of hyperparameters (best parameters) to form a grid of hyperparameter values where we specify the range of hyperparameter values to search for, making it a costly and time-consuming method, (Bergstra & Bengio, 2012).

Ensemble Learning

We have shown that our models perform well, so it is evident that combining these models with ensemble learning techniques such as voting will likely yield better results in the field of classification.

Hard Voting

A hard voting ensemble: consists of tallying the votes for the clear classes from other models and predicting the class that has received the most votes. After implementing the hard voting ensemble method, we have obtained the following results (see Figure 22).

Soft Voting

A soft voting ensemble: consists of adding up the predicted probabilities for the classes and predicting the class with the highest total probability. After implementing the Soft voting ensemble method, we have obtained the following results (see Figure 22).

We present the results obtained using the different classifiers mentioned previously and the different techniques with and without feature engineering and with or without grid search (see Figure 16, Figure 17, Figure 18, Figure 19, Figure 20, Figure 21).

Figure 16. a) Confusion Matrix – Logistic Regression without Feature engineering, b) Confu- sion Matrix – Logistic Regression using Feature engineering, c) Confusion Matrix – Logistic Regression without Feature engineering, with GridSearch, d) Confusion Matrix – Logistic Re- gression using Feature engineering, with GridSearch

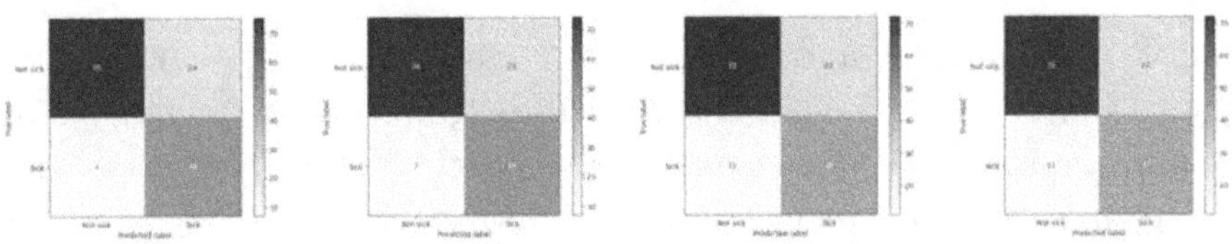

a) Confusion Matrix – Logistic Regression without Feature engineering

b) Confusion Matrix – Logistic Regression Using Feature engineering

c) Confusion Matrix – Logistic Regression without Feature engineering, with GridSearch

d) Confusion Matrix – Logistic Regression using Feature engineering, with GridSearch

Table 2 above presents the various classification models, including logistic regression, naive Bayes, SVMs, decision trees, and random forests. We had to test different techniques on each model to see if they improve the results. The columns of the table represent, respectively, the name of the model used, whether feature engineering is used in each model, whether grid search is utilized to fine-tune the best hyperparameter or not, and the last columns for different types of classification measures such as accuracy, precision, recall, F1 score, MCC.

Figure 17. a) Confusion Matrix – SVM without Feature engineering, b) Confusion Matrix – SVM using Feature engineering, c) Confusion Matrix – SVM without Feature engineering, with GridSearch, d) Confusion Matrix – SVM using Feature engineering, with GridSearch

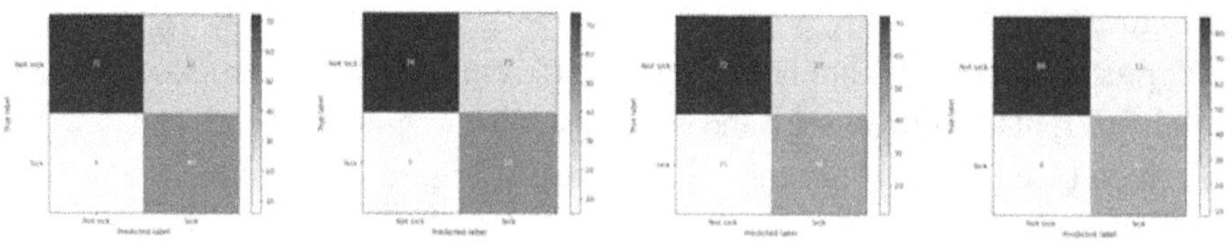

a) Confusion Matrix – Support Vector Machine without Feature engineering

b) Confusion Matrix – Support Vector Machine using Feature engineering

c) Confusion Matrix – Support Vector Machine without Feature engineering, with GridSearch

d) Confusion Matrix – Support Vector Machine using Feature engineering, with GridSearch

Figure 18. a) Confusion Matrix – Decision tree without Feature engineering, b) Confusion Matrix – Decision tree using Feature engineering, c) Confusion Matrix – Decision tree without Feature engineering, with GridSearch, d) Confusion Matrix – Decision tree using Feature engineering, with GridSearch

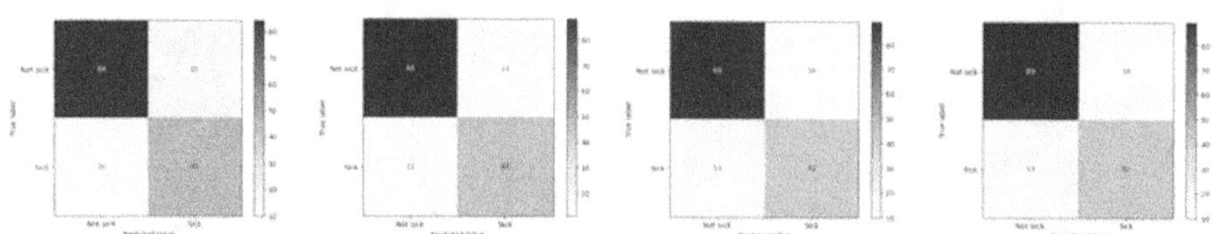

a) Confusion Matrix – Decision Tree without Feature engineering

b) Confusion Matrix – Decision Tree using Feature engineering

c) Confusion Matrix – Decision Tree without Feature engineering, with GridSearch

d) Confusion Matrix – Decision Tree using Feature engineering, with GridSearch

Figure 19. a) Confusion Matrix – Random Forest without Feature engineering, b) Confusion Matrix – Random Forest using Feature engineering, c) Confusion Matrix – Random Forest without Feature engineering, with GridSearch, d) Confusion Matrix – Random Forest using Feature engineering, with GridSearch.

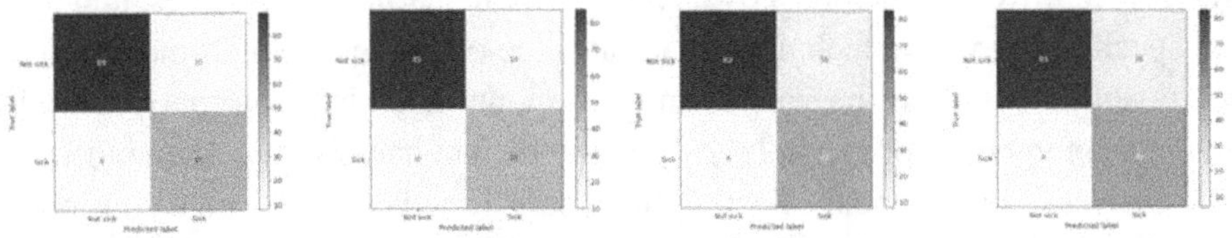

a) Confusion Matrix – Random Forest without Feature engineering

b) Confusion Matrix – Random Forest using Feature engineering

c) Confusion Matrix – Random Forest without Feature engineering, with GridSearch

d) Confusion Matrix – Random Forest using Feature engineering, with GridSearch

Discussion

In our model comparison, we will mainly focus on the recall score because the issue at hand is of a medical nature. It's about detecting whe$_2$th$_2$er a patient is diabetic or not! Therefore, it's more critical to identify individuals who are actually diabetic. Our model must, therefore, catch the maximum number of truly ill people, and for that, we need to focus specifically on recall, which is a measure of the true positive rate (number of diabetic individuals correctly identified) divided by the sum of the true positive and the false negatives (number of diabetic individuals not detected). In the following, we compare the results obtained to draw a general conclusion (see Table 1). Starting with logistic regression, we noticed that using Grid Search does not improve accuracy, but since our data is unbalanced and we have a medical issue, we don't really care about accuracy but rather recall, and we notice that Grid Search has improved our recall results by 1%. The most interesting result is that by combining the two techniques, feature engineering and grid search, we manage to accumulate the increased recall value, which is 91%, an increase of 11%. In the naive Bayes algorithm, we only used the feature engineering approach since there is no need for grid search. We can see that there is a 5% increase in all classification measures. For the SVM algorithm, grid search has improved the results of our model by more than 2% in terms of precision and the recall does not change values, which allows the model to predict a larger number of patients who are actually diabetic, feature engineering has also improved the results to a good extent and by combining the two techniques, we notice that the final recall value is 85%. Using grid search to find the best hyperparameter for the decision tree resulted in better results in all metrics, except for recall. But adding new features improved the results of all metrics, including 1% for recall. And finally, the combination of new features and grid search with 80% recall. And finally, with the random forest with an improvement after using new calculated features, with recall results of 89%. After implementing all the models and selecting the best results, we can attempt to further improve the outcomes by using ensemble learning techniques, and to be more specific, the voting technique that takes the outcomes from all models. This involves either counting the vote from each model and choosing the result with the greatest number—for example, if 'yes' the patient has diabetes, then our result would be 'yes'—or it's about selecting the results based on the average confidence probability of each model on the given results. From the two confusion matrix graphs (see Figure 21 and 22), we can see that soft voting or the idea of taking the confidence probabilities from each model yields very impressive results with an 89% recall, which can be explained by considering that some models may have more confidence in certain results, and combining this confidence can mitigate the minor differences in probability.

Figure 20. a) Confusion Matrix – Gaussian naive bayes without Feature engineering, b) Con- fusion Matrix – Gaussian naive bayes using Feature engineering

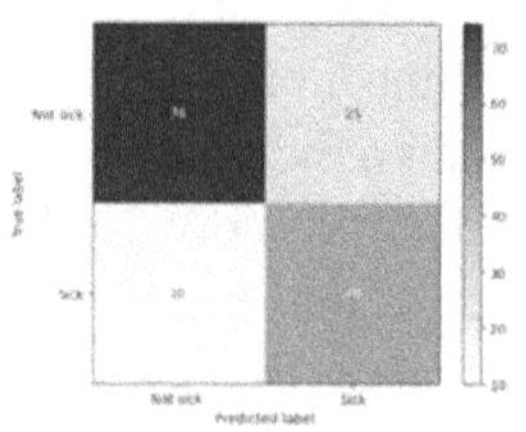

a) Confusion Matrix – Gaussian naive bayes without Feature engineering

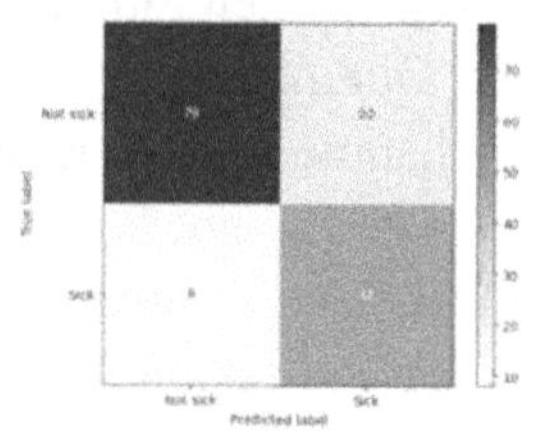

b) Confusion Matrix – Gaussian naive bayes using Feature engineering

Figure 21. ROC curves comparison

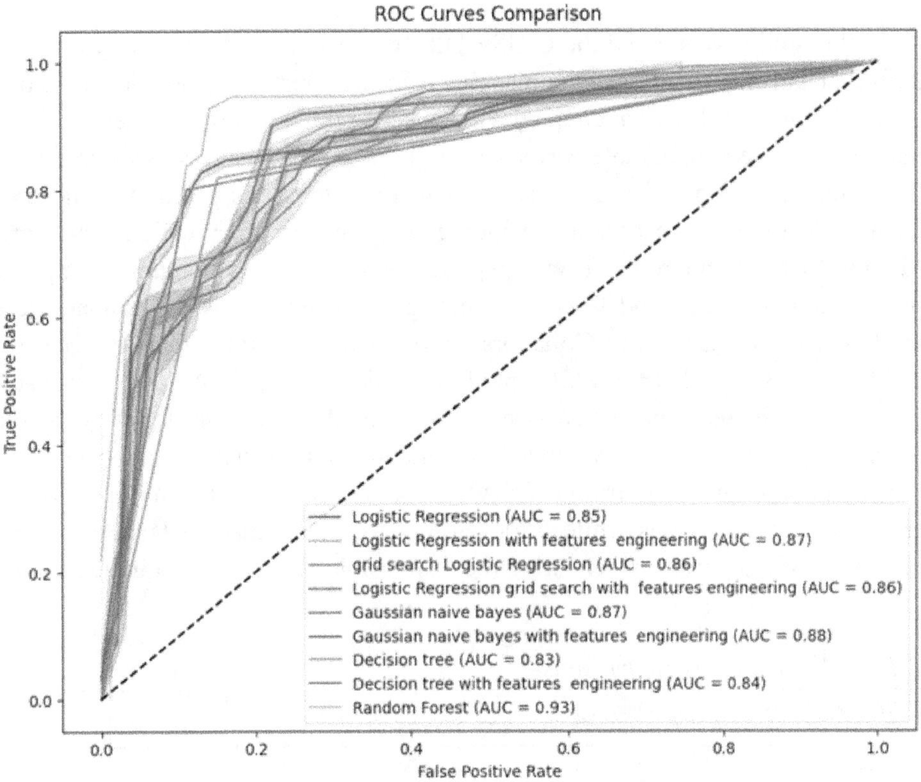

Figure 22. a) Confusion Matrix - Hard Voting, b) Confusion Matrix - Hard Voting

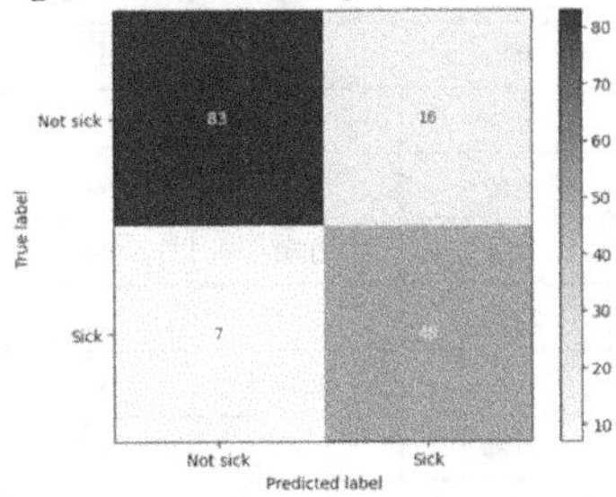

a) Confusion Matrix – Hard Voting

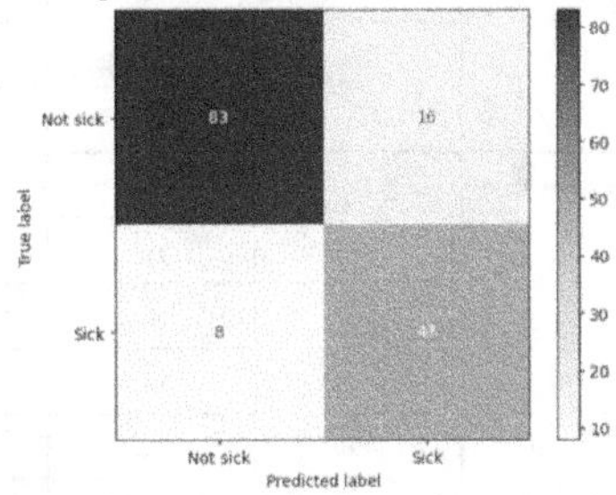

b) Confusion Matrix – Soft Voting

CONCLUSION AND FUTURE WORK

In this study, we applied the CRISP-DM framework to advance early diabetes detection and classification using machine learning. Our results demonstrated that the Decision Tree classifier, coupled with GridSearchCV and without feature engineering, achieved remarkable performance metrics: 96% recall, 94% accuracy and F1 score, and 90% precision. These findings underscore the potential of tailored machine learning approaches in enhancing diagnostic accuracy within healthcare. Moving forward, our research will explore deep learning techniques to improve pattern recognition, expand datasets for more generalized models, and validate these models in real-world settings. Collaborations with medical professionals will be crucial to refining model utility while upholding ethical standards and patient privacy. Furthermore, integrat- ing patient-specific data could pave the way for personalized medicine, ultimately enhancing treatment outcomes and reducing healthcare costs. Leveraging real-time data from IoT devices for continuous patient monitoring can enable early interventions, while the development of ex- plainable AI models will be pivotal in building trust and ensuring the responsible adoption of AI in healthcare.

Table 2. Table of classifier results

lightblue Classifier	Grid Search	Feature Engineering	Accuracy	Precision	Recall	F1 Score	MCC
Logistic Regression	No	No	0.77	0.63	0.82	0.71	0.53
		Yes	0.76	0.62	0.87	0.72	0.54
	Yes	No	0.75	0.61	0.80	0.69	0.49
		Yes	0.77	0.62	0.91	0.74	0.58
SVM	No	No	0.79	0.65	0.91	0.76	0.60
		Yes	0.80	0.66	0.91	0.76	0.61
	Yes	No	0.86	0.77	0.87	0.82	0.71
		Yes	0.86	0.77	0.85	0.81	0.69
Decision Tree	No	No	0.84	0.76	0.82	0.79	0.66
		Yes	0.85	0.78	0.82	0.80	0.67
	Yes	No	0.94	0.90	0.96	0.94	0.84
		Yes	0.88	0.82	0.88	0.79	0.76
Random Forest	No	No	0.87	0.79	0.85	0.82	0.72
		Yes	0.86	0.77	0.85	0.81	0.69
	Yes	No	0.86	0.80	0.80	0.80	0.68
		Yes	0.86	0.77	0.89	0.82	0.71
Hard Voting	Yes	No	0.86	0.8	0.8	0.8	0.68
Soft Voting	Yes	No	0.86	0.75	0.89	0.82	0.70
Gaussian Naive Bayes	No No	No	0.77	0.63	0.82	0.71	0.53
		Yes	0.81	0.69	0.85	0.76	0.61

REFERENCES

Alam, T. M., Iqbal, M. A., Ali, Y., Wahab, A., Ijaz, S., Baig, T. I., Hussain, A., Malik, M. A., Raza, M. M., & Ibrar, S. (2019). A model for early prediction of diabetes. *Informatics in Medicine Unlocked, 16*, 100204.

Barik, S., Mohanty, S., Mohanty, S., & Singh, D. (2021). Analysis of prediction accuracy of diabetes using classifier and hybrid machine learning techniques. In *Intelligent and Cloud Computing: Proceedings of ICICC 2019, Volume 2* (pp. 399–409). Springer.

Bergstra, J., & Bengio, Y. (2012). Random search for hyper-parameter optimization. *Journal of Machine Learning Research, 13*, 281–305.

Breiman, L. (2001). Random forests. *Machine Learning, 45*(1), 5–32. DOI: 10. 1023/A:1010933404324

Chawla, N. V., Bowyer, K. W., Hall, L. O., & Kegelmeyer, W. P. (2002). SMOTE: Syn- thetic minority over-sampling technique. *Journal of Artificial Intelligence Research, 16*, 321–357. DOI: 10.1613/jair.953

Cho, N. H., Shaw, J. E., Karuranga, S., Huang, Y., da Rocha Fernandes, J. D., Ohlrogge, A. W., & Malanda, B. I. D. F. (2018). IDF Diabetes Atlas: Global estimates of diabetes prevalence for 2017 and projections for 2045. *Diabetes Research and Clinical Practice, 138*, 271–281.

Cortes, C., & Vapnik, V. (1995). Support-vector networks. *Machine Learning, 20*(3), 273–297. DOI: 10.1007/BF00994018

Dagliati, A., Marini, S., Sacchi, L., Cogni, G., Teliti, M., Tibollo, V., De Cata, P., Chiovato, L., & Bellazzi, R. (2018). Machine learning methods to predict diabetes com- plications. *Journal of Diabetes Science and Technology, 12*(2), 295–302. DOI: 10.1177/1932296817710475 PMID: 28494618

Hama Saeed, M. A. (2023). Diabetes type 2 classification using machine learning algorithms with up-sampling technique. *Journal of Electrical Systems and Information Technology, 10*(1), 8.

International Diabetes Federation. (2019). *IDF Diabetes Atlas* (9th ed.). Retrieved from https://www.diabetesatlas.org

Jian, Y., Pasquier, M., Sagahyroon, A., & Aloul, F. (2021). A machine learning approach to predicting diabetes complications. *Health Care, 9*(12), 1712. PMID: 34946438

Kavakiotis, I., Tsave, O., Salifoglou, A., Maglaveras, N., Vlahavas, I., & Chouvarda, I. (2017). Machine learning and data mining methods in diabetes research. *Computational and Structural Biotechnology Journal, 15*, 104–116. https://doi.org/ . 12.005DOI: 10.1016/j.csbj.2016

Khaleel, F. A., & Al-Bakry, A. M. (2023). Diagnosis of diabetes using machine learning algorithms. *Materials Today: Proceedings*, *80*, 3200–3203.

Khanam, J. J., & Foo, S. Y. (2021). A comparison of machine learning algorithms for diabetes prediction. *ICT Express*, *7*(4), 432–439.

Lamaakal, I., El Makkaoui, K., & Ouahbi, I.. (2024). A TinyML model for gesture-based air handwriting Arabic numbers recognition. *Procedia Computer Science*, *236*, 589–596.

Lamaakal, I., Ouahbi, I., & El Makkaoui, K.. (2024). A TinyDL model for gesture-based air handwriting Arabic numbers and simple Arabic letters recognition. *IEEE Access : Practical Innovations, Open Solutions*.

Langley, P., Iba, W., & Thompson, K. (1992). An analysis of Bayesian classifiers. *Proceed- ings of the Tenth National Conference on Artificial Intelligence*, 223–228.

Mujumdar, A., & Vaidehi, V. B. (2019). Diabetes prediction using machine learning al- gorithms. *Procedia Computer Science*, *165*, 292–299.

Phongying, M., & Hiriote, S. (2023). Diabetes classification using machine learning tech- niques. *Computation (Basel, Switzerland)*, *11*(5), 96.

Quinlan, J. R. (1986). Induction of decision trees. *Machine Learning*, *1*(1), 81–106.

Smith, J. W., Everhart, J. E., Dickson, W. C., Knowler, W. C., & Johannes, R. S. (1988). Using the ADAP learning algorithm to forecast the onset of diabetes mellitus. *Proceedings of the Symposium on Computer Applications and Medical Care*, 261–265.

Walker, S. H., & Duncan, D. B. (1967). Estimation of the probability of an event as a function of several independent variables. *Biometrika*, *54*(1-2), 167–179. DOI: 10.2307/2333860 PMID: 6049533

Wee, B. F., Sivakumar, S., Lim, K. H., Wong, W. K., & Juwono, F. H. (2023). Diabetes detection based on machine learning and deep learning approaches. *Multimedia Tools and Applications*, •••, 1–33.

Wirth, R., & Hipp, J. (2000). CRISP-DM: Towards a standard process model for data mining. In *Proceedings of the 4th International Conference on the Practical Applications of Knowledge Discovery and Data Mining*.

Yuvaraj, N., & SriPreethaa, K. R. (2019). Diabetes prediction in healthcare systems using machine learning algorithms on Hadoop cluster. *Cluster Computing*, *22*(Suppl 1), 1–9.

Zimmet, P. Z., Magliano, D. J., Herman, W. H., & Shaw, J. E. (2014). Diabetes: A 21st century challenge. *The Lancet. Diabetes & Endocrinology*, *2*(1), 56–64. DOI: 10. 1016/S2213-8587(13)70112-8 PMID: 24622669

Section 3
Education, Ethics, and Cybersecurity

Chapter 6
Innovating Education 6.0 With LLM Classroom Strategies for Robotics and Computing Skills Integration in EFL Ecosystem

Muthmainnah Muthmainnah
https://orcid.org/0000-0003-3170-2374
Universitas Al Asyariah Mandar, Indonesia

Besse Darmawati
https://orcid.org/0000-0002-7555-4230
National Research and Innovation Agency, Indonesia

Abd. Rasyid
National Research and Innovation Agency, Indonesia

Sutejo Sutejo
National Research and Innovation Agency, Indonesia

Sri Haryatmo
National Research and Innovation Agency, Indonesia

Nurweni Saptawuryandari
National Research and Innovation Agency, Indonesia

Ahmad Al Yakin
https://orcid.org/0000-0003-3170-2374
Universitas Al Asyariah Mandar, Indonesia

Ismail Lamaakal
https://orcid.org/0009-0009-6532-2573
Multidisciplinary Faculty of Nador, Mohammed Premier University, Oujda, Morocco

DOI: 10.4018/979-8-3693-8387-2.ch006

ABSTRACT

The purpose of this study is to improve classroom tactics in teaching computing and robotics in an EFL environment. It seeks to investigate the integration of Large Language Models (LLM) within the Education 6.0 framework. This study contributes to the growing body of literature on the role of AI in the classroom by demonstrating that LLM can serve as a bridge between technical and language instruction. Future research should investigate the long-term effects of LLM integration on student performance and extend this strategy to other STEM-related domains within the EFL ecosystem.

INTRODUCTION

A new paradigm, known as "Education 6.0," is taking shape in response to society's changing demands brought about by the exponential growth of technological capabilities. Digital tools, automation, and artificial intelligence are reshaping traditional teaching approaches in Education 6.0, the new paradigm in education (Peláez, 2024). A branch of AI known as Large Language Models (LLMs) presents a unique opportunity to improve learning outcomes, particularly in computer science and robotics. By leveraging LLMs, educators can better prepare their students for the challenges of the Fourth Industrial Revolution (4IR) and implement new teaching practices that address the complexities of contemporary education. The ability to successfully incorporate LLMs and related technologies into classroom instruction is critical as Indonesia embarks on its journey towards digital transformation (Filippi and Motyl, 2024). Despite growing awareness of the potential of LLMs in education, there is a significant lack of studies on their use in robotics and computing classroom practices. So far, most research on AI in education has concentrated on three main areas: adaptive learning systems, personalized learning, and automated assessment.

However, researchers have not thoroughly studied the relationship between LLMs and practical, hands-on areas like robotics in teaching. There is a lack of in-depth studies that address the specific challenges and opportunities faced by developing countries like Indonesia because most studies focus on wealthy countries with more advanced education systems and technical infrastructure. Furthermore, there is a lack of focus on pedagogical frameworks that enable the integration of robotics and computing into the classroom, even though these subjects are essential for STEM education. Especially in public schools in Indonesia, the use of computers and robots in the classroom is still in its infancy. There have been efforts to promote STEM education and digital literacy, such as the "*Merdeka Belajar*" program, but major obstacles remain. Some of these issues include curricula that do not always keep up with technological changes, lack of training for teachers in emerging technologies, and inadequate access to digital infrastructure. By providing a scalable answer to the problems of inadequate teacher preparation and resource distribution, LLM and other AI-based technologies have the potential to radically transform current robotics and computing skills.

Rural schools lack the resources and teaching knowledge of urban schools, so they are unable to participate in the growing number of coding and robotics programs. The digital divide in Indonesia is a major barrier to the full potential of Education 6.0. Due to the lack of research addressing the contextual needs of these settings, including cultural considerations and local technological limitations, it is crucial to investigate the effective use of LLMs in Indonesian classrooms. There are a few promising applications of AI in the classroom, with a focus on LLMs. Research suggests that LLMs can make learning more engaging for students by tailoring lessons to their individual needs, providing immediate feedback, and allowing them to solve complex problems using only language. Robotics-based education can benefit from LLMs because they automate coding tasks, freeing students to concentrate on learning concepts and generating new ideas. Al Yakin et al. (2024). For instance, Lyu et al. (2024) conducted a study on how LLMs assisted students in debugging code and discovered that the use of AI tools significantly enhanced the learning outcomes in a computing course. Similarly, Jošt et al. (2024) found that students retained more information and learnt the basics of robotics more effectively when an AI-based tutoring system was part of a robotics course.

Western educational systems and resources are more developed and established; therefore, most of this research focusses on that region. This highlights the importance of conducting additional research in developing countries such as Indonesia, where there may be specific barriers to implementing LLM and robotics education. We need to conduct research specific to Indonesia to address these issues. We should investigate how we can modify LLM to align with the socio-economic and educational circumstances of the country. In doing so, we can help ensure that robotics and computing are more equitably and effectively integrated into the Indonesian education system. Therefore, we believe that it is imperative to investigate how LLM and AI in education can be modified to meet the unique requirements of Indonesian classrooms, especially those related to computer science and robotics, despite the increasing amount of literature on these topics worldwide. To ensure that Education 6.0 becomes a reality in a variety of learning environments, there is an opportunity to innovate in classroom practices, highlighted by gaps in the literature.

DEFINITION OF LARGE LANGUAGE MODELS (LLM) IN EDUCATION

Over the past few decades, many educational scenarios have leveraged artificial intelligence (AI) for learning and social interaction (Al Yakin, et al. 2024). Recent years have seen widespread use of learning analytics, content recommendation or as teaching materials (Muthmainnah, et al. 2024) knowledge tracking, cognitive diagnosis, and educational data mining. In addition to being a powerful paradigm in a variety of fields, large language models (LLMs) have also achieved state-of-the-art performance in a variety of educational settings (Lee et al. 2024). According to previous studies, LLMs can solve multiple-choice and free-response problems at the level of human students on standardized tests (Hwang et al. 2024) in a variety of mathematical disciplines, including physics and computer science.

Empirical research has also shown that LLMs can help students with reading and writing in the classroom (Vik, 2024). While maintaining a healthy mix of depth and breadth, a recent study (Susnjak and McIntosh, 2024) shows that ChatGPT can generate logically consistent responses across disciplines. According to (Gill, et al. 2024) study, students who used ChatGPT (considering or enhancing LLM results as their own solution) outperformed regular students in several computer security courses. Several recent perspective papers (Kahl, et al. 2024; Cherednichenk, et al. 2024) discuss other potential uses of LLM in the classroom, including student-teacher collaboration, individualized instruction, and automated evaluation. However, there are a number of potential problems with using LLM in the classroom, such as plagiarism, bias in AI-generated content, over-reliance on LLM, and unequal access for people whose first language is not English [78]. Scholars have proposed numerous survey and exploratory studies to offer a comprehensive overview of the field. In engineering education, for example (Baber, et al., 2024; Hwang et al., 2024) drew conclusions about the usefulness of ChatGPT by examining its responses to relevant pedagogical issues.

By conducting face-to-face interviews, collecting responses to online posts and user logs, and analyzing the perspectives of different groups of ChatGPT users (e.g., educators, students, and researchers), (Yan, 2024) draw conclusions about the practical applications of LLM in education. We claim that there is no literature that comprehensively summarizes LLM for education from a technological perspective, even though these works have discussed the various current uses of LLM in educational settings and offered their long-term goals for future research. This survey aims to address this need by providing a comprehensive technical evaluation of LLM for education, complete with a new technology-focused taxonomy and an overview of currently publicly available datasets and standards. To encourage innovation and understanding in the ever-changing field of LLM for education, we also summaries current difficulties and potential for additional research.

Large Language Models (LLM) are highly sophisticated artificial intelligence (AI) systems designed to understand and generate human-like text based on extensive training on various datasets (Yigci et al., 2024). In the educational context, LLMs serve as versatile tools capable of processing natural language input to generate informative and contextual responses. LLMs such as OpenAI GPT (Generative Pre-trained Transformer) and Google's BERT (Bidirectional Encoder Representations from Transformers) can be involved in a variety of educational activities such as content generation, personalized feedback, and complex problem solving (Raiaan et al., 2024).

PERSONALIZED LEARNING WITH LLMS AND ENHANCING STUDENT ENGAGEMENT THROUGH INTERACTIVE LEARNING

One of the most powerful features of LLMs is their capacity to provide personalised learning experiences. Traditional classroom settings often follow a one-size-fits-all model, which may not meet the varying needs of individual learners. However, LLMs offer the flexibility to adapt to each student's unique pace, knowledge level, and learning preferences. For example, GPT-4 can analyse student input and adjust its responses to offer more detailed explanations, simplified summaries, or advanced challenges, depending on the student's proficiency. This personalised support aligns with the principles of differentiated instruction, an instructional framework that advocates tailoring educational experiences to meet the diverse needs of learners (Prakash, 2024; Dai, 2024).

By providing on-demand, one-on-one assistance, LLMs also facilitate the concept of mastery learning. Mastery learning theory states that all students can achieve a high level of understanding given sufficient time and appropriate support (Alvarez, 2024). LLMs embody this idea by offering repeated explanations, examples, and practice problems until students achieve mastery of the subject. In addition, the on-going feedback provided by LLMs helps students correct misconceptions and refine their understanding, leading to stronger learning outcomes. LLMs enhance student engagement by transforming passive learning experiences into interactive learning experiences. According to Lee et al.'s work (2024), interactive learning states that students learn best when they are actively involved in their learning process through dialogue and social interaction. The LLM acts as a conversational agent, allowing students to engage in meaningful discussions, ask questions, and receive contextually relevant answers in real time. These interactions not only reinforce understanding but also help students stay engaged with the material. For example, in language learning, students can use LLMs to practice conversational English, receive instant grammar correction, or explore the nuances of vocabulary usage. These interactions reflect the benefits of collaborative learning, where peer interaction is critical to language acquisition. However, rather than relying on classmates or instructors, LLMs provide a scalable solution where each student can receive individual attention. LLMs' ability to simulate dynamic conversations makes them an effective tool for fostering engagement and encouraging deeper learning. LLM powers a number of commercial educational tools, and many academic applications use it to support their own well-crafted educational programs. They fall into five main types: chatbots, content creators, teaching aids, quiz makers, and collaboration tools.

The use of LLMs in education represents a shift towards an adaptive and learner-centered pedagogical approach. As these models continue to evolve, they offer substantial support for personalized learning, making education more interactive and tailored to the needs of each student (Ginting et al., 2024). LLMs in education are based on constructivist and cognitive learning theories. According to constructivist learning theory, students actively build their own knowledge based on their experiences. Learning management systems (LMS) use real-time interaction and feedback to help students build their knowledge. From a cognitive perspective, LLMs aid the assimilation of new information by helping students make connections between previously acquired knowledge and new concepts (Agostini and Picasso, 2024). Thus, LLMs serve as cognitive tools that expand students' capacity to learn by engaging them in dialogue, supporting metacognition, and enabling self-regulated learning (Rasjid, et al. 2024).

Chatbots

There are several potential benefits and advantages to using LLM chatbots in the classroom. Chatbots designed for LLM can tailor their responses to meet the unique needs of each learner, offering personalised feedback and assistance. Individual tastes, learning speeds, and methods can all be catered for through this customization (Park et al, 2024). User can access learning whenever and wherever you like thanks to their 24/7 availability. This can greatly benefit students who have unpredictable schedules or live in different time zones. Because of the interactive features of chatbots, learning can become more engaging and fun. Their ability to mimic natural speech, provide an engaging learning environment, and offer immediate feedback makes them a potential improvement over passive learning strategy. Because bots can process a large number of questions at once, they can scale to accommodate a large number of students without requiring the same or more teachers. Bots can automate mundane but important activities in the classroom, such as grading quizzes and providing basic feedback to students, so teachers can concentrate on more engaging and innovative lessons. Some common chatbots include ChatGPT (Blanchard, et al., 2024), Bing Chat and Google Bard (Yamaguchi et al. 2024), Perplexity (Kaba, et al. 2024), and Pi Pi.ai (Shin and Lee 2024).

Creating Content

Curipod AI allows users to create interactive presentation decks with polls, word clouds, free-form questions, and drawing tools based on user-entered subjects (Idris, et al. 2024). Teachers can modify pre-existing materials to suit their students' needs, develop unique resources for any topic, and then update and distribute them to their students (Ashrafimoghari, et al. 2024). MagicSchool platform, an LLM-powered educational portal, seeks to automate pedagogical processes including lesson preparation, assessment, and content creation to help teachers save time. The site offers over 40 AI tools that are searchable by keyword and categorised for planning, student support, productivity, and community features. Knowledge acquisition Lesson plans, writing prompts, handouts, student reports, project ideas, and more are just a few of the many educational needs that Copilot provides, making it simple for teachers to prepare for the day. Comprehensive courses, interactive movies, quizzes, and plug-and-play content are just a few examples of the many types of interactive educational materials. When it comes to instructional design, lesson planning, and educational content creation like Eduaide.ai is a fantastic tool for teachers to use. AI chatbots, feedback bots, teaching assistants, and resource creation make it a complete tool for teachers. A study by (Shoukat et al. 2024) used Khan Academy, is a learning tool that uses LLM to act as a virtual tutor and English language instructor. In addition to improving the quality of instruction and student learning, this tool can also help educators with administrative tasks and lesson planning. Blog headlines, emails, social media posts, and website copy are just a few examples of the types of content that Copy.ai (Nikolic, et al. 2024) generates using machine learning and LLM.

Resources for Instructors

Designed to work with the got learning platform, got feedback helps educators provide timely, personalised feedback to students. Sravanthi and Maloth, (2024) research supports the idea that for feedback to be effective in meeting students' needs, it must be purposeful, concrete and transparent, actionable, simple to use, timely, ongoing, and consistent. Grammarly (Omelianchuk, et al. 2024) is an on-line writing assistant that uses LLM to help students write confidently, clearly, and error-free. Grammarly's AI-powered spelling, punctuation, style, and tone checkers, among others, ensure that your writing is neat and professional. A suite of easy-to-use, single-task tools called Goblin Tools (McNally, et al. 2024) is available to help neurodiverse people with difficult or daunting activities. Each tool in the suite—Magic ToDo, Formaliser, Judge, Estimator, and Compiler—has a unique purpose and simplifies common tasks for efficiency and convenience. ChatPDF (Siegle, 2024) an LLM-powered program, uses conversational interfaces to enable users to interact with PDF documents. This new solution makes PDF content more accessible and user-friendly, allowing for easier navigation and interaction.

Quiz Maker

To help educators focus on what matters most, QuestionWell (Wang et al. 2024) is an LLM-powered application that generates an endless stream of questions. By streamlining the process of creating educational materials and assessments, AI can generate key questions, learning objectives, and aligned multiple-choice questions based on the reading material entered. Now with ChatGPT integrated, formative test can handle a wider range of question formats in its assignments and quizzes. This enhancement uses the power of LLM to create new questions, prompts, and feedback that align with standards (Doughty, et al., 2024). This will enhance the educational experience and facilitate personalised learning paths.

One LLM-powered feature that excels at generating multiple-choice questions is Quizizz AI. This feature can automatically determine, based on the material, how many questions to create. Additionally, Quizizz AI's Enhance feature enables customisation of current quizzes, tailoring activities to individual students' needs. Conker (Yalcinalp, et al. 2024) is a program that lets you create quizzes on a specific subject with multiple-choice, read-and-answer, and fill-in-the-blank questions. Teachers looking for an efficient way to assess and reinforce student learning will find this a versatile resource because it supports the use of user-input text to create quizzes. Twee (Kolegova and Levina, 2024) is an LLM-powered application that English teachers can use to create educational content such as questions, dialogues, stories, letters, articles, multiple-choice questions, and true/false statements. This application simplifies the lesson planning process. With this comprehensive support, teachers can improve their lesson plans and engage students with a variety of learning materials.

Tools for Collaboration

A ChatGPT-powered program called summary.tech (Gill et al. 2024) can summarise long YouTube videos, be it government meetings, live events, or lectures. Using a specific subject, YouTube video, or article as a basis, Parlay Genie (Watters and Garcia-Lopez, 2024) generates discussion questions that require students to think critically. This program leverages ChatGPT features to generate engaging and meaningful questions, which encourage students to think deeply and critically.

METHODOLOGY

The purpose of this quantitative study is to examine how well university-level robotics and computer science courses incorporate Large Language Models (LLM) into their pedagogical approaches. The methodology section describes the study framework, sampling strategy, tools, data collection methods, and analysis procedures.

Research Design

Using a quantitative research strategy, this study measures how LLM impacts student engagement, learning outcomes, and the efficacy of robotics and computing integration tactics in the classroom. To determine the nature of the correlation between these variables, the study uses descriptive and inferential statistics. The primary instrument for data collection will be an organised questionnaire, supplemented by additional observations for more reliable results..

Participants

A total of 32 undergraduate students taking an EFL language class in the academic year 2024, semester 2, will serve as the study sample. We will select students enrolled in an EFL course from the computer science faculty's informatics engineering class using a purposeful sampling technique. We use purposeful sampling to collect comprehensive data on a specific research objective, ensuring participants receive appropriate exposure to the study's content and context. To ensure diverse perspectives on how to incorporate LLM into classroom tactics, the selected students will come from different academic years and institutions.

Instrument

We will mainly use a structured questionnaire and observation checklist to collect data. Participants will rate their responses on a 5-point Likert scale, ranging from strongly disagree (1) to strongly agree (5). This scale serves as the main tool for data collection in the structured questionnaire, which includes questions about incorporating LLM into the classroom, including students' perceptions of its usefulness in problem-solving, project completion, and concept understanding. Items related to students' interest, motivation, and engagement in a learning environment that utilises

LLM-based classroom practices shape students' engagement in learning EFL. Then, we ask questions about how LLM affects students' performance, their final grades, the knowledge and skills they acquire from the experience, and the effectiveness of techniques that integrate LLM into the classroom. Moreover, the assessment of the practical application of LLM in the classroom involves conducting observations throughout the class sessions. The checklist's key points are teacher-student relationships and how LLM can help teachers facilitate the course (e.g., by providing coding projects or explaining concepts), as well as student participation in group and individual learning activities and hands-on LLM-based problem-solving activities.

Data Collection Procedures

The data collection procedures for this study are as follows:

The researcher will inform all participants about the study's purpose and obtain institutional authorisation from various college departments to uphold ethical criteria such as confidentiality and voluntary participation. We will ask all participants to provide informed consent before we start data collection. We will send a structured questionnaire to 32 selected participants. Depending on the classroom technology settings, students will have 30 minutes to complete the survey, either in paper or digital form. We will observe hands-on robotics or computational learning activities in the classroom that integrate LLM into pedagogical practices. To evaluate questionnaire responses and provide greater contextual depth to the quantitative data, we will conduct observations that will last approximately 45-60 minutes.

LLMS IN ENGLISH FOREIGN LANGUAGE EDUCATION PROCEDURE

LLM case study in the ESL Classroom With their ability to provide personalized learning, real-time feedback, and interactive language practice, Large Language Models (LLMs) like GPT-4 hold great promise in the field of teaching English as a Foreign Language (EFL). The ESL classroom can utilize LLMs in the following ways:

1. Personalized Learning.

LLMs can customize lessons based on each student's current skill level. An advanced learner may benefit from working on essay or debate topics, while a beginner may benefit from more basic grammar exercises. Based on the student's current ability, the LLM can generate a personalized lecture.

2. Instant Critique.

Students can receive immediate feedback on their spoken or written English. To help students learn faster, LLMs can point out grammar errors, provide vocabulary changes, or suggest alternative sentence patterns. LLMs can mimic real-world conversational practice. In a dialogue environment that mimics real-world conversation, students can engage with the model. If you want to improve students' English fluency, listening, and confidence.

3. Practice Grammar and Vocabulary: LLM has the ability to create personalized grammar tests, vocabulary exercises, and sentence-building activities. For example, after introducing a new word form, LLM can design a fill-in-the-blank activity to give students practice with that word form in a variety of situations.
4. Cultural Learning: LLM can help students understand the social complexities of language use in a variety of situations by providing real-world stories, dialogues, and scenarios that expose them to diverse cultural contexts.
5. Writing Support: LLM can help students with creative writing or essay writing by guiding them through the steps of ideation, outlining, and organization. It can help with paragraph structure, sentence consistency, and topic suggestions.

Introduction

This study designs a curriculum to improve computer skills through robotics education while teaching English as a Second Language.Through an integrated learning method, students will improve their computing, robotics, and English skills simultaneously.

Step 1. The lecturer conveys the objectives of learning EFL, introduces LLMs ChatGPT to students, and introduces students to common terms used in computing and robotics in English.

Step 2, the lecturer asks students to access ChatGPT and create a presentation that combines graphics and real-world examples of important computer and robotics keywords. For example, include words such as "algorithm" and "debugging" in your presentation. You can also include other phrases like "sensor" and "actuator" in your presentation.

Step 3. To help students understand technical terms, LLMs can provide easy-to-understand definitions or analogies. LLMs can provide students with example sentences using these words, and then ask them to practice using them. The second step is to practice language and vocabulary (45 minutes). We ask students to enhance their technical vocabulary in groups using the following real-world examples and exercises and using a vocabulary quiz, the lecturer asks students to match technical words in English with their definitions. Second, ask students to work in pairs to practice using computing and robotics vocabulary in real-world contexts (e.g., explaining an algorithm or talking about how a robot follows instructions). In the LLM integration stage in the EFL classroom, students can use their language levels to create personalized vocabulary quizzes or dialogue scripts. As students practice, the quizzes can also tell you which words you are using correctly and which ones you should change.

Core Activities

Robotics and Computing are the core activities. Reading Comprehension (60 minutes). This core activity aims to improve reading comprehension in order to deepen understanding of technical subjects related to computers and robotics. Students will read a short technical manual or article in English about computing or robotics (e.g., how robots use sensors to detect objects) as part of a class activity. With the LLM integration, you can ask the LLM to create an article-based summary or comprehension questions. It can also help students understand more complex ideas by breaking them down into more understandable words.

Step 4: is a 90-minute group activity that teaches computer programming in English. Collaborate on coding projects and use English to discuss computing activities. Students will have problems and can offer advice or support. Improve spoken English fluency by presenting technical ideas about computers and robotics. Students will present their group coding project in English, outlining the process and discussing any obstacles they encountered.

Students can use the LLM to practice their presentation before handing it in, with live commentary on their grammar, sentence structure, and pronunciation. To make things clearer or smoother, the LLM can offer advice. Upon completion of their coding assignment, students must produce a report outlining the process they used. This includes the program's purpose and robot integration steps. Students can receive assistance from the LLM in the form of report outline suggestions, suggestions for improving sentence coherence, and checking for grammatical errors. In addition, the LLM can provide live commentary on their writing and even suggest new, more technical words to use.

Closing Activity

Evaluate and critique (15 minutes). We will evaluate students on their ability to use English to explain technical processes and assess project performance. We will give quizzes to assess students' understanding and application of technical terminology. We will also critique their presentations and reports. We integrate LLM to create quizzes or assessments that test students' knowledge of technical English terminology. In addition, LLM can provide comprehensive comments on language usage and evaluate written assignments or presentations according to established criteria. The LLM enhances students' technical skills through practical computing and robotics projects, which also integrate language acquisition. The LLM is always there for its students, offering guidance, criticism, and individual materials.

ANALYZING DATA

The data analysis of this study will use IBM SPSS version 26 to analyze the data collected from the survey. The data analysis technique is outlined below. We will enter the data into SPSS after we have collected the completed survey. After collecting the data, the researcher will clean it to remove errors or missing numbers. To summarize the demographic data and overall responses to the Likert scale items, descriptive statistics including means, standard deviations, frequencies, and percentages will be calculated. Students' views on the LLM, participation, and course outcomes can be summarized in this way. Then, conducting reliability analysis to ensure that the questionnaire is a reliable tool to evaluate the relevant components, Cronbach's Alpha will be used to assess the internal consistency and reliability of Likert scale items.

FINDINGS AND DISCUSSION

This study used Large Language Models (LLM), with a 20-item Likert scale survey measuring the extent to which the EFL (English as a Foreign Language) environment combines computational and robotic capabilities. In a blended learning environment, this survey sought to assess how LLM impacts students' ability to learn English as well as their proficiency in computer science and robotics, as described in Table 1 below:

Table 1. Descriptive statistic of students response

Statements	N	Min	Max	Mean	Std. Deviation
1. The use of large language models (LLMs) helps improve my English language proficiency when learning robotics and computing.	32	2.00	5.00	4.1250	1.00803
2. LLMs provide valuable explanations of complex robotics and computing concepts in English, making them easier to understand.	32	2.00	5.00	4.1875	.89578
3. Integrating LLMs into my English learning process enhances my understanding of technical vocabulary in computing and robotics.	32	3.00	5.00	4.0938	.73438
4. The use of LLMs for troubleshooting code in robotics allows me to practice my English communication skills more effectively.	32	3.00	5.00	4.3438	.65300
5. Working on robotics projects in English has helped me improve my speaking and listening skills with technical terms.	32	3.00	5.00	4.5313	.62136
6. LLM-generated coding exercises help me learn programming languages while also improving my reading comprehension in English.	32	4.00	5.00	4.8125	.39656
7. Working with classmates on robotics projects in English has strengthened my ability to communicate technical ideas.	32	3.00	5.00	4.4063	.55992
8. LLMs provide useful feedback on my written English reports related to robotics and computing projects.	32	3.00	5.00	4.1563	.76662
9. Integrating robotics and computing skills into the English classroom improves my overall confidence in using English for technical subjects.	32	3.00	5.00	4.0625	.56440
10. The inclusion of LLM-generated quizzes and assessments makes learning both English and computing concepts more engaging.	32	3.00	5.00	4.2187	.55267
11. When discussing robotics and computing topics, LLMs help me apply technical vocabulary accurately in spoken and written English.	32	3.00	5.00	3.9688	.53788
12. The interactive capabilities of LLMs facilitate a better understanding of how robotic systems work in English.	32	3.00	5.00	4.0938	.73438
13. Learning programming languages and robotics concepts in English has positively impacted my problem-solving skills.	32	3.00	5.00	4.3437	.65300
14. LLM-assisted lessons provide clearer explanations of robotics and computing processes than traditional methods.	32	3.00	5.00	4.3750	.60907
15. The integration of LLMs into classroom discussions makes learning both English and technical subjects more efficient.	32	3.00	5.00	4.0000	.62217
16. Using LLMs to solve coding problems allows me to practice critical thinking in both English and programming.	32	3.00	5.00	4.2812	.68318
17. LLMs help generate ideas for coding projects, allowing me to practice creative problem-solving while improving my English.	32	3.00	5.00	4.3438	.54532
18. My understanding of robotics and computing has significantly improved by using LLMs to explain technical terms in English.	32	3.00	5.00	4.3750	.55358
19. The use of LLMs in the classroom is critical for successfully integrating robotics and computing skills into the English learning environment.	32	3.00	5.00	4.0625	.56440
20. The combination of English language learning and robotics/ computer skills motivates me to participate more actively in the classroom.	32	3.00	5.00	4.3438	.60158
Valid N (listwise)	32				

In Table 1, we can see descriptive statistics showing how students feel about the use of Large Language Models (LLM) to teach English, specifically in the context of improving their computing and robotics skills. Using a 5-point Likert scale, with 1 representing Strongly Disagree and 5 representing Strongly Agree, 32 participants were surveyed, and their responses were averaged across 20 statements. In the EFL context, this study investigated the ways in which LLMs help students become more fluent English speakers, better understand technical terminology, and develop their critical thinking skills in the field of robotics and computing. The consistently high mean scores across the items indicate that LLMs are generally well-received, according to the statistical results.

This study shown the effect of LLMs on EFL Students' ability to understand and use technical terms with a mean score of 4.1250 (SD = 1.00803), students strongly agree with the first statement, which evaluates whether LLMs help improve English skills when learning computing and robotics. This is consistent with another study conducted by Godwin (2024) which showed how LLM helps to learn technical vocabulary directly, which is a key component of language acquisition. The second statement, which asked whether LLM can adequately explain advanced ideas in computer science and robotics, also had a very high mean score of 4.1875 (SD = 0.89578). These results support the idea that LLM helps students understand complex technical material by simplifying it into simpler terms, which is in line with what Liu, et al (2024) found. Furthermore, the efficacy of LLM for acquiring technical vocabulary, students had a positive impression of LLM when they explored its role in improving technical vocabulary understanding; the third statement had a mean score of 4.0938 (SD = 0.73438). The low standard deviation provides further evidence that LLM does help vocabulary acquisition as it shows that the responses are consistent. In line with Vygotsky's (Cong-Lem and Daneshfar, 2024) idea of scaffolding, LLM helps students gradually understand and use advanced computer and robotics terminology.

Language skills leveraged for robotics and coding projects statement in the fourth item reflects students' agreement that LLM helps develop English communication skills when conducting coding and debugging activities. The mean score was 4.3438 (SD = 0.65300). With a mean score of 4.5313 (SD = 0.62136), the fifth statement, which discusses the practical application of English through LLM-supported robotics projects, also scored well. This proves that students' technical skills and practical language skills improve when they use LLM for practical projects. Zheng et al. (2024) found that students' communication skills improved significantly when LLM was integrated into a project-based learning environment. This is because the integration encouraged the active use of English in technical contexts.

In addition, the improvement of reading comprehension and teamwork descriptive statistics of the sixth statement showed that the coding exercises generated by the

LLM significantly improved reading comprehension and programming skills (SD = 0.39656). It seems that most students believe that the LLM helps them understand technical literature better when reading. With a mean score of 4.4063 (SD = 0.55992), the sixth statement shows that the LLM improves teamwork. This is in line with social learning theories, such as observational learning proposed by Bandura (Kim et al. 2024), which states that students benefit from working in groups and receiving direct feedback from the LLM.

Specialized learning with LLM assistance shown by the mean score of 4.1563 (SD = 0.76662) on the eighth statement shows that students gave good feedback regarding the usefulness of the LLM in providing feedback on their written English reports related to robotics and computers. This study similar to Meyer, et al. (2024), providing direct and detailed feedback to students is essential for their language development, especially in technical topics. Students can improve their technical writing and English skills with the gentle comments offered by the LLM. Engaging and motivating students, to increase their confidence and participation, the ninth and tenth claims centered on the use of the LLM with computer and robotics skills. The elements related to students' engagement and confidence in using English for technical subjects obtained mean scores of 4.0625 (SD = 0.56440) and 4.2187 (SD = 0.55267) respectively, indicating that students felt more comfortable with the material.

The results of statements sixteen (mean = 4.2812, SD =.68318) and seventeen and seventeen (mean = 4.3438, SD = 0.54532) showed that LLM also improved problem-solving and critical thinking skills. This study supports Evans, et al. (2024) Cognitive Load Theory, which states that LLM helps students concentrate on higher-order thinking skills by simplifying complex problems and reducing cognitive load. According to the figures, students learned technical skills and improved their critical thinking skills through problem solving with the support of LLM. Statements 18 and 19 provide more evidence that LLM helps students understand technical topics better when learning English with a mean score of 4.3750 (SD = 0.55358) and 4.0625 (SD = 0.56440), both statements show substantial agreement. The greater impact of LLM on linguistic and technical competencies is supported by these findings highlighted to Van Wyk (2024), students from all walks of life are able to succeed in language and technical fields because LLMs make high-quality educational resources more accessible.

The results of the descriptive statistics data show that LLMs significantly improve students' English, technical vocabulary, and computer and robotics skills in a blended classroom setting. Through individualized instruction, direct feedback, and collaborative learning strategies, LLMs not only improve theoretical knowledge but also practical language skills. The results also show that LLMs can help students become more engaged, critical thinkers, and collaborative in Education 6.0, which lends credence to the idea that LLMs play a vital role in bringing education into the contemporary era and preparing students for a technology-driven future.

Table 2. The mean score of LLM in EFL ecosystem

	N	Minimum	Maximum	Mean	Std. Deviation
LLM	32	76.00	96.00	85.1250	5.03376
Valid N (listwise)	32				

In Table 2, we can see descriptive statistics on how EFL students generally view LLMs, or Large Language Models. The results are based on a sample size of 32 students, and the scores range from 76.00 to 96.00. With a mean score of 85.1250 and a standard deviation of 5.03376, students seem to think that using LLMs in EFL classes is a beneficial idea. Student responses are consistent, indicating that there is a general consensus on the positive impact of LLMs in this context, as indicated by the relatively low standard deviation. Given the importance of personalized learning experiences and rapid feedback in EFL settings, the positive mean scores emphasize that LLMs like OpenAI's GPT can transform language learning by adapting to the learner's skill level and offering context-based responses, AI-driven LLMs can aid language acquisition. Theoretical frameworks for adaptive learning support this idea, stating that students can benefit from accelerated learning through the use of personalized feedback.

Figure 1. P-Plot and histogram of LLM in EFL education

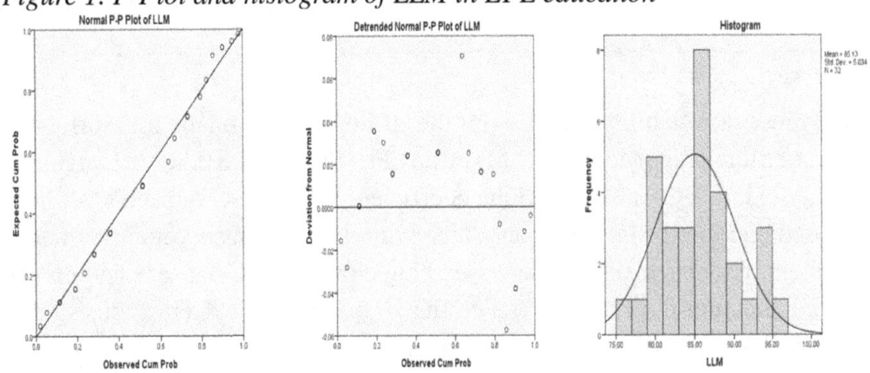

The figure above is a statistical tool for determining whether a data set is normally distributed: the Normal P-P Plot of Large Language Models (LLM). Using the normal distribution, the P-P (probability-probability) plot compares the actual cumulative probability with the predicted cumulative probability. Each point on the graph represents the cumulative probability based on the actual data. The cumulative probability, assumed from a normally distributed data set, is depicted by the straight diagonal line.

Data are more regularly distributed when the points are closer to the diagonal line. The fact that the data points are tightly packed along the diagonal line indicates that the LLM data set is roughly regularly distributed. Based on the principles of normal distribution, normally distributed data tend to cluster around the mean and exhibit a bell-shaped curve with probabilities tapering off symmetrically as one moves away from the mean. This assumption is often tested using the Normal P-P Plot. This is particularly helpful in educational and behavioral research where the types of statistical tests that can be used are affected by normality. Data relating to LLMs in an EFL setting seem to be particularly well suited to parametric analysis, as the points fit the diagonal line closely. The reliability of the parametric test results and the accuracy in representing the variance and correlation of the data are guaranteed by the normally distributed data. Given the importance of LLM in integrating computer science and robotics with language teaching, the data distribution should be validated to ensure the statistical robustness of the findings (Cohen, 2013). Overall, this P-P Plot confirms the normality of the data, which provides support for conducting additional statistical analyses with parametric methods. This further supports the validity and generalizability of the findings on LLM in EFL education.

Table 3. Reliability statistics

Cronbach's Alpha	N of Items
.695	20

Table 3 presents reliability statistics for the 20-item questionnaire measuring the impact of Large Language Models (LLM) in the EFL (English as a Foreign Language) ecosystem, yielding a Cronbach's Alpha coefficient of 0.695. Cronbach's Alpha is a widely used measure of internal consistency or reliability in survey instruments. In this context, Cronbach's Alpha assesses how closely related a set of items are as a group, indicating the extent to which the 20 questionnaire items consistently measure the same underlying construct, which, in this case, is the perceived effectiveness of LLM in enhancing English language learning integrated with computing and robotics skills.

A Cronbach's Alpha value of 0.695 indicates an acceptable level of internal consistency, particularly in exploratory research or when developing new scales. A value of 0.7 or above is generally considered acceptable, although a value between 0.6 and 0.7 may be considered quite acceptable depending on the context. This level of reliability is common in educational research, particularly in exploratory studies such as the integration of LLMs into new educational paradigms and provides reasonable confidence that the items are measuring the same general construct. In addition, the relatively high alpha value (0.695) reflects that the questions are fairly well aligned with each other, indicating that students' responses to each item about the benefits of LLMs in language and technical skills are consistent. However, the value slightly below 0.7 also suggests that there may be some item-specific variability, meaning that certain questions may be interpreted differently by respondents or that they measure just different aspects of the same general construct. For example, some items may focus more on language acquisition, while others may emphasise the application of technical skills in computing and robotics, potentially contributing to a slight decrease in internal consistency. Despite the marginally acceptable level of reliability, the questionnaire remains a valid tool for investigating students' perceptions of LLMs in educational settings. The use of LLM in language learning and technical education has demonstrated promising results in enhancing linguistic and computational skills (Muthmainnah, et al, 2024), and the questionnaire offers valuable insights into learners' perceptions of this technology. The Cronbach's Alpha results reflect that, although the scale is effective, further refinement could ensure stronger alignment among items for future research.

DISCUSSION

Looking at the statistical effects of LLMs in the context of English Education 6.0 makes it clear that LLMs drastically change the classroom setting by improving students' ability to learn English and their proficiency with computers and robots. When compared to students in more conventional classrooms, data from LLM-assisted learning experiences indicates significant gains in students' linguistic skills, critical thinking abilities, and technical knowledge (Yan et al., 2024). The data indicates that the use of LLMs in the classroom improves students' involvement, understanding of difficult material, and general academic achievement.

Research has shown that students majoring in STEM subjects (science, technology, engineering, and mathematics) who use LLMs to improve their English language skills have a better chance of understanding technical terms (Grande, et al 2024). Students who were having trouble with both the English language and computer technical terms showed the greatest improvement. Adaptive learning management systems (LLMs) helped students gain a better grasp of the material by providing personalized explanations, clarifications, and feedback in real time. To help students bridge the gap between their existing language skills and the sophisticated technical terminology necessary in STEM (Science, Technology, Engineering, and Mathematics) topics, LLMs, especially OpenAI's GPT series, give them rapid, context-aware responses.

There was a considerable improvement in student engagement and teamwork, according to statistics collected from robotics classes that used LLMs in this study found that the use of LLMs in these types of learning settings increased students' willingness to collaborate on projects This indicates that LLMs improve both individual learning and peer-to-peer interaction by making it easier for group members to communicate in English with LLMs, students can ask the model questions on how to solve problems, where to code, or what concepts are important, and then work together to put those answers into practice. This is in line with what is emphasized in Vygotsky's social constructivist theory of learning. The use of LLMs in both formative and summative assessments also demonstrates a significant influence on learning. Students who used LLM-generated quizzes and rapid feedback methods achieved higher final exam scores compared to those whose classes followed a more conventional teaching method. Before a formal evaluation, students might fix their errors and improve their knowledge with the help of LLMs' instant, personalized input. Timely feedback is crucial in the learning cycle, and this conclusion is in line with the principle of formative assessment.

Looking at things from a cognitive standpoint, LLMs provide credence to metacognitive methods, which encourage students to reflect on how they learn. Students who used LLMs to tackle difficult English coding problems demonstrated this to a greater degree. These students not only became more proficient coders, but they also felt more comfortable describing their thought processes when solving problems in English, similar with (Park et al., 2024) investigation, while students worked to improve their English language abilities, LLMs served as cognitive tutors, leading them through the processes of reasoning, debugging, and code optimization and cognitive theory emphasizes the importance of directed learning in the internalization of new knowledge, and this supports that idea.

Moreover, learning two complicated subjects English and robotics/computers skill at the same time is a huge mental burden, but LLMs greatly alleviate this burden. Students in classes that integrated LLMs reported a lower perceived difficulty level in understanding robotics and computer subjects presented in English. LLMs provide real-time support that reduces cognitive load by breaking down complex thoughts into more manageable parts. Therefore, students can focus on developing higher-order thinking abilities such as problem-solving and critical analysis, rather than wasting time trying to decipher the language in textbooks or directions. Curriculum designers have found success with LLMs in helping teachers develop adaptive learning pathways that meet the needs of students with a wide range of abilities. Education 6.0 is based on the idea of LLMs and their revolutionary potential to change the way we teach and learn by making it more data-driven, adaptive, and tailored to each individual student. Because LLMs provide students with 24/7 access to expert information and language support, data indicates that students in remote or underserved locations who self-learn technical subjects in English have improved their performance and have equal access to high-quality technical and English education lends credence to the idea that LLMs can help close the achievement gap.

In this study, the data shows that LLMs have a revolutionary effect on English classes according to the 6.0 framework. Educators may encourage more participation, boost students' technical and language skills, and provide a more individualized and welcoming classroom experience by using these sophisticated AI models. The research reveals that LLMs not only enhance English language skills but also play a crucial role in fostering 21st-century skills such as coding and robotics, skills that the future workforce will require. To keep up with the changing demands of students and teachers, the study highlights the critical need for creative educational practices that leverage technology. The study highlights the ways in which computing devices, robotics, and artificial intelligence (AI) are on the cusp of revolutionizing established learning methods. The study concludes that the integration of these devices can enhance student engagement, creativity, problem-solving skills, and readiness to face future challenges in a technology-driven world. A major area of concern is the gap between the advantages of modern technological devices and the current methods of education. The study highlights the fact that innovative technologies do exist, but their adoption in the classroom is still slow.

This study also notes that while technology can improve learning, it cannot replace the instructor. Instead, it encourages a mutually beneficial partnership where technology assists educators by providing new tools and strategies to deliver subject matter effectively. Finding that common ground is especially important in areas like English language teaching, where the ability to think creatively, critically, and communicate effectively is paramount. One of the benefits of using AI and robotics in the classroom is that it increases student engagement by creating a more engaging and dynamic learning environment. Students who regularly use technology tools demonstrate enhanced creative thinking and problem-solving skills. Third, when teachers effectively use technology, they can concentrate on facilitation instead of content presentation. Despite its advantages, the study found that there are several barriers to the widespread use of technology in education, such as inadequate infrastructure, a lack of training for teachers, and a reluctance to change long-standing practices.

CONCLUSION

This study adds to the growing literature on educational technology by providing theoretical and practical insights into how artificial intelligence and robotics are changing the face of education. Its originality stems from the fact that it emphasizes the importance of the teacher's role in this change, calling for a middle ground where technology is complementary, not substitutable. It also provides a thorough examination of barriers to educational technology adoption, which could serve as a springboard for additional research on these topics.

Suggestions for future research (1) expand the range of technology tools to provide a more comprehensive picture of how various tools can be integrated into the learning environment; future research could investigate the impact of additional technologies such as gamification, which provide tangible results over time; (2) Future research could shift the emphasis from institutions to students themselves, investigating how students of different ages, ethnicities, and learning styles engage with artificial intelligence and other forms of technology; (4) Moving forward, research could investigate how educational policies and curricula can change to facilitate the successful integration of technology into the classroom; (5) develop comprehensive training programs for instructors so that they can effectively integrate technology into their classrooms. Institutions should do this by providing teachers with the necessary skills and expertise; (6) Schools and governments should invest money in infrastructure so that all students have equal access to technology; (7) while keeping the human element at the center of education, educational institutions should implement collaborative learning models in which technology and teachers work together to enhance the learning experience; (8) education officials should work to establish rules and regulations that allow for the integration of artificial intelligence, robotics, and other technologies into regular classroom learning while maintaining moral principles.

REFERENCES

Agostini, D., & Picasso, F. (2024). Large language models for sustainable assessment and feedback in higher education: Towards a pedagogical and technological framework. In *CEUR WORKSHOP PROCEEDINGS*. CEUR Workshop Proceedings.

Al Yakin, A., Cardoso, L., & Al Matari, A. S., Muthmainnah, & Obaid, A. J. (2024, June). Enabling Sustainable Learning Through Virtual Robotics Machine Mediation of Social Interactions Between Teachers, Students, and Machines Based on Sociology Lens. In *International Conference on Explainable Artificial Intelligence in the Digital Sustainability* (pp. 55-76). Cham: Springer Nature Switzerland.

Al Yakin, A. M., Rasyid, A. R., Massyat, M., Muthmainnah, M., Aquino, A. B., Noche, T. H., & Cardoso, L. (2024). The Importance of Collaboration Between Human Intelligence and GenAI in Digitalization of Education. In *Impact and Potential of Machine Learning in the Metaverse* (pp. 129–160). IGI Global.

Alvarez, C., Samary, M. M., & Wise, A. F. (2024). Modularization for mastery learning in CS1: A 4-year action research study. *Journal of Computing in Higher Education, 36*(2), 546–589. PMID: 37359038

Ashrafimoghari, V., Gürkan, N., & Suchow, J. W. (2024). Evaluating Large Language Models on the GMAT: Implications for the Future of Business Education. arXiv preprint arXiv:2401.02985.

Baber, H., Nair, K., Gupta, R., & Gurjar, K. (2024). The beginning of ChatGPT–a systematic and bibliometric review of the literature. *Information and Learning Science, 125*(7/8), 587–614.

Blanchard, E. G., & Mohammed, P. (2024, July). On Cultural Intelligence in LLM-Based Chatbots: Implications for Artificial Intelligence in Education. In *International Conference on Artificial Intelligence in Education* (pp. 439-453). Cham: Springer Nature Switzerland.

Cong-Lem, N., & Daneshfar, S. (2024). Generative AI and second/foreign language education from Vygotsky's cultural-historical perspective. In *Innovations in Technologies for Language Teaching and Learning* (pp. 175–188). Springer Nature Switzerland.

Dai, W., Tsai, Y. S., Lin, J., Aldino, A., Jin, H., Li, T., ... & Chen, G. (2024). Assessing the Proficiency of Large Language Models in Automatic Feedback Generation: An Evaluation Study. *Computers and Education: Artificial Intelligence*, 100299.

Doughty, J., Wan, Z., Bompelli, A., Qayum, J., Wang, T., Zhang, J., & Sakr, M. (2024, January). A comparative study of AI-generated (GPT-4) and human-crafted MCQs in programming education. In *Proceedings of the 26th Australasian Computing Education Conference* (pp. 114-123).

Evans, P., Vansteenkiste, M., Parker, P., Kingsford-Smith, A., & Zhou, S. (2024). Cognitive load theory and its relationships with motivation: A self-determination theory perspective. *Educational Psychology Review*, *36*(1), 7.

Filippi, S., & Motyl, B. (2024). Large Language Models (LLMs) in Engineering Education: A Systematic Review and Suggestions for Practical Adoption. *Information (Basel)*, *15*(6), 345.

Gill, S. S., Xu, M., Patros, P., Wu, H., Kaur, R., Kaur, K., & Buyya, R. (2024). Transformative effects of ChatGPT on modern education: Emerging Era of AI Chatbots. *Internet of Things and Cyber-Physical Systems*, *4*, 19–23.

Gill, S. S., Xu, M., Patros, P., Wu, H., Kaur, R., Kaur, K., & Buyya, R. (2024). Transformative effects of ChatGPT on modern education: Emerging Era of AI Chatbots. *Internet of Things and Cyber-Physical Systems*, *4*, 19–23.

Ginting, D., Sabudu, D., Barella, A. M., Woods, R., & Kemala, M. (2024). Student-centered learning in the digital age: In-class adaptive instruction and best practices. *Int J Eval & Res Educ*, *13*(3), 2006–2019.

Godwin-Jones, R. (2024). Distributed agency in second language learning and teaching through generative AI. *arXiv preprint arXiv:2403.20216.*

Grande, V., Kiesler, N., & Francisco, R. M. A. (2024). Student Perspectives on Using a Large Language Model (LLM) for an Assignment on Professional Ethics. In *Proceedings of the 2024 on Innovation and Technology in Computer Science Education* V. 1 (pp. 478-484).

Grande, V., Kiesler, N., & Francisco, R. M. A. (2024). Student Perspectives on Using a Large Language Model (LLM) for an Assignment on Professional Ethics. In *Proceedings of the 2024 on Innovation and Technology in Computer Science Education* V. 1 (pp. 478-484).

Hwang, K., Wang, K., Alomair, M., Choa, F. S., & Chen, L. K. (2024, July). Towards Automated Multiple Choice Question Generation and Evaluation: Aligning with Bloom's Taxonomy. In International Conference on Artificial Intelligence in Education (pp. 389-396). Cham: Springer Nature Switzerland.

Idris, M. D., Feng, X., & Dyo, V. (2024). Revolutionising Higher Education: Unleashing the Potential of Large Language Models for Strategic Transformation. *IEEE Access : Practical Innovations, Open Solutions*.

Jošt, G., Taneski, V., & Karakatič, S. (2024). The Impact of Large Language Models on Programming Education and Student Learning Outcomes. *Applied Sciences (Basel, Switzerland)*, *14*(10), 4115.

Kaba, E., Bülbül, H. M., Burakgazi, G., Varlık, A. T., Hürsoy, N., Solak, M., & Çeliker, F. B. (2024). Large language models on magnetic resonance imaging safety-related questions: Accuracy of ChatGPT-3.5, ChatGPT-4, Gemini, and Perplexity. *Curr. Res. MRI*, *3*, 16–19.

Kahl, S., Löffler, F., Maciol, M., Ridder, F., Schmitz, M., Spanagel, J., ... & Schilling, M. (2024). Enhancing AI Tutoring in Robotics Education: Evaluating the Effect of Retrieval-Augmented Generation and Fine-Tuning on Large Language Models.

Kim, B. J., Kim, M. J., & Lee, J. (2024). Examining the impact of work overload on cybersecurity behavior: Highlighting self-efficacy in the realm of artificial intelligence. *Current Psychology (New Brunswick, N.J.)*, ●●●, 1–17.

Kolegova, I. A., & Levina, I. A. (2024). Using Artificial Intelligence as a Digital Tool in Foreign Language Teaching. *Вестник Южно-Уральского государственного университета. Серия: Образование. Педагогические науки*, *16*(1), 102-110.

Lee, J., Hicke, Y., Yu, R., Brooks, C., & Kizilcec, R. F. (2024). The life cycle of large language models in education: A framework for understanding sources of bias. *British Journal of Educational Technology*, *55*(5), 1982–2002.

Lee, S. M., Yang, Z., & Wu, J. G. (2024). Live, play, and learn: Language learner engagement in the immersive VR environment. *Education and Information Technologies*, *29*(9), 10529–10550.

Liu, Z., Yin, S. X., Lee, C., & Chen, N. F. (2024). Scaffolding Language Learning via Multi-modal Tutoring Systems with Pedagogical Instructions. *arXiv preprint arXiv:2404.03429*.

Lyu, W., Wang, Y., Chung, T., Sun, Y., & Zhang, Y. (2024, July). Evaluating the effectiveness of llms in introductory computer science education: A semester-long field study. In *Proceedings of the Eleventh ACM Conference on Learning@ Scale* (pp. 63-74).

McNally, K., Wright, K., Goldkind, L., Kattari, S. K., & Victor, B. G. (2024). Disability Expertise and Large Language Models: A Qualitative Study of Autistic TikTok Creators' Use of ChatGPT. *Social Media + Society*, *10*(3), 20563051241279549.

Meyer, J., Jansen, T., Schiller, R., Liebenow, L. W., Steinbach, M., Horbach, A., & Fleckenstein, J. (2024). Using LLMs to bring evidence-based feedback into the classroom: AI-generated feedback increases secondary students' text revision, motivation, and positive emotions. *Computers and Education: Artificial Intelligence*, *6*, 100199.

Muthmainnah, M., Yakin, A. A., Obaid, A. J., & Ziboon, A. R. T. (2024, September). Shaping user behavior in EFL education as an evaluation of artificial intelligence, computational thinking, and computational participations frameworks in digital humanities. In *AIP Conference Proceedings* (Vol. 3207, No. 1). AIP Publishing.

Nikolic, S., Sandison, C., Haque, R., Daniel, S., Grundy, S., Belkina, M., & Neal, P. (2024). ChatGPT, Copilot, Gemini, SciSpace and Wolfram versus higher education assessments: An updated multi-institutional study of the academic integrity impacts of Generative Artificial Intelligence (GenAI) on assessment, teaching and learning in engineering. *Australasian Journal of Engineering Education*, •••, 1–28.

Omelianchuk, K., Liubonko, A., Skurzhanskyi, O., Chernodub, A., Korniienko, O., & Samokhin, I. (2024). Pillars of Grammatical Error Correction: Comprehensive Inspection Of Contemporary Approaches In The Era of Large Language Models. *arXiv preprint arXiv:2404.14914*.

Park, J., Bae, J., Lee, U., Ahn, T., Lee, S., Kim, D., . . . Kim, H. (2024). How to Align Large Language Models for Teaching English? Designing and Developing LLM based-Chatbot for Teaching English Conversation in EFL, Findings and Limitations. *arXiv preprint arXiv:2409.04987*.

Park, J., Bae, J., Lee, U., Ahn, T., Lee, S., Kim, D., . . . Kim, H. (2024). How to Align Large Language Models for Teaching English? Designing and Developing LLM based-Chatbot for Teaching English Conversation in EFL, Findings and Limitations. *arXiv preprint arXiv:2409.04987*.

Peláez-Sánchez, I. C., Velarde-Camaqui, D., & Glasserman-Morales, L. D. (2024, June). The impact of large language models on higher education: Exploring the connection between AI and Education 4.0. [). Frontiers Media SA.]. *Frontiers in Education*, *9*, 1392091.

Prakash, K., Rao, S., Hamza, R., Lukich, J., Chaudhari, V., & Nandi, A. (2024, June). Integrating LLMs into Database Systems Education. In *Proceedings of the 3rd International Workshop on Data Systems Education: Bridging education practice with education research* (pp. 33-39).

Raiaan, M. A. K., Mukta, M. S. H., Fatema, K., Fahad, N. M., Sakib, S., Mim, M. M. J., & Azam, S. (2024). A review on large Language Models: Architectures, applications, taxonomies, open issues and challenges. *IEEE Access : Practical Innovations, Open Solutions.*

Shin, D., & Lee, J. H. (2024). Moving from off-the-shelf chatbots to a user-designed bespoke L2 chatbot.

Shoukat, S., Mamoon, R., & Arif, M. F. (2024). Enhancing Language Proficiency Through TPACK Model and AI Applications A Study on Effective Integration Strategies in English Language Instruction. *Pakistan Languages and Humanities Review*, *8*(2), 540–554.

Siegle, D. (2024). Using Artificial Intelligence (AI) Technology to Support the Three Legs of Talent Development. *Gifted Child Today*, *47*(3), 221–227.

Sravanthi, C., & Maloth, U. (2024, June). Digital classroom: Tech-friendly academic model for teaching english. In *AIP Conference Proceedings* (Vol. 2971, No. 1). AIP Publishing.

Susnjak, T., & McIntosh, T. R. (2024). ChatGPT: The end of online exam integrity? *Education Sciences*, *14*(6), 656.

Van Wyk, M. M. (2024). Is ChatGPT an opportunity or a threat? Preventive strategies employed by academics related to a GenAI-based LLM at a faculty of education. *Journal of applied learning and teaching, 7*(1).

Vik, B. (2024). *Large Language Models in L2 English Teaching: Exploring Teachers' Understanding and Utilisation* (Master's thesis, The University of Bergen).

Wang, S., Xu, T., Li, H., Zhang, C., Liang, J., Tang, J., . . . Wen, Q. (2024). Large language models for education: A survey and outlook. *arXiv preprint arXiv:2403.18105.*

Watters, J. B., & Garcia-Lopez, A. (2024). Artificial Intelligence in Education: Transforming Learning and Teaching Julie A. Delello iD https://orcid. org/0000-0002-4326-8096. *Disruptive Technologies in Education and Workforce Development*, 1.

Yalcinalp, S., Türkoğlu, H., Koc, S. E., & Ersoy, H. (2024). Utilization of Artificial Intelligence in Education: A Perspective on Learning Strategies.

Yamaguchi, S., Morishita, M., Fukuda, H., Muraoka, K., Nakamura, T., Yoshioka, I., & Awano, S. (2024). Evaluating the efficacy of leading large language models in the Japanese national dental hygienist examination: A comparative analysis of ChatGPT, Bard, and Bing Chat. *Journal of Dental Sciences*. PMID: 39347065

Yan, D. (2024). Feedback seeking abilities of L2 writers using ChatGPT: A mixed method multiple case study. *Kybernetes*.

Yan, L., Sha, L., Zhao, L., Li, Y., Martinez-Maldonado, R., Chen, G., & Gašević, D. (2024). Practical and ethical challenges of large language models in education: A systematic scoping review. *British Journal of Educational Technology*, *55*(1), 90–112.

Yigci, D., Eryilmaz, M., Yetisen, A. K., Tasoglu, S., & Ozcan, A. (2024). Large Language Model-Based Chatbots in Higher Education. *Advanced Intelligent Systems*, •••, 2400429.

Zheng, C., Yuan, K., Guo, B., Hadi Mogavi, R., Peng, Z., Ma, S., & Ma, X. (2024, May). Charting the Future of AI in Project-Based Learning: A Co-Design Exploration with Students. In *Proceedings of the CHI Conference on Human Factors in Computing Systems* (pp. 1-19).

Chapter 7
Ethical and Societal Implications of Large Language Models: Can We Trust Machines With Human Language?

Wasswa Shafik
https://orcid.org/0000-0002-9320-3186
Dig Connectivity Research Laboratory (DCRLab), Uganda & School of Digital Science, Universiti Brunei Darussalam, Brunei

ABSTRACT

Large language models (LLMs) are powerful AI tools with broad applications, but they also pose significant ethical and societal challenges. These include risks of inherent bias in training data, leading to biased outputs that may amplify stereotypes or unfair treatment. LLMs raise concerns regarding data privacy, as they may inadvertently use sensitive or personally identifiable information. Additionally, the widespread use of LLMs for generating disinformation poses threats to public trust and information integrity. Addressing these issues requires transparent model development, responsible data use, and strong ethical guidelines to mitigate risks while maximizing the societal benefits of LLMs.

INTRODUCTION

Large language models[1] (LLM) have become increasingly prominent, from state-of-the-art performance in commercial technology to their status as objects of general interest and concern. Companies use millions of dollars to sophisticate and

DOI: 10.4018/979-8-3693-8387-2.ch007

parade their models as both indicators of technological sophistication and guides for personal improvement (Pijeira-Díaz et al., 2024). At the same time, discussions surrounding their detrimental impacts on society feature prominently in news stories, blog posts, and journals. Misinformation, disinformation, adversarial, and dangerous uses of artificial intelligence[2] (AI), as well as the treatment of AI ethics as the primary strategy in mitigating these impacts, are becoming regular conversations among scholars, practitioners, and industry stakeholders (Jiang et al., 2024).

Although the research in ethical and data-driven concerns is growing, none of the existing literature has systematically mapped the potential harms and benefits of these models, the actors involved, and the plausible consequences of societal uptake. In this chapter, we discuss a range of concerns that industry, technologists, policymakers, and society, more generally, must confront when discussing and using language models at scale (Khan et al., 2024). There is an increasing need to take seriously the challenges that modern language models pose, in addition to the growing public concern for the societal impacts. Thus, we focus the scope of this paper on language models. We demonstrate the risks and benefits of modern language models and map out logistic, distributive, communal, epistemic, and power asymmetries at play. We contend that modern language models are both a danger to society and its stakeholders as well as a force for potential benefits (Smetana et al., 2024).

The use of large language models has significantly broadened the scope of modern natural language processing, becoming a dominant approach over the last few years. In essence, these models are solving tasks by predicting the probability of the words they generate, making use of past words in the sequence. As such, they tend to "learn" patterns in language, ranging from common spelling patterns to abstract notions over millions of tokens. In short, the text generation capabilities of these models have the potential to be disruptive in the AI community and, by extension, in society (Zietsch et al., 2024). As language models continue to advance, questions about the ethics of developing and using systems with the potential to influence society become both more important and more immediate.

But while research on language models, in general, has rapidly accelerated, research on their implications and ethical considerations similarly lags. Given the state of AI and the need to continue working out what it means to algorithmically manipulate language, quantify truth, strip privacy from communication, blur work with play, and shift how people connect with technology, thinking about the consequences of releasing a large language model is an essential next step. The following paper thus seeks to answer two fundamental but thorny questions. First, what new ethical, social, political, and practical risks or challenges arise from the use of large language models? Second, who should be accountable for those risks or challenges? These questions weave together an array of issues that hide beneath the headline, and it is essential to examine them across a range of applications and institutions, supported with different artificial intelligence, as demonstrated in Figure 1.

Figure 1. types of artificial intelligence

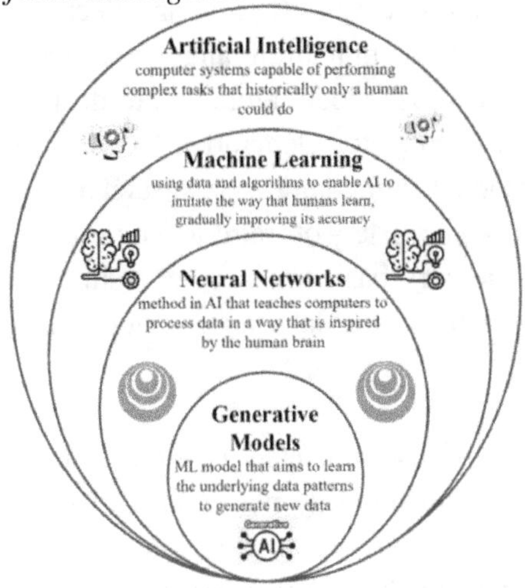

Background and Overview of Large Language Models

Language models, a type of AI system designed to understand and produce human-like text, have been researched and developed for many years. Technological advances in neural network architectures and increased access to vast amounts of text data have led to the development of increasingly more prominent, single-purpose models suitable for a wide variety of natural language processing tasks. Knowing that language models can draft convincing articles, developers have sought to improve the conceptual and fact-based knowledge of larger language models to engage the public in meaningful debates (Kirchner et al., 2024). To achieve polished and grammatically accurate results, the latest pre-trained models rely on transformer-layered architectures, specifically a scaled-up variant of the Generative Pre-trained Transformer[3].

Many companies have tasked these AI teams to replace classic search engines with question-answering systems that use highly scaled-up language models to answer user questions in natural language directly. Large language models have become functional, often serving as a starting point in further training or fine-tuning on narrower domains. Pathologies related to scaling, inappropriate and sequestered training data, and potential usability from maintenance and shifting use cases were highlighted (Ding et al., 2024). The increasing influence and reliance on language models for communication and accessing information have brought to the forefront the societal and ethical implications of these powerful technologies.

Natural language processing[4] (NLP) research has improved and continues to work towards the challenges of understanding, reasoning, and generation. Notable advances include the development of efficient architectures such as transformers, which efficiently model context in natural language processing and have been the basis of large language models. Model architecture design continues to advance; iterations on model architecture for Generative Pre-training Transformer[5] (GPT) include more diverse model scaling approaches, such as hierarchical sparse model scaling (Helm et al., 2024). A variety of training data sets could be used to pre-train language models using the same basic transformer architecture approach. Typically, language models treat language as a flat sequence of tokens. This chapter presented the following contributions:

- Analyzes the ethical risks associated with the opaque decision-making processes of LLMs and their impact on accountability.
- Assesses the ethical tensions between innovation and regulation in the development and deployment of LLMs at scale.
- Critically examines how LLMs replicate and potentially amplify societal biases embedded in training data.
- Examines a multidisciplinary framework for evaluating LLM impacts across education, law, media, and public discourse.
- Explores the societal implications of misinformation, disinformation, and hallucination generated by LLMs in high-stakes domains.
- Highlights the role of data provenance, consent, and surveillance in shaping the trustworthiness of language-based AI systems.
- Investigates the consequences of anthropomorphizing LLMs and the erosion of human agency in automated communication.
- Offers actionable recommendations for ethical design, transparent governance, and culturally sensitive deployment of LLMs.

ETHICAL CONSIDERATIONS

A potential concern is that ethical and moral reasoning systems are being encoded in language models. A user querying such models could be misinformed due to the adversarial behavior of the model or the training data. Essential questions regarding the influence of language models on ethical reasoning are whether particular versions of ethical stances have become embodied in the system and to what extent the development of language models embodies and exacerbates some social and moral dilemmas or ethical positions (Wan et al., 2024). Biased decision-making based on the characteristics of the user can lead to unfair outcomes. AI systems might store, process, and exchange personal user data, which, given inappropriate use and security leaks of the data, can lead to societal harm. With AI systems influencing daily human activities, there is a risk for scenarios when AI steers behavior in one or more directions, causing implications at the societal level. How the developed AI is socially accepted reflects how intensely perceived ethical perceptions and values are included (Chow et al., 2024).

When considering fair AI, we have to include two questions: “Fair with respect to what?” and “Which aspects of society and human bias should be represented in the design of AI systems?” It is notoriously challenging to develop methodological operationalizations of fairness, measures for equality, social bias, and accountability, proposing different statistical definitions of fairness used in literature, such as non-discrimination, demographic parity, and equality of opportunity. The no-free-lunch theorem highlights the limitations in guaranteeing the fairness of the system. This is due to the fact that fairness can depend on complex, nuanced considerations and local or situational factors that are not aggregable (Benítez et al., 2024; Roberts et al., 2024). As such, we need to consider how to measure fairness in a system and propose different ways to evaluate whether the AI system meets the fairness requirement amidst several applications as sampled in Figure 2.

Figure 2. Artificial intelligence application

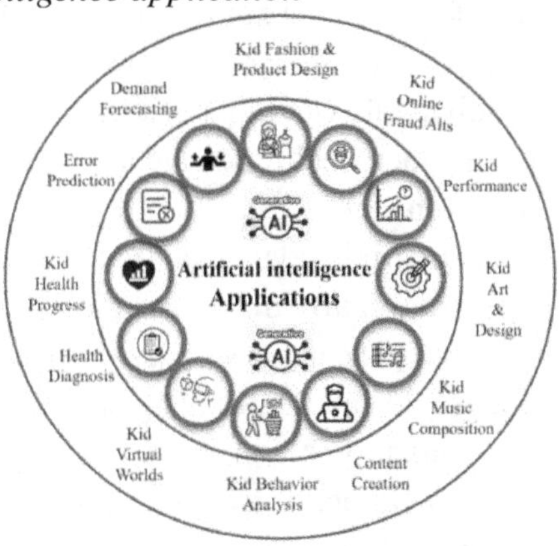

Bias and Fairness

Bias in the outputs of large language models can emerge from sources of bias present in the training data or from the model’s inability to reflect diverse cultural practices in its output. Datasets commonly reflect and reproduce historical or culturally localized biases towards, for example, certain ethnic groups or marginalized sexual and gender identities, or they lack diverse linguistic data. The inability of models to represent all demographic and geographic groups equally raises concerns about the fairness of language generation (Tian et al., 2024). For instance, a language model fine-tuned on specific data has a higher likelihood of associating women with the home domain and men with the career domain. Recent initiatives have introduced tools to monitor the concept association between, for example, gender and profession across a variety of models, including large language models. It is argued that aggregate output can shift societal norms and that media organizations have a responsibility to monitor and potentially address bias in their reporting continually (Park et al., 2024). We similarly argue for developing processes for continued evaluation and monitoring of the outputs of large language models.

Privacy and Security

It is essential to understand what privacy and security risks arise from the use of large language models. They process personal data both when learning from the data present in the model and when generating outputs that can be about or attributed to known individuals. Relying on providing access to a large volume of data to work correctly may be seen as a requirement for a breach to occur. As regards the decision of setting a policy of not considering a breach to have occurred if the unauthorized access has been rectified before the data are further used, there are at least two potential points of discussion (Hidayatullah et al., 2023; Shafik, 2023). One refers to the confidentiality[6] that individuals would have if the data were not disseminated. This is of particular concern when dealing with data in sensitive contexts from the point of view of data protection law.

The other point, more directly related to legal issues in data protection, has to do with the classification as personal data of the information of the legal representatives. If such information is not a specific category of data based on processing, revealing the representative involved would entail not having personal data that would need to be protected under rules. Acquisition of personal data subject to processing serves as the basis for processing operations (Takemoto, 2024). Given that privacy and data protection are fundamental requirements for all AI innovation and deployment, organizations must adopt a security and privacy-by-design approach when adopting language models and other large machine learning[7] (ML) algorithms. Legally, such AI may be based on information about individuals and for individuals, who are natural persons, to interpret a result in combination with privacy as the control over one's data as interpreted by lawyers and ethicists (Tian et al., 2024).

Under the General Data Protection Regulation[8] (GDPR), "personal data" means any information relating to an identified or identifiable natural person; an identifiable person can be identified, directly or indirectly, in particular by reference to an identifier such as a name, an identification number, location data, online identifier, among others. A legal entity has no privacy rights but data protection rights to the extent that their information and data about them are personal data subject to protection. With language models in AI as a function of the algorithm[9], it is challenging to attribute risk as they can process personal data of various levels of sensitivity (Kretschmer et al., 2024; Zietsch et al., 2024). In practice, "user privacy models run the gamut from very conservative and risk-averse to speculative." As a matter of fact, it is a matter of how language models are used. For instance, those trained on proprietary company data in sensitive areas such as finance or healthcare should be scrutinized with a higher standard and go even beyond the current state-of-the-art in data privacy for models. In those cases, training data could be subject to regulations both in the U.S. and in Europe. In Europe, AI may be subject to more stringent rules under the GDPR, and specific AI surveillance technology may not be admitted (Takemoto, 2024).

Moral and Legal Responsibility

The research community does not have consensual answers to the question of who should be responsible when AI systems produce harmful and misleading output. Responsibilities can be variously assigned between the developers, developers' organizations (which have goals, capabilities, and incentives codified in their policies and guidelines), and end users. End users are capable of influencing the output generated by the models by choosing to use or refrain from using them in accordance with the guidelines that followed the development of the model. This multilayered moral and legal responsibility assignment to founders, developers, information technology[10] (IT) experts, research scientists, and model end users is in line with current theories of legal responsibility focused primarily on notions of rea and actus reus (Hubert et al., 2024). Other proposals have suggested taking a class economic approach in order to discuss the accounting of responsibility. This approach analyzes the consequences of enterprises' wrongdoing with regard to shareholders, creditors, employees, or suppliers.

A classic legal framework could also be used to frame AI-related harm by distinguishing between subject and object components of responsibility. The term 'liability' refers to the legal basis on which the harm can be addressed. In strict liability, manufacturers are held liable for any defect in the product without the need to prove any carelessness, lack of skill, or deliberate intent. Instead, in negligence liability, the plaintiff is required to prove that the defendant failed to exercise reasonable care, violating a duty owed to the plaintiff, resulting in damage to the plaintiff (Gilson et al., 2024; Tai et al., 2024). Of course, principles of liability often contain only tort norms that indicate categories of those who are allowed to claim, such as consumers, end users, competitors, or public bodies. According to specific rules, a company is responsible primarily for maximizing benefits to shareholders, and this ought to involve little or no attention to the social consequences of its activities (Dal Molin, 2024; Lehman et al., 2024). Ethical AI principles are guidelines that various groups, institutions, and corporations design. They should be respected by all those who operate a large language model and translated into enforceable rules, laws, or guidelines chosen. In this way, if the guidelines of the ethical development principles are translated and adopted as law, that law will control the entire AI development as any other law, and the problem of individual and producer responsibility will be solved (Gilson et al., 2024; Hadar-Shoval et al., 2024).

Dataset Bias and Application Fairness

Many everyday activities, ranging from simple to nuanced, can become ethically problematic when they involve language models trained on huge datasets[11]. The datasets reflect existing social inequalities, so the model risks reproducing such biases in its outputs or, worse, creating new stereotypes. For example, a language model can join two variables with knowledge of binary gender and also state which activity is most likely associated with such a person (Lee & Park, 2024; Yan et al., 2024). Akin to a simple query to the model, prompts that reflect popular stereotypes about communities or groups can make the model reproduce such myths: when asked to list the most minor and most potent jobs out of three and presented with the stereotype associations, the model exhibited confirmation bias by agreeing that women are more often assigned jobs the model rates as the least powerful and men as more powerful jobs when compared to other genders. Ensuring that the model makes decisions based on actual capabilities and the relevance of the candidates, rather than biased training data, is a significant challenge (Llanes-Jurado et al., 2024; Ma et al., 2024; Takemoto, 2024). Ensuring that automated decision-making systems are fair is not only a matter of avoiding legal repercussions but is a topic embedded in a larger conversation about justice, among the application of ChatGPT as presented in Figure 3.

Figure 3. Application of ChatGPT

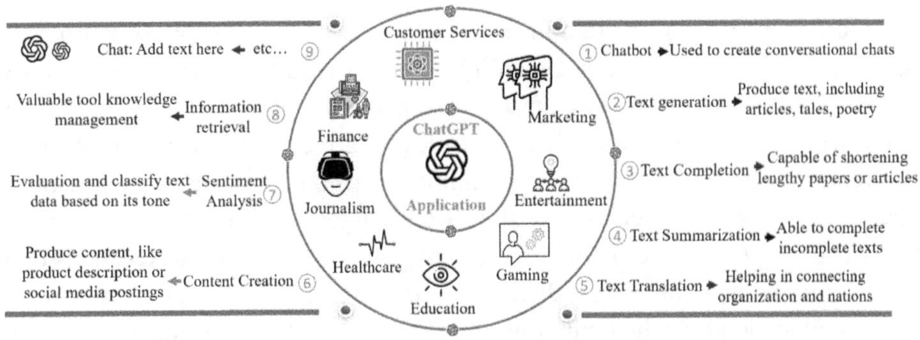

The ethical risks associated with biased language models when deployed for a multitude of tasks are substantial, including for the people and communities who are discriminated against. The mere creation of such technologies is ethically problematic as well. To mitigate the propagation of bias, first and foremost, commercially released language models must be trained on varied, inclusive, and representative datasets; however, this data-centric measure cannot dispense with the need for explicitly auditing language models according to their behavior. The corrective measures of these audits are yet an open challenge (Tai et al., 2024). So far, certainty in measuring and thus fixing the bias in a system remains elusive. However, some discourses suggest removing bias from these models altogether might be undesirable, so we are still left without a clear way forward. Whether a future of debiasing models is desirable or not requires severe discussion and debates within communities (Dal Molin, 2024).

SOCIETAL IMPACT

Implying economic losses, the deployment of large language models might affect not only productivity but also the complete landscape of many occupational areas. Occupations such as legal and healthcare services, rapidly adopting AI enhancements, have to date experienced little automation. A broad consensus of economists exists that consistent technological change is a primary driver behind shifts in the labor market that have led to both a reduction in available jobs and a decrease in demand for many low-skill occupations, causing economic inequality (Hadar-Shoval et al., 2024; Lau, 2024). Similarly, shifts away from certain occupations that are more easily automated can also drastically change the distribution of wages. In the U.S., for example, when certain trade agreements were enacted, low-skilled labor demand doubled while the average wage fell (Ashrafimoghari & Gürkan, 2024; Yan et al., 2024).

AI-driven technologies are impacting various areas in ways that sometimes go unnoticed. A prominent one not highlighted so far is in the sphere of culture. AI models have already started to shape social and cultural narratives significantly. In our truly globalized world, sharing stories with individuals from dramatically different backgrounds has become common. With the growing influence of AI writers, it is possible to encounter significant language model-generated content as if written by people from other educational, cultural, or class backgrounds or as someone living in a completely different country (Bezzi, 2024). These new forms of communication blur the boundaries of culture by making certain conversations more accessible and flattening hierarchies. This also applies to education through the unconscious conveyance of societal norms and values since culture can be transmitted formally and informally in an academic setting. The content of large language models has the potential to shift public opinion and influence cultural documents. Consequently, the deployment of large language models has solid societal and cultural implications for the construction and preservation of knowledge that might not be immediately apparent (Laato et al., 2023). This emerging new media landscape needs to be approached proactively.

Labor Displacement and Economic Inequality

Widespread unemployment is commonly considered a key concern arising from AI technologies and extensive language model deployment. Substantial potential, therefore, exists for jobs in various sectors, including finance, legal services, technical fields, health, and education, allowing creative services to be carried out by humans to be undertaken by AI. Including AI coping with customer service at help desks, chatbots, schools, and universities calling, grading, and in companies from reception to research may lead to a significant decrease in demand for human work in these areas (Epstein & Dexter, 2023; Lau, 2024). Fundamental changes in the current fabric of human society are entailing them at a time when these job markets are faced with significant turmoil. AI is created at a time of economic polarization and joblessness.

Economic inequality and lack of opportunities. Work substitution by large language systems is likely to result in devastating job loss, which will have a broader, differential effect on society. It will be easier to replace service work and other low-skill jobs with AI, so positions that require formal education and training, which equal reasonable remuneration in the context of human society, are less feasible for large-scale language AI to promote (Dwivedi et al., 2023; Kenthapadi et al., 2023). Indeed, community health care, service personnel that tend to earn less than national averages are likely to be crowded out where there is a mismatch in their education and practice. At the same time, the transition may lead to lower productivity and reliance on established employees. Decentralized workers with only school and in-service instruction, such as in services or other practical areas, should experience some of the most adverse cumulative social and economic effects of work displacement (Gumilyov, 2023; Liyanage & Ranaweera, 2023). Entrenched ranks of the intelligence service may also face considerable displacement.

Cultural Influence and Globalization

A lot of media concern has surrounded the idea of AI learning from existing cultural narratives and then replicating or remixing them. One example is the appropriation of or differing views on folklore by culturally alien algorithms. While some researchers are working on ways to limit this influence through design, others are reveling in the ways that large language models can be used to facilitate international cultural exchange without specialist translators. AI can facilitate and propagate interactions between and understanding of different cultural values, making it easier to share lawsuits and compensate researchers across cultures fairly (Hagendorff & Danks, 2023; Tokayev, 2023).

Because models may also be trained to mimic other cultures, care must be taken to ensure inclusivity and representation in resultant work. This raises questions of who gets to represent different cultures in models. On the one hand, AI can and does work to preserve traditional knowledge and languages; it highlighted the ability of voice recognition systems to understand 500 languages and dialects, fifty of which are minority languages. Digitizing and labeling voice data in such languages are contributing to the preservation and advancement of diverse and marginalized languages and dialects across the globe (Uzun, 2023). It also creates new demand for those seeking to digitize historical texts and preserve marginalized languages, which in the past have only received attention from a small subset of the data community. On the other hand, AI could potentially have a homogenizing effect alongside globalization, reducing the most interesting differences between cultures and limiting the ability of some groups to pass on oral traditions. These questions have no easy answers because AI itself is a neutral technology that happens to enable other cultural influences to spread more quickly (Bahammam et al., 2023).

Questions about how to balance change and preservation, global and local narratives, and interconnectedness and distinctiveness have arisen over and over in human history. In fact, interactions between emerging communication technologies and individual societies are the subject of entire fields of scholarship. On the one hand, the bookkeeping technologies that underpinned the accounting, tax, and administrative systems of ancient civilizations were gradually adopted by others

(Liyanage & Ranaweera, 2023). Approximately 3,000 years later, the arrival of the printing press facilitated cultural cross-pollination, imperialism, and colonization by efficiently disseminating influential texts. In a more popular context, the radio, highway, and mass automobile industries created a snapshot of American middle-class life that was more influential than the cultural narratives of the time. The crux of both these anecdotes is that the available technology is only part of the question. The tools must also be in the hands of people and societies motivated to share, or at least open to, direct, meaningful exchange (Gumilyov, 2023).

Disinformation and Misinformation

Disinformation is defined as deliberately misleading information meant to evoke specific emotional responses or guide behavior and beliefs in one direction, while misinformation refers to inaccurate information that is shared through sincere social interactions. The technology of today generally addresses disinformation in public conversation more so than misinformation. The central problem is that large language models will likely be used to generate and spread disinformation and misinformation due to the high quality of their output, which might be used to deceive people at scale. In recent years, some tools and services using AI for generating persuasive texts have emerged, but increasing the output of these models and broadening potential languages can lower the bar for entry to produce this kind of content (Caselli et al., 2023; Kenthapadi et al., 2023).

Following the recent wave of discussion about the ethical and societal implications of language models, as the field of AI has gradually started addressing the risks and limitations of large language models, misinformation has surfaced as a critical use case of large language models to society. As misinformation can lead to harmful, sometimes catastrophic, consequences for society and the economy, it is vital to discuss the spread of misinformation and how humans can be brought to this misleading content (Laato et al., 2023). As a practical matter, governments, companies, and nonprofits seeking to mitigate deepfake risks will commonly need to address misleading content of all types. Relatedly, the rise of misinformation has generated significant interest among researchers and practitioners in ways to improve algorithms and detect and counter misinformation. This is motivation enough for us to identify, differentiate, and explore pathways to belief in our significant language model-generated piece of misinformation (Ashrafimoghari & Gürkan, 2024). In short, what concrete mechanisms contribute to the spread of harmful ideas in language?

Economic-Technological Divide

AI technologies and automation enabled by AI-based language models are transforming significant sectors of the economy. When used in the workplace, language models have the potential to lower the time and energy required for a wide range of tasks by making it easier to understand ambiguities, navigate large document corpora, and automate many repetitive data entry and extraction tasks. At a macroeconomic level, these efficiencies can be used to solve new problems, provide new goods, or drive down costs (Hadar-Shoval et al., 2024). However, labor market reports point to wage and job polarization due to automation, even as AI language models are offering the potential to augment a wide variety of high-skill jobs. The economic theory on the future of work offers two main possibilities: either the machines will complement human labor or the machines will replace humans for many tasks. Opinions remain divided, but there is broad agreement that augmenting human potential requires industry, government, and educational institutions to engage in the reskilling of workers to enable them to make effective use of powerful new toolkits and to change jobs throughout their careers potentially (Gilson et al., 2024; Lehman et al., 2024).

Even if AI can be used to create demand elsewhere in the economy, the short-run challenges of reallocation have societal and moral implications. Already in the U.S. labor market, there is mounting evidence that it is disproportionately the economically vulnerable who are in harm's way from automation. Technological change looks to be a central driver of income and wealth inequality as even high-skill sectors of the workforce see wages pushed downwards. Additionally, the pace of skill change in the modern economy is accelerating (Takemoto, 2024). Industry composition is now shifting towards more dynamic sectors, like health care and STEM (science, technology, engineering and mathematics) fields. AI language models are driving further diversification in our economic landscape just as the cutting edge of AI research is increasingly turning to real-world applications. In short, automation is likely to upend a number of sectors and will likely create new workers in some sectors even as it displaces others (Lehman et al., 2024).

Labor Market Effects

Language models have the potential to automate certain elements of a wide range of jobs, including aspects of writing, customer relations, human–human, and human–system communication. Therefore, it is conceivable that large language models could have a significant impact on the labor market. Like all major technological innovations, there are both negative and positive labor market impacts. Historically, major technological innovations have disrupted existing industries and led to the loss of many jobs, only for new industries and jobs to be created, driven by the new technology (Bezzi, 2024; Cheung & Co, 2023). A survey of historical technical literature suggests that technological automation may displace workers in many fields, especially when the work being done is intermittent and subject to significant quality fluctuations.

Many of these displaced workers may find new employment in the many new roles and businesses that large language models are likely to create. Therefore, the big drawdowns in employment are likely to be temporary for most workers, though they can still be highly destructive for the workers who find themselves in the wrong part of the labor market at the wrong time. The industries where we might expect to see significant employment changes include relatively well-rewarded fields like law and medicine, since the work currently done by junior staff in these industries can be highly automated (Epstein & Dexter, 2023; Fecher et al., 2023). The increased efficiency these models will bring, alongside the many valuable products and services they will enable, should create opportunities for growth that will outweigh these negative effects in the long run. The provision of adequate education and retraining, however, may be required for displaced workers to transition to new opportunities in the AI-driven economy. There may thus be a role for governments to play in increasing opportunities for vocational education and providing subsidies or tax credits to firms that undertake in-work training. Regional differences in job growth and declines may occur, and any government policies should consider this (Kenthapadi et al., 2023). There may be significant displacement despite the new jobs created. Given the social and political aspects of inequality and technological change, these policies ought to consider equity issues, not only efficiency concerns. Governments may also need to run compensatory policies, for example, improving the social security system and the insurance market. Long term, displaced workers may also need skills upgrades to get new types of work in these new sectors. As with many settings of technical change, a tension exists between unlocking significant economic gains—like increased system productivity and tax revenue—and social responsibility dimensions—such as adequate help for the displaced workforce (Dwivedi et al., 2023; Kenthapadi et al., 2023). Current global norms constrain some of the economic benefits that technological innovation might yield. Ignoring these norms is likely to lead to suboptimal outcomes, assuming all stakeholders act rationally in response.

Energy Consumption

Training and deploying large language models result in substantial levels of energy consumption. This cost arises from both the training phase and the deployment phase, with larger costs incurred in the training phase. Cloud computing and relevant data infrastructure contribute largely to the energy cost. While data processing and optimizing large language models also bring energy costs and carbon emissions, the relative increase in consumption attributed to model development is relatively small. Global energy consumption generated by internet use and data infrastructure is growing rapidly (Jun et al., 2021; Shafik & Tufail, 2023; Zhao et al., 2022). There is a popular concern regarding the environmental impact of training and using large language models, and the dilemma between training models at scale and the planet's future. Some researchers propose monitoring the carbon emissions of AI model development and usage based on various criteria in discussing the environmental impact of AI.

There may be several potential approaches to address such concerns. Firstly, from a technical perspective, optimizing the data and algorithms, which may not solely be the pursuit of reducing the model size and computational complexity, would potentially contribute to energy-efficient model training. From an infrastructure perspective, using green energy in the training phase and designing data infrastructures with lower energy usage are also potential solutions (Lehman et al., 2024). Additionally, researching more AI model architectures that require much less energy or building dedicated hardware specifically designed for maintaining low energy usage will also potentially address the issues. The central attribute is that the process tends to raise public attention to the energy usage of AI model research and development and pushes energy usage optimization as a technical research target. In the pursuit of a sustainable view of language model research and design, the energy consumption induced by the entire cycle of language model deployment, from model training and storage to inference, should be a concern to be addressed (Takemoto, 2024).

LEGAL AND REGULATORY FRAMEWORKS

Various existing legal and regulatory tools could be applied in principle to large language models, including rules pertaining to unfair commercial practices, advertising, and competition. While there is considerable heterogeneity in how possible concerns with such systems are addressed across jurisdictions, a number of gaps have been identified, including the predictability and proportionality of general consumer and non-discrimination laws. Given the aforementioned challenges with law making and enforcement, a number of expert reports have argued that a regulatory approach for AI should focus not on ex-ante rules specifying minimum standards for certain applications, but rather on creating a general background of liability and obligation when it comes to the deployment of AI or AI systems or the generation of AI-generated services or goods (Llanes-Jurado et al., 2024).

In addition, while not legally enforced, the EU has established a number of best practices for trustworthy AI, focusing on a number of different domains such as recruitment and employment, personalized pricing and content, or judicial decision making and processes. Governments, firms, and civil society have the capacity, and therefore the responsibility, to help frame the rules of responsible and fair AI, given the significant consequences of its use (Dal Molin, 2024). Moreover, these practices highlighted significant gaps in the legal protection offered to end users of language models, which have the potential to leave consumers and the broader society exposed to significant risks. These risks, such as deception through synthetic media or persuasion tactics that are currently under-regulated, require urgent action. As traditional ex-ante legal frameworks focused on the input have shown their limitations, the report now points to the development of output-focused legal frameworks that take into account the foreseeable impact of AI generation on people and societies (Ma et al., 2024; Nay et al., 2024).

Current Regulations and their Adequacy

Current regulations are not prepared to deal with LLG and its implications for society. Some of them do not distinguish between AI technologies, making it impossible to conduct a contextual analysis. In the Spanish context, there is a draft of the AI Regulation. The Spanish AI Draft does not provide for specific measures regarding large language models, nor is its first draft based on the European one. Current regulations set different obligations for individuals or entities that develop or operate AI technologies. In this regard, LLG carriage entails several obligations if the obligations are transposed to the LLG system load, such as a description of its architecture, an estimation of its capacity to interact with individuals or its abilities, the documentation of its assessment showing such abilities, how it will be carried out, and how they overcome the risks associated with this dataset (Hubert et al., 2024; Polverini & Gregorcic, 2024).

Certain regulations require confirming the intervention of concerned parties when it comes to their development or application of AI technologies. For instance, the Spanish Law on climate change and energy transition requires the successive participation of citizens in the preparation of impact studies which could prove contradictory to the development of LLG systems. Most of the achievements in the Spanish AI Regulation follow the guidelines presented by the European Commission. National laws will have to achieve an all-encompassing reform in order to address the inadequacy of regulation in the field of AI, as well as involving all stakeholders to guarantee its feasibility in the light of existing technologies, keeping in mind the failings derived from the application of current regulations (Gilson et al., 2024; Hadar-Shoval et al., 2024). Once the adequacy of the legal framework is discussed, it is valuable to review some particular cases in which the legal system has been restructured in order to accommodate significant legal developments. This could be a good criterion to follow when it comes to AI development.

MITIGATION STRATEGIES

Mitigation strategies may include a number of considerations in the design and deployment of large language models. The best manner to approach such strategies is to integrate them into the system from the ground up. This includes not only ethical considerations but also practical ones: if systems that use large language models are designed to be highly verifiable, then standard systems created using language models may also inspire greater confidence (Esmaeilzadeh, 2023; Noguer i Alonso, 2023). One example of a potentially useful mitigation strategy in this area is explanation: to what extent models are able to explain their outputs, or at least their decision-making process.

More generally, if the models are treated as "black boxes," and they make a prediction that is wrong or unethical, then one may be left with no means available to understand what happened. Even a wrong but ethical prediction by the systems has the potential to be harmful, given the large number of instances in which these models are employed. Another potential mitigation strategy may be to encourage greater granular control over filtering and censorship decisions. Researchers have reviewed methods to ameliorate the filtering and censorship challenges faced by social platforms and search engines, and argued that machine learning and natural language processing researchers should consider these issues as part of AI's risk landscape (Hagendorff & Danks, 2023). Mitigation strategies should focus on involving many different stakeholders in the process, including the AI-using organizations. Different recommendations ranging from public advisories about fraud and AI analysis and monitoring to percentage AI usage limits based on workforce size were developed. Researchers from industry, government, and academia have been discussing and formulating visions of how to mitigate the risks associated with AI and to ensure the benefits of the technology can be shared by all. The impetus for these actions is to build guidelines and best practices to safeguard the access and use of AI in a manner that benefits society and the economy (Tokayev, 2023). Finally, public consultation and education may both be a useful and necessary form of mitigation strategy, even without technical interventions. It is possible that only a tiny fraction of potential "AI harms" can be addressed in the technical design of AI systems, and this proportion is likely to decline as the performance of AI systems continues to improve. Moreover, public reactions can shape incentives for AI companies, AI users, and others. It could therefore be very important to shape favorable public attitudes affecting responsible AI design and use (Caselli et al., 2023).

Current mitigation strategies for the risks and harms of AI use include measures to ensure AI developers and AI-using organizations are held accountable. Indeed, policy interventions have long sought to increase the transparency of and oversight over AI-algorithmic systems to enable this accountability. Through these measures, governments seek to enforce the duty of care responsibilities of organizations with respect to the adverse outcomes and wider societal impacts of their outputs. This may include ensuring ethical practice when developing AI-led services and products (Bahammam et al., 2023). Further innovative ways of mitigating AI output risks could potentially be achievable through industry and academic cooperation to share best practices and make AI use safer, better, and more secure. Governments can support these efforts through investment in the academic research infrastructure that highlights pathways to risk reduction, and possibly, though not necessarily, by creating incentives for AI-using organizations. However, the research and investments need to be able to adapt via continuation to coincide with evolving AI technologies (Hagendorff & Danks, 2023).

Algorithmic Transparency and Accountability

Large language models are designed to mimic the way human brains process information. Although recent breakthroughs in natural language processing set new records for specific tasks, large language models raise many ethical and societal questions. Algorithmic transparency and accountability is the concept representing the degree to which information is disclosed regarding the existence, structure, and operation of algorithms, and there is a need to attribute liability for the decisions and outcomes of algorithms. In digital trust, algorithmic transparency is essential to users' willingness to put their trust in a system (Hagendorff & Danks, 2023; Liyanage & Ranaweera, 2023). It can allow for an opening up of AI systems, demystify how they work, and help potential non-experts—potential adversaries, potential users, and the public—to understand and hypothesize in broader terms what an AI system might be capable of in an adversarial situation.

For AI systems that are designed to impact the real world or have significant ethical implications, developers of AI models have an obligation to ensure that the systems they build are accountable; that someone can audit their systems, hold them accountable for performance, point out inconsistencies, and contest the system's learned censorship decisions. Given that, ensuring systems are accountable from the design phase down to deployment, even if there is resistance to transparency or resistance to improving models, can be done up front and remains one of the key activities of transparency (Bahammam et al., 2023; Liyanage & Ranaweera, 2023). Transparency and evaluation, more generally, should be a core concern addressing the hundreds of non-AI researchers and technologists working to hold the systems accountable and maintain checks and balances. There are calls and statements that demand interdisciplinary investment in questions in such areas, except in the intervention state. Process-focused strategies for embedding processes into systems and preventing vulnerabilities are essential.

The stronger the reliance on AI systems in the intervention state and social media space, and moreover, the potential harms, the stronger such efforts are needed. Indeed, a number of research papers have underlined the development of mistranslation and algorithm development concerns. Researchers have shown why algorithmic audits, tests, and publicly accessible performance measures are increasingly relevant in AI safety, liability, and security across AI domains (Gilson et al., 2024; Ma et al., 2024). Current AI research holds up the idea of transparency and accountability as a fundamental part of the underlying logic of AI development, not just a potential side effect—but also a range of practical issues. In other work, researchers argue that the infallibility of an AI model should call for transparency as they design models. Indeed, legal implications for lack of transparency have been detailed in the case of court decisions at this time. Although there has been little in AI regulation that demands transparency, it is likely that there will be increasingly affected fields, especially when there are concerns about the largest algorithmic harms, for example, enforced error or democratic error, and storage bias in social media; unfair race issues, such as facial recognition or loan applications (Smetana et al., 2024). In view of current high-stakes developments in AI, long-term and remedial investments in reproducibility analysis will be valuable.

Regulatory Initiatives - National and International Frameworks

Currently, at the national and international levels, there are few regulations and public initiatives under consideration addressing in silico. Examples exist of a number of conventions and guidelines that are intended to provide a framework for ethical uses of AI. The majority of these mention transparency, accountability, and fairness as important issues that should be considered by AI developers if they wish to create ethical products. Although the scope of these regulations, conventions, and public initiatives is similar, there are important differences that are worth elaborating (Ding et al., 2024). The legislation addressing the ethical usage of AI that is currently in development proposes additional research into both AI's potential for harm and existing regulatory gaps. They also attempt to balance the importance of investment into AI technologies with the enforcement of ethical standards. To finish, although the knowledge-based economy - among the digital and artificial intelligence pillars

- is integral for the European Union, it would prevent the spread of malicious AI applications or unintended accidents (Jiang et al., 2024; Pijeira-Díaz et al., 2024).

Shortcomings and Areas that Require Improvement

Current regulations are inadequate to address the novel threats induced by misuse of AI, such as large language models designed to manipulate individuals and institutions. Although certain AI practices are considered illegal, such as deepfakes and disinformation, these are not specifically associated with AI. Instead, usually, the issue of large language models is closely associated with illegal malpractices. There is a need for industry guidelines establishing best practices based on respective field research data (Benítez et al., 2024). It is not enough for the developers or manufacturers of AI applications to understand their conduct; the same applies also to policymakers, businesses that utilize such products, and the wider community. Thus, a concerted effort is needed to create guidelines that will inform businesses as to when and how they can and should use AI and AI applications in a responsible manner. The choice between "force, bargaining, or industry standard" paths is considered to present challenges of either controversial acceptance, even by industry insiders, and with little practical effect of implementation, or slow adoption (Lau, 2024).

Given that bad actors can make unauthorized use of these models with current advances in adversarial machine learning and text-pretraining models, or that intended end-users could mistakenly or through malice use them to harm others, AI ethics cannot focus solely on the operational aspects of model outputs. Other parties must be taken into consideration aside from the AI developer (Ashrafimoghari & Gürkan, 2024; Bezzi, 2024). Consequently, a broader array of stakeholder voices must be heard in the industry, and we must be aware of how civil society groups, governments, and human rights organizations can influence and be influenced by such practices. As AI, and particularly large language models, constitute a fast-growing field, it is essential that any international regulatory breakthrough in AI be adaptable to rapid, yet incremental, innovation. Although its primary concern should be the present state-of-the-art with broad legal and ethical principles, a larger policy should retain the prerogative of amicable expansion, with tribunals open for expanding charging options if and when necessary (Zietsch et al., 2024). This endowment, however, needs careful consideration in order not to stifle innovation by overwhelming legal abstraction.

FUTURE DIRECTIONS

A number of emerging technologies, such as more sophisticated neural network designs, data processing capabilities, and language processing at scale, are expected to be sources of change in the AI landscape in the coming years. The ethical implications of these technologies should be examined further. While it is important to foster innovation, it is also important that this is done responsibly. Discussions of future possibilities (both promising and concerning) are a preventative form of "ethical foresight," and in the context of the present work, such discussions can include both researchers and industry stakeholders, regulators, and others who may benefit from a more "flash-in-the-pan" look at potential risks and benefits that are as current as possible given the speed of AI research.

Societal and Ethical Design Principles

In addition to the development of new language technologies, large language models are likely to have significant implications for society. Some of these implications, such as changes to job markets, are difficult to plan for in advance, but may be made more manageable if anticipated beforehand. More research is needed to model the likely societal changes that must be prepared for. Furthermore, crafters who can swiftly publish content before the review process will have a disproportionately large influence on public narratives (Kretschmer et al., 2024). This will have impacts in a number of political and public health contexts. In essence, while very large language models are still the source of much speculation, they exist now, and the potential costs and benefits of their development need to be considered. It is the belief that the potential costs should be better understood and mitigated given the increasing accessibility of such powerful language models. Future efforts, in the current context of primarily understanding risk and mitigation, can be related to the current approach and be directed towards outlier mitigation measures (Roberts et al., 2024).

Future applications of such work might include models of recruiting content creators or using those with the current traits and opinions of popular creators to seek extra work. More collaborative approaches between researchers, stakeholders, and policymakers are also important. The current models that aid the discussion about risks and benefits in the field of large language models should be considered. An in-house body for considering the ethics and implications of work in social, economic, and ecological domains has already been included. Additionally, further dialogue between industry, researchers, participants, and policymakers should be taken as language models come under wider scrutiny in the coming years, and they become more ubiquitous in both commercial and consumer products (Park et al., 2024; Tian et al., 2024). Ongoing dialogue concerning how they are engineered, the ethical development and use of such systems, and the details of the mitigations discussed above should be integral to both deciphering the risks and ensuring their ethical use.

Emerging Technologies and Their I Implications

Machines' abilities to produce human-like text and to hold conversations are rapidly getting better and being increasingly used in different applications. Recent improvements in machine learning algorithms and models have been recognized as one of the most important contributing factors. They can explore and identify complex patterns in data features that can only be described statistically, like language. These phenomena have uncovered a spate of ethical and societal issues. AI systems' access to individuals' personal information and ability to share or use it to communicate with people raises privacy concerns (Ma et al., 2024). Language models may perpetrate discrimination or social bias by representing or generating text that discriminates against individuals. In recent years, an interdisciplinary community has started to investigate possible remedies, including flagging undesirable outputs and restricting certain uses of AI (Cheung & Co, 2023; Gilson et al., 2024). We have yet to understand how these promising technologies are shaped by the whims of corporations as well as the positive or negative norms that societies build around technologies.

In this light, numerous legal and ethical problems are associated with emerging technologies and new applications of old ones. One should ask: Does a new subfield of machine learning algorithms deserve a special spotlight on prescient ethical and societal analysis? Our answer resoundingly is: yes. Moreover, scholarly analysis of the negative societal ramifications of machine learning models underscores a clear need for multidisciplinary studies. Interdisciplinary investigating committees can pick apart the engineering, the relevant ethics and strategy, racial, gender, and financial equity issues, as well as other issues worth considering that often fall well outside the range of expertise frequently represented in AI ethics literature (Esmaeilzadeh, 2023; Noguer i Alonso, 2023). Many agree on the ethical and legal requirements we should place on society-wide systems of conversational AI. These arguments are anticipated to levy stressed AI systems so one can vividly envisage their ethical quandaries and browse the training systematics that design how their culture will evolve in the exact run. Every issue of legal caliber can also functionally be an ethical issue, and ethical arguments are anticipated to be more persuasive when supplemented by legal arguments (Uzun, 2023; Yue Zhuo et al., 2023). Absorbing criticism of developing industrial conversational AI provides a vivid encasing example of the species of ethical complaints that ought to accompany most cogent legal ones.

Ethical Design Principles

Large language models, like other AI models, can impact society profoundly through many pathways, including exacerbation of social inequality, perpetuation of oppression, deepening of unfair corporate practices, the spread of disinformation, and so on. As such, we believe that it is crucial to bake ethical considerations into every stage of the model life cycle: from the design and data collection to training and post-deployment usage and maintenance. This view is in line with the existing discussions in fairness, accountability, and transparency, and we consider language AI part of this broader effort (Hagendorff & Danks, 2023). The development of an ethical design framework for language AI will necessarily involve many stakeholders, so for now we can only articulate some high-level principles regarding how we should involve society in the development of the ethical framework. These principles are: integrating societal concerns into the very early stage in which we establish the research questions and design decisions; doing so using a bottom-up approach that starts by involving the communities that are expected to be directly affected by our work; and finally, developing mechanisms to track the societal impact of the research as it evolves at every stage of the process, and to use this information to revise our goals, methods, and expected impact so as to intervene and reformulate our approach and correct for misalignments as they arise (Narayanan Venkit, 2023).

The above set of principles rests on the assumption that ethical design and deployment of AI models will require first to define some values that are worth protecting—an ethical framework—and then to figure out the practical implications that the implementation of these values could have on AI software. Importantly, it is an incremental and iterative process, rather than a one-size-fits-all solution: research on language AI has already gone through some of these steps and has shown that it will be a complex, ongoing negotiation between language technology and societal stakeholders (Pijeira-Díaz et al., 2024). This report will help shed light on the array of diverse moral and social values that are implicated in AI research and application, and to spur discussion in this space. As the AI community both within academia and industry continues working to make progress, and as we develop more eclectic models that are rich in novel capabilities, new questions are likely to emerge that raise important ethical and social considerations (Smetana et al., 2024; Zietsch et al., 2024). So, while the release of this document represents only one snapshot of the considerations that ought to inform the ethical development of advanced AI technology, we hope that it is, at the very least, an influential image that captures and reveals much of the moral and social work that has already been undertaken.

User-Oriented, Explainable Artificial Intelligence

This should be done through interdisciplinary conversations and working groups involving researchers, industry, policymakers, social scientists, philosophers, and other influential organizations. This working group would stake out the range of different ethico-social principles, the socio-ontological underpinnings of these principles, and create an agenda for evaluating their implications with AI more generally. This could help ensure that future advanced technologies are developed with clear guidelines where 'lines' are not only technically possible but should inform the faith of development. This, in turn, can help to shape societal expectations and legitimate AI governance (Benítez et al., 2024). Moving forward, AI research and application need to be grounded in the need to be understood and made transparent. Researchers and policymakers should focus on user-oriented, explainable AI, setting norms and standards for transparency and accountability of such systems. More research focus is needed for developing bias detection and bias mitigation tools, developing thorough consultations on a global level – including a diverse range of voices containing different worldviews, value assumptions, and ethical backgrounds (Roberts et al., 2024; Tian et al., 2024).

Different countries, governments, and stakeholders will use this input for shaping policy at a local level through ideas on realistic policy recommendations and feasible systems of measurement, indicators, and assessments. The final research question comes down to the broader engagement with non-dominant and marginalized user groups, involving them in inclusive design processes considering their needs, rights, and acceptance towards new voice-generating AI technologies (Pijeira-Díaz et al., 2024). This could be operationalized in the form of various actions in the development of the technology, or even issues related to their cultural, religious, and practical ethical implications of creating a voice modeled after a religious figure or a deceased family member. Solutions to these ethical dilemmas need to be found in the next steps of responsible innovation in the AI sector (Ma et al., 2024; Nay et al., 2024). In the future, AI ethics need to take on board the analyses and solutions of current ethical improprieties, to focus on proactive bridge-building and to engage in forward-looking collaborations.

CONCLUSION

This paper has framed and examined the societal and ethical implications of increasingly large language models. We have emphasized inherent uncertainties about the future trajectory of such technologies. Such uncertainty does not, however, provide a license for policy stasis. Risks are emerging now that require urgent attention, and as AI capabilities and infrastructures continue to evolve, there is a vital role for interdisciplinary investigation into the full impacts and ethical questions that they pose. We undertook a factual review of the literature and our own expertise on AI technologies, specifically in NLP, in order to identify possible risks and opportunities. While the list of associated societal and ethical implications was by no means exhaustive, we identified a variety of intrinsic risks that large language models and future systems may pose. In this conclusion, we are able to highlight related risks and opportunities that emerged from this analysis. The ethical risks of using these systems have been documented, and the benefits and opportunities to society are detailed.

Large language models could present societal benefits by contributing to the development of a future in which large-scale AI technologies are designed and governed responsibly. The intelligent systems being developed have great potential to serve societal goals in numerous ways. AI could contribute to the generation of ambient, data-driven knowledge that is supportive, critical of systems of power and control, and opposed to misinformation and disinformation. Policymakers should develop adaptive rather than static or precautionary approaches, emphasizing careful examination of uncertainty and capacity for adaptation. Informed and much broader public engagement with larger and more diverse investments in public processes are required. These efforts must be genuinely inclusive and, as much as possible, representative. Withdrawal or divestment would result in the siloing and reduced transparency of important agents in the AI development community. We envisage a flourishing research and development environment and a potential AI world where less harm is done. Researchers and funders should together encourage the development of enhanced clarification mechanisms in the explanatory interface. This should include finding new ways to maintain and enhance a free, constructive dialogue between AI technologists, communities, and countries. Additionally, we support researchers and other actors seeking to spawn new efforts to curtail the social misuse of AI, for example, by supporting various strategies to provide tools for grassroots and collective empowerment and accountability, in addition to the enhancement of national and international legal frameworks.

REFERENCES

Ashrafimoghari, V., & Gürkan, N. (2024). Evaluating Large Language Models on the GMAT: Implications for the Future of Business Education. SSRN *Electronic Journal.* DOI: 10.2139/ssrn.4681307

Bahammam, A. S., Trabelsi, K., Pandi-Perumal, S. R., & Jahrami, H. (2023). Adapting to the Impact of Artificial Intelligence in Scientific Writing: Balancing Benefits and Drawbacks while Developing Policies and Regulations. *Journal of Nature and Science of Medicine*, *6*(3). Advance online publication. DOI: 10.4103/jnsm.jnsm_89_23

Benítez, T. M., Xu, Y., Boudreau, J. D., Kow, A. W. C., Bello, F., Van Phuoc, L., Wang, X., Sun, X., Leung, G. K. K., Lan, Y., Wang, Y., Cheng, D., Tham, Y. C., Wong, T. Y., & Chung, K. C. (2024). Harnessing the potential of large language models in medical education: Promise and pitfalls. *Journal of the American Medical Informatics Association : JAMIA*, *31*(3). Advance online publication. DOI: 10.1093/jamia/ocad252 PMID: 38269644

Bezzi, M. (2024). Large Language Models and Security. *IEEE Security and Privacy*, *22*(2). Advance online publication. DOI: 10.1109/MSEC.2023.3345568

Caselli, T., Lieto, A., Nissim, M., & Patti, V. (2023). They are just words. ChatGPT: Anatomy and recommendations for use. *Sistemi Intelligenti*, *35*(2). Advance online publication. DOI: 10.1422/108131

Cheung, B. H. H., & Co, M. T. H. (2023). Large language models: implications of rapid evolution in medicine. In *Hong Kong Medical Journal* (Vol. 29, Issue 6). https://doi.org/DOI: 10.12809/hkmj2310890

Chow, J. C. L., Wong, V., & Li, K. (2024). Generative Pre-Trained Transformer-Empowered Healthcare Conversations: Current Trends, Challenges, and Future Directions in Large Language Model-Enabled Medical Chatbots. In *BioMedInformatics* (Vol. 4, Issue 1). DOI: 10.3390/biomedinformatics4010047

Dal Molin, L. (2024). Notes towards infrastructure governance for large language models. *First Monday*, *29*(2). Advance online publication. DOI: 10.5210/fm.v29i2.13567

Ding, Q., Ding, D., Wang, Y., Guan, C., & Ding, B. (2024). Unraveling the landscape of large language models: A systematic review and future perspectives. *Journal of Electronic Business & Digital Economics*, *3*(1). Advance online publication. DOI: 10.1108/jebde-08-2023-0015

Dwivedi, Y. K., Kshetri, N., Hughes, L., Slade, E. L., Jeyaraj, A., Kar, A. K., Baabdullah, A. M., Koohang, A., Raghavan, V., Ahuja, M., Albanna, H., Albashrawi, M. A., Al-Busaidi, A. S., Balakrishnan, J., Barlette, Y., Basu, S., Bose, I., Brooks, L., Buhalis, D., & Wright, R. (2023). "So what if ChatGPT wrote it?" Multidisciplinary perspectives on opportunities, challenges and implications of generative conversational AI for research, practice and policy. *International Journal of Information Management, 71*. Advance online publication. DOI: 10.1016/j.ijinfomgt.2023.102642

Epstein, R. H., & Dexter, F. (2023). Variability in Large Language Models' Responses to Medical Licensing and Certification Examinations. Comment on "How Does ChatGPT Perform on the United States Medical Licensing Examination? The Implications of Large Language Models for Medical Education and Knowledge Assessment." In *JMIR Medical Education* (Vol. 9). DOI: 10.2196/48305

Esmaeilzadeh, P. (2023). The role of ChatGPT in disrupting concepts, changing values, and challenging ethical norms: A qualitative study. *AI and Ethics*. Advance online publication. DOI: 10.1007/s43681-023-00338-w

Fecher, B., Hebing, M., Laufer, M., Pohle, J., & Sofsky, F. (2023). Friend or foe? Exploring the implications of large language models on the science system. *AI & Society*. Advance online publication. DOI: 10.1007/s00146-023-01791-1

Gilson, A., Safranek, C. W., Huang, T., Socrates, V., Chi, L., Taylor, R. A., & Chartash, D. (2024). Correction: How Does ChatGPT Perform on the United States Medical Licensing Examination (USMLE)? The Implications of Large Language Models for Medical Education and Knowledge Assessment. *JMIR Medical Education, 10*. Advance online publication. DOI: 10.2196/57594 PMID: 38412478

Gumilyov, L. N. (2023). Ethical Implications of Large Language Models A Multidimensional Exploration of Societal, Economic, and Technical Concerns. In *International Journal of Social Analytics*.

Hadar-Shoval, D., Asraf, K., Mizrachi, Y., Haber, Y., & Elyoseph, Z. (2024). Assessing the Alignment of Large Language Models With Human Values for Mental Health Integration: Cross-Sectional Study Using Schwartz's Theory of Basic Values. *JMIR Mental Health, 11*(1). Advance online publication. DOI: 10.2196/55988 PMID: 38593424

Hagendorff, T., & Danks, D. (2023). Ethical and methodological challenges in building morally informed AI systems. *AI and Ethics, 3*(2). Advance online publication. DOI: 10.1007/s43681-022-00188-y

Helm, P., Bella, G., Koch, G., & Giunchiglia, F. (2024). Diversity and language technology: How language modeling bias causes epistemic injustice. *Ethics and Information Technology, 26*(1). Advance online publication. DOI: 10.1007/s10676-023-09742-6

Hidayatullah, A. F., Kalinaki, K., Aslam, M. M., Zakari, R. Y., & Shafik, W. (2023). Fine-Tuning BERT-Based Models for Negative Content Identification on Indonesian Tweets. *ICITDA 2023 - Proceedings of the 2023 8th International Conference on Information Technology and Digital Applications*. DOI: 10.1109/ICITDA60835.2023.10427046

Hubert, K. F., Awa, K. N., & Zabelina, D. L. (2024). The current state of artificial intelligence generative language models is more creative than humans on divergent thinking tasks. *Scientific Reports, 14*(1). Advance online publication. DOI: 10.1038/s41598-024-53303-w PMID: 38341459

Jiang, M., Bacchi, S., Kovoor, J., Stretton, B., & Chan, W. O. (2024). Response to Jin and Dobry's "ChatGPT for health care providers and patients: Practical implications within dermatology." In *Journal of the American Academy of Dermatology* (Vol. 90, Issue 3). DOI: 10.1016/j.jaad.2023.10.038

Jun, Y., Craig, A., Shafik, W., & Sharif, L. (2021). Artificial Intelligence Application in Cybersecurity and Cyberdefense. In *Wireless Communications and Mobile Computing* (Vol. 2021). https://doi.org/DOI: 10.1155/2021/3329581

Kenthapadi, K., Lakkaraju, H., & Rajani, N. (2023). Generative AI meets Responsible AI: Practical Challenges and Opportunities. *Proceedings of the ACM SIGKDD International Conference on Knowledge Discovery and Data Mining*. DOI: 10.1145/3580305.3599557

Khan, A. A., Yunus, R., Sohail, M., Rehman, T. A., Saeed, S., Bu, Y., Jackson, C. D., Sharkey, A., Mahmood, F., & Matyal, R. (2024). Artificial Intelligence for Anesthesiology Board–Style Examination Questions: Role of Large Language Models. In *Journal of Cardiothoracic and Vascular Anesthesia* (Vol. 38, Issue 5). DOI: 10.1053/j.jvca.2024.01.032

Kirchner, K., Laue, R., Edwards, K., & Lantow, B. (2024). Patterns for modeling process variability in a healthcare context. *Business Process Management Journal, 30*(1). Advance online publication. DOI: 10.1108/BPMJ-10-2022-0500

Kretschmer, M., Margoni, T., & Oruç, P. (2024). Copyright Law and the Lifecycle of Machine Learning Models. *IIC International Review of Intellectual Property and Competition Law, 55*(1). Advance online publication. DOI: 10.1007/s40319-023-01419-3

Laato, S., Morschheuser, B., Hamari, J., & Bjorne, J. (2023). AI-Assisted Learning with ChatGPT and Large Language Models: Implications for Higher Education. *Proceedings - 2023 IEEE International Conference on Advanced Learning Technologies, ICALT 2023*. DOI: 10.1109/ICALT58122.2023.00072

Lau, M. (2024). Is ChatGPT taking over the language classroom? *Working Papers in Applied Linguistics and Linguistics at York, 4*. https://doi.org/DOI: 10.25071/2564-2855.36

Lee, S., & Park, G. (2024). Development and validation of ChatGPT literacy scale. *Current Psychology (New Brunswick, N.J.), 43*(21). Advance online publication. DOI: 10.1007/s12144-024-05723-0

Lehman, J., Gordon, J., Jain, S., Ndousse, K., Yeh, C., & Stanley, K. O. (2024). *Evolution Through Large Models*. DOI: 10.1007/978-981-99-3814-8_11

Liyanage, U. P., & Ranaweera, N. D. (2023). Ethical Considerations and Potential Risks in the Deployment of Large Language Models in Diverse Societal Contexts. *Journal of Computational Social Dynamics*, *8*(11).

Llanes-Jurado, J., Gómez-Zaragozá, L., Minissi, M. E., Alcañiz, M., & Marín-Morales, J. (2024). Developing conversational Virtual Humans for social emotion elicitation based on large language models. *Expert Systems with Applications*, *246*. Advance online publication. DOI: 10.1016/j.eswa.2024.123261

Ma, J., Song, J., Young, N. D., Chang, B. C. H., Korhonen, P. K., Campos, T. L., Liu, H., & Gasser, R. B. (2024). "Bingo" - a large language model- and graph neural network-based workflow for the prediction of essential genes from protein data. *Briefings in Bioinformatics*, *25*(1). Advance online publication. DOI: 10.1093/bib/bbad472 PMID: 38152979

Narayanan Venkit, P. (2023). *Towards a Holistic Approach: Understanding Sociodemographic Biases in NLP Models using an Interdisciplinary Lens*. DOI: 10.1145/3600211.3604754

Nay, J. J., Karamardian, D., Lawsky, S. B., Tao, W., Bhat, M., Jain, R., Lee, A. T., Choi, J. H., & Kasai, J. (2024). Large language models as tax attorneys: A case study in legal capabilities emergence. *Philosophical Transactions. Series A, Mathematical, Physical, and Engineering Sciences*, *382*(2270). Advance online publication. DOI: 10.1098/rsta.2023.0159 PMID: 38403061

Noguer i Alonso, M. (2023). A Framework for the Evaluation of Large Language Models. SSRN *Electronic Journal*. https://doi.org/DOI: 10.2139/ssrn.4649866

Park, Y. J., Pillai, A., Deng, J., Guo, E., Gupta, M., Paget, M., & Naugler, C. (2024). Assessing the research landscape and clinical utility of large language models: A scoping review. *BMC Medical Informatics and Decision Making*, *24*(1). Advance online publication. DOI: 10.1186/s12911-024-02459-6 PMID: 38475802

Pijeira-Díaz, H. J., Braumann, S., van de Pol, J., van Gog, T., & de Bruin, A. B. H. (2024). Towards adaptive support for self-regulated learning of causal relations: Evaluating four Dutch word vector models. *British Journal of Educational Technology*, *55*(4). Advance online publication. DOI: 10.1111/bjet.13431

Polverini, G., & Gregorcic, B. (2024). How understanding large language models can inform the use of ChatGPT in physics education. *European Journal of Physics*, *45*(2). Advance online publication. DOI: 10.1088/1361-6404/ad1420

Roberts, J., Baker, M., & Andrew, J. (2024). Artificial intelligence and qualitative research: The promise and perils of large language model (LLM) 'assistance.'. *Critical Perspectives on Accounting*, *99*. Advance online publication. DOI: 10.1016/j.cpa.2024.102722

Shafik, W. (2023). *Introduction to ChatGPT*. In *Advanced Applications of Generative AI and Natural Language Processing Models*. DOI: 10.4018/979-8-3693-0502-7.ch001

Shafik, W., & Tufail, A. (2023). Energy Optimization Analysis on Internet of Things. In *Environmental Science and Engineering*. https://doi.org/DOI: 10.1007/978-3-031-25662-2_1

Smetana, M., Salles de Salles, L., Sukharev, I., & Khazanovich, L. (2024). Highway Construction Safety Analysis Using Large Language Models. *Applied Sciences (Switzerland)*, *14*(4). Advance online publication. DOI: 10.3390/app14041352

Tai, R. H., Bentley, L. R., Xia, X., Sitt, J. M., Fankhauser, S. C., Chicas-Mosier, A. M., & Monteith, B. G. (2024). An Examination of the Use of Large Language Models to Aid Analysis of Textual Data. *International Journal of Qualitative Methods*, *23*. Advance online publication. DOI: 10.1177/16094069241231168

Takemoto, K. (2024). The moral machine experiment on large language models. *Royal Society Open Science*, *11*(2). Advance online publication. DOI: 10.1098/rsos.231393 PMID: 38328569

Tian, D., Jiang, S., Zhang, L., Lu, X., & Xu, Y. (2024). The role of large language models in medical image processing: a narrative review. In *Quantitative Imaging in Medicine and Surgery* (Vol. 14, Issue 1). DOI: 10.21037/qims-23-892

Tokayev, K.-J. (2023). Ethical Implications of Large Language Models A Multidimensional Exploration of Societal, Economic, and Technical Concerns. *International Journal of Stochastic Analysis*, *8*(9).

Uzun, L. (2023). Are Concerns Related to Artificial Intelligence Development and Use Really Necessary: A Philosophical Discussion. *Digital Society : Ethics, Socio-Legal and Governance of Digital Technology*, *2*(3). Advance online publication. DOI: 10.1007/s44206-023-00070-2

Wan, Q., Hu, S., Zhang, Y., Wang, P., Wen, B., & Lu, Z. (2024). "It Felt Like Having a Second Mind": Investigating Human-AI Co-creativity in Prewriting with Large Language Models. *Proceedings of the ACM on Human-Computer Interaction*, *8*(CSCW1). DOI: 10.1145/3637361

Yan, L., Sha, L., Zhao, L., Li, Y., Martinez-Maldonado, R., Chen, G., Li, X., Jin, Y., & Gašević, D. (2024). Practical and ethical challenges of large language models in education: A systematic scoping review. In *British Journal of Educational Technology* (Vol. 55, Issue 1). DOI: 10.1111/bjet.13370

Zhao, L., Zhu, D., Shafik, W., Matinkhah, S. M., Ahmad, Z., Sharif, L., & Craig, A. (2022). Artificial intelligence analysis in cyber domain: A review. In *International Journal of Distributed Sensor Networks* (Vol. 18, Issue 4). DOI: 10.1177/15501329221084882

Zhuo, Y. T., Huang, Y., Chen, C., & Xing, Z. (2023). Exploring AI Ethics of ChatGPT: A Diagnostic Analysis. *ArXiv Preprint ArXiv:2301.12867.*

Zietsch, J., Kulaga, R., Held, H., Herrmann, C., & Thiede, S. (2024). Multi-layer edge resource placement optimization for factories. *Journal of Intelligent Manufacturing*, *35*(2). Advance online publication.

ENDNOTES

1. https://www.ibm.com/topics/large-language-models
2. https://cloud.google.com/learn/what-is-artificial-intelligence
3. https://en.wikipedia.org/wiki/Generative_pre-trained_transformer
4. https://www.ibm.com/topics/natural-language-processing
5. https://en.wikipedia.org/wiki/GPT

6 https://en.wikipedia.org/wiki/Confidentiality

7 https://www.ibm.com/topics/machine-learning

8 https://gdpr-info.eu/

9 https://en.wikipedia.org/wiki/Algorithm

10 https://www.cisco.com/c/en/us/solutions/enterprise-networks/it-information-technology-explained.html

11 https://www.databricks.com/glossary/what-is-dataset

Chapter 8
Assessing Security and Privacy Concerns in LLM Applications:
Legal and Social Concerns

Bhupinder Singh
https://orcid.org/0009-0006-4779-2553
Sharda University, India

Arunima Shastri
https://orcid.org/0000-0002-6260-1253
Christ University, Bangalore, India

Saurabh Chandra
https://orcid.org/0000-0003-4172-9968
Bennett University, Greater Noida, India

ABSTRACT

Large language models (LLMs) like Open AI's GPT-4 have transformed many industries, including natural language processing. But, still the applications of these need a properly secure mechanism as it is getting attached to everyday technology at on an extensive rate and large security & privacy risk are encapsulated in its use which must be controlled for safe and ethical use. LLM models are trained with an avalanche of data, often from web-scraped sources that could be handling personal and sensitive content. This may inadvertently have the LAZ model hold on to, and possibly leak, some private data of users who use the API. Having measures to address them through comprehensive strategies and conforming with regulations are important in the responsible usage of LLM applications.

DOI: 10.4018/979-8-3693-8387-2.ch008

INTRODUCTION

Ensuring that training data are indeed well-vetted and fully anonymized is essential to avoid these risks. The input data which the users provide to an LLM can be sensitive in nature (Dinesh Arokia Raj et al., 2024). These interactions are managed by infrastructure, and a compromise of that result in data breaches (Yue & Shyu, 2024). To prevent unauthorized access, user inputs should be handled and stored securely. The primary step to secured LLM applications is universal encryption and secures data transmission s (Mithas et al., 2022). The LLMs can also be vulnerable to adversarial attacks, where they are supplied with the inputs which have been crafted in such a way that it changes its behavior (Ivanov et al., 2019). They can vary from input manipulations causing the model to generate harmful or misleading content, all the way up to extracting sensitive information for advanced attackers (Javaid et al., 2022). Strong security measures, such as vigilant monitoring and updating of models are essential to identify/adapt against adversarial activities like this (Fraga-Lamas et al., 2021).

Apart from the obvious technical security issues LLMs bring along a whole raft of ethical considerations - and specifically around bias, discrimination (Asadollahi-Yazdi et al., 2020). These models can both learn from previous data and thus inherits any biases that were present within the training data, as well as propagate this potential societal bias (Meyendorf et al., 2023). This results in outputs that perpetuate stereotypes or unjustly target certain groups (Zhong et al., 2017). This is something which needs continuous work and we will need to audit the models again to fine tune them for fairness, bias reduction (Angelopoulos et al., 2019). That is why it must be regulated to protect the privacy and security of consumers, as more LLMs are used (Lu et al., 2020). For LLM applications, regulatory compliance in the areas of data protection such as General Data Protection Regulation (GDPR) is a must (Chander et al., 2022). These laws require specific data care and transparency standards so that users know when their information is used or stored (Kasowaki & Ahmet, 2024). Though LLMs and Transformers of this sort do wonderful tasks, they introduce really large security and privacy issues (Sima et al., 2020). Tempted with an example, a model trained on not anonymized datasets could generate responses that contain private information thus becoming the privacy time bomb. But as technology changes, the challenge evolves and vigilance in perpetuity appears to be a necessity if we are going to protect the privacy of being tracked by these powerful tools (Tseng et al., 2021).

Relevance of the Security and Privacy Concerns in LLM Applications

The security of Large Language Model applications is mainly a data issue because LLMs can manage a lot of data, have large computational powers, and can affect decision-making aggressively. A potential risk is regarding data privacy, where LLMs could accidently memorize and produce sensitive or proprietary information that exists in the training datasets. Prompt injection attacks and adversarial inputs are two methods through which the model can be used to generate harmful, biased or misleading outputs. Also, more troubling yet is that model hallucination creating fake but credible information can be risky in te domain of high stakes such as healthcare, law and finance. LLMs can also be misused by bad actors to automate Phishing, Social Engineering or Deepfake Text. At the same time, bias and fairness are ongoing challenges as models learn from data that embodies societal biases, so they can be discriminative against certain groups. Intellectual property violations can happen if the model reproduces copyrighted content. Model extraction attacks, in which adversaries extract LLMs to clone capabilities without permission for this to be possible; it is of utmost importance to have the highest levels of security protocols, data anonymization and output moderation in place with continuous vulnerability testing. Applying ethical governance frameworks, regulatory compliance, and explainable AI (XAI) approaches to LLM can help to ensure that these applications are also trustworthy and compliant with safety and societal values.

The rapid development and deployment of large language models (LLMs) such as GPT-4 have revolutionized various sectors, including healthcare, finance, and technology (Anastasi et al., 2021). However, these advancements bring with them significant security and privacy concerns, especially given the sensitive nature of the data these models process (Dwivedi et al., 2021). This paper critically examines these concerns, focusing on the legal and social implications that arise from the widespread use of LLMs (Majstorovic & Mitrovic, 2019). Through a comprehensive review of the existing literature, analysis of regulatory frameworks, and exploration of case studies, this chapter identifies key challenges, including the risk of data breaches, adversarial attacks, and violations of data privacy (Badri et al., 2018). Legal loopholes and the lack of robust regulatory frameworks further exacerbate these issues, leaving users vulnerable to exploitation (Xu et al., 2018). The findings highlight the urgent need for enhanced security measures, legal reforms, and ethical guidelines to ensure the responsible use of LLMs. Thus, this chapter proposes several recommendations to mitigate these risks, including technical solutions, legal reforms, and strategies to raise public awareness about the potential dangers of LLM applications (Bhuiyan et al., 2020). However, the significant development of LLM technology also has brought some considerable concerns related to security and privacy (Reier Forradellas & Garay Gallastegui, 2021). With the growing integration of such models in multiple applications, it is important to identify and mitigate the legal as well as social concerns linked with their use (Singh Rajawat et al., 2021). Also, the security and privacy concerns raised by LLM applications, with a focus on legal and social aspects. The potential risks, vulnerabilities, and ethical concerns depend on the deployment of LLMs across a variety of domains including health, finance, social media, etc. (Leng et al., 2020).

Figure 1. Dimensions of the introduction section (Original)

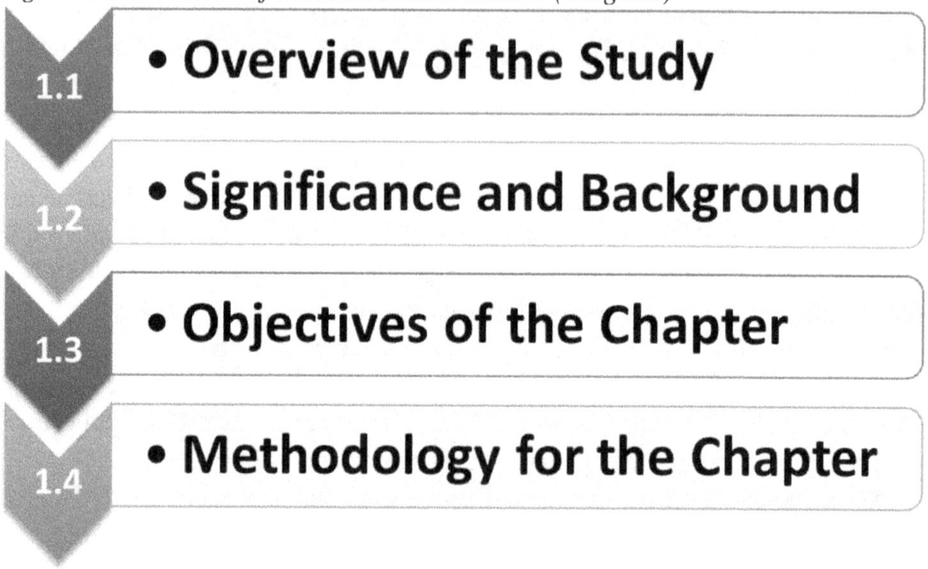

Overview of the Study

The Large Language Models (LLMs) such as GPT-4, and BER are transforming the industries and pushing ahead of natural language processing, content generation customer support & predictive analysis solutions (Javaid et al., 2021). Working based on analyzing extensive data sets and outputting text similar to a human's words, these models have become essential for companies or organizations. Nevertheless, extensive data use results in severe security and privacy issues (Hassoun et al., 2023). Also, this Chapter elaborates on these aspects, particularly highlighting the potential threats and issues involved in LLM performances (Aoun et al., 2021). Firstly, the paper discusses security concerns such as data leaks and adversarial attacks or model exploitation associated with LLMs, all of which resulted from their complex architecture and extensive usage of large-scale datasets (Arden et al., 2021). Under privacy the various scrutiny done like data exposure, an opt-out clause for informed consent, and then independent loading of different legal frameworks such as GDPR or CCPA (Rane, 2023). The larger social and ethical problems with LLMs, such as bias, discrimination, transparency control, accountability concerns, and their effect on job work and employee relationships and trust in general (Awan et al., 2021). Based on an analysis of these dimensions, the paper aspires to provide a comprehensive view in real contexts regarding various legal and social challenges posed by LLMs with recommendations for measures against them effectively aiming at preventing unethical deployment of such systems across sectors (Kumar et al., 2020).

Significance and Background of the Chapter

Also, LLM integration has been contentious and even setting ethics aside, the very nature of these model's data-hungry monoliths that in many cases contain deeply personal & sensitive information about individuals served by proprietary algorithms at a colossal scale is cause for concern on privacy and security grounds. There are many risks in using LLM applications including data breaches, adversarial attacks, and misuse of AI-generated content. For a while now, the legislation providing for data protection and privacy has been struggling to keep up with AI technology since they are not moving at break-neck speed as the technology itself. In brief, the LLMs are powered by big datasets potentially containing personal data, drawing critical questions about privacy, consent, and misuse. Addressing both the legal, and more general social-scientific questions surrounding the use of LLM, there are several key aspects such as transparency or accountability in the spirit. This also helps policymakers as well as developers and users, both contributing to the safe and responsible integration of LLMs into society.

Objectives of the Chapter

This chapter has the following objectives which are as follows to:

- assess the privacy implications of LLM usage such as unintended data exposure, and informed consent problems, and well-established techniques such as differential privacy protect them (Li et al., 2017).
- review & Critique Legal Frameworks to evaluate existing legal frameworks governing data privacy based on LLMs like GDPR, and CCPA and identify lacunae that may necessitate certain modifications to enhance the protection of user data (Kurniawan et al., 2022).

- understand the broader social and ethical considerations of LLM deployment, addressing such topics as bias, discrimination transparency accountability end consequences to public trust and fair representation in society (Jakka et al., 2022).
- proactively develop and recommend effective methods to mitigate the underlying security, and privacy issues with technical, legal, and ethical procedures delivery based on a more responsible model (Xing et al., 2021).

Methodology for the Chapter

The methodology adopted in this chapter is primarily doctrinal research that remains fundamental when analyzing the security and privacy concerns of LLM applications, especially any legal or social element (Shi et al., 2020). This strategy includes detailed research of the status quo, looking into existing legal frameworks, case laws, and regulations as well as scholarly commentary to understand how good currently applicable laws are at solving problems posed by LLMs (Finance et al., 2015). The method of systematically reviewing legal texts helps detect lacunae within the law and ambiguities as to what has legal force, which permits how it was most likely meant, together with assessing enforcement compliance for LLM applications (Saeed et al., 2023). As a person who has an interest in tech policy, doctrinal research is also useful to some extent as it contextualizes the way courts have addressed concepts like data privacy and informed consent but can be supplemented by empirical methods (Kumar & Mallipeddi, 2022). About social concerns, this process allows for the examination of how the legal norms and ethics (bias, discrimination, trust) intertwine in a way that creates fundamental grounds for reforming laws based on moral principles that are vital for LLMs as seen through their complexities (Bag & Pretorius, 2022).

SECURITY CONCERNS IN LLM APPLICATION

Large Language Model (LLM) applications deal with issues tainted by legality such as privacy, responsibility for harassment, and adherence to country-specific rules (Morgan et al., 2021). However, data privacy has become a major concern. Because LLMs typically handle significant volumes of personal data, adhering to the requirements in regard to compliance and privacy matters prescribed by GDPR specialists or CCPA's highest-paid attorney is critical. These legislations enforce powerful user consent, data anonymizing systems, and the access or deletion of one's personal information which is a bit difficult to accommodate into LLM (Nica & Stehel, 2021). Additionally, there are intellectual property concerns as LLMs produce what appears to be copyrighted content (Borowski, 2021). It is essential to have LLM applications that are not only copyright law compliant but also do not violate other intellectual property rights (Ahmad et al., 2021). Ultimately, legal standards are required to manage and mitigate these new challenges as current legislation in this area fails to address the extensive nuances of LLM technology (Wamba-Taguimdje et al., 2020). To ensure a responsible and lawful utilization of LLM applications, it is necessary to create an appropriate framework for comprehensive regulations on these concerns (Popov et al., 2022). To mitigate these threats, nontrivial data protection, model robustness against these attacks, and strict access control must all be met at scale. There are some best practices to address LLM vulnerabilities and reduce any associated risks while maintaining a strong security posture are as follows-

Data Security and Privacy

The biggest problem in LLM applications is the risk of data leaks and unauthorized access to classified information. LLMs have been trained on much more data than just your personal, financial, or medical records (Lu, 2019). If this data is not well protected, it can also be exploited by people who want to use your personal information against you (Borowski, 2021). Also, LLMs can output sensitive information that may inadvertently be exposed to unauthorized consumers. Organizations must, as an imperative guard data with encryption and access controls which anonymize the text to avoid context loss (Lim et al., 2021). Performing regular risk assessments and penetration testing can help to identify vulnerabilities so that they are done away with in LLM systems (Vogt, 2021).

Model Security and Integrity

LLMs can additionally be targeted by integrity attacks or adversaries aiming to bias their final samples. For instance, adversarial attacks can leverage a model's architectural inadequacy to produce incorrect or biased outputs (Gadekar et al., 2022). Prompt injection attacks may also be applied to generate harmful or unethical content by having the attacker craft a prompt that provokes the model into creating a statement accordingly (Tao et al., 2021). The best defense against these attacks is for systems to employ both front-end and back-end input validation followed by sanitization activities that aim at cleansing the suspected malicious content (Chen et al., 2022). Resource limits and the use of rate limiting or intentional throttling can help guard against DoS attacks that seek to flood a system. Keeping an eye on all of the transactions being made along with performing anomaly detection can be great tools to indicate suspicious behavior (Mourtzis et al., 2022).

Ethical Considerations

The deployment of LLMs also raises existential ethical questions, especially around the themes of bias, fairness, and transparency. However, LLMs may exacerbate and reproduce societal biases in the data they are trained on, hence introducing biased outputs or decisions (Wan et al., 2018). LLM systems are often regarded as black boxes, a status that is not only elusive to regulators but also difficult for adversaries or lawyers to determine the evidence of its outputs (Cioffi et al., 2020). As for these concerns, companies need to take steps to lead ethical AI with fairness, accountability, and transparency (Laskurain-Iturbe et al., 2021). Key aspects of these systems involve responsively collecting unbiased training data, bias testing, and mitigation methods in model development around decision-making transparency for AI so that we can know why our algorithms react the way they do (Brock & Von Wangenheim, 2019).

Legal Concerns in LLM Application

Large Language Model (LLM) applications deal with issues tainted by legality such as privacy, responsibility for harassment, and adherence to country-specific rules (Nguyen et al., 2020). However, data privacy has become a major concern. Because LLMs typically handle significant volumes of personal data, adhering to the requirements in regard to compliance and privacy matters prescribed by GDPR specialists or CCPA highest paid attorney is critical (Hassoun et al., 2022). These legislations enforce powerful user consent, data anonymizing systems, and the access or deletion of one's personal information which is a bit difficult to accommodate into LLM. A highly crucial aspect of this is to what extent the developers should be accredited or if any accountability lies with those who use the model, as well as how much responsibility we can attribute to "the model" (Nahavandi, 2019).

Privacy Regulations and Laws

Governments are increasingly introducing data protection and privacy laws that apply to the use of LLMs. These laws place rigorous demands on the collection, storage and processing of data including sensitive data that might be harnessed for training or employing LLM technologies (Zhou et al., 2021). Organizations must take steps to ensure that their applications are compliant with regulations aiming at protecting personal data, such as obtaining consent from individuals or the person in charge of that individual and providing concise notice about how applicant information is used by communities including restrictions on retention. This means that failure to comply with these laws can subject you to fines of significant amounts and legal actions (de la Pena Zarzuelo et al., 2020).

IP and Trade Secrets

LLMs can also pose intellectual property and trade secret issues. The training data to create LLMs may include copyrighted work or sensitive information, which could be replicated in the outputs of a model (Sanchez-Sotano et al., 2020). Furthermore, the exact algorithms and architectures used to construct LLMs may be legitimately protected as trade secrets at best or stolen, infringed upon, and counterfeited by others in a worstcase scenario. Because LLM applications may run on the same computers where sensitive information is processed in other ways and would be impractical for companies to simply turn off when they are also handling regulated data, the secrecy of IP owned or being used through a license must still be carefully considered (Bokhari & Myeong, 2023).

Liability and Accountability

With the increasing deployment of LLM applications, there are mounting concerns over who is responsible if these systems inflict harm (Ali et al., 2022). The user interacts with the model, and if that LLM begins to conclude things that result in actual harm figuring out who's responsible is ambiguous regulators and legal scholars have begun to contemplate the frameworks by which liability can be allocated and accountability established for LLM-related harms. It could require new legal or regulatory frameworks at the industry level and best practices for responsible development and implementation of LLM applications (Kuzior, 2022).

Figure 2. Points on security concerns in LLM application (Original)

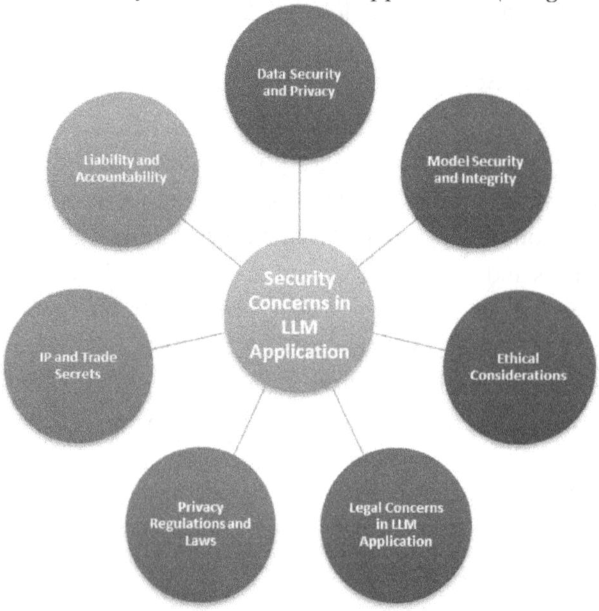

SOCIAL CONCERNS IN LLM APPLICATIONS

Misinformation and Disinformation

A significant social issue associated with LLM applications is their capacity to create and spread false and misleading information. LLMs can generate your fake news articles, social media posts, or anything that looks authentic but is untrue (Bongomin et al., 2020). This erodes public confidence, diminishes social unity, and has the possibility to impact political processes. Organizations need to put content moderation protocols, such as validating with fact-checkers and sources or sharing of authentic digital watermarks and signatures in place for protection against misinformation behavior (Pivoto et al., 2021). The use of LLMs in generating and distributing content is being considered for regulation by both policymakers as well as social media platforms (Gupta, 2023).

Algorithmic Discrimination Bias

LLMs can inherit social biases within their training data that are re-used to generate predictions, which may lead to fair or unfair outputs. In many contexts such as hiring, lending, or healthcare these decisions can lead to significant harm when LLM-powered systems take actions that are disadvantageous to certain individuals or groups. Fairness and nondiscrimination must be a priority in developing and deploying LLM applications to counter the effects of algorithmic bias or discrimination (Dorfleitner & Braun, 2019).

Job Loss or Unemployment

Job displacement and subsequent unemployment due to high rates of LLMs serving in various industries become a growing concern. As LLMs become more competent at doing human work like writing, analysis, and customer service there is the chance that this will replace or severely retrain some jobs (Nassiry, 2018). But to offset those risks, policymakers and industries should collaborate in constructing paths that allow for the reskilling and redeployment of workers disrupted by LLM adoption. This will necessitate investments in up-skilling and re-training, new job creation in future industries, and social safety nets to safeguard workers against the vagaries of economic transition.

Figure 3. Social concerns in LLM applications (Original)

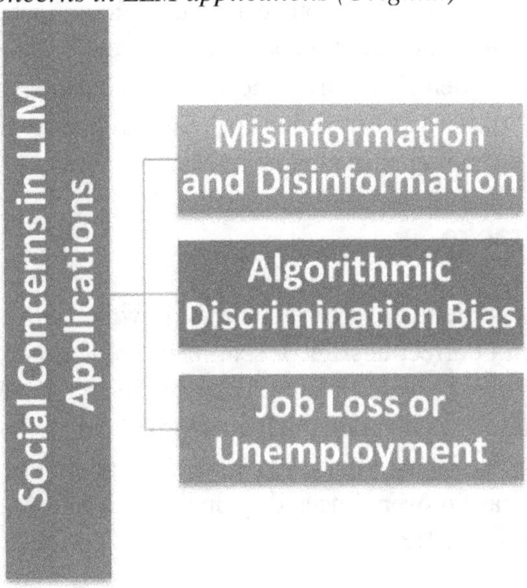

LIMITATIONS OF ASSESSING SECURITY AND PRIVACY IN LLM APPLICATIONS

Security and privacy analysis on Large Language Model (LLM) applications face various difficulties, which also well represents the difficulty and evolution of LLM technologies. This points to a need for a subtler appreciation of the LLM technology itself, as well as attention to applicable supervisory regimes (Chen & Volz, 2021).

Complexity of LLMs

The main difficulty with LLMs in terms of evaluating security and privacy concerns is the fact that they are highly complex. These models use complex architectures to generate human-like text trained on massive amounts of data (Yang et al., 2021). The complexity makes it tough to grasp what LLMs are like and how they may behave in different situations. The "black-box" nature of LLMs makes it difficult to examine potential security vulnerabilities and privacy concerns (Zhang et al., 2018).

Data Privacy Concerns

LLMs are trained on large datasets which may include highly private data about individuals. This large amount of data means one thing, and that is a huge challenge protecting this resource in compliance with privacy regulations (Migliorelli & Dessertine, 2019). There are, of course techniques to mitigate privacy risks such as data anonymization and encryption but a certain lack of a secure environment is clear. For example, re-identification can occur even with anonymized data through de-anonymization attacks and encryption does not mitigate the risk of exposure that exists during model training or deployment (Naderi & Tian, 2022).

Adversarial Attacks

LLMs are susceptible to adversarial attacks, in which clever stimuli cause the model output from a correct answer or sentiment prediction to entirely different orders of magnitude responses. The attacks target the architecture of the model or weaknesses in its training data, potentially compromising both security and privacy. The problem is creating strong enough barriers to protect against these attacks, which the enemies have proven time and again that they are always getting smarter and trickier (Thomason 2018).

Existing Data Protection Laws (GDPR, CCPA)

The main issues for LLM applications are compliance with existing data protection laws. The regulations further outline laws around how data is handled, requiring firms to have explicit user consent and the demand for access to personal information (Liu et al., 2022). The difficulty is that the essential nature of LLMs makes applying such regulations to them much more complicated. A great example is the right to be forgotten in GDPR, which can prove technically difficult as it might be challenging or impossible to manually delete every instance of a particular data point from large amounts of training examples that were used (Yan et al., 2022).

Liability and Accountability

The complex legal question of attribution and liability for AI generated content if an LLM yields damaging or misleading results, it is frequently unclear which party the developers, users, and the model itself are to blame. This ambiguity makes enforcing accountability and redress for harm resulting from LLM applications more difficult. In case of an attack, legal frameworks have to be standardized so that roles and responsibilities are made crystal clear (Bayram et al., 2022).

Bias and Fairness

LLM bias is an enormous problem as well Since these models are often trained on biased datasets that reflect societal prejudices, this bias would result in producing inappropriate or discriminatory content (Sachs et al., 2019). The sheer magnitude of data and the complexity in LLMs, makes identifying bias decidedly non-trivial. Moreover, some of the bias analytics are not capturing all necessary dimensions effectively to address issues optimally leaving much room for a need in research and development (Campbell-Verduyn, 2023).

Transparency and Explainability

LLMs are frequently accused of being uninterpretable and opaque. Interpreting the internal mechanism behind which those models output some results in a certain manner is difficult because of these complex architectures. This lack of transparency is problematic because it leaves regulators, developers and end users to guess how well an embedding performs at capturing the information contained in data needed for processing a model (Schulz & Feist, 2021).

Interdisciplinary Challenges

The security and privacy issues in LLMs is a multidiscipline subject, involving at least computer science, law, and ethics (Kalaiarasi & Kirubahari, 2023). Understanding each other type of expertise can be difficult because technically focused experts might tend to think in terms that are practical or technological and the legal types will use law informed language (Chueca Vergara & Ferruz Agudo, 2021). Solutions that work are necessarily interdisciplinary, drawing upon the lessons learned from all of these adjoining territories (Radanliev, 2024).

CONCLUSION AND FUTURE SCOPE

The progress in LLM technology has many advantages and at the same time develops severe concerns like security, privacy, legality, and social impact. As LLMs are increasingly being integrated within applications in organizations, responsible development and deployment of these technologies is imperative. And all of this needs to factor in strong data security and model integrity, ethical AI practices that obey the law, literal laws and regulation compliance when necessary as well as steps taken with potential stakeholders to address societal matters. These simple steps could help us leverage the benefits of LLMs while mitigating risks to ensure that these technologies are used safely, ethically, and in a way as beneficial to society at large. As the area of LLM advances, it is imperative that policymakers legal experts, and industry leaders collaborate in developing clear guidelines standards, and regulations for LLM use. This will help to ensure that the application of LLMs is done in a way that respects individual rights, enhances fairness and non-discrimination, and increases societal welfare. In the end, all types of LLM experiences will live and die on how well organizations can address this tangle of security, privacy, legal, and social considerations. Adopting these principles, and taking the necessary measures to address each of them in a timely manner will enable us to fully unleash LLM technology while ensuring that it is implemented in a responsible ethical way that benefits all. Since LLMs will be applied across sectors, creating robust security standards is paramount. In future work, we hope to build strong defenses against a wide range of attacks such as data breaches, adversarial examples, and model stealing. Also, growing attention to data privacy, in order to improve our work further research will need better solutions for both preserving and protecting it that are more efficient such as utilizing new forms of differentially private information-sharing or federated learning. Global Standards for LLM Development: As correspondence transcends borders, global standards are required to ensure the ethical and legal use of large language models. An important role is reserved for the establishment and coordination of international laws as well as economic guidelines that are able to be adopted by LLM applications all over the world in a consistent way.

REFERENCES

Ahmad, T., Zhang, D., Huang, C., Zhang, H., Dai, N., Song, Y., & Chen, H. (2021). Artificial intelligence in sustainable energy industry: Status Quo, challenges and opportunities. *Journal of Cleaner Production*, *289*, 125834.

Ali, A., Septyanto, A. W., Chaudhary, I., Al Hamadi, H., Alzoubi, H. M., & Khan, Z. F. (2022, February). Applied Artificial Intelligence as Event Horizon Of Cyber Security. In *2022 International Conference on Business Analytics for Technology and Security (ICBATS)* (pp. 1-7). IEEE.

Anastasi, S., Madonna, M., & Monica, L. (2021). Implications of embedded artificial intelligence-machine learning on safety of machinery. *Procedia Computer Science*, *180*, 338–343.

Angelopoulos, A., Michailidis, E. T., Nomikos, N., Trakadas, P., Hatziefremidis, A., Voliotis, S., & Zahariadis, T. (2019). Tackling faults in the industry 4.0 era—A survey of machine-learning solutions and key aspects. *Sensors (Basel)*, *20*(1), 109. PMID: 31878065

Aoun, A., Ilinca, A., Ghandour, M., & Ibrahim, H. (2021). A review of Industry 4.0 characteristics and challenges, with potential improvements using blockchain technology. *Computers & Industrial Engineering*, *162*, 107746.

Arden, N. S., Fisher, A. C., Tyner, K., Lawrence, X. Y., Lee, S. L., & Kopcha, M. (2021). Industry 4.0 for pharmaceutical manufacturing: Preparing for the smart factories of the future. *International Journal of Pharmaceutics*, *602*, 120554. PMID: 33794326

Asadollahi-Yazdi, E., Couzon, P., Nguyen, N. Q., Ouazene, Y., & Yalaoui, F. (2020). Industry 4.0: Revolution or Evolution? *American Journal of Operations Research*, *10*(06), 241.

Awan, U., Sroufe, R., & Shahbaz, M. (2021). Industry 4.0 and the circular economy: A literature review and recommendations for future research. *Business Strategy and the Environment*, *30*(4), 2038–2060.

Badri, A., Boudreau-Trudel, B., & Souissi, A. S. (2018). Occupational health and safety in the industry 4.0 era: A cause for major concern? *Safety Science*, *109*, 403–411.

Bag, S., & Pretorius, J. H. C. (2022). Relationships between industry 4.0, sustainable manufacturing and circular economy: Proposal of a research framework. *The International Journal of Organizational Analysis*, *30*(4), 864–898.

Bayram, O., Talay, I., & Feridun, M. (2022). Can FinTech promote sustainable finance? Policy lessons from the case of Turkey. *Sustainability, 14*(19), 12414.

Bhuiyan, A. B., Ali, M. J., Zulkifli, N., & Kumarasamy, M. M. (2020). Industry 4.0: Challenges, opportunities, and strategic solutions for Bangladesh. *International Journal of Business and Management Future*, *4*(2), 41–56.

Bokhari, S. A. A., & Myeong, S. (2023). The influence of artificial intelligence on e-Governance and cybersecurity in smart cities: A stakeholder's perspective. *IEEE Access : Practical Innovations, Open Solutions*.

Bongomin, O., Gilibrays Ocen, G., Oyondi Nganyi, E., Musinguzi, A., & Omara, T. (2020). Exponential disruptive technologies and the required skills of industry 4.0. *Journal of Engineering*, *2020*, 1–17.

Borowski, P. F. (2021). Innovative processes in managing an enterprise from the energy and food sector in the era of industry 4.0. *Processes (Basel, Switzerland)*, *9*(2), 381.

Borowski, P. F. (2021). Digitization, digital twins, blockchain, and industry 4.0 as elements of management process in enterprises in the energy sector. *Energies*, *14*(7), 1885.

Brock, J. K. U., & Von Wangenheim, F. (2019). Demystifying AI: What digital transformation leaders can teach you about realistic artificial intelligence. *California Management Review*, *61*(4), 110–134.

. Campbell-Verduyn, M. (2023). Conjuring a cooler world? Imaginaries of improvement in blockchain climate finance experiments. *Environment and Planning C: Politics and Space*, 23996544231162858.

. Chander, B., Pal, S., De, D., & Buyya, R. (2022). Artificial intelligence-based internet of Things for industry 5.0. *Artificial intelligence-based internet of things systems*, 3-45.

Chen, Y., Lu, Y., Bulysheva, L., & Kataev, M. Y. (2022). Applications of blockchain in industry 4.0: A review. *Information Systems Frontiers*, •••, 1–15.

Chen, Y., & Volz, U. (2021). Scaling up sustainable investment through blockchain-based project bonds. *ADB-IGF Special Working Paper Series "Fintech to Enable Development, Investment, Financial Inclusion, and Sustainability.*

Chueca Vergara, C., & Ferruz Agudo, L. (2021). Fintech and sustainability: Do they affect each other? *Sustainability*, *13*(13), 7012.

Cioffi, R., Travaglioni, M., Piscitelli, G., Petrillo, A., & De Felice, F. (2020). Artificial intelligence and machine learning applications in smart production: Progress, trends, and directions. *Sustainability*, *12*(2), 492.

de la Peña Zarzuelo, I., Soeane, M. J. F., & Bermúdez, B. L. (2020). Industry 4.0 in the port and maritime industry: A literature review. *Journal of Industrial Information Integration*, *20*, 100173.

Dinesh Arokia Raj, A., Jha, R. R., Yadav, M., Sam, D., & Jayanthi, K. (2024). Role of Blockchain and Watermarking Toward Cybersecurity. In *Multimedia Watermarking: Latest Developments and Trends* (pp. 103–123). Springer Nature Singapore.

. Dorfleitner, G., & Braun, D. (2019). Fintech, digitalization and blockchain: possible applications for green finance. *The rise of green finance in Europe: opportunities and challenges for issuers, investors and marketplaces*, 207-237.

Dwivedi, Y. K., Hughes, L., Ismagilova, E., Aarts, G., Coombs, C., Crick, T., & Williams, M. D. (2021). Artificial Intelligence (AI): Multidisciplinary perspectives on emerging challenges, opportunities, and agenda for research, practice and policy. *International Journal of Information Management*, *57*, 101994.

Finance, A. T. C. C. (2015). *Industry 4.0 Challenges and solutions for the digital transformation and use of exponential technologies. Finance, audit tax consulting corporate*. Swiss.

Fraga-Lamas, P., Lopes, S. I., & Fernández-Caramés, T. M. (2021). Green IoT and edge AI as key technological enablers for a sustainable digital transition towards a smart circular economy: An industry 5.0 use case. *Sensors (Basel)*, *21*(17), 5745. PMID: 34502637

Gadekar, R., Sarkar, B., & Gadekar, A. (2022). Key performance indicator based dynamic decision-making framework for sustainable Industry 4.0 implementation risks evaluation: Reference to the Indian manufacturing industries. *Annals of Operations Research*, *318*(1), 189–249. PMID: 35910040

Gupta, R. (2023). Industry 4.0 adaption in indian banking Sector—A review and agenda for future research. *Vision (Basel)*, *27*(1), 24–32. PMID: 36977304

Hassoun, A., Aït-Kaddour, A., Abu-Mahfouz, A. M., Rathod, N. B., Bader, F., Barba, F. J., & Regenstein, J. (2023). The fourth industrial revolution in the food industry—Part I: Industry 4.0 technologies. *Critical Reviews in Food Science and Nutrition*, *63*(23), 6547–6563. PMID: 35114860

Hassoun, A., Prieto, M. A., Carpena, M., Bouzembrak, Y., Marvin, H. J., Pallares, N., & Bono, G. (2022). Exploring the role of green and Industry 4.0 technologies in achieving sustainable development goals in food sectors. *Food Research International*, •••, 112068. PMID: 36461323

Ivanov, D., Dolgui, A., & Sokolov, B. (2019). The impact of digital technology and Industry 4.0 on the ripple effect and supply chain risk analytics. *International Journal of Production Research*, *57*(3), 829–846.

Jakka, G., Yathiraju, N., & Ansari, M. F. (2022). Artificial Intelligence in Terms of Spotting Malware and Delivering Cyber Risk Management. *Journal of Positive School Psychology*, *6*(3), 6156–6165.

Javaid, M., Haleem, A., Singh, R. P., Khan, S., & Suman, R. (2021). Blockchain technology applications for Industry 4.0: A literature-based review. *Blockchain: Research and Applications*, *2*(4), 100027.

Javaid, M., Haleem, A., Singh, R. P., Suman, R., & Gonzalez, E. S. (2022). Understanding the adoption of Industry 4.0 technologies in improving environmental sustainability. *Sustainable Operations and Computers*, *3*, 203–217.

Kalaiarasi, H., & Kirubahari, S. (2023). Green finance for sustainable development using blockchain technology. In *Green Blockchain Technology for Sustainable Smart Cities* (pp. 167–185). Elsevier.

. Kasowaki, L., & Ahmet, S. (2024). *Shielding the Virtual Ramparts: Understanding Cybersecurity Essentials* (No. 11700). EasyChair.

Kumar, S., & Mallipeddi, R. R. (2022). Impact of cybersecurity on operations and supply chain management: Emerging trends and future research directions. *Production and Operations Management*, *31*(12), 4488–4500.

Kumar, S. H., Talasila, D., Gowrav, M. P., & Gangadharappa, H. V. (2020). Adaptations of Pharma 4.0 from Industry 4.0. *Drug Invention Today*, *14*(3).

Kurniawan, T. A., Maiurova, A., Kustikova, M., Bykovskaia, E., Othman, M. H. D., & Goh, H. H. (2022). Accelerating sustainability transition in St. Petersburg (Russia) through digitalization-based circular economy in waste recycling industry: A strategy to promote carbon neutrality in era of Industry 4.0. *Journal of Cleaner Production*, *363*, 132452.

Kuzior, A. (2022). Technological unemployment in the perspective of Industry 4.0. *Virtual Economics*, *5*(1), 7–23.

Laskurain-Iturbe, I., Arana-Landín, G., Landeta-Manzano, B., & Uriarte-Gallastegi, N. (2021). Exploring the influence of industry 4.0 technologies on the circular economy. *Journal of Cleaner Production*, *321*, 128944.

Leng, J., Ye, S., Zhou, M., Zhao, J. L., Liu, Q., Guo, W., & Fu, L. (2020). Blockchain-secured smart manufacturing in industry 4.0: A survey. *IEEE Transactions on Systems, Man, and Cybernetics. Systems*, *51*(1), 237–252.

Li, B. H., Hou, B. C., Yu, W. T., Lu, X. B., & Yang, C. W. (2017). Applications of artificial intelligence in intelligent manufacturing: A review. *Frontiers of Information Technology & Electronic Engineering*, *18*, 86–96.

Lim, C. H., Lim, S., How, B. S., Ng, W. P. Q., Ngan, S. L., Leong, W. D., & Lam, H. L. (2021). A review of industry 4.0 revolution potential in a sustainable and renewable palm oil industry: HAZOP approach. *Renewable & Sustainable Energy Reviews*, *135*, 110223.

Liu, H., Yao, P., Latif, S., Aslam, S., & Iqbal, N. (2022). Impact of Green financing, FinTech, and financial inclusion on energy efficiency. *Environmental Science and Pollution Research International*, •••, 1–12. PMID: 34705207

Lu, C., Lyu, J., Zhang, L., Gong, A., Fan, Y., Yan, J., & Li, X. (2020). Nuclear power plants with artificial intelligence in industry 4.0 era: Top-level design and current applications—A systemic review. *IEEE Access : Practical Innovations, Open Solutions*, *8*, 194315–194332.

Lu, Y. (2019). Artificial intelligence: A survey on evolution, models, applications and future trends. *Journal of Management Analytics*, *6*(1), 1–29.

Majstorovic, V. D., & Mitrovic, R. (2019). Industry 4.0 programs worldwide. In *Proceedings of the 4th International Conference on the Industry 4.0 Model for Advanced Manufacturing: AMP 2019 4* (pp. 78-99). Springer International Publishing.

Meyendorf, N., Ida, N., Singh, R., & Vrana, J. (2023). NDE 4.0: Progress, promise, and its role to industry 4.0. *NDT & E International*, •••, 102957.

Migliorelli, M., & Dessertine, P. (2019). The rise of green finance in Europe. *Opportunities and challenges for issuers, investors and marketplaces. Cham. Palgrave Macmillan*, *2*, 2019.

Mithas, S., Chen, Z. L., Saldanha, T. J., & De Oliveira Silveira, A. (2022). How will artificial intelligence and Industry 4.0 emerging technologies transform operations management? *Production and Operations Management*, *31*(12), 4475–4487.

Morgan, J., Halton, M., Qiao, Y., & Breslin, J. G. (2021). Industry 4.0 smart reconfigurable manufacturing machines. *Journal of Manufacturing Systems, 59*, 481–506.

Mourtzis, D., Angelopoulos, J., & Panopoulos, N. (2022). A Literature Review of the Challenges and Opportunities of the Transition from Industry 4.0 to Society 5.0. *Energies, 15*(17), 6276.

. Naderi, N., & Tian, Y. (2022). Leveraging Blockchain Technology and Tokenizing Green Assets to Fill the Green Finance Gap. *Energy Research Letters, 3*(3).

Nahavandi, S. (2019). Industry 5.0—A human-centric solution. *Sustainability, 11*(16), 4371.

Nassiry, D. (2018). *The role of fintech in unlocking green finance: Policy insights for developing countries* (No. 883). ADBI working paper.

Nguyen, T., Gosine, R. G., & Warrian, P. (2020). A systematic review of big data analytics for oil and gas industry 4.0. *IEEE Access : Practical Innovations, Open Solutions, 8*, 61183–61201.

Nica, E., & Stehel, V. (2021). Internet of things sensing networks, artificial intelligence-based decision-making algorithms, and real-time process monitoring in sustainable industry 4.0. *Journal of Self-Governance and Management Economics, 9*(3), 35–47.

Pivoto, D. G., de Almeida, L. F., da Rosa Righi, R., Rodrigues, J. J., Lugli, A. B., & Alberti, A. M. (2021). Cyber-physical systems architectures for industrial internet of things applications in Industry 4.0: A literature review. *Journal of Manufacturing Systems, 58*, 176–192.

Popov, V. V., Kudryavtseva, E. V., Kumar Katiyar, N., Shishkin, A., Stepanov, S. I., & Goel, S. (2022). Industry 4.0 and digitalisation in healthcare. *Materials (Basel), 15*(6), 2140. PMID: 35329592

. Rane, N. (2023). Transformers in Industry 4.0, Industry 5.0, and Society 5.0: Roles and Challenges.

Reier Forradellas, R. F., & Garay Gallastegui, L. M. (2021). Digital transformation and artificial intelligence applied to business: Legal regulations, economic impact and perspective. *Laws, 10*(3), 70.

Sachs, J. D., Woo, W. T., Yoshino, N., & Taghizadeh-Hesary, F. (2019). Importance of green finance for achieving sustainable development goals and energy security. *Handbook of green finance: Energy security and sustainable development, 10*, 1-10.

Saeed, S., Altamimi, S. A., Alkayyal, N. A., Alshehri, E., & Alabbad, D. A. (2023). Digital transformation and cybersecurity challenges for businesses resilience: Issues and recommendations. *Sensors (Basel), 23*(15), 6666. PMID: 37571451

Sánchez-Sotano, A., Cerezo-Narváez, A., Abad-Fraga, F., Pastor-Fernández, A., & Salguero-Gómez, J. (2020). Trends of digital transformation in the shipbuilding sector. In *New Trends in the Use of Artificial Intelligence for the Industry 4.0*. IntechOpen.

Schulz, K., & Feist, M. (2021). Leveraging blockchain technology for innovative climate finance under the Green Climate Fund. *Earth System Governance, 7*, 100084.

Shi, Z., Xie, Y., Xue, W., Chen, Y., Fu, L., & Xu, X. (2020). Smart factory in Industry 4.0. *Systems Research and Behavioral Science, 37*(4), 607–617.

Sima, V., Gheorghe, I. G., Subić, J., & Nancu, D. (2020). Influences of the industry 4.0 revolution on the human capital development and consumer behavior: A systematic review. *Sustainability, 12*(10), 4035.

Singh Rajawat, A., Bedi, P., Goyal, S. B., Shukla, P. K., Zaguia, A., Jain, A., & Monirujjaman Khan, M. (2021). Reformist framework for improving human security for mobile robots in industry 4.0. *Mobile Information Systems, 2021*, 1–10.

Tao, F., Akhtar, M. S., & Jiayuan, Z. (2021). The future of artificial intelligence in cybersecurity: A comprehensive survey. *EAI Endorsed Transactions on Creative Technologies, 8*(28), e3–e3.

Thomason, J., Ahmad, M., Bronder, P., Hoyt, E., Pocock, S., Bouteloupe, J., & Shrier, D. (2018). Blockchain—powering and empowering the poor in developing countries. In *Transforming climate finance and green investment with blockchains* (pp. 137–152). Academic Press.

Tseng, M. L., Tran, T. P. T., Ha, H. M., Bui, T. D., & Lim, M. K. (2021). Sustainable industrial and operation engineering trends and challenges Toward Industry 4.0: A data driven analysis. *Journal of Industrial and Production Engineering, 38*(8), 581–598.

Vogt, J. (2021). Where is the human got to go? Artificial intelligence, machine learning, big data, digitalisation, and human–robot interaction in Industry 4.0 and 5.0: Review Comment on: Bauer, M.(2020). Preise kalkulieren mit KI-gestützter Onlineplattform BAM GmbH, Weiden, Bavaria, Germany. *AI & Society, 36*(3), 1083–1087.

Wamba-Taguimdje, S. L., Fosso Wamba, S., Kala Kamdjoug, J. R., & Tchatchouang Wanko, C. E. (2020). Influence of artificial intelligence (AI) on firm performance: The business value of AI-based transformation projects. *Business Process Management Journal*, *26*(7), 1893–1924.

Wan, J., Yang, J., Wang, Z., & Hua, Q. (2018). Artificial intelligence for cloud-assisted smart factory. *IEEE Access : Practical Innovations, Open Solutions*, *6*, 55419–55430.

. Xing, K., Cropley, D. H., Oppert, M. L., & Singh, C. (2021). Readiness for digital innovation and industry 4.0 transformation: studies on manufacturing industries in the city of salisbury. *Business Innovation with New ICT in the Asia-Pacific: Case Studies*, 155-176.

Xu, L. D., Xu, E. L., & Li, L. (2018). Industry 4.0: State of the art and future trends. *International Journal of Production Research*, *56*(8), 2941–2962.

Yan, C., Siddik, A. B., Yong, L., Dong, Q., Zheng, G. W., & Rahman, M. N. (2022). A two-staged SEM-artificial neural network approach to analyze the impact of FinTech adoption on the sustainability performance of banking firms: The mediating effect of green finance and innovation. *Systems*, *10*(5), 148.

Yang, Y., Su, X., & Yao, S. (2021). Nexus between green finance, fintech, and high-quality economic development: Empirical evidence from China. *Resources Policy*, *74*, 102445.

Yue, Y., & Shyu, J. Z. (2024). A paradigm shift in crisis management: The nexus of AGI-driven intelligence fusion networks and blockchain trustworthiness. *Journal of Contingencies and Crisis Management*, *32*(1), e12541.

Zhang, X., Aranguiz, M., Xu, D., Zhang, X., & Xu, X. (2018). Utilizing blockchain for better enforcement of green finance law and regulations. In *Transforming climate finance and green investment with blockchains* (pp. 289–301). Academic Press.

Zhong, R. Y., Xu, X., Klotz, E., & Newman, S. T. (2017). Intelligent manufacturing in the context of industry 4.0: A review. *Engineering*, *3*(5), 616–630.

Zhou, J., Zhang, S., Lu, Q., Dai, W., Chen, M., Liu, X., . . . Herrera-Viedma, E. (2021). A survey on federated learning and its applications for accelerating industrial internet of things. *arXiv preprint arXiv:2104.10501*.

Compilation of References

Agostini, D., & Picasso, F. (2024). Large language models for sustainable assessment and feedback in higher education: Towards a pedagogical and technological framework. In *CEUR WORKSHOP PROCEEDINGS*. CEUR Workshop Proceedings.

Ahmad, T., Zhang, D., Huang, C., Zhang, H., Dai, N., Song, Y., & Chen, H. (2021). Artificial intelligence in sustainable energy industry: Status Quo, challenges and opportunities. *Journal of Cleaner Production*, *289*, 125834.

Akhtar, Z. Bin. (2024). Unveiling the evolution of generative AI (GAI): a comprehensive and investigative analysis toward LLM models (2021–2024) and beyond. *Journal of Electrical Systems and Information Technology 2024 11:1, 11*(1), 1–21. https://doi.org/DOI: 10.1186/S43067-024-00145-1

Al Yakin, A., Cardoso, L., & Al Matari, A. S., Muthmainnah, & Obaid, A. J. (2024, June). Enabling Sustainable Learning Through Virtual Robotics Machine Mediation of Social Interactions Between Teachers, Students, and Machines Based on Sociology Lens. In *International Conference on Explainable Artificial Intelligence in the Digital Sustainability* (pp. 55-76). Cham: Springer Nature Switzerland.

Al Yakin, A. M., Rasyid, A. R., Massyat, M., Muthmainnah, M., Aquino, A. B., Noche, T. H., & Cardoso, L. (2024). The Importance of Collaboration Between Human Intelligence and GenAI in Digitalization of Education. In *Impact and Potential of Machine Learning in the Metaverse* (pp. 129–160). IGI Global.

Al-Amin, M., Ali, M. S., Salam, A., Khan, A., Ali, A., Ullah, A., & Chowdhury, S. K. (2024). History of generative Artificial Intelligence (AI) chatbots: past, present, and future development. arXiv preprint arXiv:2402.05122.

Alammar, J. (2018, June 27). The illustrated transformer. *Jay Alammar's Blog*. https://jalammar.github.io/illustrated-transformer/

Alammar, J. (2019, August 31). The illustrated GPT-2. *Jay Alammar's Blog*. https://jalammar.github.io/illustrated-gpt2/

Alammar, J. (2020, January 13). Interfaces for explaining transformer language models. *Jay Alammar's Blog*. https://jalammar.github.io/explaining-transformers/

Alammar, J. (2023). The Transformer Family: Variants, Applications, and Limitations. *Proceedings of the IEEE Conference on Neural Networks*, 29(2), 299-313.

Alam, T. M., Iqbal, M. A., Ali, Y., Wahab, A., Ijaz, S., Baig, T. I., Hussain, A., Malik, M. A., Raza, M. M., & Ibrar, S. (2019). A model for early prediction of diabetes. *Informatics in Medicine Unlocked, 16*, 100204.

Ali, A., Septyanto, A. W., Chaudhary, I., Al Hamadi, H., Alzoubi, H. M., & Khan, Z. F. (2022, February). Applied Artificial Intelligence as Event Horizon Of Cyber Security. In *2022 International Conference on Business Analytics for Technology and Security (ICBATS)* (pp. 1-7). IEEE.

Alvarez, C., Samary, M. M., & Wise, A. F. (2024). Modularization for mastery learning in CS1: A 4-year action research study. *Journal of Computing in Higher Education, 36*(2), 546–589. PMID: 37359038

Anastasi, S., Madonna, M., & Monica, L. (2021). Implications of embedded artificial intelligence-machine learning on safety of machinery. *Procedia Computer Science, 180*, 338–343.

Angelopoulos, A., Michailidis, E. T., Nomikos, N., Trakadas, P., Hatziefremidis, A., Voliotis, S., & Zahariadis, T. (2019). Tackling faults in the industry 4.0 era—A survey of machine-learning solutions and key aspects. *Sensors (Basel), 20*(1), 109. PMID: 31878065

Aoun, A., Ilinca, A., Ghandour, M., & Ibrahim, H. (2021). A review of Industry 4.0 characteristics and challenges, with potential improvements using blockchain technology. *Computers & Industrial Engineering, 162*, 107746.

Arden, N. S., Fisher, A. C., Tyner, K., Lawrence, X. Y., Lee, S. L., & Kopcha, M. (2021). Industry 4.0 for pharmaceutical manufacturing: Preparing for the smart factories of the future. *International Journal of Pharmaceutics, 602*, 120554. PMID: 33794326

Asadollahi-Yazdi, E., Couzon, P., Nguyen, N. Q., Ouazene, Y., & Yalaoui, F. (2020). Industry 4.0: Revolution or Evolution? *American Journal of Operations Research, 10*(06), 241.

Ashrafimoghari, V., & Gürkan, N. (2024). Evaluating Large Language Models on the GMAT: Implications for the Future of Business Education. SSRN *Electronic Journal*. DOI: 10.2139/ssrn.4681307

Ashrafimoghari, V., Gürkan, N., & Suchow, J. W. (2024). Evaluating Large Language Models on the GMAT: Implications for the Future of Business Education. arXiv preprint arXiv:2401.02985.

Awadalla, A., Xue, L., Lo, O., Shu, M., Lee, H., Kumar Guha, E., Jordan, M., Shen, S., Awadalla, M., Savarese, S., Xiong, C., Xu, R., Choi, Y., & Schmidt, L. (2024). MINT-1T: Scaling Open-Source Multimodal Data by 10x: A Multimodal Dataset with One Trillion Tokens (arXiv:2406.11271). https://arxiv.org/abs/2406.11271

Awan, U., Sroufe, R., & Shahbaz, M. (2021). Industry 4.0 and the circular economy: A literature review and recommendations for future research. *Business Strategy and the Environment*, *30*(4), 2038–2060.

Azunre, P. (2021). *Transfer learning for natural language processing*. Simon and Schuster.

Baber, H., Nair, K., Gupta, R., & Gurjar, K. (2024). The beginning of ChatGPT–a systematic and bibliometric review of the literature. *Information and Learning Science*, *125*(7/8), 587–614.

Badri, A., Boudreau-Trudel, B., & Souissi, A. S. (2018). Occupational health and safety in the industry 4.0 era: A cause for major concern? *Safety Science*, *109*, 403–411.

Bag, S., & Pretorius, J. H. C. (2022). Relationships between industry 4.0, sustainable manufacturing and circular economy: Proposal of a research framework. *The International Journal of Organizational Analysis*, *30*(4), 864–898.

Bahammam, A. S., Trabelsi, K., Pandi-Perumal, S. R., & Jahrami, H. (2023). Adapting to the Impact of Artificial Intelligence in Scientific Writing: Balancing Benefits and Drawbacks while Developing Policies and Regulations. *Journal of Nature and Science of Medicine*, *6*(3). Advance online publication. DOI: 10.4103/jnsm.jnsm_89_23

Bao, H., Dong, L., Wei, F., Wang, W., Yang, N., Liu, X., & Hon, H. W. (2020, November). Unilmv2: Pseudo-masked language models for unified language model pre-training. In International conference on machine learning (pp. 642-652). PMLR.

Bardhan, I., Chen, H., & Karahanna, E. (2020). Connecting systems, data, and people: A multidisciplinary research roadmap for chronic disease management. *Management Information Systems Quarterly*, *44*(1).

Barik, S., Mohanty, S., Mohanty, S., & Singh, D. (2021). Analysis of prediction accuracy of diabetes using classifier and hybrid machine learning techniques. In *Intelligent and Cloud Computing: Proceedings of ICICC 2019, Volume 2* (pp. 399–409). Springer.

Barman, K. G., Wood, N., & Pawlowski, P. (2024). Beyond transparency and explainability: On the need for adequate and contextualized user guidelines for LLM use. *Ethics and Information Technology*, *26*(3), 1–12. DOI: 10.1007/S10676-024-09778-2/METRICS

Bartoldson, B. R., Kailkhura, B., & Blalock, D. (2023). Compute-efficient deep learning: Algorithmic trends and opportunities. *Journal of Machine Learning Research*, *24*(122), 1–77.

Bayram, O., Talay, I., & Feridun, M. (2022). Can FinTech promote sustainable finance? Policy lessons from the case of Turkey. *Sustainability*, *14*(19), 12414.

Benítez, T. M., Xu, Y., Boudreau, J. D., Kow, A. W. C., Bello, F., Van Phuoc, L., Wang, X., Sun, X., Leung, G. K. K., Lan, Y., Wang, Y., Cheng, D., Tham, Y. C., Wong, T. Y., & Chung, K. C. (2024). Harnessing the potential of large language models in medical education: Promise and pitfalls. *Journal of the American Medical Informatics Association : JAMIA*, *31*(3). Advance online publication. DOI: 10.1093/jamia/ocad252 PMID: 38269644

Bergstra, J., & Bengio, Y. (2012). Random search for hyper-parameter optimization. *Journal of Machine Learning Research*, *13*, 281–305.

Bezzi, M. (2024). Large Language Models and Security. *IEEE Security and Privacy*, *22*(2). Advance online publication. DOI: 10.1109/MSEC.2023.3345568

Bhuiyan, A. B., Ali, M. J., Zulkifli, N., & Kumarasamy, M. M. (2020). Industry 4.0: Challenges, opportunities, and strategic solutions for Bangladesh. *International Journal of Business and Management Future*, *4*(2), 41–56.

Blanchard, E. G., & Mohammed, P. (2024, July). On Cultural Intelligence in LLM-Based Chatbots: Implications for Artificial Intelligence in Education. In *International Conference on Artificial Intelligence in Education* (pp. 439-453). Cham: Springer Nature Switzerland.

Bojanowski, P., Grave, E., Joulin, A., & Mikolov, T. (2016). Bag of tricks for efficient text classification. *arXiv*. https://arxiv.org/abs/1607.01759

Bokhari, S. A. A., & Myeong, S. (2023). The influence of artificial intelligence on e-Governance and cybersecurity in smart cities: A stakeholder's perspective. *IEEE Access : Practical Innovations, Open Solutions*.

Bommasani, R., Hudson, D., Adeli, E., & Altman, R.. (2022). On the Opportunities and Risks of Foundation Models. *Communications of the ACM*, *65*(3), 55–64.

Bommasani, R., Hudson, D., & Brundage, M.. (2022). Foundations of Large Language Models: A Comprehensive Overview. *Journal of Artificial Intelligence Research*, *75*, 1–48.

Bongomin, O., Gilibrays Ocen, G., Oyondi Nganyi, E., Musinguzi, A., & Omara, T. (2020). Exponential disruptive technologies and the required skills of industry 4.0. *Journal of Engineering*, *2020*, 1–17.

Borowski, P. F. (2021). Digitization, digital twins, blockchain, and industry 4.0 as elements of management process in enterprises in the energy sector. *Energies*, *14*(7), 1885.

Borowski, P. F. (2021). Innovative processes in managing an enterprise from the energy and food sector in the era of industry 4.0. *Processes (Basel, Switzerland)*, *9*(2), 381.

Borrows, L. (2022). The Land is Our Casebook: Revitalizing Indigenous Law in Relation with the Living World.

Breiman, L. (2001). Random forests. *Machine Learning*, *45*(1), 5–32. DOI: 10. 1023/A:1010933404324

Brock, J. K. U., & Von Wangenheim, F. (2019). Demystifying AI: What digital transformation leaders can teach you about realistic artificial intelligence. *California Management Review*, *61*(4), 110–134.

Brown, T. B., Mann, B., Ryder, N., Subbiah, M., Kaplan, J. D., Dhariwal, P., Neelakantan, A., Shyam, P., Sastry, G., Askell, A., & Associates. (2020). Language models are few-shot learners. In *Advances in Neural Information Processing Systems* (Vol. 33). NeurIPS.

Bubeck, S., Eldan, R., Li, Y., ... (2023). Sparks of Artificial General Intelligence: Early Experiments with GPT-4. arXiv preprint arXiv:2303.12712.

Buffart, M., Croidieu, G., Kim, P. H., & Bowman, R. (2020). Even winners need to learn: How government entrepreneurship programs can support innovative ventures. *Research Policy*, *49*(10), 104052.

Caselli, T., Lieto, A., Nissim, M., & Patti, V. (2023). They are just words. ChatGPT: Anatomy and recommendations for use. *Sistemi Intelligenti*, *35*(2). Advance online publication. DOI: 10.1422/108131

Chawla, N. V., Bowyer, K. W., Hall, L. O., & Kegelmeyer, W. P. (2002). SMOTE: Syn- thetic minority over-sampling technique. *Journal of Artificial Intelligence Research*, *16*, 321–357. DOI: 10.1613/jair.953

Chen, Y., & Volz, U. (2021). Scaling up sustainable investment through blockchain-based project bonds. *ADB-IGF Special Working Paper Series "Fintech to Enable Development, Investment, Financial Inclusion, and Sustainability.*

Chen, Z. Z., Ma, J., Zhang, X., Hao, N., Yan, A., Nourbakhsh, A., & Wang, W. Y. (2024). A Survey on Large Language Models for Critical Societal Domains: Finance, Healthcare, and Law. arXiv preprint arXiv:2405.01769.

Chen, Y., Lu, Y., Bulysheva, L., & Kataev, M. Y. (2022). Applications of blockchain in industry 4.0: A review. *Information Systems Frontiers*, •••, 1–15.

Cheung, B. H. H., & Co, M. T. H. (2023). Large language models: implications of rapid evolution in medicine. In *Hong Kong Medical Journal* (Vol. 29, Issue 6). https://doi.org/DOI: 10.12809/hkmj2310890

Cho, K., Merrienboer, B., Gulcehre, C., Bahdanau, D., Schwenk, H., & Bengio, Y. (2014). Learning phrase representations using RNN encoder–decoder for statistical machine translation. In *Proceedings of the 2014 Conference on Empirical Methods in Natural Language Processing* (pp. 1724–1734). Association for Computational Linguistics.

Cho, N. H., Shaw, J. E., Karuranga, S., Huang, Y., da Rocha Fernandes, J. D., Ohlrogge, A. W., & Malanda, B. I. D. F. (2018). IDF Diabetes Atlas: Global estimates of diabetes prevalence for 2017 and projections for 2045. *Diabetes Research and Clinical Practice*, *138*, 271–281.

Chow, J. C. L., Wong, V., & Li, K. (2024). Generative Pre-Trained Transformer-Empowered Healthcare Conversations: Current Trends, Challenges, and Future Directions in Large Language Model-Enabled Medical Chatbots. In *BioMedInformatics* (Vol. 4, Issue 1). DOI: 10.3390/biomedinformatics4010047

Chu, Z., Wang, Z., & Zhang, W. (2024). Fairness in Large Language Models: A Taxonomic Survey. *arXiv preprint arXiv:2404.01349.*

Chueca Vergara, C., & Ferruz Agudo, L. (2021). Fintech and sustainability: Do they affect each other? *Sustainability*, *13*(13), 7012.

Cioffi, R., Travaglioni, M., Piscitelli, G., Petrillo, A., & De Felice, F. (2020). Artificial intelligence and machine learning applications in smart production: Progress, trends, and directions. *Sustainability*, *12*(2), 492.

Comber, S. (2021). *Retail Research in the Age of Big Data: Guiding the Search for Answers.* The University of Liverpool.

Cong-Lem, N., & Daneshfar, S. (2024). Generative AI and second/foreign language education from Vygotsky's cultural-historical perspective. In *Innovations in Technologies for Language Teaching and Learning* (pp. 175–188). Springer Nature Switzerland.

Corallo, G., & Papotti, P. (2024). Finch: Prompt-guided key-value cache compression (arXiv:2408.00167). https://arxiv.org/abs/2408.00167

Cornuéjols, A., & Vrain, C. (2020). Designing algorithms for machine learning and data mining. In A Guided Harke, G., Shishlenin, M., & Koppisetti, S. (2020). Application of Algorithmic Trading Strategies for Retail Investors. Available at SSRN 3904097.

Cortes, C., & Vapnik, V. (1995). Support-vector networks. *Machine Learning*, *20*(3), 273–297. DOI: 10.1007/BF00994018

Cruz, C. (2021). From digital disparity to educational excellence: Closing the opportunity and achievement gaps for low-income, Black and Latinx students. *Harv. Latinx L. Rev.*, *24*, 33.

Dagliati, A., Marini, S., Sacchi, L., Cogni, G., Teliti, M., Tibollo, V., De Cata, P., Chiovato, L., & Bellazzi, R. (2018). Machine learning methods to predict diabetes com- plications. *Journal of Diabetes Science and Technology*, *12*(2), 295–302. DOI: 10.1177/1932296817710475 PMID: 28494618

Dai, W., Tsai, Y. S., Lin, J., Aldino, A., Jin, H., Li, T., ... & Chen, G. (2024). Assessing the Proficiency of Large Language Models in Automatic Feedback Generation: An Evaluation Study. *Computers and Education: Artificial Intelligence*, 100299.

Dal Molin, L. (2024). Notes towards infrastructure governance for large language models. *First Monday*, *29*(2). Advance online publication. DOI: 10.5210/fm.v29i2.13567

Dao, T., Fu, D. Y., Ermon, S., Rudra, A., & Ré, C. (2022). FlashAttention: Fast and memory-efficient exact attention with IO-awareness. *arXiv*. https://arxiv.org/abs/2205.14135

Dawson, A. G. (2024). Algorithmic Adjudication and Constitutional AI—The Promise of A Better AI Decision Making Future? *SMU Science and Technology Law Review*, *27*(1), 11.

Dawson, N. (2021). *Changing labour market dynamics in Australia: skill shortages, job transitions, and artificial intelligence technology adoption*. University of Technology Sydney.

de la Peña Zarzuelo, I., Soeane, M. J. F., & Bermúdez, B. L. (2020). Industry 4.0 in the port and maritime industry: A literature review. *Journal of Industrial Information Integration, 20*, 100173.

Devlin, J., Chang, M. W., Lee, K., & Toutanova, K. (2018). BERT: Pre-training of Deep Bidirectional Transformers for Language Understanding. *NAACL HLT 2019 - 2019 Conference of the North American Chapter of the Association for Computational Linguistics: Human Language Technologies - Proceedings of the Conference, 1*, 4171–4186. https://arxiv.org/abs/1810.04805v2

Dinesh Arokia Raj, A., Jha, R. R., Yadav, M., Sam, D., & Jayanthi, K. (2024). Role of Blockchain and Watermarking Toward Cybersecurity. In *Multimedia Watermarking: Latest Developments and Trends* (pp. 103–123). Springer Nature Singapore.

Ding, Q., Ding, D., Wang, Y., Guan, C., & Ding, B. (2024). Unraveling the landscape of large language models: A systematic review and future perspectives. *Journal of Electronic Business & Digital Economics, 3*(1). Advance online publication. DOI: 10.1108/jebde-08-2023-0015

Doughty, J., Wan, Z., Bompelli, A., Qayum, J., Wang, T., Zhang, J., & Sakr, M. (2024, January). A comparative study of AI-generated (GPT-4) and human-crafted MCQs in programming education. In *Proceedings of the 26th Australasian Computing Education Conference* (pp. 114-123).

Du, F., Ma, X.-J., Yang, J.-R., Liu, Y., Luo, C.-R., Wang, X.-B., Jiang, H.-O., Jing, X., Du, F., Ma, X.-J., Yang, J.-R., Liu, Y., Luo, C.-R., Wang, X.-B., Jiang, H.-O., & Jing, X. (2024). A Survey of LLM Datasets: From Autoregressive Model to AI Chatbot. *Journal of Computer Science and Technology, 2024, Vol. 39, Issue 3, Pages: 542-566, 39*(3), 542–566. https://doi.org/DOI: 10.1007/S11390-024-3767-3

Dwivedi, Y. K., Hughes, L., Ismagilova, E., Aarts, G., Coombs, C., Crick, T., & Williams, M. D. (2021). Artificial Intelligence (AI): Multidisciplinary perspectives on emerging challenges, opportunities, and agenda for research, practice and policy. *International Journal of Information Management, 57*, 101994.

Dwivedi, Y. K., Kshetri, N., Hughes, L., Slade, E. L., Jeyaraj, A., Kar, A. K., Baabdullah, A. M., Koohang, A., Raghavan, V., Ahuja, M., Albanna, H., Albashrawi, M. A., Al-Busaidi, A. S., Balakrishnan, J., Barlette, Y., Basu, S., Bose, I., Brooks, L., Buhalis, D., & Wright, R. (2023). "So what if ChatGPT wrote it?" Multidisciplinary perspectives on opportunities, challenges and implications of generative conversational AI for research, practice and policy. *International Journal of Information Management, 71*. Advance online publication. DOI: 10.1016/j.ijinfomgt.2023.102642

Dwivedi, Y. K., Kshetri, N., Hughes, L., Slade, E. L., Jeyaraj, A., Kar, A. K., Baabdullah, A. M., Koohang, A., Raghavan, V., Ahuja, M., Albanna, H., Albashrawi, M. A., Al-Busaidi, A. S., Balakrishnan, J., Barlette, Y., Basu, S., Bose, I., Brooks, L., Buhalis, D., & Wright, R. (2023). Opinion Paper: "So what if ChatGPT wrote it?" Multidisciplinary perspectives on opportunities, challenges and implications of generative conversational AI for research, practice and policy. *International Journal of Information Management*, *71*, 102642. DOI: 10.1016/J.IJINFOMGT.2023.102642

Easop, B. A. (2022). Education Equity during COVID-19: Analyzing In-Person Priority Policies for Student with Disabilities. *Stanford Law Review*, *74*, 223.

Epstein, R. H., & Dexter, F. (2023). Variability in Large Language Models' Responses to Medical Licensing and Certification Examinations. Comment on "How Does ChatGPT Perform on the United States Medical Licensing Examination? The Implications of Large Language Models for Medical Education and Knowledge Assessment." In *JMIR Medical Education* (Vol. 9). DOI: 10.2196/48305

Esmaeilzadeh, P. (2023). The role of ChatGPT in disrupting concepts, changing values, and challenging ethical norms: A qualitative study. *AI and Ethics*. Advance online publication. DOI: 10.1007/s43681-023-00338-w

Evans, P., Vansteenkiste, M., Parker, P., Kingsford-Smith, A., & Zhou, S. (2024). Cognitive load theory and its relationships with motivation: A self-determination theory perspective. *Educational Psychology Review*, *36*(1), 7.

Fecher, B., Hebing, M., Laufer, M., Pohle, J., & Sofsky, F. (2023). Friend or foe? Exploring the implications of large language models on the science system. *AI & Society*. Advance online publication. DOI: 10.1007/s00146-023-01791-1

Feng, Y., Xie, M., Tian, Z., Wang, S., Lu, Y., & Shu, J. Mobius: Fine tuning large-scale models on commodity gpu servers. In *Proceedings of the 28th ACM International Conference on Architectural Support for Programming Languages and Operating Systems*, Volume 2, pages 489–501, 2023.

Filippi, S., & Motyl, B. (2024). Large Language Models (LLMs) in Engineering Education: A Systematic Review and Suggestions for Practical Adoption. *Information (Basel)*, *15*(6), 345.

Finance, A. T. C. C. (2015). *Industry 4.0 Challenges and solutions for the digital transformation and use of exponential technologies. Finance, audit tax consulting corporate*. Swiss.

Fraga-Lamas, P., Lopes, S. I., & Fernández-Caramés, T. M. (2021). Green IoT and edge AI as key technological enablers for a sustainable digital transition towards a smart circular economy: An industry 5.0 use case. *Sensors (Basel), 21*(17), 5745. PMID: 34502637

Gadekar, R., Sarkar, B., & Gadekar, A. (2022). Key performance indicator based dynamic decision-making framework for sustainable Industry 4.0 implementation risks evaluation: Reference to the Indian manufacturing industries. *Annals of Operations Research, 318*(1), 189–249. PMID: 35910040

Gill, S. S., Xu, M., Patros, P., Wu, H., Kaur, R., Kaur, K., & Buyya, R. (2024). Transformative effects of ChatGPT on modern education: Emerging Era of AI Chatbots. *Internet of Things and Cyber-Physical Systems, 4*, 19–23.

Gilson, A., Safranek, C. W., Huang, T., Socrates, V., Chi, L., Taylor, R. A., & Chartash, D. (2024). Correction: How Does ChatGPT Perform on the United States Medical Licensing Examination (USMLE)? The Implications of Large Language Models for Medical Education and Knowledge Assessment. *JMIR Medical Education, 10.* Advance online publication. DOI: 10.2196/57594 PMID: 38412478

Ginting, D., Sabudu, D., Barella, A. M., Woods, R., & Kemala, M. (2024). Student-centered learning in the digital age: In-class adaptive instruction and best practices. *Int J Eval & Res Educ, 13*(3), 2006–2019.

Godwin-Jones, R. (2024). Distributed agency in second language learning and teaching through generative AI. *arXiv preprint arXiv:2403.20216.*

Grande, V., Kiesler, N., & Francisco, R. M. A. (2024). Student Perspectives on Using a Large Language Model (LLM) for an Assignment on Professional Ethics. In *Proceedings of the 2024 on Innovation and Technology in Computer Science Education* V. 1 (pp. 478-484).

Gu, Q. (2023). LLM-Based Code Generation Method for Golang Compiler Testing. *ESEC/FSE 2023 - Proceedings of the 31st ACM Joint Meeting European Software Engineering Conference and Symposium on the Foundations of Software Engineering*, 2201–2203. https://doi.org/DOI: 10.1145/3611643.3617850

Gumilyov, L. N. (2023). Ethical Implications of Large Language Models A Multidimensional Exploration of Societal, Economic, and Technical Concerns. In *International Journal of Social Analytics.*

Guo, H., Singh, R., & Ferris, A.. (2022). Adapting Pretrained Transformers for Question Answering. *Journal of Natural Language Engineering, 28*(3), 291–310.

Gupta, R. (2023). Industry 4.0 adaption in indian banking Sector—A review and agenda for future research. *Vision (Basel)*, *27*(1), 24–32. PMID: 36977304

Hadar-Shoval, D., Asraf, K., Mizrachi, Y., Haber, Y., & Elyoseph, Z. (2024). Assessing the Alignment of Large Language Models With Human Values for Mental Health Integration: Cross-Sectional Study Using Schwartz's Theory of Basic Values. *JMIR Mental Health*, *11*(1). Advance online publication. DOI: 10.2196/55988 PMID: 38593424

Hagan, J., McCarthy, B., & Herda, D. (2022). *Chicago's Reckoning: Racism, Politics, and the Deep History of Policing in an American City*. Oxford University Press.

Hagendorff, T., & Danks, D. (2023). Ethical and methodological challenges in building morally informed AI systems. *AI and Ethics*, *3*(2). Advance online publication. DOI: 10.1007/s43681-022-00188-y

Haldorai, A., Murugan, S., & Balakrishnan, M. (2024). Bi-Model Emotional AI for Audio-Visual Human Emotion Detection Using Hybrid Deep Learning Model. In *Artificial Intelligence for Sustainable Development* (pp. 293–315). Springer Nature Switzerland.

Hama Saeed, M. A. (2023). Diabetes type 2 classification using machine learning algorithms with up-sampling technique. *Journal of Electrical Systems and Information Technology*, *10*(1), 8.

Han, H., Kim, J., Yoo, J., Lee, Y., & Hwang, S.-w. (2024). ArchCode: Incorporating software requirements in code generation with large language models [arXiv:2408.00994]. arXiv. https://arxiv.org/abs/2408.00994

Hart, S. N., Hoffman, N. G., Gershkovich, P., Christenson, C., McClintock, D. S., Miller, L. J., & Brodsky, V. (2023). Organizational preparedness for the use of large language models in pathology informatics. *Journal of Pathology Informatics*, •••, 100338.

Hassan, A. O. (2021). Interactive Vocabulary Learning Application for Children with Autism Spectrum Disorder: A Participatory Design Study (Master's thesis, Hamad Bin Khalifa University (Qatar)).

Hassoun, A., Aït-Kaddour, A., Abu-Mahfouz, A. M., Rathod, N. B., Bader, F., Barba, F. J., & Regenstein, J. (2023). The fourth industrial revolution in the food industry—Part I: Industry 4.0 technologies. *Critical Reviews in Food Science and Nutrition*, *63*(23), 6547–6563. PMID: 35114860

Hassoun, A., Prieto, M. A., Carpena, M., Bouzembrak, Y., Marvin, H. J., Pallares, N., & Bono, G. (2022). Exploring the role of green and Industry 4.0 technologies in achieving sustainable development goals in food sectors. *Food Research International*, •••, 112068. PMID: 36461323

Helm, P., Bella, G., Koch, G., & Giunchiglia, F. (2024). Diversity and language technology: How language modeling bias causes epistemic injustice. *Ethics and Information Technology*, *26*(1). Advance online publication. DOI: 10.1007/s10676-023-09742-6

Hidayatullah, A. F., Kalinaki, K., Aslam, M. M., Zakari, R. Y., & Shafik, W. (2023). Fine-Tuning BERT-Based Models for Negative Content Identification on Indonesian Tweets. *ICITDA 2023 - Proceedings of the 2023 8th International Conference on Information Technology and Digital Applications*. DOI: 10.1109/ICITDA60835.2023.10427046

Hinton, G. E., Dean, J., & Young, T.. (2023). A Survey of Large Language Models. *Proceedings of the National Academy of Sciences of the United States of America*, *120*(3), 1038–1045.

Hoffmann, J., Borgeaud, S., Mensch, A., Buchatskaya, E., Cai, T., Rutherford, E., de Las Casas, D., Hendricks, L. A., Welbl, J., Clark, A., Hennigan, T., Noland, E., Millican, K., van den Driessche, G., Damoc, B., Guy, A., Osindero, S., Simonyan, K., Elsen, E., & Sifre, L. (2022). Advances in Neural Information Processing Systems: Vol. 35. *Training Compute-Optimal Large Language Models*., https://arxiv.org/abs/2203.15556v1

Horsey, K., & Rackley, E. (2023). Casebook on Tort Law. oxford university press.

Huang, H., Wu, S., Liang, X., Wang, B., Shi, Y., Wu, P., Yang, M., & Zhao, T. (2023). Towards Making the Most of LLM for Translation Quality Estimation. *Lecture Notes in Computer Science (Including Subseries Lecture Notes in Artificial Intelligence and Lecture Notes in Bioinformatics), 14302 LNAI*, 375–386. https://doi.org/DOI: 10.1007/978-3-031-44693-1_30

Hubert, K. F., Awa, K. N., & Zabelina, D. L. (2024). The current state of artificial intelligence generative language models is more creative than humans on divergent thinking tasks. *Scientific Reports*, *14*(1). Advance online publication. DOI: 10.1038/s41598-024-53303-w PMID: 38341459

Hwang, K., Wang, K., Alomair, M., Choa, F. S., & Chen, L. K. (2024, July). Towards Automated Multiple Choice Question Generation and Evaluation: Aligning with Bloom's Taxonomy. In International Conference on Artificial Intelligence in Education (pp. 389-396). Cham: Springer Nature Switzerland.

Ibrahim, A., Nnaji, C., & Shakouri, M. (2021). Influence of sociodemographic factors on construction fieldworkers' safety risk assessments. *Sustainability*, *14*(1), 111.

Idris, M. D., Feng, X., & Dyo, V. (2024). Revolutionising Higher Education: Unleashing the Potential of Large Language Models for Strategic Transformation. *IEEE Access : Practical Innovations, Open Solutions*.

International Diabetes Federation. (2019). *IDF Diabetes Atlas* (9th ed.). Retrieved from https://www.diabetesatlas.org

Işıkdemir, Y. E. (2024). NLP TRANSFORMERS: ANALYSIS OF LLMS AND TRADITIONAL APPROACHES FOR ENHANCED TEXT SUMMARIZATION. *Journal of Engineering and Architecture Faculty of Eskisehir Osmangazi University*, *32*(1), 1140–1151. DOI: 10.31796/OGUMMF.1303569

Ivanov, D., Dolgui, A., & Sokolov, B. (2019). The impact of digital technology and Industry 4.0 on the ripple effect and supply chain risk analytics. *International Journal of Production Research*, *57*(3), 829–846.

Jakka, G., Yathiraju, N., & Ansari, M. F. (2022). Artificial Intelligence in Terms of Spotting Malware and Delivering Cyber Risk Management. *Journal of Positive School Psychology*, *6*(3), 6156–6165.

Javaid, M., Haleem, A., Singh, R. P., Khan, S., & Suman, R. (2021). Blockchain technology applications for Industry 4.0: A literature-based review. *Blockchain: Research and Applications*, *2*(4), 100027.

Javaid, M., Haleem, A., Singh, R. P., Suman, R., & Gonzalez, E. S. (2022). Understanding the adoption of Industry 4.0 technologies in improving environmental sustainability. *Sustainable Operations and Computers*, *3*, 203–217.

Jiang, M., Bacchi, S., Kovoor, J., Stretton, B., & Chan, W. O. (2024). Response to Jin and Dobry's "ChatGPT for health care providers and patients: Practical implications within dermatology." In *Journal of the American Academy of Dermatology* (Vol. 90, Issue 3). DOI: 10.1016/j.jaad.2023.10.038

Jian, Y., Pasquier, M., Sagahyroon, A., & Aloul, F. (2021). A machine learning approach to predicting diabetes complications. *Health Care*, *9*(12), 1712. PMID: 34946438

Joksimović, S., Marshall, R., Rakotoarivelo, T., Ladjal, D., Zhan, C., & Pardo, A. (2021). Privacy-driven learning analytics. In *Manage your own learning analytics: Implement a Rasch modelling approach* (pp. 1–22). Springer International Publishing.

Jošt, G., Taneski, V., & Karakatič, S. (2024). The Impact of Large Language Models on Programming Education and Student Learning Outcomes. *Applied Sciences (Basel, Switzerland)*, *14*(10), 4115.

Jun, Y., Craig, A., Shafik, W., & Sharif, L. (2021). Artificial Intelligence Application in Cybersecurity and Cyberdefense. In *Wireless Communications and Mobile Computing* (Vol. 2021). https://doi.org/DOI: 10.1155/2021/3329581

Kaba, E., Bülbül, H. M., Burakgazi, G., Varlık, A. T., Hürsoy, N., Solak, M., & Çeliker, F. B. (2024). Large language models on magnetic resonance imaging safety-related questions: Accuracy of ChatGPT-3.5, ChatGPT-4, Gemini, and Perplexity. *Curr. Res. MRI*, *3*, 16–19.

Kahl, S., Löffler, F., Maciol, M., Ridder, F., Schmitz, M., Spanagel, J., ... & Schilling, M. (2024). Enhancing AI Tutoring in Robotics Education: Evaluating the Effect of Retrieval-Augmented Generation and Fine-Tuning on Large Language Models.

Kalaiarasi, H., & Kirubahari, S. (2023). Green finance for sustainable development using blockchain technology. In *Green Blockchain Technology for Sustainable Smart Cities* (pp. 167–185). Elsevier.

Kaplan, J., McCandlish, S., & Henighan Open, A. I. T., Brown OpenAI, T. B., Chess OpenAI, B., Child OpenAI, R., Gray OpenAI, S., Radford OpenAI, A., Wu OpenAI, J., & Amodei OpenAI, D. (2020). *Scaling Laws for Neural Language Models*. https://arxiv.org/abs/2001.08361v1

Kasneci, E., Sessler, K., Küchemann, S., Bannert, M., Dementieva, D., Fischer, F., Gasser, U., Groh, G., Günnemann, S., Hüllermeier, E., Krusche, S., Kutyniok, G., Michaeli, T., Nerdel, C., Pfeffer, J., Poquet, O., Sailer, M., Schmidt, A., Seidel, T., & Kasneci, G. (2023). ChatGPT for good? On opportunities and challenges of large language models for education. *Learning and Individual Differences*, *103*, 102274. DOI: 10.1016/J.LINDIF.2023.102274

Kavakiotis, I., Tsave, O., Salifoglou, A., Maglaveras, N., Vlahavas, I., & Chouvarda, I. (2017). Machine learning and data mining methods in diabetes research. *Computational and Structural Biotechnology Journal*, *15*, 104–116. https://doi.org/ . 12.005DOI: 10.1016/j.csbj.2016

Kenthapadi, K., Lakkaraju, H., & Rajani, N. (2023). Generative AI meets Responsible AI: Practical Challenges and Opportunities. *Proceedings of the ACM SIGKDD International Conference on Knowledge Discovery and Data Mining*. DOI: 10.1145/3580305.3599557

Khaleel, F. A., & Al-Bakry, A. M. (2023). Diagnosis of diabetes using machine learning algorithms. *Materials Today: Proceedings*, *80*, 3200–3203.

Khan, A. A., Yunus, R., Sohail, M., Rehman, T. A., Saeed, S., Bu, Y., Jackson, C. D., Sharkey, A., Mahmood, F., & Matyal, R. (2024). Artificial Intelligence for Anesthesiology Board–Style Examination Questions: Role of Large Language Models. In *Journal of Cardiothoracic and Vascular Anesthesia* (Vol. 38, Issue 5). DOI: 10.1053/j.jvca.2024.01.032

Khanam, J. J., & Foo, S. Y. (2021). A comparison of machine learning algorithms for diabetes prediction. *ICT Express*, *7*(4), 432–439.

Khanna, S., & Srivastava, S. (2020). Patient-centric ethical frameworks for privacy, transparency, and bias awareness in deep learning-based medical systems. *Applied Research in Artificial Intelligence and Cloud Computing*, *3*(1), 16–35.

Khan, R. K. (2023). Arbitration in the Digital Age: The Growing use of Technology in International Arbitration. *PLR*, *14*, 1.

Kim, B. J., Kim, M. J., & Lee, J. (2024). Examining the impact of work overload on cybersecurity behavior: Highlighting self-efficacy in the realm of artificial intelligence. *Current Psychology (New Brunswick, N.J.)*, •••, 1–17.

Kirchner, K., Laue, R., Edwards, K., & Lantow, B. (2024). Patterns for modeling process variability in a healthcare context. *Business Process Management Journal*, *30*(1). Advance online publication. DOI: 10.1108/BPMJ-10-2022-0500

Kolegova, I. A., & Levina, I. A. (2024). Using Artificial Intelligence as a Digital Tool in Foreign Language Teaching. *Вестник Южно-Уральского государственного университета. Серия: Образование. Педагогические науки, 16*(1), 102-110.

Kretschmer, M., Margoni, T., & Oruç, P. (2024). Copyright Law and the Lifecycle of Machine Learning Models. *IIC International Review of Intellectual Property and Competition Law*, *55*(1). Advance online publication. DOI: 10.1007/s40319-023-01419-3

Kronenfeld, J. P., Saberi, R. A., Cioci, A. C., Urrechaga, E. M., Ryon, E. L., Thorson, C. M., & Sands, L. R. (2023). Implementation of a Surgical Problem-Based learning curriculum: A one-year single-center experience. *The American Surgeon*, *89*(5), 1807–1813.

Kumar, S. H., Talasila, D., Gowrav, M. P., & Gangadharappa, H. V. (2020). Adaptations of Pharma 4.0 from Industry 4.0. *Drug Invention Today*, *14*(3).

Kumar, S., & Mallipeddi, R. R. (2022). Impact of cybersecurity on operations and supply chain management: Emerging trends and future research directions. *Production and Operations Management*, *31*(12), 4488–4500.

Kuperberg, G. R., & Jaeger, T. F. (2016). What do we mean by prediction in language comprehension? *Language, Cognition and Neuroscience*, *31*(1), 32–59. DOI: 10.1080/23273798.2015.1102299 PMID: 27135040

Kurniawan, T. A., Maiurova, A., Kustikova, M., Bykovskaia, E., Othman, M. H. D., & Goh, H. H. (2022). Accelerating sustainability transition in St. Petersburg (Russia) through digitalization-based circular economy in waste recycling industry: A strategy to promote carbon neutrality in era of Industry 4.0. *Journal of Cleaner Production*, *363*, 132452.

Kuzior, A. (2022). Technological unemployment in the perspective of Industry 4.0. *Virtual Economics*, *5*(1), 7–23.

Laato, S., Morschheuser, B., Hamari, J., & Bjorne, J. (2023). AI-Assisted Learning with ChatGPT and Large Language Models: Implications for Higher Education. *Proceedings - 2023 IEEE International Conference on Advanced Learning Technologies, ICALT 2023*. DOI: 10.1109/ICALT58122.2023.00072

Lamaakal, I., El Makkaoui, K., & Ouahbi, I.. (2024). A TinyML model for gesture-based air handwriting Arabic numbers recognition. *Procedia Computer Science*, *236*, 589–596.

Lamaakal, I., Ouahbi, I., & El Makkaoui, K.. (2024). A TinyDL model for gesture-based air handwriting Arabic numbers and simple Arabic letters recognition. *IEEE Access : Practical Innovations, Open Solutions*.

Langley, P., Iba, W., & Thompson, K. (1992). An analysis of Bayesian classifiers. *Proceed- ings of the Tenth National Conference on Artificial Intelligence*, 223–228.

Laskurain-Iturbe, I., Arana-Landín, G., Landeta-Manzano, B., & Uriarte-Gallastegi, N. (2021). Exploring the influence of industry 4.0 technologies on the circular economy. *Journal of Cleaner Production, 321*, 128944.

Lau, M. (2024). Is ChatGPT taking over the language classroom? *Working Papers in Applied Linguistics and Linguistics at York, 4*. https://doi.org/DOI: 10.25071/2564-2855.36

Lee, J., Hicke, Y., Yu, R., Brooks, C., & Kizilcec, R. F. (2024). The life cycle of large language models in education: A framework for understanding sources of bias. *British Journal of Educational Technology*, *55*(5), 1982–2002.

Lee, S. M., Yang, Z., & Wu, J. G. (2024). Live, play, and learn: Language learner engagement in the immersive VR environment. *Education and Information Technologies, 29*(9), 10529–10550.

Lee, S., & Park, G. (2024). Development and validation of ChatGPT literacy scale. *Current Psychology (New Brunswick, N.J.), 43*(21). Advance online publication. DOI: 10.1007/s12144-024-05723-0

Lehman, J., Gordon, J., Jain, S., Ndousse, K., Yeh, C., & Stanley, K. O. (2024). *Evolution Through Large Models*. DOI: 10.1007/978-981-99-3814-8_11

Leng, J., Ye, S., Zhou, M., Zhao, J. L., Liu, Q., Guo, W., & Fu, L. (2020). Blockchain-secured smart manufacturing in industry 4.0: A survey. *IEEE Transactions on Systems, Man, and Cybernetics. Systems, 51*(1), 237–252.

Li, X., Peng, L., Wang, Y., & Zhang, W. (2024). Open Challenges and Opportunities in Federated Foundation Models Towards Biomedical Healthcare. arXiv preprint arXiv:2405.06784.

Li, B. H., Hou, B. C., Yu, W. T., Lu, X. B., & Yang, C. W. (2017). Applications of artificial intelligence in intelligent manufacturing: A review. *Frontiers of Information Technology & Electronic Engineering, 18*, 86–96.

Lim, C. H., Lim, S., How, B. S., Ng, W. P. Q., Ngan, S. L., Leong, W. D., & Lam, H. L. (2021). A review of industry 4.0 revolution potential in a sustainable and renewable palm oil industry: HAZOP approach. *Renewable & Sustainable Energy Reviews, 135*, 110223.

Lin, C. (2020). Understanding cultural diversity and diverse identities. *Quality education*, 929-938.

Liu, Z., Yin, S. X., Lee, C., & Chen, N. F. (2024). Scaffolding Language Learning via Multi-modal Tutoring Systems with Pedagogical Instructions. *arXiv preprint arXiv:2404.03429*.

Liu, D., Honoré, A., Chatterjee, S., & Rasmussen, L. K. (2020). Powering hidden markov model by neural network based generative models. In *ECAI 2020* (pp. 1324–1331). IOS Press.

Liu, H., Yao, P., Latif, S., Aslam, S., & Iqbal, N. (2022). Impact of Green financing, FinTech, and financial inclusion on energy efficiency. *Environmental Science and Pollution Research International*, •••, 1–12. PMID: 34705207

Liu, Y., Han, T., Ma, S., Zhang, J., Yang, Y., Tian, J., He, H., Li, A., He, M., Liu, Z., Wu, Z., Zhao, L., Zhu, D., Li, X., Qiang, N., Shen, D., Liu, T., & Ge, B. (2023). Summary of ChatGPT-Related research and perspective towards the future of large language models. *Meta-Radiology*, *1*(2), 100017. DOI: 10.1016/J.METRAD.2023.100017

Liyanage, U. P., & Ranaweera, N. D. (2023). Ethical Considerations and Potential Risks in the Deployment of Large Language Models in Diverse Societal Contexts. *Journal of Computational Social Dynamics*, *8*(11).

Llanes-Jurado, J., Gómez-Zaragozá, L., Minissi, M. E., Alcañiz, M., & Marín-Morales, J. (2024). Developing conversational Virtual Humans for social emotion elicitation based on large language models. *Expert Systems with Applications*, *246*. Advance online publication. DOI: 10.1016/j.eswa.2024.123261

Lu, C., Lyu, J., Zhang, L., Gong, A., Fan, Y., Yan, J., & Li, X. (2020). Nuclear power plants with artificial intelligence in industry 4.0 era: Top-level design and current applications—A systemic review. *IEEE Access : Practical Innovations, Open Solutions*, *8*, 194315–194332.

Lu, J., Holleis, T., Zhang, Y., Aumayer, B., Nan, F., Bai, F., Ma, S., Ma, S., Li, M., Yin, G., Wang, Z., & Pang, R. (2023). ToolSandbox: A stateful, conversational, interactive evaluation benchmark for LLM tool use capabilities. arXiv. https://arxiv.org/abs/2306.11500

Lu, Y. (2019). Artificial intelligence: A survey on evolution, models, applications and future trends. *Journal of Management Analytics*, *6*(1), 1–29.

Lv, W., Xia, X., & Huang, S.-J. (2023). CodeACT: Code adaptive compute-efficient tuning framework for code LLMs. Pages. 34 https://arxiv.org/abs/2408.02193

Lyu, W., Wang, Y., Chung, T., Sun, Y., & Zhang, Y. (2024, July). Evaluating the effectiveness of llms in introductory computer science education: A semester-long field study. In *Proceedings of the Eleventh ACM Conference on Learning@ Scale* (pp. 63-74).

Ma, W. (2024). Mitigating Safety Issues in Pre-trained Language Models: A Model-Centric Approach Leveraging Interpretation Methods.

Ma, J., Song, J., Young, N. D., Chang, B. C. H., Korhonen, P. K., Campos, T. L., Liu, H., & Gasser, R. B. (2024). "Bingo" - a large language model- and graph neural network-based workflow for the prediction of essential genes from protein data. *Briefings in Bioinformatics*, *25*(1). Advance online publication. DOI: 10.1093/bib/bbad472 PMID: 38152979

Majstorovic, V. D., & Mitrovic, R. (2019). Industry 4.0 programs worldwide. In *Proceedings of the 4th International Conference on the Industry 4.0 Model for Advanced Manufacturing: AMP 2019 4* (pp. 78-99). Springer International Publishing.

McNally, K., Wright, K., Goldkind, L., Kattari, S. K., & Victor, B. G. (2024). Disability Expertise and Large Language Models: A Qualitative Study of Autistic TikTok Creators' Use of ChatGPT. *Social Media + Society*, *10*(3), 20563051241279549.

Meyendorf, N., Ida, N., Singh, R., & Vrana, J. (2023). NDE 4.0: Progress, promise, and its role to industry 4.0. *NDT & E International*, •••, 102957.

Meyer, J., Jansen, T., Schiller, R., Liebenow, L. W., Steinbach, M., Horbach, A., & Fleckenstein, J. (2024). Using LLMs to bring evidence-based feedback into the classroom: AI-generated feedback increases secondary students' text revision, motivation, and positive emotions. *Computers and Education: Artificial Intelligence*, *6*, 100199.

Migliorelli, M., & Dessertine, P. (2019). The rise of green finance in Europe. *Opportunities and challenges for issuers, investors and marketplaces. Cham. Palgrave Macmillan*, *2*, 2019.

Mikolov, T., Karafiát, M., Burget, L., Černocký, J., & Khudanpur, S. (2010). Recurrent neural network based language model. In *Proceedings of Interspeech 2010* (pp. 1045–1048). ISCA., https://www.isca-archive.org/interspeech_2010/mikolov10_interspeech.html

Mikolov, T., Sutskever, I., Chen, K., Corrado, G. S., & Dean, J. (2013). Efficient estimation of word representations in vector space. In *Proceedings of the International Conference on Learning Representations (ICLR).*

Minaee, S., Mikolov, T., Nikzad, N., Chenaghlu, M., Socher, R., Amatriain, X., & Gao, J. (2024). Large language models: A survey. arXiv preprint arXiv:2402.06196.

Minaee, S., Kalchbrenner, N., Cambria, E., Nikzad, N., Chenaghlu, M., & Gao, J. (2021, April). Deep learning–based text classification: A comprehensive review. *ACM Computing Surveys*, *54*(3).

Mithas, S., Chen, Z. L., Saldanha, T. J., & De Oliveira Silveira, A. (2022). How will artificial intelligence and Industry 4.0 emerging technologies transform operations management? *Production and Operations Management*, *31*(12), 4475–4487.

Morgan, J., Halton, M., Qiao, Y., & Breslin, J. G. (2021). Industry 4.0 smart reconfigurable manufacturing machines. *Journal of Manufacturing Systems*, *59*, 481–506.

Mourtzis, D., Angelopoulos, J., & Panopoulos, N. (2022). A Literature Review of the Challenges and Opportunities of the Transition from Industry 4.0 to Society 5.0. *Energies, 15*(17), 6276.

Mujumdar, A., & Vaidehi, V. B. (2019). Diabetes prediction using machine learning al- gorithms. *Procedia Computer Science, 165*, 292–299.

Muthmainnah, M., Yakin, A. A., Obaid, A. J., & Ziboon, A. R. T. (2024, September). Shaping user behavior in EFL education as an evaluation of artificial intelligence, computational thinking, and computational participations frameworks in digital humanities. In *AIP Conference Proceedings* (Vol. 3207, No. 1). AIP Publishing.

Nahavandi, S. (2019). Industry 5.0—A human-centric solution. *Sustainability, 11*(16), 4371.

Narayanan Venkit, P. (2023). *Towards a Holistic Approach: Understanding Sociodemographic Biases in NLP Models using an Interdisciplinary Lens*. DOI: 10.1145/3600211.3604754

Nassiry, D. (2018). *The role of fintech in unlocking green finance: Policy insights for developing countries* (No. 883). ADBI working paper.

Nay, J. J., Karamardian, D., Lawsky, S. B., Tao, W., Bhat, M., Jain, R., Lee, A. T., Choi, J. H., & Kasai, J. (2024). Large language models as tax attorneys: A case study in legal capabilities emergence. *Philosophical Transactions. Series A, Mathematical, Physical, and Engineering Sciences, 382*(2270). Advance online publication. DOI: 10.1098/rsta.2023.0159 PMID: 38403061

Nejjar, M., Zacharias, L., Stiehle, F., & Weber, I. (2023). LLMs for science: Usage for code generation and data analysis. *Journal of Software (Malden, MA), 2723*. Advance online publication. DOI: 10.1002/SMR.2723

Nguyen, T., Gosine, R. G., & Warrian, P. (2020). A systematic review of big data analytics for oil and gas industry 4.0. *IEEE Access : Practical Innovations, Open Solutions, 8*, 61183–61201.

Ni, A., Yin, P., Zhao, Y., Riddell, M., Feng, T., Shen, R., Yin, S., & Liu, Y. Semih Yavuz, ◇, Xiong, C., Joty, S., Zhou, Y., Radev, D., & Cohan, A. (2023). *L2CEval: Evaluating Language-to-Code Generation Capabilities of Large Language Models*. https://arxiv.org/abs/2309.17446v2

Nica, E., & Stehel, V. (2021). Internet of things sensing networks, artificial intelligence-based decision-making algorithms, and real-time process monitoring in sustainable industry 4.0. *Journal of Self-Governance and Management Economics, 9*(3), 35–47.

Nikolic, S., Sandison, C., Haque, R., Daniel, S., Grundy, S., Belkina, M., & Neal, P. (2024). ChatGPT, Copilot, Gemini, SciSpace and Wolfram versus higher education assessments: An updated multi-institutional study of the academic integrity impacts of Generative Artificial Intelligence (GenAI) on assessment, teaching and learning in engineering. *Australasian Journal of Engineering Education*, •••, 1–28.

Noguer i Alonso, M. (2023). A Framework for the Evaluation of Large Language Models. SSRN *Electronic Journal*. https://doi.org/DOI: 10.2139/ssrn.4649866

Omelianchuk, K., Liubonko, A., Skurzhanskyi, O., Chernodub, A., Korniienko, O., & Samokhin, I. (2024). Pillars of Grammatical Error Correction: Comprehensive Inspection Of Contemporary Approaches In The Era of Large Language Models. *arXiv preprint arXiv:2404.14914.*

Park, J., Bae, J., Lee, U., Ahn, T., Lee, S., Kim, D., . . . Kim, H. (2024). How to Align Large Language Models for Teaching English? Designing and Developing LLM based-Chatbot for Teaching English Conversation in EFL, Findings and Limitations. *arXiv preprint arXiv:2409.04987.*

Park, Y. J., Pillai, A., Deng, J., Guo, E., Gupta, M., Paget, M., & Naugler, C. (2024). Assessing the research landscape and clinical utility of large language models: A scoping review. *BMC Medical Informatics and Decision Making*, *24*(1). Advance online publication. DOI: 10.1186/s12911-024-02459-6 PMID: 38475802

Patwary, M. (2022). Using DeepSpeed and Megatron to train Megatron-Turing NLG 530B, a large-scale generative language model. *arXiv*. https://arxiv.org/abs/2201.11990

Pavlick, E. (2022). Semantic structure in deep learning. *Annual Review of Linguistics*, *8*(1), 447–471.

Peláez-Sánchez, I. C., Velarde-Camaqui, D., & Glasserman-Morales, L. D. (2024, June). The impact of large language models on higher education: Exploring the connection between AI and Education 4.0. [). Frontiers Media SA.]. *Frontiers in Education*, *9*, 1392091.

Peng, B., Alcaide, E., Anthony, Q. G., Albalak, A., Arcadinho, S., Biderman, S., Cao, H., Cheng, X., Chung, M. N., & Derczynski, L. (2023). RWKV: Reinventing RNNs for the transformer era. *arXiv*. https://arxiv.org/abs/2305.13048

Pennington, J., Socher, R., & Manning, C. D. (2014). GloVe: Global vectors for word representation. In *Proceedings of the 2014 Conference on Empirical Methods in Natural Language Processing* (pp. 1532–1543). Association for Computational Linguistics.

Perconti, P., & Plebe, A. (2020). Deep learning and cognitive science. *Cognition, 203*, 104365.

Phongying, M., & Hiriote, S. (2023). Diabetes classification using machine learning tech- niques. *Computation (Basel, Switzerland), 11*(5), 96.

Phuong, M., & Hutter, M. (2022). Formal algorithms for transformers. *arXiv*. https://arxiv.org/abs/2207.09238

Pijeira-Díaz, H. J., Braumann, S., van de Pol, J., van Gog, T., & de Bruin, A. B. H. (2024). Towards adaptive support for self-regulated learning of causal relations: Evaluating four Dutch word vector models. *British Journal of Educational Technology, 55*(4). Advance online publication. DOI: 10.1111/bjet.13431

Pivoto, D. G., de Almeida, L. F., da Rosa Righi, R., Rodrigues, J. J., Lugli, A. B., & Alberti, A. M. (2021). Cyber-physical systems architectures for industrial internet of things applications in Industry 4.0: A literature review. *Journal of Manufacturing Systems, 58*, 176–192.

Polverini, G., & Gregorcic, B. (2024). How understanding large language models can inform the use of ChatGPT in physics education. *European Journal of Physics, 45*(2). Advance online publication. DOI: 10.1088/1361-6404/ad1420

Popov, V. V., Kudryavtseva, E. V., Kumar Katiyar, N., Shishkin, A., Stepanov, S. I., & Goel, S. (2022). Industry 4.0 and digitalisation in healthcare. *Materials (Basel), 15*(6), 2140. PMID: 35329592

Prakash, K., Rao, S., Hamza, R., Lukich, J., Chaudhari, V., & Nandi, A. (2024, June). Integrating LLMs into Database Systems Education. In *Proceedings of the 3rd International Workshop on Data Systems Education: Bridging education practice with education research* (pp. 33-39).

Quinlan, J. R. (1986). Induction of decision trees. *Machine Learning, 1*(1), 81–106.

Raffel, C., Shazeer, N., Roberts, A., Lee, K., Narang, S., Matena, M., Zhou, Y., Li, W., & Liu, P. J. (2020). Exploring the limits of transfer learning with a unified text-to-text transformer. *Journal of Machine Learning Research, 21*(140), 1–67.

Raiaan, M. A. K., Mukta, M. S. H., Fatema, K., Fahad, N. M., Sakib, S., Mim, M. M. J., & Azam, S. (2024). A review on large Language Models: Architectures, applications, taxonomies, open issues and challenges. *IEEE Access : Practical Innovations, Open Solutions.*

Ramirez, E. A. B., & Esparrell, J. A. F. (2024). Artificial Intelligence (AI) in Education: Unlocking the Perfect Synergy for Learning. *Educational Process: International Journal, 13*(1), 35–51.

Rao, V. P. (2020). Reap the Rewards Of Intelligent Automation. In *Energy Sector Without Injecting Risk Using Design Thinking*. Service Design Network.

Razavi, S. (2021). Deep learning, explained: Fundamentals, explainability, and bridgeability to process-based modelling. *Environmental Modelling & Software, 144*, 105159.

Reier Forradellas, R. F., & Garay Gallastegui, L. M. (2021). Digital transformation and artificial intelligence applied to business: Legal regulations, economic impact and perspective. *Laws, 10*(3), 70.

Riyadh, M., & Shafiq, M. O. (2023). Towards Automatic Evaluation of NLG Tasks Using Conversational Large Language Models. *IFIP Advances in Information and Communication Technology, 676 IFIP*, 425–437. https://doi.org/DOI: 10.1007/978-3-031-34107-6_34

Roberts, A., Raffel, C., Shazeer, N., & Lee, K.. (2022). Exploring the Limits of Transfer Learning with a Unified Text-to-Text Transformer. *Journal of Artificial Intelligence Research, 74*, 67–85.

Roberts, J., Baker, M., & Andrew, J. (2024). Artificial intelligence and qualitative research: The promise and perils of large language model (LLM) 'assistance.'. *Critical Perspectives on Accounting, 99*. Advance online publication. DOI: 10.1016/j.cpa.2024.102722

Robertson, S. E., & Sparck Jones, K. (1976). Simple, proven approaches to text retrieval. *The Journal of Documentation, 32*(1), 30–48.

Ruan, S. S. (2021). *Smart tutoring through conversational interfaces*. Stanford University.

Sachs, J. D., Woo, W. T., Yoshino, N., & Taghizadeh-Hesary, F. (2019). Importance of green finance for achieving sustainable development goals and energy security. *Handbook of green finance: Energy security and sustainable development, 10*, 1-10.

Saeed, S., Altamimi, S. A., Alkayyal, N. A., Alshehri, E., & Alabbad, D. A. (2023). Digital transformation and cybersecurity challenges for businesses resilience: Issues and recommendations. *Sensors (Basel), 23*(15), 6666. PMID: 37571451

Sánchez-Sotano, A., Cerezo-Narváez, A., Abad-Fraga, F., Pastor-Fernández, A., & Salguero-Gómez, J. (2020). Trends of digital transformation in the shipbuilding sector. In *New Trends in the Use of Artificial Intelligence for the Industry 4.0*. IntechOpen.

Sarker, I. H. (2024). LLM potentiality and awareness: A position paper from the perspective of trustworthy and responsible AI modeling. *Discover Artificial Intelligence*, *4*(1), 1–7. DOI: 10.1007/S44163-024-00129-0/FIGURES/1

Schaeffer, R., Miranda, B., & Koyejo, S. (2023). Are Emergent Abilities of Large Language Models a Mirage? https://arxiv.org/abs/2304.15004v2

Schoenegger, P., & Park, P. S. (2023). *Large Language Model Prediction Capabilities: Evidence from a Real-World Forecasting Tournament*. https://arxiv.org/abs/2310.13014v1

Schulz, K., & Feist, M. (2021). Leveraging blockchain technology for innovative climate finance under the Green Climate Fund. *Earth System Governance*, *7*, 100084.

Sennrich, R., Haddow, B., & Birch, A. (2016). Neural machine translation of rare words with subword units. In *Proceedings of the 54th Annual Meeting of the Association for Computational Linguistics* (Vol. 1, pp. 1715–1725). Association for Computational Linguistics.

Shafik, W. (2023). *Introduction to ChatGPT*. In *Advanced Applications of Generative AI and Natural Language Processing Models*. DOI: 10.4018/979-8-3693-0502-7.ch001

Shafik, W., & Tufail, A. (2023). Energy Optimization Analysis on Internet of Things. In *Environmental Science and Engineering*. https://doi.org/DOI: 10.1007/978-3-031-25662-2_1

Shakir, U. (2023). A Novel Method for Thematically Analyzing Student Responses to Open-ended Case Scenarios.

Shanks, K. W. (2020). Machine Learning and Critical Thinking: Applying Machine Learning Algorithms to the Scoring of the Critical Thinking Assessment Test (CAT) (Doctoral dissertation, Tennessee Technological University).

Shannon, C. E. (1948). A mathematical theory of communication. *The Bell System Technical Journal*, *27*(3), 379–423.

Shen, T., Jin, R., Huang, Y., Liu, C., Dong, W., Guo, Z., & Xiong, D. (2023). Large language model alignment: A survey. arXiv preprint arXiv:2309.15025.

Shin, D., & Lee, J. H. (2024). Moving from off-the-shelf chatbots to a user-designed bespoke L2 chatbot.

Shi, Z., Xie, Y., Xue, W., Chen, Y., Fu, L., & Xu, X. (2020). Smart factory in Industry 4.0. *Systems Research and Behavioral Science*, *37*(4), 607–617.

Shoukat, S., Mamoon, R., & Arif, M. F. (2024). Enhancing Language Proficiency Through TPACK Model and AI Applications A Study on Effective Integration Strategies in English Language Instruction. *Pakistan Languages and Humanities Review*, *8*(2), 540–554.

Siegle, D. (2024). Using Artificial Intelligence (AI) Technology to Support the Three Legs of Talent Development. *Gifted Child Today*, *47*(3), 221–227.

Sima, V., Gheorghe, I. G., Subić, J., & Nancu, D. (2020). Influences of the industry 4.0 revolution on the human capital development and consumer behavior: A systematic review. *Sustainability*, *12*(10), 4035.

Singh Rajawat, A., Bedi, P., Goyal, S. B., Shukla, P. K., Zaguia, A., Jain, A., & Monirujjaman Khan, M. (2021). Reformist framework for improving human security for mobile robots in industry 4.0. *Mobile Information Systems*, *2021*, 1–10.

Smetana, M., Salles de Salles, L., Sukharev, I., & Khazanovich, L. (2024). Highway Construction Safety Analysis Using Large Language Models. *Applied Sciences (Switzerland)*, *14*(4). Advance online publication. DOI: 10.3390/app14041352

Smith, J. W., Everhart, J. E., Dickson, W. C., Knowler, W. C., & Johannes, R. S. (1988). Using the ADAP learning algorithm to forecast the onset of diabetes mellitus. *Proceedings of the Symposium on Computer Applications and Medical Care*, 261–265.

Song, X., Salcianu, A., Song, Y., Dopson, D., & Zhou, D. (2021). Fast WordPiece tokenization. In *Proceedings of the 2021 Conference on Empirical Methods in Natural Language Processing* (pp. 2089–2103). Association for Computational Linguistics.

Sravanthi, C., & Maloth, U. (2024, June). Digital classroom: Tech-friendly academic model for teaching english. In *AIP Conference Proceedings* (Vol. 2971, No. 1). AIP Publishing.

Sun, L., Chan, A., Chang, Y. S., & Dow, S. P. (2024, March). ReviewFlow: Intelligent Scaffolding to Support Academic Peer Reviewing. In Proceedings of the 29th International Conference on Intelligent User Interfaces (pp. 120-137). Tour of Artificial Intelligence Research: Volume II: AI Algorithms (pp. 339-410). Cham: Springer International Publishing.

Susnjak, T., & McIntosh, T. R. (2024). ChatGPT: The end of online exam integrity? *Education Sciences*, *14*(6), 656.

Tai, R. H., Bentley, L. R., Xia, X., Sitt, J. M., Fankhauser, S. C., Chicas-Mosier, A. M., & Monteith, B. G. (2024). An Examination of the Use of Large Language Models to Aid Analysis of Textual Data. *International Journal of Qualitative Methods, 23*. Advance online publication. DOI: 10.1177/16094069241231168

Takemoto, K. (2024). The moral machine experiment on large language models. *Royal Society Open Science, 11*(2). Advance online publication. DOI: 10.1098/rsos.231393 PMID: 38328569

Tamkin, A., & Brundage, M. (2021). *3, J. C., & Ganguli, D.* Understanding the Capabilities, Limitations, and Societal Impact of Large Language Models.

Tan, Y., Min, D., Li, Y., Li, W., Hu, N., Chen, Y., & Qi, G. (2023). Can ChatGPT Replace Traditional KBQA Models? An In-Depth Analysis of the Question Answering Performance of the GPT LLM Family. *Lecture Notes in Computer Science (Including Subseries Lecture Notes in Artificial Intelligence and Lecture Notes in Bioinformatics), 14265 LNCS*, 348–367. https://doi.org/DOI: 10.1007/978-3-031-47240-4_19

Tao, F., Akhtar, M. S., & Jiayuan, Z. (2021). The future of artificial intelligence in cybersecurity: A comprehensive survey. *EAI Endorsed Transactions on Creative Technologies*, *8*(28), e3–e3.

Thomason, J., Ahmad, M., Bronder, P., Hoyt, E., Pocock, S., Bouteloupe, J., & Shrier, D. (2018). Blockchain—powering and empowering the poor in developing countries. In *Transforming climate finance and green investment with blockchains* (pp. 137–152). Academic Press.

Tian, D., Jiang, S., Zhang, L., Lu, X., & Xu, Y. (2024). The role of large language models in medical image processing: a narrative review. In *Quantitative Imaging in Medicine and Surgery* (Vol. 14, Issue 1). DOI: 10.21037/qims-23-892

Tokayev, K.-J. (2023). Ethical Implications of Large Language Models A Multidimensional Exploration of Societal, Economic, and Technical Concerns. *International Journal of Stochastic Analysis*, *8*(9).

Tseng, M. L., Tran, T. P. T., Ha, H. M., Bui, T. D., & Lim, M. K. (2021). Sustainable industrial and operation engineering trends and challenges Toward Industry 4.0: A data driven analysis. *Journal of Industrial and Production Engineering*, *38*(8), 581–598.

Tuggener, L., Sager, P., Taoudi-Benchekroun, Y., Grewe, B. F., & Stadelmann, T. (2024). So you want your private LLM at home?: a survey and benchmark of methods for efficient GPTs. *11th IEEE Swiss Conference on Data Science (SDS), Zurich, Switzerland*, 30-31 May 2024, 205–212. https://doi.org/DOI: 10.1109/SDS60720.2024.00036

Uzun, L. (2023). Are Concerns Related to Artificial Intelligence Development and Use Really Necessary: A Philosophical Discussion. *Digital Society : Ethics, Socio-Legal and Governance of Digital Technology*, *2*(3). Advance online publication. DOI: 10.1007/s44206-023-00070-2

Van Wyk, M. M. (2024). Is ChatGPT an opportunity or a threat? Preventive strategies employed by academics related to a GenAI-based LLM at a faculty of education. *Journal of applied learning and teaching, 7*(1).

Vaswani, A., Shazeer, N., Parmar, N., Uszkoreit, J., Jones, L., Gomez, A. N., Kaiser, Ł., & Polosukhin, I. (2017). Attention is all you need. In *Advances in Neural Information Processing Systems* (Vol. 30). NeurIPS.

Vaswani, A., Shazeer, N., Parmar, N., & Uszkoreit, J.. (2022). Attention is All You Need. *Neural Computation*, *34*(4), 681–689.

Vik, B. (2024). *Large Language Models in L2 English Teaching: Exploring Teachers' Understanding and Utilisation* (Master's thesis, The University of Bergen).

Vogt, J. (2021). Where is the human got to go? Artificial intelligence, machine learning, big data, digitalisation, and human–robot interaction in Industry 4.0 and 5.0: Review Comment on: Bauer, M.(2020). Preise kalkulieren mit KI-gestützter Onlineplattform BAM GmbH, Weiden, Bavaria, Germany. *AI & Society*, *36*(3), 1083–1087.

Walker, S. H., & Duncan, D. B. (1967). Estimation of the probability of an event as a function of several independent variables. *Biometrika*, *54*(1-2), 167–179. DOI: 10.2307/2333860 PMID: 6049533

Wamba-Taguimdje, S. L., Fosso Wamba, S., Kala Kamdjoug, J. R., & Tchatchouang Wanko, C. E. (2020). Influence of artificial intelligence (AI) on firm performance: The business value of AI-based transformation projects. *Business Process Management Journal*, *26*(7), 1893–1924.

Wan, Q., Hu, S., Zhang, Y., Wang, P., Wen, B., & Lu, Z. (2024). "It Felt Like Having a Second Mind": Investigating Human-AI Co-creativity in Prewriting with Large Language Models. *Proceedings of the ACM on Human-Computer Interaction*, *8*(CSCW1). DOI: 10.1145/3637361

Wang, S., Xu, T., Li, H., Zhang, C., Liang, J., Tang, J., . . . Wen, Q. (2024). Large language models for education: A survey and outlook. *arXiv preprint arXiv:2403.18105*.

Wang, S., & Jiang, J. (2016). Learning natural language inference with LSTM. In *Proceedings of the 2016 Conference on Empirical Methods in Natural Language Processing* (pp. 1442–1451). Association for Computational Linguistics.

Wan, J., Yang, J., Wang, Z., & Hua, Q. (2018). Artificial intelligence for cloud-assisted smart factory. *IEEE Access : Practical Innovations, Open Solutions*, *6*, 55419–55430.

Watters, J. B., & Garcia-Lopez, A. (2024). Artificial Intelligence in Education: Transforming Learning and Teaching Julie A. Delello iD https://orcid. org/0000-0002-4326-8096. *Disruptive Technologies in Education and Workforce Development*, 1.

Wee, B. F., Sivakumar, S., Lim, K. H., Wong, W. K., & Juwono, F. H. (2023). Diabetes detection based on machine learning and deep learning approaches. *Multimedia Tools and Applications*, •••, 1–33.

Wirth, R., & Hipp, J. (2000). CRISP-DM: Towards a standard process model for data mining. In *Proceedings of the 4th International Conference on the Practical Applications of Knowledge Discovery and Data Mining*.

Wu, J., Zhu, J., & Qi, Y. (2024). Medical Graph RAG: Towards Safe Medical Large Language Model via Graph Retrieval-Augmented Generation. arXiv:2408.04187v1 [cs.CV]. Retrieved from https://arxiv.org/abs/2408.04187

Xu, L. D., Xu, E. L., & Li, L. (2018). Industry 4.0: State of the art and future trends. *International Journal of Production Research*, *56*(8), 2941–2962.

Yalcinalp, S., Türkoğlu, H., Koc, S. E., & Ersoy, H. (2024). Utilization of Artificial Intelligence in Education: A Perspective on Learning Strategies.

Yamaguchi, S., Morishita, M., Fukuda, H., Muraoka, K., Nakamura, T., Yoshioka, I., & Awano, S. (2024). Evaluating the efficacy of leading large language models in the Japanese national dental hygienist examination: A comparative analysis of ChatGPT, Bard, and Bing Chat. *Journal of Dental Sciences*. PMID: 39347065

Yan, L., Sha, L., Zhao, L., Li, Y., Martinez-Maldonado, R., Chen, G., Li, X., Jin, Y., & Gašević, D. (2024). Practical and ethical challenges of large language models in education: A systematic scoping review. In *British Journal of Educational Technology* (Vol. 55, Issue 1). DOI: 10.1111/bjet.13370

Yan, C., Siddik, A. B., Yong, L., Dong, Q., Zheng, G. W., & Rahman, M. N. (2022). A two-staged SEM-artificial neural network approach to analyze the impact of FinTech adoption on the sustainability performance of banking firms: The mediating effect of green finance and innovation. *Systems*, *10*(5), 148.

Yan, D. (2024). Feedback seeking abilities of L2 writers using ChatGPT: A mixed method multiple case study. *Kybernetes*.

Yang, J., Jin, H., Tang, R., Han, X., Feng, Q., Jiang, H., & Hu, X. (2024). Harnessing the power of llms in practice: A survey on chatgpt and beyond. *ACM Transactions on Knowledge Discovery from Data*, *18*(6), 1–32.

Yang, J., Jin, H., Tang, R., Han, X., Feng, Q., Jiang, H., Zhong, S., Yin, B., & Hu, X. (2024). Harnessing the Power of LLMs in Practice: A Survey on ChatGPT and Beyond. *ACM Transactions on Knowledge Discovery from Data*, *18*(6), 32. DOI: 10.1145/3649506/ASSET/D2038F72-9808-4957-BF9D-FB4E05F82081/ASSETS/GRAPHIC/TKDD-2023-06-0236-F02.JPG

Yang, Y., Su, X., & Yao, S. (2021). Nexus between green finance, fintech, and high-quality economic development: Empirical evidence from China. *Resources Policy*, *74*, 102445.

Yan, L., Sha, L., Zhao, L., Li, Y., Martinez-Maldonado, R., Chen, G., & Gašević, D. (2024). Practical and ethical challenges of large language models in education: A systematic scoping review. *British Journal of Educational Technology*, *55*(1), 90–112.

Ye, J., Xu, H., Liu, H., Hu, A., Yan, M., Qian, Q., Zhang, J., Huang, F., & Zhou, J. (2024). mPLUG-Owl3: Towards long image-sequence understanding in multi-modal large language models (arXiv:2408.04840v2). https://arxiv.org/abs/2408.04840

Yigci, D., Eryilmaz, M., Yetisen, A. K., Tasoglu, S., & Ozcan, A. (2024). Large Language Model-Based Chatbots in Higher Education. *Advanced Intelligent Systems*, •••, 2400429.

Yilmaz, R., Yurdugül, H., Yilmaz, F. G. K., Şahin, M., Sulak, S., Aydin, F., & Ömer, O. R. A. L. (2022). Smart MOOC integrated with intelligent tutoring: A system architecture and framework model proposal. *Computers and Education: Artificial Intelligence*, *3*, 100092.

Yue, Y., & Shyu, J. Z. (2024). A paradigm shift in crisis management: The nexus of AGI-driven intelligence fusion networks and blockchain trustworthiness. *Journal of Contingencies and Crisis Management*, *32*(1), e12541.

Yuvaraj, N., & SriPreethaa, K. R. (2019). Diabetes prediction in healthcare systems using machine learning algorithms on Hadoop cluster. *Cluster Computing*, *22*(Suppl 1), 1–9.

Zaman, K. S., Reaz, M. B. I., Ali, S. H. M., Bakar, A. A. A., & Chowdhury, M. E. H. (2021). Custom hardware architectures for deep learning on portable devices: A review. *IEEE Transactions on Neural Networks and Learning Systems*, *33*(11), 6068–6088.

Zhang, Y., & Wallace, B. (2016). A study on neural network language modeling. *arXiv*. https://arxiv.org/abs/1708.07252

Zhao, L., Zhu, D., Shafik, W., Matinkhah, S. M., Ahmad, Z., Sharif, L., & Craig, A. (2022). Artificial intelligence analysis in cyber domain: A review. In *International Journal of Distributed Sensor Networks* (Vol. 18, Issue 4). DOI: 10.1177/15501329221084882

Zheng, C., Yuan, K., Guo, B., Hadi Mogavi, R., Peng, Z., Ma, S., & Ma, X. (2024, May). Charting the Future of AI in Project-Based Learning: A Co-Design Exploration with Students. In *Proceedings of the CHI Conference on Human Factors in Computing Systems* (pp. 1-19).

Zhong, S., Gao, S., Huang, Z., Wen, W., Zitnik, M., & Zhou, P. (2024). MoExtend: Tuning new experts for modality and task extension. Retrieved from https://aclanthology.org/2024.acl-srw.8.pdf

Zhong, R. Y., Xu, X., Klotz, E., & Newman, S. T. (2017). Intelligent manufacturing in the context of industry 4.0: A review. *Engineering*, *3*(5), 616–630.

Zhou, J., Zhang, S., Lu, Q., Dai, W., Chen, M., Liu, X., . . . Herrera-Viedma, E. (2021). A survey on federated learning and its applications for accelerating industrial internet of things. *arXiv preprint arXiv:2104.10501.*

Zhuo, Y. T., Huang, Y., Chen, C., & Xing, Z. (2023). Exploring AI Ethics of ChatGPT: A Diagnostic Analysis. *ArXiv Preprint ArXiv:2301.12867.*

Zietsch, J., Kulaga, R., Held, H., Herrmann, C., & Thiede, S. (2024). Multi-layer edge resource placement optimization for factories. *Journal of Intelligent Manufacturing*, *35*(2). Advance online publication.

Zimmet, P. Z., Magliano, D. J., Herman, W. H., & Shaw, J. E. (2014). Diabetes: A 21st century challenge. *The Lancet. Diabetes & Endocrinology*, *2*(1), 56–64. DOI: 10. 1016/S2213-8587(13)70112-8 PMID: 24622669

Zuzul, T., & Tripsas, M. (2020). Start-up inertia versus flexibility: The role of founder identity in a nascent industry. *Administrative Science Quarterly*, *65*(2), 395–433.

About the Contributors

Ismail Lamaakal (Member, IEEE) received a Master of Science degree in Computer Science from the Multidisciplinary Faculty of Nador, University Mohammed Premier, Oujda, Morocco. He is currently advancing towards his Ph.D. in Computer Science at the same esteemed institution. As an Artificial Intelligence Scientist, his research primarily focuses on the innovative integration of Tiny Machine Learning, the Internet of Things (IoT), Human-computer interaction, and Embedded Systems. His work is characterized by its pioneering approach in the field, emphasizing practical applications and advancements in these interconnected domains. His contributions are marked by a commitment to pushing the boundaries of AI and its applications in the modern technological landscape.

Yassine Maleh is a PhD of the University Hassan 1st in Morocco in the field of Internet of Things Security and privacy, since 2013. He is Senior Member of IEEE, Member of the International Association of Engineers IAENG and The Machine Intelligence Research Labs. Dr Maleh has made contributions in the fields of information security and privacy, Internet of Things Security, Wireless and Constrained Networks Security. His research interests include Information Security and Privacy, Internet of Things, Networks Security, Information system and IT Governance. He has published over than 50 papers (Book chapters, international journals and conferences/workshops), and 4 edited books and 1 authored book. He is the editor in chief of the International Journal of Smart Security Technologies (IJSST). He serves as an Associate Editor for IEEE Access (2019 Impact Factor 4.098), the International Journal of Digital Crime and Forensics (IJDCF) and the International Journal of Information Security and Privacy (IJISP). He was also a Guest Editor of a special issue on Recent Advances on Cyber Security and Privacy for Cloud-of-Things of the International Journal of Digital Crime and Forensics (IJDCF), Volume 10, Issue 3, July-September 2019. He has served and continues to serve on executive and technical program committees and as a reviewer of numerous international conference and journals such as Elsevier Ad Hoc Networks, IEEE Network Magazine, IEEE Sensor Journal, ICT Express, and Springer Cluster Computing. He was the Publicity chair of BCCA 2019 and the General Chair of the MLBDACP 19 symposium.

Khalid El Makkaoui received his master's degree in networks and systems and a Ph.D. in computer science from Hassan 1st University, Settat, Morocco, in 2014 and 2018. Since 2019, he has been an Associate Professor with the Department of Computer Science at the Multidisciplinary Faculty of Nador, University Mohammed Premier, Oujda, Morocco. His research interests focus on cybersecurity and artificial intelligence. He has published over 40 papers (book chapters, international journals, and conferences).

Ibrahim Ouahbi is a professor of computer science at the Multidisciplinary Faculty of Nador, University Mohammed Premier, Oujda, Morocco. He received his Ph.D. in didactics of informatics in 2018 from Sidi Mohammed Ben Abdellah University, Fez, Morocco. He was a professor of educational technologies at the Faculty of Educational Sciences, Mohammed V University of Rabat, in 2019. His research interests include artificial intelligence, cybersecurity, and ICT integration in science education and learning.

Ahmed A. Abd El-Latif graduated with distinction from the Harbin Institute of Technology, China, in 2013, earning a Ph.D. Since then, he has led and participated in several successful research projects and secured grants in Egypt, the Russian Federation, Saudi Arabia, China, Malaysia, and Tunisia. Currently, Dr. Abd El-Latif holds staff positions at Menoufia University, Egypt, and Prince Sultan University, Saudi Arabia. With over 18 years of professional experience, he has published approximately 300 papers in journals and conference proceedings, including 12 books, with over 10,000 citations. Since 2022, he has served as Head of the MEGANET 6G Lab Research in the Russian Federation. Dr. Abd El-Latif holds several leadership positions, including Vice Chair of the EIAS Research Lab, Founder and Deputy Director of the Center of Excellence in Quantum & Intelligent Computing (Prince Sultan University, Saudi Arabia). He has received several awards, including the State Encouragement Award in Engineering Sciences from the Arab Republic of Egypt in 2016, the Best Ph.D. Student Award from the Harbin Institute of Technology, China, in 2013, and the Young Scientist Award from Menoufia University, Egypt, in 2014. Dr. Abd El-Latif actively participates in the scientific community, serving as Chair/Co-Chair of several Scopus/EI conferences. He also holds editorial positions, including Editor-in-Chief of the International Journal of Information Security and Privacy, Series Editor of Quantum Information Processing and Computing, and Series Editor of Advances in Cybersecurity Management. Additionally, he serves as an academic editor or associate editor for many indexed journals in the Web of Science (WoS) and Scopus, covering various quartiles. Dr. Abd El-Latif's research interests span quantum communications and cryptography, cybersecurity, artificial intelligence of things (AIoT), AI-based image processing, information hiding, and applications of dynamical systems (discrete-time models: chaotic systems and quantum walks) in cybersecurity.

***

Saurabh Chandra is an accomplished legal scholar and currently serves as an Associate Professor & Assistant Dean at the School of Law, Bennett University, India. With a robust academic foundation, he earned his Bachelor of Arts and Bachelor of Laws (B.A. LL.B.) from the prestigious Aligarh Muslim University (A.M.U.). He further specialized in Business Laws, completing his Master of Laws (LL.M.) at the renowned National Law School of India University (NLSIU), Bangalore. Dr. Chandra's academic journey culminated in a Doctorate in Law (Ph.D.) from the esteemed National Law University (NLU) Delhi. In addition to his impressive legal education from some of India's most prestigious institutions, Dr. Saurabh Chandra also holds a master's degree in Management with specialization in Human Resources in Management and another in Journalism and Mass Communication. With 16 years of teaching experience, he has established himself as an expert in Business and Corporate Laws, with numerous publications to his credit. Dr. Saurabh Chandra is a distinguished expert in Business and Corporate Laws, with a profound understanding of the intricate legal frameworks that govern the business world. His expertise is complemented by a robust portfolio of scholarly publications, which underscores his commitment to advancing knowledge in his field. Throughout his career, Dr. Chandra has consistently produced high-impact research that addresses critical issues in Business and Corporate Law. His publications are widely recognized for their depth of analysis, innovative perspectives, and practical relevance. He has contributed extensively to leading journals, where his work has often set new standards for legal scholarship. His publications not only reflect his scholarly rigor but also his dedication to addressing contemporary challenges faced by businesses and policymakers. By bridging the gap between theoretical insights and real-world applications, Dr. Chandra's work serves as a valuable resource for academics, legal practitioners, and industry professionals alike. Dr. Chandra brings a wealth of experience in Academic Administration, having successfully held various key administrative positions. His diverse qualifications and extensive experience make him a distinguished figure in the academic and legal communities.

Besse Darmawati, she is a senior researcher at Badan Riset dan Inovasi Nasional (National Research and Innovation Agency), Indonesia. She has extensive experience as a researcher and global speaker in international conferences. She is an accomplished author, having written 77 national and International publications in journals, proceedings, books and book chapters which have been published by global reputable journals and proceedings, esteemed book publishers such as Taylor and Francis. She serves as an international board member for various scientific innovation research professional groups, such as Perhimpunan Periset Indonesia and Association Moslem Community in ASEAN). She is also a member of the United Nations volunteers' roster and the advisory board of Indonesian education share to care volunteers. Her research interests include developing literary work; learning language, literature, and literacy; and Literature Interdisciplinary. With her extensive experience and outstanding track record, Besse Darmawati is open to international collaborations and teamwork.

Rashmi Gupta received the Ph.D. degree in computer applications from the National Institute of Technology, Raipur. Currently, she is an Assistant Professor with the Department of Computer Science and Application, Atal Bihari Vajpayee University, Bilaspur, Chhattisgarh. She has published more than 20 research papers, conference papers, and book chapters. She has undertaken peer-reviewing responsibilities for esteemed publishers. She received grants from AICTE, to organize the ATAL Faculty Development Program; and the Science and Engineering Research Board, DST, for conducting high-end workshops and internships. She has successfully organized numerous faculty development programs under the AIU-AADC Centre, ABVV. Demonstrating her commitment to mentorship, she has guided over 30 PG and 20 UG students in their research-related major projects.. Additionally, she has been invited as a resource person to deliver lectures at various workshops and faculty development programs.

Anandakumar Haldorai serves as a Professor in CSE and Associate Dean – Research at Sri Eshwar College of Engineering. He has 18 years of experience in Engineering Education. He has received his Master's in Software engineering from PSG College of Technology, Coimbatore and PhD in Information and Communication Engineering from PSG College of Technology. His research areas include Big Data, Cognitive Radio Networks,Mobile Communications and Networking Protocols. He has authored more than 172 research papers in reputed International Journals and IEEE conferences. He has authored 14 books and many book chapters with reputed publishers such as Springer and IGI. He is a passionate researcher and also Editor in Chief Keai – Elsevier – IJIN, Associate Editor IEEE Access, Area Editor – EAI Energy Web and served as a reviewer for IEEE, IET,

Springer, Inderscience and Elsevier journals. He is also the guest editor of many journals with Elsevier, Springer, Inderscience, etc. He had been the General Chair, Session Chair, and Panelist in several conferences. He is a senior member of IEEE, IET, ACM and Fellow member of EAI research group.

Sri Haryatmo His works have been published in several national and international journals. Some of her writings have also been collected in several seminar proceedings national and international. His books that have been published include (1) Interpreting Unen-Unen Semut Ireng Anak-anak Sapi With An Intertext Approach, (2) Understanding the Meaning, Function and Role of Angel Stories in Literary Literature (3) The Transformation of the Book of Pararaton in the Novel Romance of Blood Ken Arok - Ken Dedes, and the Conception of Contemporary Leadership . In addition, he has also written several children's stories. Sri Haryatmo is a member of the Indonesian Researchers Association (PPI) and the Indonesian Scholars-Literature Association (HISKI).

Jeetendra Kumar has Ph.D. received the M.Sc. and M.Tech. degrees in computer science. He was an Assistant Professor with the Department of Computer Science and Application, Atal Bihari Vajpayee University, Bilaspur, Chhattisgarh, India, for the last ten years. He has completed two research projects sponsored by the State Planning Commission, C. G., and Commonwealth Media Centre for Asia (CEMCA) New Delhi, and Atal Bihari Vajpayee University. He has published various research articles in reputed journals and conferences, including topics such as sentiment analysis, fall detection using machine learning techniques, IoT applications, and automatic question generation. He has also contributed book chapters on topics related to neuroscience, smartphone applications, and fog computing in healthcare. He is a member of ISCA, IAENG, the ICSES, and IAASSE.

Abd. Rasyid is a researcher at the National Research and Innovation Agency, Indonesia. As a researcher and author, he has published several other works: (1) Ethno Medicine Bugis Traditional Medicine (2021), (2) The Structure of Conflict Resolution in the Bugis Wajo Community Story from the Perspective of Levi Strauss (2022), (3) Lexical Deviation in the Novel: A Stylistic Study (2023, high reputation international journal), (4) Unravelling the Meaning of Vernacular Settlements Through Linguistic Threads: A Case of Ngapak Dialect in Indonesia (2024). His specific interests include: literature, interdisciplinary or multidisciplinary studies, literary documentation, and literature literacy.

Nurweni Saptawuryandari is a senior researcher at the National Research and Innovation Agency. Her works have been published in several national and international journals. Some of her writings have also been collected in several seminar proceedings national and international. Her books that have been published include (1) Understanding Children's Stories: A Case Study of Bobo, Ananda, and Amanah Magazines, (2) The Form, Content, and Function of Children'sToy Poetry Texts, (3) Literary and Literary Works. In addition, he has also written several children's stories. Nurweni Saptawuryandari is a member of the Indonesian Researchers Association (PPI) and the Indonesian Scholars-Literature Association (HISKI).

Wasswa Shafik (Member, IEEE) received a Bachelor of Science degree in information technology from Ndejje University, Uganda, a Master of Engineering degree in Information Technology (Computer and Communication Networks) from Yazd University, Iran, and a PhD in Computer Science with the School of Digital Science, Universiti Brunei Darussalam, Brunei Darussalam. He is also the Founder and Research Director of the Dig Connectivity Research Laboratory (DCRLab) after serving as a Research Associate at the Network Interconnectivity Research Laboratory at Yazd University. Prior to this, he worked as a Community Data Analyst at Population Services International (PSI-Uganda), a Community Data Officer at the Programme for Accessible Health Communication (PACE-Uganda), a Research Assistant at the Socio-Economic Data Centre (SEDC-Uganda), Uganda, an Assistant Data Officer at TechnoServe, Kampala, IT Support at Thurayya Islam Media, Uganda, and Asmaah Charity Organization. He has hundreds of publications with renowned publishers. His research interests include Computer Vision, Explainable AI, Smart Agriculture, Health and ecological informatics, Security and Privacy.

Suvarna Sharma has received her B.Sc. and M.Sc. degree in Computer Science from Jiwaji University, Gwalior, Madhya Pradesh in the year 2005 and 2007. She has received M.Tech. Degree from DAVV, Indore, Madhya Pradesh in the year 2013. She has done PhD from MANIT Bhopal, Madhya Pradesh in the year 2020. She is currently working as Assistant Professor in the Department of Computer Science and Engineering, Chitkara University, Rajpura, Punjab, India. Her research interests include Data Mining, Information Retrieval, Web Mining, Blockchain Technology and Big Data.

Arunima Shastri is a legal academic with a focus on the intersections of law, technology, and social justice. She holds an LL.M. in Corporate and Commercial Law from NLU Odisha and is currently completing her Ph.D. at Gujarat National Law University, where her research critically explores the interplay between intellectual property rights, visual art, deepfakes, and digital expression. Her teaching and research interests include intellectual property law, data privacy, blockchain regulation, and human rights law, with a particular emphasis on LGBTQ+

rights. Through her work, she bridges doctrinal legal analysis with contemporary technological and cultural developments, contributing to scholarship and curriculum development in emerging areas of law.

Bhupinder Singh working as Professor at Sharda University, India. Also, Honorary Professor in University of South Wales UK and Santo Tomas University Tunja, Colombia. His areas of publications as Smart Healthcare, Medicines, fuzzy logics, artificial intelligence, robotics, machine learning, deep learning, federated learning, IoT, PV Glasses, metaverse and many more. He has 3 books, 139 paper publications, 163 paper presentations in international/national conferences and seminars, participated in more than 40 workshops/FDP's/QIP's, 25 courses from international universities of repute, organized more than 59 events with international and national academicians and industry people's, editor-in-chief and co-editor in journals, developed new courses. He has given talks at international universities, resource person in international conferences such as in Nanyang Technological University Singapore, Tashkent State University of Law Uzbekistan; KIMEP University Kazakhstan, All'ah meh Tabatabi University Iran, the Iranian Association of International Criminal law, Iran and Hague Center for International Law and Investment, The Netherlands, Northumbria University Newcastle UK,

Sutejo is an intermediate expert researcher at the National Research and Innovation Agency of Indonesia. He graduated from Universitas Jember as a bachelor of Indonesian linguistics and literature in 1993. His topic interest is in the field of interdisciplinary linguistics. The title of an internationally published article he wrote was "Language Choices and Digital Identity of High School Student Text Messages in the New Capital City of Indonesia: Implication for Language Education".

Muthmainnah Yakin is a senior lecturer at Universitas Al Asyariah Mandar in West Sulawesi, Indonesia. She has extensive experience as a lecturer, global speaker, and international leader. Muthmainnah has held numerous positions at her university, including Chairman of the Indonesian Language Department, Public Relations Officer, Director of Women's Centre Studies, Deputy Director of Quality Assurance Unit, and currently, Deputy Director of the Language and Character Development Institute. Muthmainnah is also an accomplished author, having written 80 national and International books, published by esteemed publishers such as IGI Global, Springer, Emerald, Wiley, Taylor and Francis. She serves as an international board member for various scientific innovation research groups, adjunct faculty of MAAUN Nigeria, adjunct faculty at Buriram Rajabhat university (BRU) Thailand and adjunct faculty at MANIPAL Global Ntx Malaysia Muthmainnah has won over 100+ international awards, including Outstanding Professor, Outstanding

Leadership, Best International Influencer, Best Emerging Professor of the Year, International Award for Working Women, and SDGs Warrior. She is also an honorary doctorate degree holder from Layahe University and the recipient of the Doctor of Excellence award from the Philippines. Moreover, Muthmainnah is a member of the United Nations volunteers' roster and the advisory board of Indonesian education share to care volunteers. Her research interests include developing literary work, instructional teaching material, assurance of learning (Assure), TESOL (Teaching English to Speakers of Other Languages), ICT in education, digital education, GenAI and cybergogy. Muthmainnah is an outstanding scholar with a Sinta (Indonesian Ministry of education and culture) score overall of 4256 and h-index 20. Her position as External examiner for PhD students at 3 A+ accredited campuses in India, Malaysia, Cyprus Europe, USA and Australia. She is a strong believer in international collaboration and teamwork, making her an ideal candidate for various academic and leadership roles. With her extensive experience and outstanding track record, Muthmainnah is open to international collaborations and teamwork.

Index

A

B

D

E

F

G

H

L

M

N

P

R

S

T

www.ingramcontent.com/pod-product-compliance
Lightning Source LLC
LaVergne TN
LVHW061540290926
849162LV00004B/854